ESSAYS ON POETRY

ESSAYS ON POETRY
by Ralph J. Mills, Jr.

Introduction by Michael Anania

DALKEY ARCHIVE PRESS

Portions of this book have appeared in earlier form between the late 1950s and the early 1980s. Thanks to the editors at: *Accent, American Poetry Review, Boundary 2, Chicago Review, The Christian Century*, Wm. B. Eerdmans, *Iowa Review, Ironwood, Modern Age, Northeast, TriQuarterly, Renascence*, and Texas Christian University Press.

Library of Congress Cataloging-in-Publication Data:

Mills, Ralph J.
    Essays on poetry / Ralph J. Mills, Jr. ; introduction by Michael Anania.— 1. ed.
    p. cm.
    ISBN 1-56478-294-8 (pbk. : alk. paper) — ISBN 1-56478-295-6 (cloth : alk. paper)
    1. American Poetry—20th century—History and criticism. 2. English poetry—20th century—History and criticism. 3. Poetry. I. Title.

    PS323.5.M25 2003
    811.509—dc21

                                                    2002041573

Partially funded by grants from the Lannan Foundation and the Illinois Arts Council, a state agency.

Dalkey Archive Press books are published by the Center for Book Culture, a nonprofit organization.

www.centerforbookculture.org

Printed on permanent/durable acid-free paper and bound in the United States of America.

For   Richard Ellmann
Donald Torchiana
Esther Wagner
Gordon Milne—

in memory.

CONTENTS

The Exercise of Reverence

THE POET-CRITIC ALLEN TATE SAID, DESCRIBING HIS OWN CRITICAL ESSAYS, "I simply conducted my education in public." Although Tate may have been being purposefully ingenuous, it's a useful way to think about the best literary critics, not as tastemakers or judges, but as readers who allow us to share in their evolving understanding of what they are reading. The literary essay, in this sense, is not so much a means of explanation, but of exploration, a matter of engaged reading that moves among its chosen texts as an informed but enthusiastic traveler might move, more pilgrim than tourist, more cartographer than pilgrim, at once knowledgeable, attentive, passionate and exacting. The first pleasure of Ralph Mills's essays lies in his ability to give us clear, gracefully written access to his thinking about literature. Mills is not offering us puzzles he alone can solve or poetic encryptions he is meant to decipher. The sense here is that the essay is reading turned outward, an exchange carefully raised out of reading's essential privacy toward conversation. Mills's assumption is that literature makes understanding possible that would not be as available elsewhere. That its issues—life, love, spirit, waste, death—are our issues, still, and that having them configured for us in poems and stories is a privilege. This conviction, and his open interest in sharing the awareness it brings, allows Mills to take up writers from a variety of literary schools with equal seriousness. In every case, Mills's attention as reader and critic is, to use a Denise Levertov expression, an "exercise of reverence," meant to honor the terms with which the writer treats the world.

Mills devoted most of his thirty-year career as a critic of contemporary American poetry. He wrote on fiction, of course. An early, wonderfully clear, thorough piece on Beckett's *Three Novels* is included in this collection. Two essays from Mills's work on modern English poets, on Edith Sitwell and

Kathleen Raine, are also included. His essay on René Char and Henri
Michaux represents Mills's broader critical reach. Almost incidentally, it
provides as clear a sense of the legacy of surrealism as anyone has ever man-
aged. Very little of Mills's work as a book reviewer is included in this collection, though for years he wrote reviews for *Poetry, Christian Century, American Poetry Review*, and the *Chicago Sun-Times*. My sense is that the reviews—
at least in poetry—provided him the reflexive reading that led him to the
subjects of his longer essays.

English and American poetry changed in extraordinary ways during the
period in which Mills was most active as a critic. The modernist masters—
Yeats, Pound, Eliot, Williams, Stevens, and Auden—as overbearing as they
were, left a chaotic legacy: impersonal, anti-Romantic, classical, allusive,
experimental, arcane, immediate, spare, luxuriant, imagistic, epical, ironic,
Christian, pagan. For a time in the mid-1950s poetry seemed, at least in the
quarterlies, to have settled into a concern for craft, for the sufficiency of the
individual poem as a keenly observant device for wit and insinuated judgment. The precise but morally suggestive poems of Richard Wilbur belong
to this period, as do the wryly observant poems of Karl Shapiro on haircuts,
Buicks and car wrecks, so do early Lowell, Berryman and Bishop with their
emphasis on control and the rich lyricisms of Theodore Roethke and James
Wright, as well as wits as different as J. V. Cunningham, Howard Nemerov
and Reed Wittimore. By the end of the 1950s, this brief sense of poetic
certainty had completely collapsed. The principle anthology of established
poetry, Hall, Pack, and Simpson's *New Poets of England and America* in two
very successful editions, was countered by Donald Allen's *The New American Poetry*, which focused on the Beats, the Black Mountain poets and the
New York School. Two features, in some ways at odds with each other,
emerged among Allen's poets, a conscious identification with the experi-
mentalisms of the first part of the twentieth century and an unabashed interest in the poet and the occasion of the poem as a moment in the poet's
life. The personal made a raucous reappearance in Allen, but it was already
becoming an informing concern among the Hall, Pack, and Simpson poets.
It is the personal, in the somber guise of "confessionalism," in the playful,
abstract expressionist immediacies of the New York School or in the theory-
heavy ideas of the heart, breath and body among the Black Mountain poets, that Mills takes up in "Creation's Very Self," this collection's opening
essay.

Mills's method of dealing with this fairly radical shift in the poetic center
of gravity was to treat poets and the range of their work, to step, that is,
away from a concern with the individual poem as either balanced rhetorical
structure or complex, metaphoric algebra and examine how poems continued to emerge from poems. The goal becomes clear early in Mills's criticism,

in the essay on Roethke, where he describes, "a poetic world of recurring themes and preoccupations into which the individual poems fit and within which they are comprehended." The personal, as Mills defines it, does not involve the imposition of biography or biographical detail onto the poem. Biography only incidentally comes into play. For Mills, the personal is contained in, even defined by, the poetry. Person, as his titles ("Creation's Very Self" and *The Cry of the Human*) suggest, is what emerges in the excited speech of the poem and is understood in the terms the poet uses to configure his poetic interests across a developing body of work. It is easy to understand Mills's great popularity among poets. As a critic he turned his extraordinary learning and his subtlety as a reader in the direction of his poets' own most serious concern, not to one poem out of many or to literary lineage but to the ongoing purposes of a poetic career.

The two poets whose careers Mills knows best are Theodore Roethke and David Ignatow. The literary and stylistic space between them is a good indication of the breadth of Mills's enthusiasms. Mills edited Roethke's letters and Ignatow's notebooks for publication, and the scholarly and editorial work that lies behind his essays on these two poets is enormous. Still, it is never intrusive or overbearing. Mills finds his way through the densely lyric, often Yeatsian, terrain of Roethke and the terse, skeptical, cityscape of Ignatow with equal skill. The heavy foliage of Roethke's settings, his traditional sonorities and his desire to find a language at once "strict and pure" seem a universe away from Ignatow's New York where the mundane part of existence defines existence ("To be alive is to carry a wallet and shake hands"). Roethke's sense of the poem's space as a place for the reintegration of self ("I am gathered together once more") seems radically different than Ignatow's recurrent, almost disciplined sense of separation and negation ("Against the evidence, I live by choice" and "The song is to emptiness"). What Mills examines is how the assertion of self in poetry, the "closely woven pattern" of imagery and aspiration, identification and alienation evolve in both poetries. Similar distances in poetic style and lineage could be drawn between Karl Shapiro and Galway Kinnell, between Isabella Gardner and Hilda Morley, Stanley Kunitz and Philip Levine. I am particularly fond of the essay on Levertov because it defined the scope of her interests so early but also because Denise was so fond of it. It was, she said, an essay that informed her as much as it pleased or flattered her.

In the 1980s, Ralph Mills stopped writing criticism and devoted himself entirely to his own poetry, the succession of successively more beautiful books that culminated in *Grasses Standing: Selected Poems* (2000), which won the William Carlos Williams prize from the Poetry Society of America. Of course, he has continued to read poetry, and his reading has taken new and surprising directions. You can trace his recent interests through the dedications to his poems—Robert Desnos, Jules Superville, Phillippe Jaccottet, Lorine Niedecker, Larry Eigner, John Jacob, Ted Enslin and James Schuyler. Sadly, there are no essays for this group of poets—sad for us because it would have been marvelous to read Mills on the surrealists in this group and to have seen how he would read the self's presence in Objectivists like Enslin and Eigner and sadder still for the poets, of course. When Ralph Mills moved from criticism to poetry, it was a loss for poets, particularly for those who hoped they might be next in line for one of his long, attentive essays, but a gain for poetry. In this strange period in which everything but poetry seems to have been settled on for critical scrutiny (rugby team fight songs, coffee bar orders and sitcom theme songs come immediately to mind), we are fortunate to have these wonderful, patient, literate essays, their lessons and their delights.

Michael Anania
2003

One

1

Creation's Very Self: On the Personal Element in Recent American Poetry

Behind the poem is the human being . . .
—RICHARD LEWIS

CATEGORIES AND CLASSIFICATIONS ARE AMONG THE DEHUMANIZING EVILS OF OUR time. Almost anywhere we turn in these bleak, disordered days of recent history there lies in wait one kind of mechanism or other which has as its end the obscuration or destruction of what is unique and particular, unmistakably itself: the very identity of a person, an experience, an object. Since nothing keeps alive our awareness of the concrete and specific more than poetry, it is the worst sort of folly to force it into convenient patterns or to make it demonstrate some invented principle. Such efforts are nets to catch the wind, a wind which has sacred sources because it is the Muse's or the spirit's motion, or, following Charles Olson's definition of the poetic line, because it is "the breathing of the man who writes, at the moment that he writes."[1] In spite of every attempt to do something with or to it, as W. H. Auden says in his elegy for Yeats, poetry "survives, / A way of happening, a mouth." And so it should be. The few distinctions and delineations that I make in the following pages are loose, not rigid, and are designed for the exigencies of the occasion. My purpose here will be neither that of the scholar nor the theorist, but, if you will, that of the enthusiast-commentator who wishes to bring to attention some contemporary poets and their poems, to remark on certain qualities that seem prominent and characteristic, and to disappear, leaving the reader, I hope, with a desire to know recent poetry better.

One distinction I do think necessary to draw before we can discuss current writing separates *modernist* poetry from *contemporary* poetry. I shall presume that the modernist poets are those whose names spring first to mind

when we think of poetry in English in this century, the great pioneer figures
such as Yeats, Eliot, Pound, Stevens, W. C. Williams, and Marianne Moore,
most of them born a decade or more before the turn of the century and all
but a few now dead. These modernists have in common the fact that each
of them, in his or her own way, participated in the poetic revolution which
cast aside the vestiges of Victorianism and outworn literary conventions,
infused new vigor into diction and rhythm, disclosed new possibilities of
form, and brought poetry into meaningful relationship with the actualities
of modern life—a relationship which is being renewed by poets today. Having accomplished all this, the modernist poets proceeded into the years of
their maturity and produced some of their finest work long after that revolutionary movement of what Randall Jarrell once aptly called "irregularly
cooperative experimentalism"[2] was over. So, in a period ostensibly belonging to their successors, those poets who are the first of the ones I shall call
contemporaries, we find extraordinary achievements such as Eliot's *Four
Quartets*, Pound's later *Cantos*, Williams's *Paterson, and* Stevens's *The Auroras of Autumn* looming intimidatingly over the poetic landscape.

What separates the contemporaries from the modernists, to begin with, is
the simple fact of being born too late to join in that radical movement
which, beginning around 1910, overthrew reigning literary modes and aesthetic tastes, and, with increasing help from literary critics, itself solidified
into an establishment. Not only did these younger poets emerge in the wake
of a full-scale artistic revolution whose chief participants were still alive
and still quite productive but they were also confronted with fresh versions
of the literary past and a variety of prospects for using it which Eliot's notion of tradition, the practice of his poetry, and an expanding body of literary criticism made available. The liberating influence of William Carlos
Williams was yet to be felt.

So it was that Stanley Kunitz, Richard Eberhart, Theodore Roethke, John
Berryman, Robert Lowell, Karl Shapiro, Randall Jarrell, and others who
began to write in the 1930s had to seek their own voices, searching them
out through the arduous process of trying on and discarding models, guides,
and influences from the poetic tradition and from modernist writers alike,
without the benefit of any shared aesthetic principle or revolutionary artistic purpose. They did have in common a dogged attentiveness to the inner
necessities of imaginative vision and to the difficult struggle for style. In
this situation there were both burdens and blessings. If these poets, and
many others who followed them in the late 1940s and the 1950s felt over-
shadowed by most of their elders and confined by what Donald Hall terms a
critical "orthodoxy" which required "a poetry of symmetry, intellect, irony,
and wit,"[3] they were freed as individuals from the demands created by literary movements to an energetic and single-minded concentration on the

making of poems, a concentration that brought, in due time, Roethke in *The Lost Son*, Lowell in *Life Studies*, Berryman in *Homage to Mistress Bradstreet* and *The Dream Songs*, and Shapiro in *The Bourgeois Poet*, for example, to the kind of poetic breakthrough James Dickey calls "The Second Birth"— an intense imaginative liberation, achieved at great personal cost, in which the poet, like a snake shedding his dead skin, frees himself of the weight of imposed styles and current critical criteria to come into the place of his own authentic speech. The secret of this renewal, Dickey observes, does not, of course, reside in a complete originality, which does not and could not exist. It dwells, rather, in the development of the personality, with its unique weight of experience and memory, as a writing instrument, and in the ability to give literary influence a new dimension which has the quality of this personality as informing principle. The Second Birth is largely a matter of self-criticism and endless experiment, presided over by an unwavering effort to ascertain what is most satisfying to the poet's self as it develops, or as it remains more clearly what it has always been."[4]

It is precisely here, with Dickey's notion of the poet's personality "as informing principle," that I want to note an important difference between the critical views derived from the modernist movement and the practice of many contemporaries—a difference which has been heightened in the last decade and a half by the appearance of the Beat poets, the Projectivists, the confessional poets, the so-called New York School, and what is often called a new Surrealism or poetry of the unconscious. I have used in my chapter title the term "personal element," which is purposely more general than Dickey's "personality," so it might apply equally to the work of a number of poets who have differing aims and emphases. But both terms oppose the view handed down from Eliot and the New Criticism that poetry and the emotions it conveys are, or should be, impersonal, and that an author's personality and life ought to be excluded from his writings. In many of their poems Eliot, Pound, Stevens, and others stress the poet's anonymity by employing fictional masks invented speakers or *personae*, thus enforcing a division between writer and work. The original motive for such objectivity seems genuine enough: to rid poetry of biographical excesses and the residue of the Romantics' preoccupation with personality which had seduced attention from the true object of interest, the poem itself. In his famous 1917 essay, "Tradition and the Individual Talent," Eliot declares, "The more perfect the artist, the more completely separate in him will be the man who suffers and the mind which creates"; and again he says, "The progress of the artist is a continual self-sacrifice, a continual extinction of personality."[5] While it cannot be gone into here, much of what Eliot says has great value and will continue to speak to later generations. But the emphasis on the poet as an impersonal or anonymous "medium" (actually, as various commentators have shown, to permit deeper, unconscious sources to aid in shaping poetic imagery and speech) passed out of Eliot's essay to become an important factor of the modern critical atmosphere. Subsequently, the poem came to be considered a neutral object, a vessel filled with the feelings of nobody, what Louis Simpson names "the so-called 'well-made' poem that lends itself to the little knives and formaldehyde of a graduate school."[6]

Among the pioneer modernists, William Carlos Williams, with his anti-academicism, interest in the immediacies of experience and the American spoken language, and sense of the singularity of form in the poem, and William Butler Yeats, with his insistence on the poet's creation of his personality, his anti-self, stand out in marked contrast to Eliot. The decidedly personal character of Yeats's voice, growing bolder and more idiosyncratic as his career lengthened out, could serve as a masterly example for Roethke, Kunitz, Lowell, Berryman, Nemerov, and other contemporary poets in quest of a personal idiom, a speech vibrating with their lives—something which Eliot's poetry does equally, though in perhaps subtler fashion, and in spite of his views. Writing in his autobiographies of what he saw in Dante and Villon, the Irish poet might have been describing the figure he makes in his own poems. "Such masters," he observes, "would not, when they speak through their art, change their luck; yet they are mirrored in all the suffering of desire. The two halves of their nature are so completely joined that they seem to labour for their objects, and yet to desire whatever happens, being at the same time predestinate and free, creation's very self. We gaze at such men in awe, because we gaze not at a work of art, but at the recreation of the man through that art. . . ."[7]

Contemporary poets, then, with a few forerunners providing guidance, begin to cultivate their own inwardness as material for poetry or to look to the immediacies of their own situation for valid experience. In reaction to impersonality and rationalism, critical prescription and dissection, they seek a personal mode of utterance to embody perceivings and intuitions very much their own. As Robert Creeley comments, "Confronting such *rule* [i.e., a critical rule of rationality and taste], men were driven back upon the particulars of their own experience, the literal *things* of an immediate environment, wherewith to acknowledge the possibilities of their own lives."[8] With rare exceptions like Robert Duncan, poets no longer translate subjective experience into the kind of larger symbolic or metaphysical frameworks sustained by some of the modernists. Contemporary poets frequently give the impression of beginning their poems nearer the brink of private intuition and feeling, and of trying, for the sake of authentic testimony, to remain as close to it as they are able. Nor do these poets hesitate to speak in their poems as themselves, for the individual voice is likewise to be understood as a sign of authenticity. In general, there is a distrust among contemporaries of systematizing; those who have known some sort of visionary or mystical experience—Roethke or Eberhart, say—refuse to account for it by intellectual means or to locate it within some comprehensive explanation of things. Instead, these experiences are enclosed in the heart of the poems which sprang from them; as a result, they are not divisible from the selves to whom they occurred.

Contemporary poets might take one of their chief mottoes from Wordsworth. In the preface to the *Lyrical Ballads* of 1800 after asking himself "What is a Poet?" and "To whom does he address himself?" he answers unequivocally, "He is a man speaking to men." And we can add to this statement—thinking not only of Lowell, Eberhart, or Roethke, but also of more recent poets, of Anne Sexton or John Logan, Gary Snyder or Frank O'Hara, Denise Levertov or William Stafford—that each poet wishes to speak to us, without impediment, from the deep center of a personal engagement with existence. For the contemporary poet enters into himself and the particulars of his experience in order to bring into being in his work that true poetic "self which [he] is waiting to be," to borrow a phrase from Ortega y Gassett[9] that confirms Yeats's remarks. The activity in which he engages is not just the construction of objects but the fashioning of a language that will ultimately awaken and transform the inner world of his readers. We approach here Martin Buber's description of "the primary word *I— Thou*" which "can be spoken only with the full being." The artist who creates, in Buber's thought, "may withhold nothing of himself."[10] So, for our contemporary poets, we can perhaps say that poetic creation moves toward an intimacy, a communion of selves made available to the reader, if he will assume his part in it, through the agency of the unique poetic self we encounter speaking to us there. The contemporary poem requires dialogue to fulfill itself; once received, it inhabits us, unfolds a space within where we meet another presence, the poet's, through the order and resonance of words and images he has formed. "So," Kenneth Rexroth can rightly observe, "speech approaches in poetry not only the directness and the impact but the unlimited potential of act."[11]

Recent American poetry, with its chosen precursors in Whitman, Williams, Pound, Hart Crane, and the writing of European and Latin American poets influenced by Surrealism and Expressionism, as well as Chinese and Japanese verse, discards artificial barriers that put distance between poet, poem, and reader; searches out new kinds of informality in the attempt to be more congruent with the shapes of experience. The contemporary poet re-creates himself as a personality, an identifiable self within his poetry, that is, of course, a self who has been selected and heightened in the process, captured in essence, and so is not perhaps a full likeness of the author as a physical, workaday person outside the poem yet could not be mistaken for someone else. As we read the poems of our contemporaries, we recognize a certain magnanimous gesture in their acts of creation, a profoundly touching and human gesture through which the poet voluntarily stands exposed as "creation's very self" before us. In an age in which inner disorientation occurs because the individual's acts and thoughts appear to have no issue bearing his stamp, instead being swallowed by the vast technical apparatus of social, economic, and political forces that comprise our monolithic city-states, the poet invites us to share in his pursuit of identity; to witness the dramatization of the daily events of his experience—so closely resembling our own; to be haunted by the imagery of his dreams or the flowing stream of his consciousness; to eavesdrop on conversations with friends and lovers; to absorb the shock of his deep-seated fears and neuroses, even mental instability and madness, and through them to realize the torments of our time; and finally to reach with him that redeeming state of what Denise Levertov calls "Attention," which is no less than "the *exercise* of Reverence for the 'other forms of life that want to live.'"[12]

For the rest, let us see, in the abbreviated manner imposed by our limitations, some specific instances of the personal element in several poets and kinds of poetry of the last three decades. My first choice is Theodore Roethke, who died prematurely at the height of his powers in 1963. He produced work of such high quality that I feel sure he must be ranked as one of the finest American lyric poets. Appropriately enough for our subject, too, the pattern of his writing demonstrates in advance of many of his contemporaries the trying process of a "Second Birth," after an earlier period which merely hints at the penetrating experience he has yet to realize. The poems of his first collection, *Open House* (1941), show fundamental gifts: a fine ear, close acquaintance with the natural world, a good sense of language. But in spite of worthy pieces, one feels that all sorts of resources and energies remain still to be tapped. The declarations of the title poem support this feeling:

> My truths are all foreknown,
> This anguish self-revealed.
> I'm naked to the bone,
> With nakedness my shield.
> Myself is what I wear:
> I keep the spirit spare.

"Myself is what I wear"—the announcement might have been made somewhere in *Leaves of Grass;* however, Roethke has not quite earned the right to this declaration yet. In the next half-dozen years he broke through, in the so-called greenhouse poems, to those deeper layers of himself that would draw him on to the radical experimentation of "The Lost Son" and the subsequent poems of his childhood sequence. Commenting on the above-quoted passage three decades later, and only a few months before his death, Roethke remarked:

> This poem is a clumsy, innocent, desperate asseveration. I am not speaking of the empirical self, the flesh-bound ego; it's a single word: *myself*, the aggregate of the several selves, if you will. The spirit or soul—should we say the self, once perceived, *becomes* the soul?—this I was keeping "spare" in my desire for the essential. But the spirit need not be spare: it can grow gracefully and beautifully like a tendril, like a flower.[13]

With the 1940s Roethke started shattering the restraints upon his previous work, pressing beyond the surfaces of experience toward the hidden sources. What he was to discover was, of course, himself, or those "several selves" he mentions, through a return in memory and imagination to his childhood, his family's floral establishment with its huge green-houses and the acreage of woods and fields beyond, his uncle's suicide and his father's death from cancer when the poet was only fifteen.[14] This return to the past, which was simultaneously a descent into himself, his psyche, could prove agonizing, if poetically rewarding, as he says in "The Return":

> A cold key let me in
> That self-infected lair;
> And I lay down with my life,
> With the rags and rotting clothes,
> With a stump of scraggy fang
> Bared for a hunter's boot.

But past experience which came alive then in his imagination finds a language that carries it to the page with the urgency and sensuous imme-diacy of life itself. At first, Roethke scrutinizes the lives of flowers and plants, even the tiny insects inhabiting their leaves. Yet he does not render this "vegetable realm" completely by itself; everywhere the presence of the poet, both as child-observer (since the poems draw upon vivid memories) and imaginative participant, can be felt, however obliquely. In "Cuttings (*Later*)" he claims his affinity with this world: the struggling into life visible there parallels his efforts to renew and complete himself:

> I can hear, underground, that sucking and sobbing,
> In my veins, in my bones, I feel it,—
> The small waters seeping upward,
> The tight grains parting at last.
> When sprouts break out,

> Slippery as fish,
> I quail, lean to beginnings, sheath-wet.

The childhood sequence opening with "The Lost Son," which takes a poetic leap beyond the greenhouse pieces, dramatizes what is now Roethke's imaginative preoccupation—the evolution and identity of the self. Through daring formal combinations, these poems convey a direct apprehension of inner and outer experience, the progressions and reversals of psychic life as the self seeks identity and spiritual reality. Beginning with early years, they proceed through adolescence, the pains of sexuality, the loss of the father, and on toward phases of illumination in which the self attains an ecstatic, mystical communion with the surrounding animate and inanimate cosmos. Though Roethke indicates that the anonymous protagonist of these poems is meant to serve as a universal figure or everyman, both biographical detail and the intensity of the poetic experience reveal the poet's personal involvement with the speaker, whose consciousness and preconsciousness are realized in all their complexity through an impressive array of poetic devices. He lists their "ancestors" as "German and English folk literature, particularly Mother Goose; Elizabethan and Jacobean drama, especially the songs and rants; the Bible; Blake and Traherne; Dürer."[15] In these poems Roethke avoids at all costs the intervention of explanation, interpretation, or judgment. As readers, we are compelled to live through the experiences of the self, its sufferings and joys, presented directly, until we recognize that they are the poet's and our own. Roethke also brings us to what technological man has forgotten—the inmost being of things, the essential existence we share with creation:

> Arch of air, my heart's original knock,
> I'm awake all over:
> I've crawled from the mire, alert as a saint or a dog;
> I know the back-stream's joy, and the stone's eternal
>   pulseless longing.
> Felicity I cannot board.
> My friend, the rat in the wall, brings me the clearest
>   messages;
> I bask in the bower of change;
> The plants wave me in, and the summer apples;
> My palm-sweat flashes gold;
> Many astounds before, I lost my identity to a pebble;
> The minnows love me, and the humped and spitting creatures.
> —from *Praise to the End!*

In his love poems and later meditative pieces and metaphysical lyrics Roethke continues his relentless pursuit of personal unity of being through the relationship of self to the beloved, to the cosmos, and finally to God. Some of the last poems, written with an instinctive awareness of approaching death, disclose a solitary confrontation with the Divine which becomes an excruciating course of self-annihilation before it turns into a mystical union achieved at the very boundaries of human life. My example here is "In a Dark Time," the initial poem *of Sequence, Sometimes Metaphysical:*

> In a dark time, the eye begins to see,
> I meet my shadow in the deepening shade;
> I hear my echo in the echoing wood—
> A lord of nature weeping to a tree.
> I live between the heron and the wren,
> Beasts of the hill and serpents of the den.
>
> What's madness but nobility of soul
> At odds with circumstance? The day's on fire!
> I know the purity of pure despair,
> My shadow pinned against a sweating wall.
> That place among the rocks—is it a cave,
> Or winding path? The edge is what I have.
>
> A steady storm of correspondences!
> A night flowing with birds, a ragged moon,
> And in broad day the midnight come again!
> A man goes far to find out what he is—
> Death of the self in a long, tearless night,
> All natural shapes blazing unnatural light.
>
> Dark, dark my light, and darker my desire.
> My soul, like some heat-maddened summer fly,
> Keeps buzzing at the sill. Which I is *I?*
> A fallen man, I climb out of my fear.
> The mind enters itself, and God the mind,
> And one is One, free in the tearing wind.

While our limitations do not permit detailed comment at this point,[16] let us anyway recognize in the poem an archetypal pattern of death and rebirth, of descent by the poet into his own nature, there to face its confusions, complexities, and impurities personified in the figure of his "shadow" or double, and to learn the agony of being parted from that in himself which must be abandoned through a type of ritual or symbolic dying to oneself— if he is to find renewal in the form of communion with God, a communion that is likewise a moment of self-integration or unity of being. The poem gathers strength from the oppositions and perils of spiritual quest, but these qualities would not impress us so much were it not for the feeling of the

poet's individual involvement with them. To be sure, the imagery and thematic design of the poem evoke abundant associations from various traditions of religious thought. Yet it is when we grasp these meanings as essential portions of a lived experience which is the poet's that they speak with
undeniable conviction, the conviction born of personal witness. Roethke,
in a symposium, says of the poem that it was "dictated . . . something given,
scarcely mine at all. For about three days before its writing I felt disembod-
ied, out of time; then the poem virtually wrote itself, on a day in summer,
1958."[17] The phrase "scarcely mine at all" does not, once we reflect on it in
the context of this specific poem, contradict what I have been saying by
separating the poet from his work. Rather, it points to an unusually heightened subjectivity, articulated in its totality from those regions of inwardness
where the poem was prepared in secret. Roethke might also have commented
on this poem, as on all of his poetry, with Whitman's words from "Song of
Myself": "I am the man, I suffer'd, I was there. . . ."

Glancing around the current literary scene, we observe a number
of younger poets who in certain ways stand in a line of descent from Roethke,
though I should say at once that I am not speaking of direct imitation or
obvious stylistic influence. Instead, I have in mind some of those poets who,
however different from one another (and these differences are frequently
considerable), create a poetry which depends heavily upon intuitive association, dreams, the preconscious and the unconscious, discontinuous or
elliptical imagery; a poetry highly responsive to the techniques of modern
French, German, Spanish, and Latin American poets; a poetry which proceeds by a "logic of the imagination" rather than a "logic of concepts," to
borrow Eliot's distinction with respect to St.-John Perse's work."[18] Whether
treating in some form or other the fusion of outer and inner life, as, say, in
various poems by Frank O'Hara, A. R. Ammons, David Ignatow, William
Stafford, Galway Kinnell, Donald Justice, and John Logan; exploring avenues opened up by the possibilities of Surrealism, as in the work of John
Ashbery and the recent poetry of Donald Hall; entering into the being of
other creatures or men by an imaginative extension, as in James Dickey's
writing; giving voice to the hidden dream life of America, as some of the
poems by Robert Bly, Louis Simpson, and James Wright do; or fashioning a
rich but hermetic language of association, evocation, and prophecy, like W.
S. Merwin's, this poetry continues to disclose its highly personal character.
In each instance the poet, tired of the betrayal of his deepest feelings and
most significant experiences by attempting to force them into conventional
forms, tired of the intrusion of intellect and reason (Roethke called the
latter "That dreary shed, that hutch for grubby schoolboys!" and countered,
"The hedgewren's song says something else.")[19] upon the free exercise of
imagination, tired of the arid critical formulations of the academies, has

moved in the direction of the purely intuitive, the illogical and irrational, the private and the intimate. Louis Simpson calls this tendency Surrealist, though he clearly disavows any identification with the rigid theories and formulations proposed by André Breton. In a recent anthology Simpson writes: "The next step—it is already occurring—is to reveal the movements of the subconscious. The Surrealist poet—rejecting on the one hand the clichés of the rational mind, and on the other, a mere projection of irrational images—will reveal the drama and narrative of the subconscious. The images move, with the logic of dreams."[20]

We know at once from this statement that Simpson does not wish merely to revive the Surrealist practice of automatic writing. In a later article he insists that "poetry represents not unreason but the total mind, including both reason and unreason,"[21] by which he perhaps means the shaping powers of the conscious mind at work upon the materials provided by the subconscious. The French Surrealist poet Paul Eluard, who *is* convinced of the value of automatic writing, has a passage which is helpful in clarifying differences between dream and poem, the images issuing from below consciousness and the sensations which still come from without. In spite of certain discrepancies between Simpson's and Eluard's statements, both aim at a new fusion of interior and exterior experience which will result in radically altered poetic imagery. Eluard says:

> You don't take the story of a dream for a poem. Both are living reality, but the first is a memory, immediately altered and transformed, an adventure, and of the second nothing is lost, nothing is changed. The poet desensitizes the universe to the advantage of human faculties, permits man to see differently other things. His former vision *is* dead, or false. He discovers a new world, he becomes a new man.
>
> People have thought that automatic writing makes poems useless. On the contrary! It increases or develops the domain of examination of poetic awareness, by enriching it. If awareness is perfect, the elements which automatic writing draws from the inner world and the elements of the outer world are balanced. Thus made equal, they mingle and merge in order to form poetic unity.[22]

By whatever methods they proceed, the poets I am grouping very loosely here, as well as a great number not named (think of Michael Benedikt, Stephen Berg, Charles Simic, or Mark Strand, for example, as members of a still younger generation), tend to create work that develops with "the logic of dreams," to repeat Louis Simpson's phrase, or to achieve a transformation of outer reality through its assimilation by the inward self. Unlike Roethke, who had no talent for languages, most of them have been engaged in a considerable amount of translating, as well as reading, of foreign poets. In this respect they follow the lead not only of Pound and Eliot, but also of such extraordinarily accomplished poet/translators as Ben Belitt and Kenneth Rexroth. While it is not, as a rule, easy to indicate with assurance the influence of one poet upon another, familiarity with important modern poets from other countries, among them Neruda, Lorca, Vallejo, Char, Bonnefoy, Michaux, Trakl, Rilke, Benn, Mayakovsky, Pasternak, and Voznesensky, has helped to liberate American poetry from the confinements of logic and wit, "epithets and opinions."[23]

At this point, let me offer a brief anthology of poetic effects deriving from these tendencies. I offer it with some (but not too much) comment, since such poetry, coming as it does from the "total mind" of the poet, needs first to be taken in by the reader's or listener's "total mind."

In the poems of the late Frank O'Hara, whose accidental death at the age of forty cut off a great talent, there is considerable variety but also, in the end, a unity of impression. Like his friends Kenneth Koch, John Ashbery, and James Schuyler (each of whom writes a very different kind of poem), he gives the reader a sense of being talked to, rather than simply overheard. In fact, O'Hara thought of his writing in terms of just such direct address, a communication from one individual to another. In his work a voice speaks to us, or to someone of the poet's acquaintance whose person we share while reading the poem. This voice may be gay, breezy, and whimsical; it may be elegiac or remorseful, tender and erotic; or it may pour forth in a rich, bizarre stream the contents of the poet's consciousness in its ceaseless flow. As is often noted, O'Hara has close affinities with contemporary painters, especially those named Abstract Expressionists or the New York action painters: Jackson Pollock, Franz Kline, Willem de Kooning, Philip Guston, and others. Pollock, in a written statement, tells why he prefers his canvases laid out on the floor rather than on easel or wall: "I feel nearer, more a part of the painting, since this way I can walk around it, work from the four sides, and literally be *in* the painting."[24] These remarks apply equally to O'Hara, I think, in whose poems the poet's self is very evident, moving about freely, uninhibited by rules, concerned only with the realization of personal experience in language. "What is happening to me, allowing for lies and exaggerations which I try to avoid, goes into my poems," he explains in a statement on his poetics. "I don't think my experiences are clarified or made beautiful for myself or anyone else, they are just there in whatever form I can find them."[25] That form is the unpredictable, unliterary but highly poetic form of life itself. The poem "The Day Lady Died" begins with the rather trivial events surrounding O'Hara's preparations for a weekend out of New York visiting friends. Almost at the poem's conclusion he buys a newspaper, along with two cartons of cigarettes, and reads of the death of the great jazz singer Billie Holliday (nicknamed Lady Day, which adds to the implications of the title). In the closing lines a memory of her singing overwhelms the poet, as did the original occasion, though now her death leaves him with only that recollection of an extraordinary moment:

It is 12:20 in New York a Friday
three days after Bastille day, yes
it is 1959 and I go get a shoeshine
because I will get off the 4:19 in Easthampton
at 7:15 and then go straight to dinner
and I don't know the people who will feed me

I walk up the muggy street beginning to sun
and have a hamburger and a malted and buy
an ugly NEW WORLD WRITING to see what the poets
in Ghana are doing these days
                                        I go on to the bank

and Miss Stillwagon (first name Linda I once heard)
doesn't even look up my balance for once in her life
and in the GOLDEN GRIFFIN I get a little Verlaine
for Patsy with drawings by Bonnard although I do
think of Hesiod, trans. Richmond Lattimore or
Brendan Behan's new play or *Le Balcon* or *Les Nègres*
of Genet, but I don't, I stick with Verlaine
after practically going to sleep with quandariness

and for Mike I just stroll into the PARK LANE
Liquor Store and ask for a bottle of Strega and
then I go back where I came from to 6th Avenue
and the tobacconist in the Ziegfeld Theatre and
casually ask for a carton of Gauloises and a carton
of Picayunes, and a NEW YORK POST with her face on it

and I am sweating a lot by now and thinking of
leaning on the john door in the 5 SPOT
while she whispered a song along the keyboard
to Mal Waldron and everyone and I stopped breathing

By way of contrast with the disarming openness of O'Hara's approach, a few stanzas from W. S. Merwin's "A Scale in May" suggest the poet's embarkation on a trying interior journey, frightening in its solitude and challenge, for the goal is some kind of honest understanding of existence, which is always threatened by death and nothingness. Traveling light, Merwin takes with him only the possibility of poetry and a resolute integrity. The subjective nature of the poem's statements, their division into separate sections of

three lines, each having the quality of a gnomic utterance, lead us to believe we have chanced upon the poet in profound conversation with himself and are trespassers of his inner world. But that is not really the case.
Once we begin to listen to what he is saying, its strange obliquity becomes
at once evocative; its indefiniteness belongs to the elusive nature of spiritual quests. Then we cross over into the world which Merwin has so beautifully realized through what he calls "the great language itself, the vernacu-
lar of the imagination":[26]

> Now all my teachers are dead except silence
> I am trying to read what the five poplars are writing
> On the void

> Of all the beasts to man alone death brings justice
> But I desire
> To kneel in a doorway empty except for the song

> Who made time provided also its fools
> Strapped in watches and with ballots for their choices
> Crossing the frontiers of invisible kingdoms

> To succeed consider what is as though it were past
> Deem yourself inevitable and take credit for it
> If you find you no longer believe enlarge the temple

> Through the day the nameless stars keep passing the door
> That have come all that way out of death
> Without questions

   In a note written for the dust jacket of his collection *Drowning with Others* (1962) James Dickey declares, "My subject matter is inevitably my own
life, my own obsessions, possessions and renunciations." He later adds, "In
these poems I have tried to come into that place in myself which is mine."
One of the most compelling features of Dickey's poetry is a power of imagination which enables him to feel or enter into the being of others as if it
were his own, to be haunted by the living and the dead, and to perceive the
universe as animistic, charged with forces and presences. Ordinary objects,
situations, or patterns of nature in his poems suddenly assume the confor-
mations of myth or participate in rituals of initiation and transformation,
interchanging identities, and progressing toward transcendent revelations.

Here, to be specific, are the opening lines of "The Dream Flood," where the imaginative reenactment of archetypal details in a fluid, magical cosmos provides the aspect of personally experienced myth:

> I ask and receive
> The secret of falling unharmed
> Forty nights from the darkness of Heaven,
> Coming down in sheets and in atoms
> Until I descend to the moon
>
> Where it lies on the ground
> And finds in my surface the shining
> It knew it must have in the end.
> No longer increasing, I stand
> Taking sunlight transmitted by stone,
>
> And then begin over fields
> To expand like a mind seeking truth . . .

Less cosmic in its proportions, Louis Simpson's brief poem "The Morning Light" projects, through a few suggestive images, those private associations by means of which the imagination quickens a sense of our individual lives or destinies:

> In the morning light a line
> Stretches forever. There my unlived life
> Rises, and I resist,
> Clinging to the steps of the throne.
>
> Day lifts the darkness from the hills,
> A bright blade cuts the reeds,
> And my life, pitilessly demanding,
> Rises forever in the morning light.

In a poem of this sort, as Jacques Maritain would say, "the conceptual utterances have either disappeared or they are reduced to a minimum or are merely allusive. . .there is no longer any *explicit* intelligible sense, even carried by the images. The intelligible sense drawing in the images is . . . *implicit*."[27] That is to say, if we try to translate into logical prose sense the substance of what we might call the poetic thought (as distinct from straightforward rational thought) in this poem, we will come up with very little, for it is inherent in an imagery completely implicated with inward feeling. We can only understand these images by immersing ourselves in their reality. If we do so, allowing imagination and intuition to lead us, Louis Simpson's poem takes on new aspects, and we experience them with an intimacy close to bodily sensation. There occurs to us a sense of something like pictorial space in the poem, but it is an interior space we see, an arena of desires, fears, frustrations, and possibilities glimpsed as a barely sketched landscape suffused with "morning light." In keeping with his own conviction that "the deepest image, if it does not move, is only an object,"[28] Simpson sets the poem in motion. The tension between his life's possibilities and demands, associated with the light of day and the indefinite horizon, and the resistance to them, the wish to remain motionless, "clinging to the steps of the throne," increases with the awareness of "rising light." Indeed, the general movement within the space disclosed by the poem is upward—until the gesture of the "bright blade," stroking horizontally across this vertical tendency, severs the poet's "life" like a balloon from its mooring, and "pitilessly demanding," it ascends eternally into the brightened heavens, presumably drawing him after or at least compelling his undistracted gaze. Having said these things about the poem, we have still hardly touched the suggestiveness of the images and their movements. Their sense is "implicit," to repeat Maritain's term, and will be apparent to us only when we place ourselves within the poem's precincts.

A new sort of political poem has emerged from the new poetry of dream, surrealist inclination, or pure imagination which we have been discussing. It likewise relies upon an imagery of the subconscious or of affective association; but now this imagery must reflect something of the buried collective life of the nation, even as Louis Simpson's or W. S. Merwin's poems grow from submerged areas of their individual lives. Kenneth Patchen's explosive poetry of political and social horror, with its juxtapositions of brutality, irrationalism, outraged innocence, and savage satire, together with Weldon Kees's ominous, unrelenting poems of decay and destruction are chief among the forerunners of more recent work by others. Standing alone, independent and fierce, as an exemplary precursor in this respect is the figure of Stanley Kunitz, whose work is a dramatic embodiment of his own personal life, with its torments and anxieties, and the character of the age in which he exists. Subjective existence and apocalyptic vision accumulate terrible force, as in these first lines from "Open the Gates":

> Within the city of the burning cloud,
> Dragging my life behind me in a sack,
> Naked I prowl, scourged by the black
> Temptation of the blood grown proud.

Among the chief acknowledged influences for this poetry of political and historical interest are such poets as Whitman, Pasternak, Neruda, and Vallejo. Robert Bly, an eloquent proponent and a practitioner of this sort of writing, makes some useful remarks in an essay, "On Political Poetry," where he stresses the need for poets to "penetrate the husk around their own personalities" and probe the lower regions of the psyche. "Once inside the psyche," Bly maintains, "[they] can speak of inward and political things with the same assurance. . . . Paradoxically, what is needed to write true poems about the outward world is inwardness."[29] He wants to divorce such poems from "personal" poems or poems of political "opinions"; however, his very definition of the requirements of inwardness implies that political poems of the kind he favors are at the same time personal as well, for the psyche of the poet is inseparable from its intuitions of the nation's psyche:

> The life of the country can be imagined as a psyche larger than the psyche of anyone living, a larger sphere, floating above everyone. In order for the poet to write a true political poem, he has to be able to have such a grasp of his own concerns that he can leave them for a while, and then leap up, like a grasshopper, into this other psyche. In that sphere he finds strange plants and curious many-eyed creatures which he brings back with him. This half-visible psychic life he entangles in his language.[30]

With the reservations I have expressed, let me abandon theoretical disagreement and permit these statements by Bly to stand by themselves without further comment, then place next to them James Wright's "Confession to J. Edgar Hoover," which reveals this poet's almost unbearably intense human concerns, his undeniably personal involvement with the substance of the poem, coupled with an imaginative capacity for raising into view levels of existence invisible to the naked eye and unavailable to the reasoning mind. Wright by-passes headlines, news reports, speeches, and platitudes to sound those mysterious depths of the self where the guilt, terror, alienation, and anxiety that make themselves felt in the external affairs of society in other forms have their dark, tentacular roots:

> Hiding in the church of an abandoned stone,
> A Negro soldier
> Is flipping the pages of the Articles of War,
> That he can't read.

> Our father,
> Last evening I devoured the wing
> Of a cloud.
> And, in the city, I sneaked down
> To pray with a sick tree.

> I labor to die, father,
> I ride the great stones,

I hide under stars and maples,
And yet I cannot find my own face.
In the mountains of blast furnaces,
The trees turned their backs on me.

Father, the dark moths
Crouch at the sills of the earth, waiting.

And I am afraid of my own prayers.
Father, forgive me.
I did not know what I was doing.

Departing these twilight regions of the psyche—without, it must be said, trying here to specify other forms of commitment to social themes in such poets as David Ignatow, Philip Levine, Charles Reznikoff, or Carl Rakosi, to mention but a few names—for different areas of consciousness equally tense with disturbance, we are faced with a large, impressive body of writing which has earned in the past decade the title of "confessional" poetry or, as it has been called by the British critic A. Alvarez, "Extremist art."[31] While the term "confessional" is now widely applied, its origin with respect to contemporary poetry lies in the startling transition which occurred in Robert Lowell's career with the publication of *Life Studies* in 1959. Since that book first appeared, Lowell's work has continued to change and to be exploratory, but it has taken on a new surge of power, as a result both of an unsparing scrutiny of his own life, family, and background, and of an open confrontation with our perilous moment in history. The reader must imagine for himself at what cost Lowell effected this alteration in his poetry (though the recent work has obvious connections and continuities with the earlier books), an alteration which recalls exactly Yeats's previously quoted notion of "the recreation of the man through [his] art."

In his early poetry Lowell displays considerable rhythmic and imagistic strength, which operates in the service of a somber, apocalyptic vision of life, growing out of the conflict between his New England heritage and his conversion to Roman Catholicism. That vision is conveyed with great rhetorical force in the poems of *Lord Weary's Castle* (1946). This style becomes, I think, overworked and rather heavy-handed in his third book, *The Mills of the Kavanaughs* (1951), and it is a sign of Lowell's poetic intelligence, imagination, and inner resourcefulness that he could remake himself and his art together in the years immediately following. *Life Studies* gives us a poetry which seems the living tissue of the man who has written it, for he is never completely out of sight. As he says in a later poem, "one life, one writing."

Not only are the new poems of this volume freer, prosier in style; many of them are also unashamedly autobiographical. They are composed of intimate details, close sketches and glimpses of the poet's parents and grandparents, his friends, several other writers he has known or admired, his wife, and himself. But their most radical and unsettling aspect remains the candid, often frightening revelations of the poet's mental illness and hospitalization in such poems as "Waking in the Blue" and "Skunk Hour." Lowell's admitted interest in the possibilities of prose narrative (which he explores in the memoir "91 Revere Street," included in *Life Studies*); his liking for the masters of Russian realism, Tolstoy and Chekov, for example; his acquaintance with the poems of his student W. D. Snodgrass (whose first collection, *Heart's Needle*, also was published in 1959) which treat the details and crises of private life[32] —all these factors point the way toward a transformation of his writing into a manner closer to existence itself and less literary or artificial.

Lowell is extremely frank about himself and his family, though he is perhaps outdone in this respect by Anne Sexton, the late Sylvia Plath, and John Berryman in books such as his *Love & Fame* (1970). What he says may or may not be true in every detail to the actual lives and personalities he portrays, but we cannot be judges of that. What we know are the poems alone. We may object to the use of such private material in poetry, but I believe we must prove our objections on the grounds of the poem—that is, whether the use of the material is justified by what is made of it.

To my mind, the poems do justify themselves, for wry and critical or disturbingly self-revealing as some may be, they are conceived in clarity of vision and tempered with compassion and love. If we think of the poems as sketches or studies, in the way of the visual artist, not as finished portraits, final and irrevocable, we will observe in them the benefits of freedom and informality Lowell is seeking which will permit him to achieve, in his words, "some breakthrough back into life."[33] And these poems vibrate with life, its changing moods and order, the pain and pleasure of close relationship, the humor and bittersweetness of remembrance and loss; and through all of these elements of existence, the sweep of time, the knowledge of death.

The poem "Grandparents," for instance, begins humorously, even flippantly, though that is hardly its main line of feeling. As it proceeds, a few images taken from memories of his adolescence help to evoke the poet's grandmother and grandfather, and to give their world an impression of remoteness from our own. The first stanza ends by echoing the opening of an elegiac poem by the seventeenth-century English poet Henry Vaughan which starts, "They are all gone into the world of light! / And I alone sit ling'ring here." Then we learn that the poet has inherited his grandparents' farm and now visits it by himself, only to be haunted by recollections of the past. The poetic echo from Vaughan actually sounds an alteration in mood as returning memories continue to build up emotional pressure in the poet, until he recognizes what we all know intellectually but don't really understand without experiencing its forceful blows upon our deepest affections, our hidden but vital loves: he perceives the irreversible nature of time and events. This realization creates the sudden emotional climax of the poem, which is Lowell's momentary anguished cry of love and need hurled against the inevitable deprivations that our lives accumulate. His emotion released, however, he becomes once more the whimsical, slightly irreverent self we encountered at the outset of the poem. His idle doodling with a pencil at the poem's close indicates, in spite of persistent affections, the sharp division prevailing between the poet's attitudes and his grandparents' luxurious but trivial mode of living, shut off from the harsher realities of the world and secure in a religiousness that ignored them. The poem compels us to acknowledge the complex ties between past and present in an individual, as well as the wide range of feelings those ties can generate:

> They're altogether otherworldly now,
> those adults champing for their ritual Friday spin
> to pharmacist and five-and-ten in Brockton.
> Back in my throwaway and shaggy span
> of adolescence, Grandpa still waves his stick
> like a policeman;
> Grandmother, like a Mohammedan, still wears her thick
> lavendar mourning and touring veil;
> the Pierce Arrow clears its throat in a horse-stall.
> Then the dry road dust rises to whiten
> the fatigued elm leaves—
> the nineteenth century, tired of children, is gone.
> They're all gone into a world of light; the farm's my own.
>
> The farm's my own!
> Back there alone,
> I keep indoors, and spoil another season.
> I hear the rattley little country gramophone
> racking its five foot horn:
> "O Summer Time!"
> Even at noon here the formidable
> *Ancien Régime* still keeps nature at a distance. Five
> green shaded light bulbs spider the billiards-table;
> no field is greener than its cloth,
> where Grandpa, dipping sugar for us both,
> once spilled his demitasse.
> His favorite ball, the number three,
> still hides the coffee stain.
>
> Never again
> to walk there, chalk our cues,

insist on shooting for us both.
Grandpa! Have me, hold me, cherish me!
Tears smut my fingers. There
half my life-lease later,
I hold an *Illustrated London News*—;
disloyal still,
I doodle handlebar
mustaches on the last Russian Czar.

Of course, the poems from *Life Studies* which are most unsettling and caused the greatest stir are those treating mental breakdown and hospitalization. The title of the poem "Waking in the Blue" refers to the thoughts and sensations that occur to the poet as he wakes early in the morning in a Massachusetts mental hospital. The "azure day" he can see through his window, with its suggestions of freedom and promise, is in biting contrast to his own confined state. Lowell's poem records, among other things, that first waking when we still have a moment before full consciousness returns and we must face our daily reality, whatever it may be. But the instant of total recollection with which the first stanza concludes is a murderous thrust:

The night attendant, a B.U. sophomore,
rouses frorn the mare's-nest of his drowsy head
propped on *The Meaning of Meaning*.
He catwalks down our corridor.
Azure day
makes my agonized blue window bleaker.
Crows maunder on the petrified fairway.
Absence! My heart grows tense
as though a harpoon were sparring for the kill.
(This is the house for the "mentally ill.")

Lowell proceeds to describe the wasted lives of various patients, whose figures merely intensify his own feeling of restriction, near hopelessness; a fear for the future lurks beneath every word. The last stanza combines, in its image of the poet before the mirror, a momentary but ironical sense of jauntiness and contentment with the recurrence of quiet desperation over what is yet to be:

After a hearty New England breakfast,
I weigh two hundred pounds
this morning. Cock of the walk,
I strut in my turtle-necked French sailor's jersey
before the metal shaving mirrors,
and see the shaky future grow familiar
in the pinched, indigenous faces

> of these thoroughbred mental cases,
> twice my age and half my weight.
> We are all old-timers,
> each of us holds a locked razor.

This poem, and "Skunk Hour," which focuses on an agonized moment of mental disorder yet ends on a note of stubborn persistence in living, are terrible disclosures. In them Lowell takes a more candid, searching look at himself and his situation than most of us would care to, even under reasonably normal conditions. But such poems spring from a passion born of sheer necessity, and they strike the reader with the full force of the poet's individual being. Entering into areas usually marked "Private" in Lowell's work, we do not escape our own existence; rather, we find it and the larger life of our time reflected there, and in an aspect anything but comforting. More recently, Lowell has turned to the public world in a considerable number of poems, though here again he places himself as sensitive, tormented witness to the brutality, ugliness, frightened coldness, and power-craving of America today. "Agonies are one of my changes of garments," Whitman says in *Leaves of Grass*, and Lowell knows only too well the truth of that statement. Four stanzas from another poem of waking, a much later one called "Waking Sunday Morning," included in *Near the Ocean* (1967), give us the dilemmas of Lowell the man, conscientious, honest, spiritually bereft, in the midst of a society which has bred them. In a small New England town where Sunday church bells ring, the poet, now churchless but not irreligious, ponders the fate of belief in an America "top-heavy" with military might and envisages the country's collapse along the lines of an Old Testament precedent:

> O Bible chopped and crucified
> in hymns we hear but do not read,
> none of the milder subtleties
> of grace or art will sweeten these
> stiff quatrains shovelled out four-square—
> they sing of peace, and preach despair;
> yet they gave darkness some control,
> and left a loophole for the soul.
>
> No, put old clothes on, and explore
> the corners of the woodshed for
> its dregs and dreck: tools with no handle,
> ten candle-ends not worth a candle,
> old lumber banished from the Temple,
> damned by Paul's precept and example,
> cast from the kingdom, banned in Israel,
> the wordless sign, the tinkling cymbal.

When will we see Him face to face?
Each day he shines through darker glass.
In this small town where everything
is known, I see His vanishing
emblems, His white spire and flag-
pole sticking out above the fog,
like old white china doorknobs, sad,
slight, useless things to calm the mad.

Hammering military splendor,
top-heavy Goliath in full armor—
little redemption in the mass
liquidations of their brass,
elephant and phalanx moving
with the times and still improving,
when that kingdom hit the crash:
a million foreskins stacked like trash . . .

While resorting to formal poetic devices to maintain a certain control and emphasis, as in these stanzas, Lowell becomes simultaneously elliptic, allusive, and fast-moving. He manages to create the semblance of his mind's activity as it responds to the experience of contemporary life. Unlike Wright or Bly, who seek to articulate the voices lingering in a dark substratum of collective dreams as the means for comprehending our common condition, or Allen Ginsberg, who fashions a socio-political idiom in certain poems from a speech which incorporates elements of his private vision with others derived from Blake, the Old Testament, and Eastern mysticism, Lowell projects himself as a type of representative consciousness, absorbing and suffering the jolts and jars administered from without, and answering them with honesty, directness, and the strength of a very gifted, perceptive poet who no longer finds it possible to appeal to an order higher than the human. The spiritual order with which he had substantial familiarity in the period of his Catholic poems has not vanished entirely; rather, it has become clouded, indefinite, its signs as cryptic for him as for the protagonists of Kafka's tales. In Lowell's poetry since *Life Studies*, there is the man himself, as A. Alvarez says, "a man of great contradictions, tenderness and violence, a man obsessed equally by his own crack-ups and by the symptoms of crack-up in the society around him."[34]

Similar qualities and obsessions govern a rather extensive body of contemporary poetry which, for all the skill, inventiveness, and imagination that go into its composition, still communicates a naked revelation of tormented selfhood seemingly devoid of aesthetic intention. Prufrock's lines, with their implicit pain and frustration, characterize this poetry very well:

It is impossible to say just what I mean!
But as if a magic lantern threw the nerves in
    patterns on a screen. . . .

The most elaborate work in this canon of confessional or extremist writing is the lengthy sequence of John Berryman's *Dream Songs*, which began with the *77 Dream Songs* published in 1964 and concluded with the bulky *His Toy, His Dream, His Rest: 308 Dream Songs*, which appeared in 1968. Surely the impulse for these poems reaches from the early "Nervous Songs" and some other pieces through the startling transformation of Berryman's art initiated by his *Homage to Mistress Bradstreet*, a poem in which the author's voice alternates at times with the imagined voice of the early American poet, and where the tight, elliptic style with inverted, idiosyncratic syntax which we encounter in the *Dream Songs* makes its debut. The speaker in all of these frequently untitled poems is Henry Pussycat, middle-aged, white, and, as the sequence progresses, more and more obviously a thinly disguised *version* of Berryman himself—or, to play upon Yeats, a self which is distinctly *his* creation. Since the poems constitute a stylization of the dreaming mind, there is a constant shifting back and forth between the first, second, and third persons to correspond with altering moods and changes in the climate of consciousness, and to heighten dramatic tensions. In addition, a part of Henry occasionally adopts minstrel's black face, talks in a stagey Negro dialect, and then addresses the primary self of Henry as Mr. Bones—a traditional title which carries both social and personal overtones in terms of the whole poetic sequence. Curiously, in the second volume of *Dream Songs*, where the materials of Henry's experience seem to match so closely those of Berryman's, and where internal references to the poems themselves occur, the poet has supplied a prefatory note indicating that he is not to be mistaken for the speaker. Doubtless, as Lowell notes with respect to *Life Studies*, liberty is taken with fact, for the purposes of art. It is Berryman's consciousness remade by poetry which we inhabit, an image of his personal experience which we perceive through the sharp, difficult figure of Henry, with his tormented spirit of a lapsed Catholic (though there is an unexpected return to religious conviction, due to some visionary awareness, in the last poems of the recent book, *Love & Fame*) confronted with the spectacle of "a sickening century" of war, mass extermination, racial hatred, and power politics. Perhaps the best way to describe the complicated relationship between poet and speaker is to adopt a line from *Dream Song #370* to the purpose: "Naked the man came forth in his mask, to be."

These poems take for themes, as a rule, the details of an individual life: loves, marriages, friendship and enmity, poetry, and death. They move outward from such preoccupations into politics, the sufferings of others, various

manifestations of evil in the present age, celebrations and lamentations for
several figures, usually (though not exclusively) poets whom Berryman admires and whose loss is keenly felt: Frost, Roethke, Delmore Schwartz, Louis
MacNeice, R. P. Blackmur, and Randall Jarrell among them. Intermixed
with the toughness, harshness, irrationality, and pain in the poems are recurrent strains of comedy and tender lyricism. Underlying the sequence is a
gnawing anxiety and guilt, as well as what Berryman calls "an irreversible
loss" which Henry has suffered. The latter assumes many forms: the death
of friends, failures of love, the suicide of the poet's father, his collapsed religious faith, or the terrible nameless dread that can seize him, as in *Dream
Song #29*:

> There sat down, once, a thing on Henry's heart
> só heavy, if he had a hundred years
> & more, & weeping, sleepless, in all them time
> Henry could not make good.
> Starts again always in Henry's ears
> the little cough somewhere, an odour, a chime.
>
> And there is another thing he has in mind
> like a grave Sienese face a thousand years
> would fail to blur the still profiled reproach of. Ghastly,
> with open eyes, he attends, blind.
> All the bells say: too late. This is not for tears;
> thinking.
>
> But never did Henry, as he thought he did,
> end anyone and hacks her body up
> and hide the pieces where they may be found.
> He knows: he went over everyone, & nobody's missing.
> Often he reckons, in the dawn, them up.
> Nobody is ever missing.

Though this sequence explores private associations and the details of
personal life, rendering the most lucid and the most illogical states of mind,
nothing about it is more remarkable than Berryman's combination of formal exactness—the poems are composed around three six-line stanzas, freely
rhymed—with bold experiment—he coins words, uses slang, dialect, inverted syntax, and so forth. As a result, no matter how irrational the dream
elements may be at times, they are presented with a precision and tautness
of language which is enviable. Paul Valéry says, "It is the very one who
wants to write down his dream who is obliged to be extremely wide awake."[35]
In the eighth *Dream Song* Berryman dramatizes the nightmare of the self's
destruction by a vicious, anonymous company referred to only as "they."
These grim processes are conveyed (as also in Stanley Kunitz's "My Surgeons,"

built upon a similar theme) in a language that embodies the full nature of
what is happening without itself succumbing to emotional chaos:

> The weather was fine. They took away his teeth,
> white & helpful; bothered his backhand;
> halved his green hair.
> They blew out his loves, his interests. 'Underneath,'
> (they called in iron voices) 'understand,
> is nothing. So there.'
>
> The weather was very fine. They lifted off
> his covers till he showed, and cringed & pled
> to see himself less.
> They installed mirrors till he flowed. 'Enough'
> (murmured they) 'if you will watch Us instead,
> yet you may saved be. Yes.'
>
> The weather fleured. They weakened all his eyes,
> and burning thumbs into his ears, and shook
> his hand like a notch.
> They flung long silent speeches. (Off the hook!)
> They sandpapered his plumpest hope. (So capsize.)
> They took away his crotch.

"The way is to the destructive element submit yourself," Stein advises
Marlowe in a famous passage in Conrad's *Lord Jim*. Many of our contemporary poets seem bent on following this course, pursuing it though the attendant hazards of madness and death loom perilously near for anyone who,
through an exposed, vulnerable psyche and nervous system, tries to cross
thresholds where the self is strained beyond endurance and shatters. For
them, "the destructive element" alone, rather than Stein's survival techniques, matters—unless the act of poetry itself can become a mode of release and self-protection. Anne Sexton and Sylvia Plath, two richly endowed poets, walk such a narrow, dizzying boundary line in their work, sometimes overstepping it. The price is high—life itself—and neither of them
returns. The poetry of both these women rises from the turbulence of private emotions, mental breakdown, spiritual quandaries, and strong attrac-
tions to death. To have produced the poems they have given us, charged
with beauty and terror, and to have remade themselves as distinctive poetic
personalities within those poems by transmuting inner crises and a compulsion toward self-destruction is a moral and artistic triumph for both of them—
in spite of their tragic suicides.

   In "For the Year of the Insane," subtitled "a prayer," Anne Sexton, a con-
fessed "unbeliever," still holds in her hand a "black rosary with its silver

Christ" and addresses the Virgin Mary. The theme of her reflective speech is the passage of time, the steady encroachment of age and death, her fear, loneliness, spiritual desolation, and mental instability. No poetry could be more personal:

> Closer and closer
> comes the hour of my death
> as I rearrange my face, grow back,
> grow undeveloped and straight-haired.
> All this is death.
> In the mind there is a thin alley called death
> and I move through it as
> through water.
> My body is useless.
> It lies, curled like a dog on the carpet.
> It has given up.
> There are no words here except the half-learned,
> the *Hail Mary* and the *full of grace*.
> Now I have entered the year without words.
> I note the queer entrance and the exact voltage.
> Without words they exist.
> Without words one may touch bread
> and be handed bread
> and make no sound.
>
> O Mary, tender physician,
> come with powders and herbs
> for I am in the center.
> It is very small and the air is gray
> as in a steam house.
> I am handed wine as a child is handed milk.
> It is presented in a delicate glass
> with a round bowl and a thin lip.
> The wine itself is pitch-colored, musty and secret.
> The glass rises on its own toward my mouth
> and I notice this and understand this
> only because it has happened.
> I have this fear of coughing
> but I do not speak,
> a fear of rain, a fear of the horseman
> who comes riding into my mouth.
> The glass tilts on its own
> and I am on fire.
> I see two thin streaks burn down my chin.
> I see myself as one would see another.
> I have been cut in two.

> O Mary, open your eyelids.
> I am in the domain of silence,
> the kingdom of the crazy and the sleeper.
> There is blood here
> and I have eaten it.
> O mother of the womb,
> did I come for blood alone?
> O little mother,
> I am in my own mind.
> I am locked in the wrong house.

This experience which Anne Sexton so vividly depicts, with its intense, visionary qualities, its feeling of being divided in two, may remind us of the drama of Roethke's "In a Dark Time." Though the poem strikes into the most intimate domains of consciousness and alternates between self-examination, supplication, and a hallucination that appears to approach madness yet is also strangely ritual and sacramental (the glass changes into a chalice; the wine, as in communion, into Christ's blood or presence, which in turn brings the "fear of the horseman," or death), the mind of the poet reflects the spiritual unrest and tension in which many of us may share and the terrible frustration we feel at being trapped by the limited perspective of our own egos.

The same may be said for Sylvia Plath, particularly with respect to the poems of her posthumous collection *Ariel* (1966), where her own "controlled hallucination," as Robert Lowell calls it in his foreword to the book, and the poetic powers freed by her neuropathic state permit her entry into the most extreme conditions of awareness and emotion. These poems are filled with inexorable motion, relentless energy, abrupt, shifting imagery, and the expanding, altering identity of the poet herself. In "Getting There," for instance, conceiving herself involved in "some war or other," she is moving in a train across Russia through a veritable hell of death, destruction, and brutality. The images follow one another in rapid succession, with the poet both witnessing and participating in what occurs. At the conclusion of the poem she has survived all the desolation and carnage, as if miraculously, and is reborn. If the experience seems confused, disordered, that is Plath's imaginative intention and not the failures of the neurotic; no matter what perceptions and hallucinatory visions her mental states provoke, these are worked with consummate, determined skill and craft into her poems. As she remarked in an interview not long before her death:

> I must say I cannot sympathize with these cries from the heart that are
> informed by nothing except a needle or a knife, or whatever it is. I believe

that one should be able to control and manipulate experiences, even the most terrifying, like madness, being tortured, this sort of experience, and one should be able to manipulate these experiences with an informed and an intelligent mind. I think that personal experience is very important, but certainly it shouldn't be a kind of shut-box and mirror-looking, narcissistic experience. I believe it should be *relevant*, and relevant to the larger things, the bigger things such as Hiroshima and Dachau and so on.[36]

So the nervous and emotional illness which assails her inner life becomes for Plath a means whereby she can gain access to experience not outwardly hers; the imagination thus liberated takes on the existence of others. An identification of this sort is evident in "Getting There." The last half of the poem follows:

> How far is it?
> It is so small
> The place I am getting to, why are there these obstacles—
> The body of this woman,
> Charred skirts and deathmask
> Mourned by religious figures, by garlanded children.
> And now detonations—
> Thunder and guns.
> The fire's between us.
> Is there no still place
> Turning and turning in the middle air,
> Untouched and untouchable.
> The train is dragging itself, it is screaming—
> An animal
> Insane for the destination,
> The bloodspot,
> The face at the end of the flare.
> I shall bury the wounded like pupas,
> I shall count and bury the dead.
> Let their souls writhe in a dew,
> Incense in my track.
> The carriages rock, they are cradles.
> And I, stepping from this skin
> Of old bandages, boredoms, old faces
>
> Step to you from the black car of Lethe,
> Pure as a baby.

In the last turning that this limited survey of various manifestations of the personal element among contemporary poets will take, I want to cite the work of a few poets who have, each in his or her singular fashion, followed the leads suggested both in theory and in practice by William Carlos Williams and Ezra Pound—and to a certain extent by H. D., Louis Zukofsky, and Kenneth Rexroth as well. A number of these poets are frequently called the Black Mountain group, named after the experimental Black Mountain College, where many of them first met to study or to teach and began to formulate their notions of poetry; or they are called Projectivists, after the late Charles Olson's influential and descriptive essay on "Projective Verse." What links them together, beyond a recognition of Olson as a seminal force and leader, beyond friendships and apparently a great amount of literary correspondence, is less a close or confining similarity of poetic practice than the acceptance of Williams and the other poets mentioned as their guides and mentors. As Denise Levertov writes in "September 1961," a profound tribute to Pound, Williams, and H. D.:

> They have told us
> the road leads to the sea,
> and given
> the language into our hands.

In his essays Williams urges the abandonment of iambic pentameter, the sonnet form, and other English poetic conventions which he strongly believes prevent America from producing its own unique poetry, a poetry deriving from our native speech and its rhythms, and from developing a new and relative kind of "measure," to use his favorite term, in opposition to the fixed poetic foot. But, more than that, in his poems and prose there is a concentrated attention to particulars, to immediate environment, to objects in all their detailed concreteness and specificity which simultaneously helps to define the self perceiving them. Williams notes in the introduction to a book of his poems, *The Wedge*:

> When a man makes a poem, makes it, mind you, he takes words as he finds them interrelated about him and composes them—without distortion which would mar their exact significances—into an intense expression of his perceptions and ardors that they may constitute a revelation in the speech that he uses. It isn't what he says that counts as a work of art, it's what he makes, with such intensity of perception that it lives with an intrinsic movement of its own to verify its authenticity.[37]

In the work of Denise Levertov, Robert Creeley, Charles Olson, Robert Duncan, Gary Snyder, Edward Dorn, Larry Eigner, and Paul Blackburn, among others, we discover the poetic realization in several forms of the process Williams describes. The poet's focus is frequently on his life as a person: his daily encounter with *things*, with others; the character of his relationships, even the most intimate ones; the movements of his thought and sensation; the nature of his interior being as it emerges in dream or vision, or is interwoven with traditional and occult symbols, as in Robert Duncan's poetry, into the shape of a mythology both personal and cosmic. Finally, there is, for certain of these writers, a poetry of place. The most notable and ambitious example is Charles Olson's long sequence, *The Maximus Poems*, combining the history, geography, and topography of his native town, Gloucester, Massachusetts (the "Dogtown" of the poems), with personal perceptions, biography, and, intermingled with these, elements of various mythologies. He writes in the fourth poem: "An American / is a complex of occasions, / themselves a geometry / of spatial nature," a view which grew out of his visit, years earlier, to the Yucatan Peninsula, where he studied closely the ancient Mayan culture and set down his thoughts and discoveries in a correspondence with Robert Creeley, now included in the volume of Olson's *Selected Writings* (1966).

However personal some of the work of the Projectivists and Black Mountain poets may be, it can never be mistaken for the writing of the confessional poets. While it does not avoid the harsh actualities of present-day existence or disguise painful areas of private experience, it also does not display much interest in psychic disturbance, emotional and spiritual torment, the sense of victimization, and nervous pressures which threaten to explode into madness. For these poets the act of poetry—and all of them, I believe, are fascinated with the process of composition itself—is a matter of the most profound significance to the individual, because it is through that act that he fashions his own single identity. Becoming a proper human being and making a poem properly are two sides of the same endeavor. In Charles Olson's words:

> . . . a man, carved
> out of himself, so wrought he
> fills his given space, makes
> traceries sufficient to
> others' needs. . . .[38]

Denise Levertov, who quotes in a lecture this statement by Olson, has a remark of her own which, together with Olson's, brings out the double emphasis of their poetics: the stress on the fulfillment of the poet's self and on the poem as directed to readers. She says: "The act of realizing inner experience in material substance is in itself an action *towards others*, even when the conscious intention has not gone beyond the desire for self-expression."[39]

In Denise Levertov's poems, or Robert Creeley's, or Robert Duncan's, the reader receives an impression of having stepped into a new kind of space, an invisible but nonetheless real zone bounded by an interlocking form of

words yet acquiring its substance from the felt presence of the poet. The
first poem in Robert Duncan's important collection *The Opening of the Field*
(1960) introduces a location which is at once an amalgam of memory and
dream in the author's mind and the actual space or "field" of language the
poem creates:

> . . . a scene made-up by the mind,
> that is not mine, but is a made place,
>
> that is mine, it is so near to the heart,
> an eternal pasture folded in all thought
> so that there is a hall therein
>
> that is a made place, created by light
> wherefrom the shadows that are forms fall.

This space is, in correspondence with Charles Olson's attitudes, an essential aspect of the poet's being, a part of his life. Admittedly, what I am saying may seem difficult to understand clearly, but it can be grasped readily
through the experience of the poetry. Or we might think of how our bodies
create what we could call their own individual space around themselves as
we perform all the gestures and activities of living. It is that sense of presence, involving the total self of the writer, physical and spiritual, which
reaches us in the work of these poets.

Again I shall offer only a couple of examples out of many possible ones,
rather than to aim at comprehensiveness here. The last section of Levertov's
"The Coming Fall" blends description of an external setting with the gradual
effects of this situation as it is felt inwardly by the poet herself, coming
initially through bodily sensations:

> Down by the fallen fruit in the old orchard
> the air grows cold. The hill
> hides the sun.
>
> A sense of the present
> rises out of earth and grass,
> enters the feet, ascends
>
> into the genitals, constricting
> the breast, lightening
> the head—a wisdom,
>
> a shiver, a delight
> that what is passing

> is here, as if
> a snake went by, green in the
> gray leaves.

Here the "sense of the present," an evanescent trace of feeling and physical sensation which would normally elude words, is beautifully caught; it remains true to its origins, for there is no attempt to put intellectual constructions upon it. Levertov tries to return us, through the poem, to the moment of the experience itself. In another poem, "A Common Ground," she tells us how, ideally, poetry should so transform reality that in perceiving the elements which comprise our world, in carrying out the tasks and necessities of daily life, we would be absorbing poetry:

> Poems stirred
> into paper coffee-cups, eaten
> with petals on rye in the
> sun—the cold shadows in back,
> and the traffic grinding the
> borders of spring—entering
> human lives forever,
> unobserved, a spring element. . . .

Levertov's search, as she says in "Matins," is for "the authentic," which appears both in dreams, the inward life, and in waking actualities; it is "the known / appearing fully itself, and / more itself than one knew." In discovering the true abundance and nature of knowable reality, the poet fashions her—and our—solidarity, human community, with it.

Gary Snyder's poetry, surely some of the finest of recent years, often draws on his experiences of camping and mountain-climbing, working in logging camps in the forests of the Pacific Northwest, laboring as a tanker hand, studying the life and lore of American Indians, and, finally, spending years in Japan studying under a Zen master in Kyoto. He has remarked in a dust-jacket comment for one of his books: "As a poet I hold the most archaic values on earth. They go back to the late Paleolithic; the fertility of the soil, the magic of animals, the power-vision in solitude, the terrifying initiation and rebirth; the love and ecstasy of the dance, the common work of the tribe. I try to hold both history and wilderness in mind, that my poems may approach the true measure of things and stand against the unbalance and ignorance of our times." In certain poems from his *Riprap* (1959), for example, Snyder provides a feeling of the immensity of the wilderness, of non-human nature, of its seemingly eternal, mute history, against which human activity, culture, and consciousness appear insignificant. By his control of

rhythm and language, his accuracy and precision of detail, he resists being
overwhelmed; the poem, in turn, while re-creating the man and his experience, humanizes it, if you will. The recognition is not less disturbing but has
at least been assimilated to consciousness, made part of our awareness of
reality. To repeat Denise Levertov's words: "the known / appearing fully itself, and / more itself than one knew." One such poem of Snyder's is "Above
Pate Valley":

> We finished clearing the last
> Section of trail by noon,
> High on the ridge-side
> Two thousand feet above the creek
> Reached the pass, went on
> Beyond the white pine groves,
> Granite shoulders, to a small
> Green meadow watered by the snow,
> Edged with Aspen—sun
> Straight high and blazing
> But the air was cool.
> Ate a cold fried trout in the
> Trembling shadows. I spied
> A glitter, and found a flake
> Black volcanic glass—obsidian—
> By a flower. Hands and knees
> Pushing the Bear grass, thousands
> Of arrowhead leavings over a
> Hundred yards. Not one good
> Head, just razor flakes
> On a hill snowed all but summer,
> A land of fat summer deer,
> They came to camp. On their
> Own trails. I followed my own
> Trail here. Picked up the cold-drill,
> Pick, singlejack, and sack
> Of dynamite.
> Ten thousand years.

Something of the enormous range and vitality of American poetry today
has, I hope, impressed itself in the course of these remarks, which I intended both to distinguish certain of the pronounced personal qualities evident among contemporary poets of the last three decades or so, and to provide a partial—but only partial—survey of the very different kinds of writers and writings involved. I have avoided, as I said I would, any attempt at
close definition; that should come later, as the job of the sympathetic, imaginative literary historian. Instead, I have tried to be both suggestive and

illustrative, and to focus on examples of the poetry itself, since it, after all, is more important than anything I might have to say about it. There are other poets too numerous to name whom I should have liked to introduce here, but such an effort is impracticable, the matter for a large book. I have confined myself, more or less, to three prominent tendencies for the purposes at hand. Within the landscape of contemporary poetry, as I believe my choices demonstrated, there are many talented writers, and their styles, their notions of what a poem ought to be or do, diverge widely. Yet it is not too much to say that they have in common a concern for the experience which lies nearest them, within the radius of their actual lives: the space— to return to that metaphor—outside themselves, through which they move and possess the legacies of history, in which they act and meet others; or the space within, the interior world of dream, vision, and meditation. This concern enables them, whether consciously or not, to combat those abstracting, tabulating, depersonalizing forces which our society produces by asserting through poems the value of their unique human nature and experience. Again Denise Levertov helps us; she writes of the stages of awareness leading up to poetic activity: "The progression seems clear to me: from Reverence for Life to Attention to Life, from Attention to Life to a highly developed Seeing and Hearing, from Seeing and Hearing (faculties almost indistinguishable for the poet) to the Discovery and Revelation of Form, from Form to Song."[40] A similar process, however aware of it the poet may be, however it might differ in certain particulars, appears to me to govern the work of those poets we have discussed, and many others as well. I can say little more now except that the burden of proof is in the reading of our contemporaries, and that careful attention will be repaid by an encounter with poems bold and various in form, attitude, and insight; poems which, like the poets we discover within them, are unimpeachable in their integrity, intense in their vision. In Yeats's pregnant phrase, "creation's very self" is what we look for, and find. In the third of her "Three Meditations," Levertov offers us an image of the poet's activity in our time with which I should like to finish:

> We breathe an ill wind,
> nevertheless our kind
> in mushroom multitudes
> jostles for elbow-room
> moonwards
>
> an equalization of
> hazards
> bringing the poet

back to song
as before

to sing of death
as before
and life, while he
has it, energy

being in him a singing,
a beating of gongs, efficacious
to drive away devils,
response to

the wonder that
as before
shows a double face,

to be
what he is
being his virtue

filling his whole space
so no devil
may enter.

(1969)

NOTES

[1]Charles Olson, "Projective Verse," in *Human Universe and Other Essays*, ed. Donald M. Allen (New York, 1967), p. 54.

[2]Randall Jarrell, "The End of the Line," in *Literary Opinion in America*, ed. M. D. Zabel (New York, 1951), p. 747.

[3]*Contemporary American Poetry*, ed. Donald Hall (Baltimore, 1962), p. 17.

[4]James Dickey, *The Suspect in Poetry* (Madison, Minn., 1964), pp. 55-56.

[5]T.S. Eliot, *Selected Essays 1917-1932* (New York, 1932), pp. 8, 7

[6]Louis Simpson, "Dead Horses and Live Issues,' *The Nation* (April 24, 1967), p. 520.

[7]*The Autobiography of William Butler Yeats* (New York, 1958), p. 183.

[8]Introduction to *The New Writing in the U.S.A.*, ed. Donald M. Allen and Robert Creeley (Harmondsworth, Middlesex, 1967), p. 18.

[9]Ortega y Gassett, *The Dehumanization of Art and Other Essays* (New York, 1956), p. 175

[10]Martin Buber, *I and Thou*, trans. R. G. Smith (New York, 1958), pp. 11, 10.

[11]Kenneth Rexroth, *Bird in the Bush: Obvious Essays* (New York, 1959), p. 12.

[12]Denise Levertov, "Origins of a Poem," *Michigan Quarterly Review*, VII, 4 (Fall 1968), p. 238.

[13]"On Identity," in *On the Poet and His Craft: Selected Prose of Theodore Roethke*, ed. Ralph J. Mills, Jr. (Seattle, 1965), p. 21.

[14]An illuminating account of these years is to be found in Allan Seager, *The Glass House: The Life of Theodore Roethke* (New York, 1968).

[15]"Open Letter," in Mills, ed., *On the Poet and His Craft*, p. 41.

[16]For discussion, see *The Contemporary Poet as Artist and Critic*, ed. Anthony Ostroff (Boston, 1964); Karl Malkoff, *Theodore Roethke* (New York, 1966); *Theodore Roethke: Essays on the Poetry*, ed. Arnold Stein (Seattle, 1965).

[17]Ostroff, ed., *The Contemporary Poet as Artist and Critic*, p. 49.

[18]Preface to St.-John Perse, *Anabasis*, trans. T. S. Eliot (New York, 1949), p. 10.

[19]From "I Cry, Love! Love!" in *Collected Poems of Theodore Roethke* (New York, 1966), p.92.

[20]*The Distinctive Voice*, ed. William J. Martz (Glenview, Ill., 1966), p. 247.

[21]*The Nation* (April 24, 1967), p. 521.

[22]*Mid-Century French Poets*, ed. Wallace Fowlie (New York, 1955), p. 175.

[23]Louis Simpson in Martz, ed., *The Distinctive Voice*, p. 247.

[24]*The New American Painting* (New York, 1959), p. 64.

[25]*The New American Poetry 1945-1960*, ed. Donald M. Allen (New York, 1960), p. 419. Readers may also want to consider O'Hara's remarks in "Personism: A Manifesto," included in *An Anthology of New York Poets*, ed. Ron Padgett and David Shapiro (New York, 1970), pp. xxxi-xxxiv.

[26]Martz, ed., *The Distinctive Voice*, pp. 269-270.

[27]Jacques Maritain, *Creative Intuition in Art and Poetry* (New York, 1955), p.197.

[28]Martz, ed., *The Distinctive Voice*, p. 247.

[29]Robert Bly, "On Political Poetry," *The Nation* (April 24, 1967), p. 522.

[30]Ibid., p. 522.

[31]See A. Alvarez, *Beyond All This Fiddle* (London, 1968); also on confessional poetry, M. L. Rosenthal, *The New Poets* (New York, 1967).

[32]See Frederick Seidel's interview with Lowell, in *Robert Lowell: A Collection of Critical Essays*, ed. Thomas Parkinson (Englewood Cliffs, N.J., 1968).

[33]*Robert Lowell: A Collection of Critical Essays*, p. 19.

[34]Alvarez, *Beyond All This Fiddle*, p.14.

[35]Paul Valéry, *The Art of Poetry*, trans. Denise Folliot (New York, 1958), p. 11.

[36]*The Poet Speaks*, ed. Peter Orr (London, 1966), pp. 169-170.

[37]Selected Essays of William Carlos Williams (New York, 1954), p. 257.

[38]Quoted by Denise Levertov, *Michigan Quarterly Review* (Fall 1968), p. 236.

[39]Ibid., p. 235.

[40]Ibid., p. 238.

2

Wallace Stevens:
The Image of the Rock

I

Poets in old age, feeling the steady approach of death, often tend to organize their attitudes, to seek out some representative symbols in which these may be embodied and preserved against the dissolution that, they fear, awaits their own persons. In such efforts they retrace the patterns of all their previous work, hoping to mount a worthy crown upon it, a final image which will suffuse each poem with a new light—an illumination wrenched from a struggle on the very threshold of annihilation. This activity is, of course, restricted by the nature of individual cases and also by the disposition of the writer's mind toward the question of last things.

The concluding section of poems which Wallace Stevens appended to the collected edition of his work contains, as Randall Jarrell points out, some of his finest pieces. Almost without exception, they are meditations on death or display premonitions of that event. The title given to the group, *The Rock*, figures also as a symbolic image in a number of the more important poems, and it becomes evident that this symbol is appointed a heavy burden. It is to lend a final character to the whole body of Stevens's poetry, issuing and receiving meaning in a ceaseless flow of reciprocal relations with that body. Again, the rock is a place of spiritual entombment:

> There it was, word for word,
> The poem that took the place of a mountain.
> He breathed its oxygen,
> Even when the book lay turned in the dust of his table.[1]

The work itself resists the treachery of time. Death is time's instrument and maintains everything within an apparently endless temporal round. There is no real departure from this cycle but merely changing relations in it. In order to understand the total significance of the rock as it appears in these late poems, we must look at some of its previous manifestations and see how they contribute to that prominence.

The first notable appearance of the rock comes in "How to Live. What to Do." from *Ideas of Order* (1936). In this poem a "man and his companion," in exodus from a land and a state of life which they have left far behind, stop before "the heroic height" of an enormous rock as it stands "impure" in a strange landscape under the pale light of the moon. The human pair, who certainly more than suggest Adam and Eve cast from the Garden of Eden, are explorers of the kind we encounter in Stevens's array of *dramatis personae* searching for a tenable view of the world:

> Coldly the wind fell upon them
> In many majesties of sound:
> They that had left the flame-freaked sun
> To seek a sun of fuller fire.

The wind's incessant and derelict motion, always a harbinger of flux and change for the poet, creates the unsettled climate they have found between an old order sacrificed and a new one as yet unknown. But the rock remains the irreducible focus of the scene, bathed with the remote glare, of the pure imagination (the moon), and we are forced, along with the travelers, to accept it as *the* essential and imperfect fact:

> Instead there was this tufted rock
> Massively rising high and bare
> Beyond all trees, the ridges thrown
> Like giant arms among the clouds.

> There was neither voice nor crested image,
> No chorister, nor priest. There was
> Only the great height of the rock
> And the two of them standing still to rest.

The tone is one of awe, almost of veneration, before the austere and secret promise of the rock. There is also a mixture here of a primitive pantheism and an empiricist's recognition of the definite and physical, both circumscribed by the poet's mind. The first intimation we have of Stevens's idea of a *personal church* is contained in the imagery of these stanzas, along with the attendant god of the imagination and the notable absence of ritual or clergy.

Yet the rock cannot he bound to one meaning, and Stevens likes to clothe it in the garbs of the richest season, as he does in "Credences of Summer." In this context it turns into "the rock of summer," associated with the peak of earthly, physical existence, but once more, and from another angle, it is established as a form of objective certainty in the changing universe of Stevens's poetry:

> The rock cannot be broken. It is the truth.
> It rises from land and sea and covers them.
> It is a mountain half way green and then,
> The other immeasurable half, such rock
> As placid air becomes. But it is not
>
> A hermit's truth nor symbol in hermitage.
> It is a visible rock, the audible,
> The brilliant mercy of a sure repose,
> On this present ground, the vividest repose,
> Things certain sustaining us in certainty.

Distinguishing this symbol as real or factual in opposition to the philosopher's (the hermit's) occult conceptualization, the poet sees the rock as encompassing the natural ("green") world grasped through the sense in an intuition of sheer physical being. The "immeasurable half" of "placid air" contrasts with the shifting winds that destroy or alter things in so many of Stevens's poems and corresponds to the transparent medium in which perception and what is perceived are brought to fruitful completion. Without this transparent medium, of which the images of the "major," "glass," or "central" man are other and more concentrated instances, man falls short of his potential stature and fails to realize what has been given him—the possibilities of the created world. Outside of consciousness, the rock is his only *tangible* form of assurance: it is the layer of the actual, solid world in which he has his being. Stevens insists that we, like his two travelers, start from there. "Reality is the beginning not the end," he writes in "An Ordinary Evening in New Haven."

II

Since we are involved with questions of death and eschatology in Stevens's poetry, it is necessary to examine his theology. To say that this poet is a naturalist, rejecting the orthodox systems of Christianity or any other belief, is not to say that a certain type of theology would be irrelevant here. It is true that from *Harmonium* on Stevens frequently treats supernatural religions with irony or otherwise indicates his distrust of them, sometimes setting as his frame of reference a world not unlike Nietzsche's one of eternal recurrence, as we discover in poems such as "Description without Place," where that philosopher is briefly mentioned. Often, as C. Roland Wagner has said, the influence of Bergson is discernible. At any rate, though Stevens satirizes self-righteous and stiff-necked piety or militant puritanism, (see, for example, his treatment of Cotton Mather), he further reveals his own misconceptions of traditional Christianity. If I read him correctly, he views it as purely spiritual, as inimical to creation. This notion seems to lie behind satires like "Cortège for Rosenbloom." However, much orthodox Christian thought stresses the unity of the person rather than an unconditional division of body and soul which diminishes the worth of the former.

Whether we accept it or not, the announcement made in Nietzsche's *The Gay Science* of the destruction of God has become an integral part of our modern experience; it is the air we breathe. While Stevens assuredly holds such an attitude and has set the human as his boundary, he is, at the same time, quite unwilling to wholly discard the idea of God. There is, though, no struggle in his verse with an older kind of orthodoxy which must be shed (unless we take "Sunday Morning" as a partial exception); Christianity is simply observed in retrospect. In "The Men That Are Falling" from *The Man with the Blue Guitar* he employs the *persona* of a sleeper awakening to a vision in the darkness of his "catastrophic room," a metaphor for the mind. Dominated by the fierce moonlight of the imagination, he finds the pillow on which he gazes "more than sudarium," and there confronts the tortured visage of a man who at once represents Christ and all other martyrs to an ideal cause. Though the intentions here are partially political, the value of the human redemption Stevens attaches to this sacrifice is not entirely clear. Nonetheless, we do see that it belongs to this world, not to another. The agony and triumph are man's rather than God's, while the ideal prompting these selfless actions is the noble vision of projected human "desire." We may be struck by the similarity in this to the *immanent transcendence* in the writings of Joyce or Yeats, a transcendence achieved within the natural world yet raising the participants above the range of time and space. Stevens concludes the poem: "This death was his belief though death is a stone. / This man loved earth, not heaven, enough to die." Death in the shape of the stone is fixed within the physical order of which it is a part; beyond there is only the "blank," as we are told in "The Blue Buildings in the Summer Air." Taken as a confrontation of Christ, "The Men That Are Falling" ends in the poet's refusal to accept His divinity. Yet he places importance and value on such sacrificial acts, recognizing in them a pinnacle of heroic tragedy that still belongs to the ordonnance of human imagination.

At the same time, the extent to which the significance of mortal gestures reaches is symbolic and finds fulfillment in what Stevens calls "supreme fictions." These projected ideas by which we guide ourselves lead the poet to the borders of his own mysticism. Furthermore, the attitude toward the universe Stevens implies does not preclude deity. Not only the poetry but the more recently published prose "Adagia"—aphorisms and meditations from his notebooks—in *Opus Posthumous* disclose a preoccupation with "God." But, in keeping with the limitations he has set, Stevens maintains his deity as indwelling. The universe, therefore, receives its structure from within, not by the will of an external and; omnipotent God. In one of the adages from his collection he writes, "God is in me or else is not at all (does not exist)." Evidently then the existence of Stevens's God depends completely on the existence of man; and this God is, moreover, a creative force within him or, as the poet says, "God and the imagination are one." The transfer of generative power from the divine Logos of the Prologue of St. John's Gospel to the human spirit is accomplished in "Description without Place." The world is created, we are told in this poem, not out of nothing but, we might say, in depth or perspective through the description of it:

> Description is revelation. It is not
> The thing described, nor false facsimile.
>
> It is an artificial thing that exists
> In its own seeming, plainly visible,
>
> Yet not too closely the double of our lives,
> Intenser than any actual life could be,
>
> A text that we should be born that we might read,
> More explicit than the experience of the sun
>
> And moon, the book of reconciliation,
> Book of a concept only possible
>
> In description, canon central in itself,
> The thesis of the plentifullest John.

In that space, to use a convenient metaphor, between reality and the imagination, the flatly objective and the actively subjective, is created the "book" in which we should, Stevens says, seek our fullest being. For "the word is the making of the world," constructing out of the bare rudiments of our situation among earthly objects a richer climate of habitation. The lonely pair of "How to Live. What to Do." must write upon this naked rock of the world the meanings for life of which they are capable. With that act, which is the imagination's endeavor, they and the rock are drawn together and figured forth in a new identity.

In one respect, then, poetry is for Stevens something more than the written literature alone. It is a mode of the mind's working, a way of looking that demands the "interdependence of reality and the imagination as equals," he remarks in *The Necessary Angel*. This activity, we should understand, is not restricted to writers or artists, though craftsmanship may be; it is rather the exercise of what we have somehow received as the power to make over our situation and circumstance: "The true work of art, whatever it may be," Stevens notes in *The Necessary Angel*, "is not the work of the individual artist. It is time and it is place as these perfect themselves." Poetry is involved in the very instant of our contact with the real and factual, and serves as the agent of a new reality born of the fusion of the imagination with raw physical things: "The poem is the cry of its occasion, / Part of the res itself and not about it." God, or the divine attribute, has become man's innate ability to renew the world and to live by the abundance arising from his intercourse with the blunt facts of material being. What Stevens calls "bare fact" is transmuted into the limitless prospects offered the mind by "analogy." The scope of life's potentiality is determined by the pursuit of our ideal images, fixed in earthly distances and glittering in the sunlit air. Of his thesis the poems are "pages of illustrations" giving a human meaning to an otherwise indifferent, often hostile, world. Following this in detail, we see Stevens developing the persistent terms of his "revelation" from the elemental parts of the universe: moon, sun, stars, sea, stones, rivers, trees and vegetation, wind and rain, the cycle of the seasons—all come through frequent use to operate as heavily weighted symbols. From such disciplined repetition there arises a gospel of the natural man, as we gather in "Esthétique du Mal":

> And out of what one sees and hears and out
> Of what one feels, who could have thought to make
>
> So many selves, so many sensuous worlds,
> As if the air, the mid-day air, was swarming
> With the metaphysical changes that occur,
> Merely in living as and where we live.

This kind of man charts his explorations, visualizes his horizon, from his experience of participation in the physical world and what the expansive movements of his mind can make of that.

III

The two primary components of Stevens's poetic cosmos, the brute material fact and the imagination which lends it meaning and value, are joined in the image of the rock. These interdependent parts are plainly visible in "Credences of Summer," where the physical level of creation—and this implies all of nature—is surmounted by the curious transparent glaze of imagination, bringing our focus to bear on a central point of things in a vision of celestial majesty. Here the eye, chief organ of the imaginative facility, projects its ideal representations and thus provides the harmonious conditions under which things become their utmost selves:

> It is the rock of summer, the extreme,
> A mountain luminous half way in bloom
> And then half way in the extremest light
> Of sapphires flashing from the central sky,
> As if twelve princes sat before a king.

This image of the gods is the inhuman center or idea from which everything radiates outward. Such immaterial deities are, however, human productions and are necessary to what R. P. Blackmur has called Stevens's "platonism" for these remote, inhuman figures of the mind comprise embodiments of man's ultimate desires: they are the absolutes he fashions—impermanent ones—out of his earthly experience. It is finally the rock that receives this celestial illumination and seizes the religious sense with its brilliance and splendor—and that is exactly what Stevens wishes. The rarefied realm of ideal beings exists only to enhance life in a tangible and very human world. And so we find the rock appearing as a radiant image in some of Stevens's latest pieces, for example, "The Poem That Took The Place of a Mountain" and, naturally, "The Rock" itself.

Before we examine these last and most fully developed uses of the rock, we should understand that Stevens has also assigned this symbol a relationship to death. To help us we shall have to introduce another passage from an earlier poem; this one is from "Esthétique du Mal":

VII

> How red the rose that is the soldier's wound,
> The wounds of many soldiers, the wounds of all
> The soldiers that have fallen, red in blood,
> The soldier of time grown deathless in great size.
>
> A mountain in which no case is ever found,
> Unless indifference to deeper death
> Is ease, stands in the dark, a shadow's hill,
> And there the soldier of time has deathless rest.

The soldier, whose full title indicates the temporal order to which he properly belongs, becomes symbolic of all human life and the unavoidable conclusion awaiting it. Since it is really the dark or shadow side of the rock, the
"mountain" of this passage seems an image of the burial mound, of earthly
solidity and unity, and as the poet's version of the underworld. Though
Stevens defines here a kind of survival, it is one which depends upon the
continuity of life (and imagination) and the world rather than on any belief
in God other than that already discussed. The levels of death intimated by
the poem may identify "deeper death" with the doctrine of immortality
held by Christians and unacceptable to the poet. The "concentric circles of
shadows," derived from the traditional imagery of circles and rings associated with the idea of self-containment and eternity, take on greater clarity
as we proceed in the poem:

> The shadows of his fellows ring him round
> In the high night, the summer breathes for them
> Its fragrance, a heavy somnolence, and for him,
> For the soldier of time, it breathes a summer sleep . . .

This ceremony, so close to that of the funeral rituals of seasonal gods, brings
us back to "Sunday Morning" with its "ring of men" dancing and singing
"on a summer morn" the glory of the sun, the joys of an earthly existence
viewed as paradisiacal. Stevens says of these celebrants that "They shall
know well the heavenly fellowship / Of men that perish and of summer morn."
Apparently, if we fit the common properties of the two poems together, the
living and the dead are connected with one another in some final and unbroken relation which escapes close definition but which is deeply involved
with their mystical attachment to the earth—the fecund and voluptuous
queen of so many of the poems, and the "earthly mothers waiting, sleep-
lessly" of "Sunday Morning." The two circling groups of men in "Esthétique
du Mal" and "Sunday Morning" are in a sense one and the same; we merely
observe them from a different point of view in each poem. Life and death,
as both Richard Ellmann and Northrop Frye have said in reference to
Stevens's personal eschatology, belong to each other and flow into each
other. It is not surprising, then, to discover the poet writing in *The Necessary Angel*, "What a ghastly situation it would be if the world of the dead
was actually different from the world of the living. . . ." In Stevens's notions
of how we construct and reconstruct our world there can be no difference
because the imagination is "the will of things."

The interpenetration of life and death takes place through the only agent
possible for such metamorphoses in Stevens's scheme—the mind itself. In a
poem called "The Owl in the Sarcophagus" we are offered a somewhat heavy
prophecy of "the mythology of modern death" through a trio of representative

figures. There are "two brothers" in this oddly devised pantheon; one is "high sleep," the other, "high peace." They share the company of that archetypal woman, the queen of many disguises, who is here "the mother of us all, / The earthly mother and the mother of / The dead." The three apparitions, like the gods before them, receive their validity as projections through the imagination of human wishes. Under their aegis death brings no radical alteration to the essential nature of man's condition or the limits of his world. The earth, we are told, is the eternal feminine which enfolds us and gives us endless repose. If Yeats sometimes thought that man created all he knew and experienced, Stevens could play him a close second:

> Compounded and compounded, life by life,
> These are death's own supremest images,
> The pure perfections of parental space,
>
> The children of a desire that is the will,
> Even of death, the beings of the mind
> in the light-bound space of the mind, the floreate flare . . .
>
> It is a child that sings itself to sleep,
> The mind, among the creatures that it makes,
> The people, those by which it lives and dies.

The multiple voices of the "Interior Paramour," the voices that imagination adopts, return us to the problems attendant on the poet's separation of reality from this faculty.

Reality, or the physical, factual world, is a closed system in Stevens's cosmology, conditioned by "generations of the imagination" and bounded by the returning seasonal periods whose importance in the poetry we have previously mentioned. In "The Auroras of Autumn" the serpent, we gather, imposes both order and limitation for this world in the figure of his coiling length: "the master of the maze / Of body and air and forms and images." The snake encircles the cosmos, and so repeats that pursuit of his tail which has so long symbolized the eternal ring. Stevens again relies on the circle to suggest the completeness of our earthly being.

The imagination, though restricted in the individual person by the span of human existence, imposes itself on brute reality and extends the possibilities of what would otherwise remain a "basic slate." To account for the origins and goals of this reality and the life within it the imagination introduces figurations and images that are the spirit's interpretations and comfort. Through them the reality which is the foundation of life undergoes a radical transformation that leaves man dominating it through his images.

The fundamental reality is what it was, but has now become something more too. In time these images will fade away or be destroyed and new ones will have to replace them. Stevens believes himself to be in a transitional period: old images and beliefs have died out; others are needed. The mind's labors swell, augmented by what must be included when there is no other support. Little wonder that, lacking an external God, Stevens deified the imagination. More of the scope of this work of the mind can be seen in a late poem, "The Sail of Ulysses," from *Opus Posthumous*:

> His mind presents the world
> And in his mind the world revolves.
> The revolutions through day and night,
> Through wild spaces of other suns and moons,
> Round summer and angular winter and winds,
> Are matched by other revolutions
> In which the world goes round and round
> In the crystal atmospheres of the mind,
> Light's comedies, dark's tragedies,
> Like things produced by a climate, the world
> Goes round in the climates of the mind
> And bears its floraisons of imagery.

The mind also resembles a circle, for it matches the conditions of the cycling seasons, the coiled snake, the rings of the living and the dead. This circular cosmos is the mind's own territory. Thus Stevens can remark in *The Necessary Angel*, "We live in the center of a physical poetry, a geography that would be intolerable except for the non-geography that exists there. . . ." By "non-geography" Stevens means the spirit or mind or imagination and its activities.

The attainment of a true center of this world, both necessary and desirable under the poet's arrangement of things, is related to death and the rock in "The Owl in the Sarcophagus," III, and in "Things of August," IX, we learn that such a center of reality is the place from which meanings are perceived and made:

> A text of intelligent men
> At the center of the unintelligible,
> As in a hermitage, for us to think,
> Writing and reading the rigid inscription.

The earth itself composes the "text" of secular revelation announced earlier in "Description without Place." Created by the exercise of imagination on tangible things this sacred book preserves the ordered meanings bestowed by the mind upon a rather bleak chaos of sensory impressions. These notions are drawn together more closely in "The Hermitage at the Center" and

"The World as Meditation" from *The Rock*; and in both the figure of the earth queen serves to unify life and death.

"The Irish Cliffs of Moher" in the poem of that title stand out for Stevens as another version of the rock and the ground of our being:

> This is my father or, maybe
> It is as he was,
> A likeness, one of the race of fathers: earth
> And sea and air.

In this poem we come to the farthest backward reach of Stevens's thought about the genesis of earth, a stony foundation, seemingly without origin, permeated by the psyche's most tenacious images. To the genealogy of the fathers all will be returned, for, as we read elsewhere, "the spirit comes from the body of the world." The center toward which life always moves and whence it reappears is at the heart of the symbolic circles we have seen. The unity of the real and the imagined is caught in the anticipated embrace of Penelope and the voyager Ulysses, the "form of fire" (he is the generative sun, she the fecund earth too), never fully achieved yet forever, through the reflective mind, coming nearer and nearer in "The World as Meditation." The closing of that ring, like the knitting of the circles already discussed, makes a wholeness that includes life and death, earth and the heavens, imagination and reality, the animate and the inanimate. Stevens's belief "beyond belief," his vision of what endures, is in the persistence of this totality.

IV

The space around which the serpent winds in "The Auroras of Autumn" and which the closed circle marks is the periphery of the rock; and in the poem of that title Stevens makes an effort to give a final explanation to his attitudes. There are three sections: the first begins the course of meditation from an autobiographical basis; the second discloses the rock itself and the meanings it brings together; and the last part once again places the rock in relation to death (and here we may perhaps think of Stevens's own, so closely following) which leads the poem back to the point where it began, only on a new level.

The opening section, "Seventy Years Later," has that peculiar flavor, almost a bitterness, of old age as it examines a past which no longer appears to have any ties with the present person and his situation. Indeed, the poet gazes at this earlier self with some astonishment and disbelief; they hardly seem to be attached to one another, or care to be:

> It is an illusion that we were ever alive,
> Lived in the houses of mothers, arranged ourselves
> By our own motions in a freedom of air.

With lines of defiant beauty Stevens claims that love and human relationships, at this remove in time, are grotesque: "an embrace between one desperate clod / And another. . . ." But this "queer assertion of humanity," he
realizes, is a block against "nothingness," and it forms at least "an imperma-
nence / In its permanent cold." The barren rock is itself the substance of
this negation, until human assertions—the acts of imagination—come to
bear the "green leaves" upon it. The rock stands alone, as we first saw it in
"How to Live. What to Do." an inhuman world, and it remains meaningless, a raw fact, without the invasion of the mind and senses. The responsibility for bringing about any change lies with the lonely couple of that poem,
which is to say, with man himself. The gates of Eden have opened and, for
Stevens, God is gone; divinity is man's attribute now and the world his task.
In this coming forth there is a spring birth that is at once both purge and
blossom, we are told in "The Rock": "the lilacs came and bloomed like a
blindness cleaned, / Exclaiming bright sight. . . ." Within the range of the
eye the rock is made over, a rock upon a rock, and looms out now as a newly
won ground on which the "incessant being alive" flourishes.

Whether Stevens intended it or not, the appropriation of the image of
the rock is in keeping with his general adoption of biblical vocabulary for
secular or private purposes. The rock is, of course, for a Christian associated
with the origins of the Church in Christ's delegation of spiritual authority
to Peter; from this event there has developed an identification of the rock
symbol with the Church. We have pointed to several other uses Stevens
makes of orthodox religious terminology and concepts. Inseparable from
this practice, the vision of redemption and reconstruction—the creation of
unified being—is then allied with the harmonious function of the rock in
man's connection with it. The blossoms of green are insufficient by themselves, we find in "The Rock," Part II, "The Poem as Icon," and man must
be "cured" or transformed himself, that is, identified with the "fiction of the
leaves" he has made. Stevens's narcissism is revealed here, not as morbid
egoism or self-concern, but as the contemplation of our projected images,
in whose midst we live. Perhaps we might best think of a set of mirrors
(imagination and reality) facing each other, which in-between themselves
make a habitable world out of their blending reflections. The rock is the
space of that world, and the wholeness it comes to imply in this late poetry
contains sacramental meanings for Stevens. These meanings are bodied forth
in the images of the leaves to suggest a kind of sanctification: "the figura-
tion of blessedness, / And the icon is the man." In the lines that follow

three successive seasons are taken up as properties of the rock, and together
with it they are viewed against the backdrop of nothingness, involving the
fourth season, winter, which is omitted from the ideal seasonal pattern:

> The pearled chapelet of spring,
> The magnum wreath of summer, time's autumn snood,
> Its copy of the sun, these cover the rock.
> These leaves are the poem, the icon and the man.
> These are a cure of the ground and of ourselves,
> In the predicate that there is nothing else.

Stevens means, I believe, that we should take "cure" in its sense of a spiritual charge or curacy, as well as remedy. In spite of his naturalism he is
attempting to convey through the image of the rock a religious formulation
to replace the Christian interpretation of life which, he feels, belongs to the
past. The frequent conversion of the language of the Gospels and of biblical
incident to his own poetic needs can only be understood in the light of
some such intention. But the formulation brought about must be one that
disavows doctrine or creed and, in the poet's idea of historical relativism,
corresponds with any change, in fact, partakes of it.

At this point I think we may, borrowing from Richard Ellmann, speak of
Stevens's personal "church of the imagination," mentioned in passing at
the outset of this essay. By "church" I mean a composite of sacred values
harbored by the rock and held within the compass of the mind. These include, most broadly, the life of the natural man and the work of the imagination therein. As such, it is, as we said before, a closed system, though an
extensive one. Stevens discovers religiousness there in the desired fruition
of existence:

> In this plenty, the poem makes meanings of the rock,
> Of such mixed motion and such imagery
> That its barrenness becomes a thousand things
>
> And so exists no more.

In one of the "Adagia" from *Opus Posthumous* he writes, "After one has
abandoned a belief in god, poetry is that essence which takes its place as
life's redemption." So the distinctive lines of aesthetics and theology merge
in this church of the solitary imagination, a bulwark thrown up at the edge
of an abyss. In one respect or another, the same tendency is noticeable in
writers like Yeats and Rilke, in the Joyce of *Finnegans Wake*. The modern
poet, often divorced from a stable religious faith or communal vision, is not
only faced with the job of creating the reality of his art but finds himself

inclined by the temptations of uncertainty to make of his art the single reality, an imagined one. If this is his choice, then the artist very likely becomes the inhabitant of his work. Joyce peers out at us from the figure of Stephen Dedalus and later as Shem the Penman. Yeats continually—and successfully—dramatizes himself in his poetry, even imagines an eternity of art in which he might be enclosed. Because life and the poem are for Stevens ultimately interchangeable within the boundaries of the rock, he endows them with the same significance. In "The Poem That Took the Place of a Mountain" the rock appears as the final human resting place where the poet and his work will at last be joined with the perpetual ring of nature. Art and artist are identified with the rock they have transformed through the life of the imagination. Stevens apparently discovers in this prospect a substitute for the immortality of the soul and the resurrection of the person. Art is a vessel of the purified, essential human self; it carries that self back to the heart of reality at death. For in dying the poet will merely replace one relationship to the earth with another, more inexplicable bond.

Parallel to these notions Stevens locates Heaven and Hell, in "Esthétique du Mal," as integral areas of the mind developed from man's experience of the world rather than anything external to it. The rock is, finally, "the gray particular of man's life" and "The stone from which he rises up—and—ho, / The step to the bleaker depths of his descents. . . ." These are first and last things mentioned in "The Rock," and later in the same poem the thought of death so near stirs the memory to recall the cycle of earthly life:

> The starting point of the human and the end,
> That in which space itself is contained, the gate
> To the enclosure, day, the things illumined
>
> By day, night and that which might illumines,
> Night and its midnight-minting fragrances,
> Night's hymn of the rock, as in a vivid sleep.

These stanzas draw together the circle of existence as Stevens envisages its certainty, a circle supported by the prevailing substance of the physical world and by the poem played upon that reality throughout a lifetime—a poem that remains after death (see, on this subject, "A Postcard from the Volcano"). Out of this encounter of the creative mind with concrete reality Stevens fashions his own religious image in the form of a chapel rising above the decay of an aged cathedral. The meaning is clear in this passage from "St. Armorer's Church from the Outside":

> Its chapel rises from Terre Ensevelie,
> An ember yes among its cindery noes,

> His own: a chapel of breath, an appearance made
> For a sign of meaning in the meaningless . . .

This breath is the warmth of life, the movement of the spirit, and the medium of poetic speech. Stevens's affirmation of them all makes the structure of the chapel where he is both priest and worshipper. Set in the teeth of time, it provides shelter against the unknown, the nothingness into which death threatens to catch us.

(1958)

NOTES

[1]All quotations of poetry, unless otherwise indicated, are from *The Collected Poems* (New York: Alfred A. Knopf, 1954). Quotations from *The Necessary Angel* (New York: Alfred A. Knopf, 1951) are indicated in the text.

3

The Poetic Roles of Edith Sitwell

I
Masks and Disguises

DURING THE EARLY PART OF THE TWENTIETH CENTURY, IT BECAME INCREASINGLY the habit of the writer to seek out for himself a disguise or personality or role through which to dramatize and enforce his viewpoint in poems or novels. We can, of course, locate such a speaker in, say, Donne's poetry, too, but there he gives the impression of being contrived for use only in the particular poem in which he appears; and it is rather difficult to identify a voice, a set of attitudes and a mode of perception that make each poem participate in an imaginative universe which is the product of all of the poems together. Certainly, however, an older tradition of the poetic disguise exists in English literature, and Swift's and Pope's satires or the poems of Byron furnish prime examples of it. But the modern writer's desire to act as an outspoken commentator on his times, critic of his society and its mores, agent of a prophetic or metaphysical vision, and his simultaneous wish to maintain an objective distance, a position of aloofness and independence within the world created by his art, have led to an impressive variety of disguises and to the austere anonymity of many novelists from Flaubert to James Joyce. We need only think of the dandyism of Baudelaire, Laforgue, and Wilde; of the hermetic ritualism of Mallarmé; or of the belligerent and disorderly life lived by Rimbaud in the service of his muse to realize the importance which the roles adopted by poets have played both inside their work and out. This device of self-stylization was carried on into the present century by the writers of the post-symbolist generation who carefully and successfully exploited its abundant possibilities.

Studies have been made of the masks of Ezra Pound and W. B. Yeats; and T. S. Eliot's reluctance to reveal himself, except sparingly, as a personality in his poetry has been given critical support in his prose writings. This role or mask, whether some sort of dramatization of the poet's person—as it is with Yeats, Pound, or the later Dylan Thomas—or the disguise of the fictional speaker—as it is with Eliot and often Conrad Aiken—performs an integral rather than a decorative function in the development of a body of writing. For the assumption of such roles permits the poet to drop them when necessary, and then to take up another position with less chance of seeming inconsistent or insincere. Thus the poet as a person and the speakers of his poems apparently keep separate existences. This distinction allows the poet a desirable measure of freedom and self-protection: he can do his thinking privately and test it publicly without being pegged in one hole. An alteration in his beliefs, especially in an age when those alterations are common, will usually bring about a different conception of himself in relation to the poems he writes.

In spite of the attention by critics to the poet's masks, the poetry of Edith Sitwell has frequently been neglected by those who study the stances taken by writers of the last hundred years. Yet her writing, rich and inventive, displays several modes of expression and technique which correspond to the various stages of her thought and experience. What one might call the poetic roles of Edith Sitwell are just these prolonged but changing and maturing states of mind as they find adequate language, metaphor, image, and rhythm in which to organize and disclose themselves as poems. Her poetry falls into three broad phases, I believe, each dominated by its own peculiar interests and outlook, its own voice and rhetoric. And each phase emerges from the preceding one in an organic fashion; that is to say, a new phase of her work presents a new conception of the author's role as poet—but supported by the previous one—and an extending of themes and the means of articulating them. From the more restricted and also flamboyant manner of the early poetry to the different achievement of "Gold Coast Customs" and then to the later phase of the prophetic odes and songs, there is an accompanying expansion of range and technique, as well as a growth in the poet's role from ironist and satirist to the purveyor of a religious vision embracing all mankind.

Though she was never a writer of fashionable proportions or following (and she seems to have preferred it this way), Dame Edith Sitwell marked her debut on the English literary scene at about the same time as T. S. Eliot. Her first book of poems, *The Mother*, appeared in 1915; Eliot's initial book, *Prufrock and Other Observations*, came out two years later; and by then Dame

Edith had published another collection of verse and had launched with her brother the poetry anthology, *Wheels*, which continued until 1921. Thus she had a place at the beginning of the radical movement that overturned English poetry during the war years and just before, but she always practiced on her own independent terms. Reading her early prose writings, such as the book of tales recreated from the Russian ballet (1920) and her columns for the weekly, *The New Age* (1921-22), one gathers that she immersed herself (as she has indicated in her autobiography and elsewhere) in the writings of Baudelaire, Rimbaud, and Laforgue, where she discovered, just as Eliot did, things profitable to her own verse. While echoes of these French poets may sound here and there in her poems for a time, Dame Edith is always hard at work in the creation of her own poetic universe, one that receives a certain natural impetus from her reading, but one that still depends most heavily on her ability to formulate a world out of the direct experience of life, particularly from her unusual childhood circumstance.

That childhood was not an easy one, as Osbert Sitwell suggests in his autobiographies and as Dame Edith makes quite clear in *Taken Care Of* (1965), her posthumously published memoirs. Sensitive and imaginative, devoted to music and literature at an early age, Dame Edith found her family atmosphere uncongenial and oppressive. Life on the great country estate of Renishaw was isolated; relations with her parents were difficult; but the immense gardens with their rich variety of fruits and flowers and birds through which she walked and dreamed made an impression deep enough for her to transform them into the setting of most of her earlier poems, of the long poem, *The Sleeping Beauty*, and of the pastoral portions of her novel based on Jonathan Swift's life, *I Live Under a Black Sun* (1937). A good deal of time was also spent with her family in another house they owned at the sedate seaside resort of Scarborough, which she frequently mocks in satirical poems. One can guess that, shifting from one location to another, involved in her reading, she began slowly to build in her imagination the green pastoral realm of many of the poems in her first few volumes, though to this she added the wry artifice which makes of this fictional world a critical image of the one she knew so well.

This element of artifice is an essential ingredient of Dame Edith's poetry; and her idea of the modern age and how it should be portrayed in verse manifests itself in visions of a shallow universe of toys and puppets dressed up in the costumes of folk ballet or as types of *Commedia dell'arte* figures:

> Summer afternoon in Hell!
> Down the empty streets it fell,
> Pantaloon and Scaramouche—
> Tongues like flames and shadows louche—
> Flickered down the street together

> In the spangled weather.
> Flames, bright singing-birds that pass,
> Whistled wares as shrill as grass
> (Landscapes clear as glittering glass) . . .
>   ("Singerie")

The frivolous notion of hell in this and other of Dame Edith's poems of the period does not simply denote a light, whimsical frame of mind in the writer, though she would perhaps like us *halfway* to think it does—but only *half-way*. Hell as the place of the damned and as a state of the soul is given a new character. If we think of what hell meant to Dante—a repository for the spirits of those who opposed the will of God, including some who did so deliberately—the contrast with the beliefs of our contemporary world is sharply defined. The modern individual, often without belief in God or in the metaphysical idea of sin, cannot even achieve the stature of one who has chosen infernal punishment by his own volition. Since we have cast off such theology, Dame Edith intimates, the material world has closed in about us and we have made a hell of our own surroundings and lives. Rooms of glass shot through with glimmerings of cold light which suddenly change into "jungles splashed with violent light, / Promenades all hard and bright," inhabited by apes dressed in lace and tail coats who play mandolins and pianos—these are the brilliant, quick flashes of demonic imagery we first discover in Dame Edith's poetry. The tendency to talk only of the rhythmical experimentation in these early poems, including those in *Bucolic Comedies* and *Façade*, puts us in danger of considering them merely as exercises in sound with no meaning to speak of.

But any reading of the poetry which does not begin with a predisposition to find more than what Dame Edith has called "patterns in sound" will fail to uncover her barbed criticisms of life that have their parallels with the dazzling irony of Cocteau and the acidity of Baudelaire and Laforgue. The first role she conceives for herself is that of ironist, whose artificial but pointed frivolity and gaiety enable her to criticize not only in *what* she says but also in her manner of saying it. The interest in sound rather than sense so quickly and obviously attributed to her poems—and Dame Edith has occasionally lent support to it (what could more swiftly unsettle the comfortable British middle-class reading public?)—and the introduction of theatrical techniques, dizzying performances reminiscent of the scandalous pyrotechnics of the Picasso-Satie-Cocteau *Parade* in her *Façade* are the planned results of a poetic role that creates an atmosphere in which to operate effectively. Beneath these sensational surfaces lies the forceful presence of this poet's intelligence, confronting and brooding upon the empty, mechanized reality dramatized metaphorically by the poems. In "Clowns' Houses" she brings together her favorite figure of the clown with the streets and buildings of a city that lacks physical substance and seems more like the false front of a movie set than anything else. Here, too, are some devices familiar to readers or Laforgue's "lunar parodies," marionettes and Pierrot the moon:

> Beneath the flat and paper sky
> The sun, a demon's eye,
> Glowed through the air, that mask of glass;
> All wand'ring things that pass
>
> Seemed out of tune, as if the light
> Were fiddle-strings pulled tight.
> The market square with spire and bell
> Clanged out the hour in Hell.
>
> The busy chatter of the heat
> Shrilled like a parokeet;
> And shuddering at the noonday light
> The dust lay dead and white
>
> As powder on a mummy's face,
> Or fawned with simian grace
> Round booths with many a hard bright toy
> And wooden brittle joy . . .

These opening stanzas create as powerful an image of the setting of contemporary life as Dame Edith achieves until "Gold Coast Customs," where she is more direct, less derivative. The startling imagery, which reminds us of Eliot's methods in "Prufrock" and *The Waste Land* as well as of Laforgue, admits us again to hell; but it is a hell equipped with pasteboard imitations of the furnishings of any provincial city where the church bells toll the hours. The contrived feeling of the poem, with its flavor of artifice, its synesthetic effects, and its controlled but shrill frivolity, allows occasional glimpses of an underlying reality that reveals itself through the curious activities of the sun, the heat and light, and the dust, all of which act and react upon one another. Dame Edith's ability to animate the inanimate she demonstrated right through her final work, though at this point she has yet to use this animation within the frame of as full a vision as she commands in the years after 1940. Here she lets the animated elements generate suggestions of a vacuousness, a pattern of manipulated appearances without depth or tangible life. Instead of exposing the nothingness of this world, the harsh light gives it a spurious semblance of life, just enough to cover the real emptiness behind paper houses. With nightfall, "Pierrot moon steals slyly in" to alter the scene with his strange illumination; the distractions of daylight dissolve to leave the shallow town naked in darkness:

Then underneath the veiled eyes
Of houses, darkness lies,—
Tall houses; like a hopeless prayer
They cleave the sly dumb air.

Blind are those houses, paper-thin;
Old shadows hid therein,
With sly and crazy movements creep
Like marionettes, and weep.

Tall windows show Infinity;
And, hard reality,
The candles weep and pry and dance
Like lives mocked at by Chance.

The rooms are vast as Sleep within:
When once I ventured in,
Chill Silence, like a surging sea,
Slowly enveloped me.

The agony of the poet's feeling strains through the Laforguean noncha-
lance of tone, until in the final stanza the calm relating of this discovery of
silence is like a shriek held back in the mind, lurking under the words. By
the publication of "Gold Coast Customs" nine years later, that perception
of absence or void at the center of the reality we have fashioned for ourselves has transmuted Dame Edith's poetry into an open indictment of a
society caught and twisted in the violent, jerking rhythms of an unnatural
life.

Clowns, puppets, dwarfs, marionettes—all that is mechanical, determined,
or alienated becomes symbolic, in both the poetry and the prose writings, of
debilitated human states. Sister M. Jeremy has remarked in an essay on
Edith Sitwell the affinity which the poet bears to the painter Georges
Rouault, whose tortured clowns capture the loneliness and fear of the unknown permeating daily life. But a further resemblance to the stylized abstract figures in the paintings of Gris, Picasso, and Duchamp ought to be
mentioned, for their geometrical techniques find a correspondence in the
mechanized parody of existence Dame Edith imagines. And Wallace Fowlie,
who has discussed the clown as a key figure in much modern writing, says in
The Clown's Grail, "Modern man is the clown forgetful of who he is. . . . The
hero has become the weak and pity-inspiring creature who is all men." The
ragged and tattered crowds moving through the night world of great cities
like London in Dame Edith's poems and in her novel illustrate the injustice
bred by a civilization continuously industrializing itself, becoming more and
more greedy, and casting out many who must then float, penniless and alone,

straw men in the wind. Only in her later poems is she able to envisage a means of restoration for these lost persons. The clown is for Dame Edith the model of the scapegoat; and he has the advantage of provoking tears *and* laughter, an ironical confusion of emotions at the dilemmas we have provided ourselves. Not only that, but, as she writes in an essay on Stravinsky's *Petrouchka* in 1921, the clown is a tangible example of the discrepancy between the highly-colored countenance we turn outward to the world and the disturbed, spiritless inner lives we lead:

> We had become accustomed to seeing a Clown that is, perhaps, the clearest symbol of the modern world, showing, as he does, the terrible difference between his heightened exterior, so intensely restricted, and the limitless dark of his mind. He is, above all, the man with nowhere to hide—the homeless one—as he stands in the pitiful glare of the stage, trying to cover his misery and defiance with the bright-painted rags of the limelight. He has not even the right to his own flesh, for that is painted into cubes like the cubes of empty houses; and his laughter must not be human; it must be the mechanical action of a switchback. . . .

This contrast between exteriors and interiors is of the same kind we saw in the treatment of the city in "Clowns' Houses"; reality is everywhere a thin fabric of phenomena strung on wires and pulleys, or Dame Edith's metaphor, "a thin matchboard flooring over a shallow hell." The lack of any spiritual affirmations, of any connection with nature on the part of such figures as appear, points to the futility of an existence without aim, running automatically from birth to death in the grooves of modern industrial and social interest. The laughter of the clown, like that of the poet, is an effective weapon against an overwhelming despair at this situation.

Against despair, the act of poetic composition is also a defense and a method of moral assertion, as Dame Edith proves by her continued output. Like so many modern poets, she originally viewed organized religion as an inseparable part of the society she was rejecting in her art; later, however, she came to belief in her own way, a way which fills out and completes the last phase of her writing. But in the early poems she has no solution to problems of emptiness and automation, and she has some sharp verses on "Thäis in Heaven" and "Materialism; or Pastor—Takes the Restaurant Car for Heaven." The concluding stanzas of the second piece attain effects reminiscent of the best of Eliot's or e. e. cummings's satires:

> Down endless tubes of throats we squeeze
> Our words, lymphatic paint to please
>
> Our sense of neatness, neutralize
> The overtint and oversize.

> I think it true that Heaven should be
> A narrow train for you and me,
>
> Where we perpetually must haunt
> The moving oblique restaurant
>
> And feed on foods of other minds
> Behind the hot and dusty blinds.

We can understand readily enough from these lines Dame Edith's sympathy with the tragic and energetic mind behind Swift's writings and with the moral outrage Pope sharpened to a deadly point in his poetry. Her imagination is partially an eighteenth-century one, baroque elements aside, and combines the kind of elegance and intellectual acumen we associate with writers of that period with many of the techniques and goals of the symbolist movement. Her later prophetic poems of the years of World War II and after reveal strong similarities with Blake's work of the same order and also with Christopher Smart.

The poems of *Façade*, for all their striking music and surface glitter, reach even further than the theme of "Clowns' Houses" or the jazzy staccato of a piece chosen by chance—"The Wind's Bastinado," for example—from the whole group of poems would suggest:

> The wind's bastinado
> Whipt on the calico
> Skin of the Macaroon
> And the black Picaroon
> Beneath the galoon
> Of the midnight sky.

The audience that reacted with so much violence and indignation to the first public performance of *Façade* in 1923 was rightly scandalized, but for more reasons than it probably knew. Stage settings, music, and the difficulty of the poems brought the crowd to a pitch of fury. They must have felt that an enormous hoax was being perpetrated at their expense and in the name of culture. Confronted by a curtain with painted archways and two painted masks of different sizes upon it, they listened to poetry recited through a kind of megaphone fitted into the mouth of the larger mask; the poet's brother, Osbert Sitwell, made introductions and announcements through a similar device in the smaller mask. While the purpose of this elaborate preparation was ostensibly to permit the audience to concentrate solely on the auditory qualities of the poems—as, in fact, any reader of them must do—there can be little doubt that this atmosphere only heightened what was surely the fundamental distaste of the audience for the complexities of contemporary verse. One can hardly believe that the Sitwells were totally unprepared for the stormy reception they met. The painted masks were quite in keeping with the studied gaiety, harsh mockery, and dreamlike world of the poems, their creation of a strange landscape populated with ridiculous—though carefully conceived—figures: apes, clowns, grotesque lords and kings, peasants and maids and servant girls who manage to fix an illusion of life while remaining always unrealistic. The life dramatized in these poems is subject to queer operations of chance or, if you like, determinism and has the logic of dreams, children's limericks, and fairy tales. The names and activities of many of these characters are certainly more than nonsensical, though, and are not always fare for children. In almost every poem, one can trace instances of evil, subtle criticisms of modern life, innuendoes of death, decay, and nothingness. To call these poems sound patterns alone is simply another irritation to an audience which looks for edifying messages in its literature and wishes to find the *status quo* confirmed there.

In the manner of the *Bucolic Comedies* (from which a number of them derive), the section of poems now called "Marine," and *The Sleeping Beauty*, the pieces of *Façade* belong to a developing poetic universe which yet undergoes periodic alterations. This universe becomes more pastoral, less parodistic, as Dame Edith proceeds; but even these changes do not bring completion or fulfillment to the author's vision. Behind the artificial framework of the early poems there doubtless lies some hesitancy on the poet's part to engage openly the basic realities of human existence implied and hinted at throughout. The poetic manner displayed in them is brilliant, incisive and critical, but it is also safe. A surplus of anger and horror finally dissolves this manner in "Gold Coast Customs," a poem which demands of Dame Edith an entire transformation of her poetic means, as well as of her attitudes and beliefs, to get beyond the place she reaches in its long, terrifying statement. The new direction her art will take is indicated at the close of that poem, but it is not until ten years after that her new style emerges.

II

Toward the Inferno

When William Butler Yeats was selecting poems for inclusion in the *Oxford Book of Modern Verse*, he wrote to his friend, Dorothy Wellesley, "In the last few days I have reread all Edith Sitwell and found her very hard to select from, poem is so dependent upon poem. It is like cutting a piece out of a tapestry." Yeats was, of course, right. Images and figures appear, disappear, and reappear with calculated irregularity throughout her poetry; and reading

her prose, one finds many phrases and images common to the poems. Repetition, it must be understood, does not signify a paucity of imagination but
rather the careful development of persistent themes through the increasing
value of the metaphorical language associated with them. Dame Edith's
sense of musical inspiration needs also to be taken into account, as certain
critics have done. Composed in this fashion, the body of her writing finally
must be viewed as one piece, though considerable variation and development are visible within the pattern of the whole.

But growth and change are gradual in Dame Edith's poetry, except perhaps in the startling advent of the last phase; and so we discover in the raw,
scathing satire of "Said King Pompey," from *Façade*, that many of the elements prominent in "Gold Coast Customs" have risen to the surface of this
earlier work:

> Said King Pompey, the emperor's ape
> Shuddering black in his temporal cape
> Of dust, 'The dust is everything—
> The heart to love and the voice to sing,
> Indianapolis
> And the Acropolis,
> Also the hairy sky that we
> Take for a coverlet comfortably.'
> Said the Bishop, 'The world is flat . . .'
> But the see-saw Crowd sent the Emperor down
> To the howling dust—and up went the Clown
> With his face that is filched from the new young Dead. . . .
> And the Tyrant's ghost and the Low-Man-Flea
> Are emperor-brothers, cast shades that are red
> From the tide of blood—(Red Sea, Dead Sea),
> And Attila's voice or the hum of a gnat
> Can usher in Eternity.

Death assumes the symbolic form of "dust" here and breaks down man and
his civilizations ("Indianapolis / And the Acropolis") into its particles, then
into spreading layers, until the soil of earth becomes the residue of human
history. The poem likewise illustrates a dialectical process in history: the
struggle for power between the Tyrant and the Low-Man-Flea; but neither
side seems capable of attaining a condition of full humanity and both are
tyrannical in rule. King Pompey's disregard for the value of life, his projection of death into all he sees, and the Bishop's outworn cosmology, which is
at odds with reality, apparently cause the ferment that leads the Crowd to
bloody revolution and replaces the monstrous "emperor's ape" with the blank
and cadaverous Clown. The closing lines indicate that the violent turnover of
civilizations comes alternately from the powerful ruler and from the supposedly

puny mob. The absolutism of both sides, the poet feels, distorts reality; the success and domination of one side merely prepares the way for attack and defeat by its opposite. The vision of evil or the demonic in the poem is enhanced by the musical effects of internal rhyme, occasional sing-song and chant—these join with the caricaturish figures to give the impression of a children's-tale world gone suddenly insane. Dame Edith's outlook on historical progress is a pessimistic one; the apocalyptic character of her later odes and songs draws its notion of human regeneration from sources outside of time which manifest themselves through temporal cycles, not from political or social ideologies. The appearance of a poem like "Said King Pompey" opens an imaginative path to further explorations of the rudimentary ailments in modern society.

The poems of *Bucolic Comedies* and *Façade* belong in their own unique manner to the tradition of Rimbaud's poetry, not only because of their use of synesthesia but in their reliance on the theatrical. The world of *Les Illuminations*, we ought to remember, is composed of a lengthy series of scenes or separate pictures; the poems are, in fact, miniature dramas by themselves. Some of them, "Scènes" for instance, prepare a half-natural, half-artificial theater in which the imaginary dramas Rimbaud dreams may be enacted. The theatricality of Rimbaud carries over into the mysterious idea of experiencing colors through various letters of the alphabet. A curious unity of sense experience, the reactions of one range of sensory perceptions felt in terms of another, tends to support the suggestion of a poetic universe where each thing partakes of something else, a universe operating by its own rules and closed within itself. The reader of Dame Edith's poetry will experience the same feeling, I think, for the artificial techniques of the theater there; and these devices, like the themes and imagery of her early and middle poems, are absorbed and completed only in the larger universe of subsequent work. And lest we believe the motives behind such experiment superficial, the poet has herself remarked on the purpose of synesthesia: "where the language of one sense was insufficient to cover the meaning, the sensation, I used the language of another, and by this means attempted to pierce down to the essence of the thing seen. . . ." Everything in a poem, then, partakes of the other things present there, and together they constitute a world, though Dame Edith's poems otherwise bear little resemblance to Rimbaud's, which were composed on the precarious border of hallucination and mystical enlightenment.

The affrontery of Dame Edith's early poems with their images of a grotesque but comical, bestial but seemingly nonsensical, society, which is, all the while, a refracted vision of the actual society she knew and observed, is strengthened by their re-ordering of conventional modes of perception, as we see in a random piece like "Trio for Two Cats and a Trombone":

> Long steel grass—
> The white soldiers pass—
> The light is braying like an ass.

But given the poet's preoccupations, the intense friction of contemporary life upon her nerves and moral sense, and the intimations of a more profound criticism contained in such poems as "Clowns' Houses," "Said King Pompey," and the lengthier "Metamorphosis" and "Elegy on Dead Fashion"—to say nothing of others—we realize now that she could only pause momentarily, as it were, in this gay and scandalous mood.

Even the devices so useful to her at this stage demand extending and deepening. What she does in the early poems puts her far ahead in the realm of musical and rhythmical experimentation; her artificial world in its beginnings serves well as an implicit condemnation of the butt-ends of post-Victorian romanticism cluttering the literary scene of the day. Still, we can see why this world was not sustained. It was not a considerable enough vehicle for Dame Edith's intensifying moral view; and, poetically speaking, the artifice could not hold its own indefinitely against the terrible pressures from without: it ran the risk of becoming finally a refuge from, not a mockery of, the hideous actuality of contemporary civilization. Clearly, too, the evidence of style and attitude in these poems places them at the outset of a literary career rather than its ending. So while she exposed the false lives of ladies at English seaside resorts and witnessed the destruction of innocence in "Colonel Fantock" and The Sleeping Beauty, Dame Edith underwent the slow preparations of the inner and imaginative life to stare Medusa full in the face. In "Gold Coast Customs" she succeeded in creating an image of her society that could not be mistaken for anything but what it was.

The publication of "Gold Coast Customs" signals a new period in Dame Edith's writings and the adoption of a new role—that of an undisguised judge of her society and its practices. The suffering, the strain upon nerves and sensibilities exacted by this role begin the long process of delineating the figure of the poet as prophet which appears in Street Songs (1942) and the poems that follow. In the poems of Façade, Troy Park, and so on, the poet is hidden behind the poems, or, to put it another way, is in the wings, manipulating scenery, dropping curtains, adjusting the lights on her theatrical productions; rarely does she step on the stage of these early pieces. But in "Gold Coast Customs" we are quite aware of her direct involvement in the action of the poem, and so we continue to be through the rest of her poetry, with of course occasional exceptions. Once the poet has pulled away her disguise, we are free to view, figuratively speaking, the reverse side of the comic and satirical mask she has worn; and we read on the inside of that mask the imprint of the poet's features, the agony of blood and sweat her pastoral poems and brittle comedies kept from sight.

"Elegy on Dead Fashion" and "Metamorphosis," both longer poems, lead toward "Gold Coast Customs" in the explicitness of their themes: the loss of imagination, of primordial innocence, of ties with nature and the sacred; the corruption and disunity of modern life; and the pervasive sense of time and death. The affinity of man and nature among the ancients bred the beautiful myths of the gods and goddesses, we are told in "Elegy on Dead Fashion," and in the fabled landscapes of that golden age man knew that "natural law and moral were but one,— / Derived from the rich wisdom of the sun." This earth-sun symbolism is picked up again after "Gold Coast Customs" and woven into the scheme of the odes, but already Dame Edith has started to enrich her poetic universe. Speaking of the pastoral element in her verse, she says, "The world I see is a country world, a universe of growing things, where magic and growth are one . . . a world of rough, fruitful suns, and the age of the innocence of man. . . ." Our industrial society has severed most of its roots in this pristine existence and its my-thology. And though it is not yet formulated as such in these poems, we recognize that what has been lost is the religious sense of existence, a con-tact with the fullness of being in things visible and invisible. Just as King Pompey or the Crowd are incapable of seeing, to use Blake's words, that "every thing that lives is Holy," so the revelation in "Elegy" of the ancient love and reverence for nature shows up the modern methods of exploiting it by open contradiction:

> Though grown from rocks and trees, dark as Saint Anne,
> The little nun-like leaves weep our small span,
> And eyeless statues in the garden weep
> For Niobe who by the founts doth sleep,
>
> In gardens of a fairy aristocracy
> That lead downhill to mountain peaks of sea,
> Where people build like beavers on the sand
> Among life's common movements understand
>
> That Troy and Babylon were built with bricks;
> They engineer great wells into the Styx
> And build hotels upon the peaks of seas
> Where the small trivial Dead can sit and freeze.

Though the valleys, groves, gorges, seashore, and riverbanks are haunted by lovely ghosts of the ancient world, the man of today erects a thriving commercial system on this landscape: what once was sacred is now for sale. Toward the end of the poem, the author sits by the edge of "the wrinkled lake" to suffer in herself the changes in man which have reduced his gods to puppets—"Psyche has become a kitchenmaid"—and made them victims of the same chance and determinism as threaten him:

> The ancient castle wall of Chaos nods.
> Through gaps of ruined air and withered pods
> A showman came; he smiles like Time and mocks
> Me, takes his marionettes from their small box——
>
> The gods, Time-crumbled into marionettes.
> Death frays their ageless bodies, hunger frets
> Them, till at last, like us, they dance
> Upon the old dull string pulled now by Chance.

The "Elegy" provides more than a lament for the loss of a mythological apprehension of nature and human existence; it suggests as well the spiritual shrinkage of our new, emergent civilization which has abolished imagination and metaphorical thinking, and so wasted man's instinct for the miraculous and beautiful by mechanizing him.

Time and death occupy Dame Edith in "Metamorphosis," published, appropriately enough, the same year as "Gold Coast Customs," 1929. This poem again releases images of a past peopled by an ideal race of men and women who lived in the natural freedom and luxuriance of the earth. But the poet's consideration of this period now directs her to reflect upon time with its strange mutations which have removed such an approach to life. The coldness and isolation of death hold the lost community of the ancients "beneath earth's blind hood" in the "eternal anguish of the skeleton." Time initiates the metamorphosis of the poem's title, wears away individual beauty and vitality, and annihilates generation after generation without relief or escape. Dame Edith discovers no tangible solution for these somber meditations; the hope for renewal will come only after she has grappled with the fundamental reality of spiritual death or death-in-life as it promotes the infernal human behavior depicted in "Gold Coast Customs." In "Metamorphosis" the poet enters on a quest for a tenable and comprehensive attitude toward existence; but like most journeys of its kind, it requires of the traveler a descent into nether regions, a confrontation of the demonic aspects of reality in order to arrive at wisdom or a knowledge of the sacred. "Metamorphosis" and "Gold Coast Customs" are the major steps in a symbolic descent; and in the latter poem the author figuratively undergoes the death of the spirit, which is the experience of our modern hell, and progresses beyond it to recover herself, in a new way, and at last to leave the underworld.

The encounter with forces of death and decay related in "Metamorphosis" exposes the poet to an unrelenting vision—similar to that of Dylan

Thomas's first poems, which appeared just a few years later—of the frenzied groping for life and consciousness on the part of all created beings, as well as the contrary instinct for death which pulls "people" toward the dust, "mouthing blindly for the earth's blind nipple." Dame Edith's single hope at the poem's conclusion remains with the generative power of the sun, as she says, "to rouse my carrion to life and move / The polar night, the boulder that rolled this, / My heart, my Sisyphus, in the abyss." But this hope is not answered, for the writing of "Gold Coast Customs" leads her on to another, and deeper abyss.

Just as T. S. Eliot in *The Waste Land* or James Joyce in *Ulysses* wished to mirror the fragmentary character of modern experience, so Dame Edith constructed her "Gold Coast Customs" around the rapidity, confusion, and violent, unfeeling conduct of life in a society which, a decade before, had been immersed in the most destructive war—up to that time—in Western history, and now continued again its commercial pursuits, its savage neglect of human responsibility, as if nothing had interrupted them. She put into this poetic effort, it is plain, all her indignation and disgust, and, technically, all she had learned from her rhythmical experiments, her devices of animation and synesthesia, in earlier poems. In a lecture published that year (1929) the poet comments on these radical techniques and their connection with the attitudes and behavior of contemporary man. Some of the remarks might easily serve as a preface to the poem:

> If you ask why the rhythms have become more violent [in modern poetry], the answer is: that this is an age of machinery—a wild race for time, confined within limits that are at once mad and circumscribed. Try to get out and you knock your head against the walls of materialism. This state of things is mirrored in modern syncopated dance music. . . . There is no time or space in which to dream. It is because of this that in those poems which deal with our world crumbling to dust, with materialism building monstrous shapes out of the deadened dust, I, for one, use the most complicated dance rhythms which could be found, or else syncopated rhythms which are not dance rhythms.

What Dame Edith notes is a machinery imposed upon the old natural rhythms of the seasonal cycles and their counterparts in human lives, the periodical alterations in the earth and weather that influence man in his activities, his feeling for the pattern of mortal, temporal existence. This machinery in the guise of jazz rhythms dictates the composition of "Gold Coast Customs." The poet begins, using Hegel's *Philosophy of History* and some anthropological findings as sources, by drawing a parallel between the practices of a certain cannibal tribe and the representative and symbolic figure of Lady Bamburgher, who acts as a sort of inhumane goddess of commerce presiding over the social rites of Western society. The cannibal rituals are, of course, used metaphorically (Dame Edith has clearly disavowed any suggestion of racism in her notes to the poem, and it would be a mistake to see any trace of it there) to convey the inner darkness or bestiality hidden under the veneer of civilization, much as similar methods were employed by Joseph Conrad in *Heart of Darkness* and by Charles Williams in his novel *Shadows of Ecstasy*. A convulsive music turns the entire poem into a dance of death; image flies after image, shifting focus from the cannibal tribe to Lady Bamburgher's proceedings and back again with fearful rapidity, until the two kinds of ritual blend in one furious, indistinguishable mass. The poem, as John Lehmann says, does not rely on a narrative form but like *The Waste Land* or the *Cantos* advances by thematic recurrence and by the counterpoint of images. The mechanical and determined actions of her previous clowns, puppets, and pastoral figures Dame Edith has exchanged for the orgiastic abandon of more animal types; the inhabitants of the present poem have submitted to a hypnosis of sex, money, and death, and are caught up in unappeasable appetites.

The African tribal ceremonies with which the poem starts out are explained in an epigraph as follows: in Ashantee a century before, the death of any rich or prominent person was succeeded by several days of riotous living; and the slaves and poor people were murdered so that the bones of the dead person might be bathed with their blood. This disorder and atrocity is augmented by that animation of *things* we have already seen in Dame Edith's poetry, but here the nightmare aspect of the device increases with each stanza. Non-living things and objects speak, move, and gyrate in the same diabolical ritual as the savages:

> One fantee wave
> Is grave and tall
> As brave Ashantee's
> Thick mud wall.
> Munza rattles his bones in the dust,
> Lurking in murk because he must.
>
> Striped black and white
> In the squealing light;
> The dust brays white in the market-place,
> Dead powder spread on a black skull's face.
>
> Like monkey-skin
> Is the sea—one sin
> Like a weasel is nailed to bleach on the rocks
> Where eyeless mud screeched fawning, mocks . . .

The whole setting of the poem comes alive through Dame Edith's synesthetic tricks, her theatrical sensations; and these contribute forcefully to the effect of sinister powers unleashed and hiding at every turn, in every change of image.

The three main points of focus alternate in the poem—the Ashantee tribal ceremonies, Lady Bamburgher's parties (their 'civilized,' 'modernized' reflection) and all that goes with them, and a dock scene populated with sailors and prostitutes—but the movement between these points is so swift and like the camera-work of the movies that they appear to the reader to be witnessed almost simultaneously or to be superimposed on one another. In addition, the syncopated rhythms drive the poem along at an astounding pace. But there is a controlling focus in the first person narrator, who, I believe, we must assume is the poet herself. Yet this narrator only speaks as a definite personality and reflects on what is happening from time to time; otherwise we are faced with a hideous panorama of changing scenes of degradation, to be watched with scarcely any relief. Through the reaction and commentary of this lone human voice, when we come upon it among the animal cries of death and delighted gratification choking the air, we are able to locate the writer's conscience, the moral center of the poem, with its expressions of suffering and anger, its sense of social justice, and its final assertion of a belief transcending this nightmare of brutal horror, this world, as Dame Edith says in another poem, where "there is no depth, there is no height."

The physical geography of the poem resembles that of earlier ones: a thin surface concealing a vast nothingness beneath its rags and patches:

> One house like a rat-skin
> Mask flaps fleet
> In the sailor's tall
> Ventriloquist street
> Where the rag houses flap—
> Hiding a gap.

Through this "gap," referred to several times, emptiness and death peer out. The heads of the guests at Lady Bamburgher's parties, and the costume of the tribal witch doctor who instigates the cannibals' bloody rites, are grinning skulls, but they fail to conceal the "real face rotted away" beneath them. These creatures are eviscerated beings, joined together by "strings of nerves, and the drum-taut skins." As the poem proceeds, their dance is intensified and we discover "the universal devouring Worm"—a symbol of corruption and sexuality, and the god or object of worship of the cannibals, as well as of Lady Bamburgher and her companions. Finally, the Worm incarnates itself in the festival's participants:

> The Worm's mask hid
> Her eyeless mud,
> Her shapeless love,
> The plot to escape
> From the God-ordained shape
>
> And her soul, the cannibal
> Amazon's mart,
> Where in squealing light
> And clotted black night
> On the monkey-skin black and white striped dust they
> Cackle and bray to the murdered day.

    The repetition of words and images enforces the stifling, claustrophobic atmosphere; and the poem moves forward with a continuous heightening of tensions and a more and more graphic presentation of the ferocious rituals. Yet from stanza to stanza the pattern is also one of inexorable descent into infernal regions of behavior without restraint, passion without order or humanity, where life spends itself seemingly by intent. The scrupulous degeneracy of Lady Bamburgher at last explodes into a maddened indulgence of her lusts and avarice; the whole world becomes the savage dance.

    Though the impression of unrelieved horror is strong, we cannot lose sight of the narrator, the poet, who quite early in the poem attaches herself to us and is the single guide we have through this hell. She alone prevents the poem from dissolving into the chaos it portrays. But Dame Edith is more than an observer and guide; she participates in the action of the poem and, as sole moral witness, must endure the anguish of what she sees:

> When the sun of dawn looks down on the shrunken
> Heads, drums of skin, and the dead men drunken,
> I only know one half of my heart
> Lies in that terrible coffin of stone,
> My body that stalks through the slum alone.
> And that half of my heart
> That is in your breast
> You gave for meat
> In the sailor's street
> To the rat that had only my bones to eat.

    With the poet's reappearances, we realize that she, too, is a victim of this universal life-in-death; she is numbed in spirit, not from having celebrated the cannibal rituals of Lady Bamburgher herself, but from watching them performed. Her body has turned to stone, her heart has been killed by a betrayal of whatever trust she placed in man. In later stanzas she again shows herself a victim, remarks the banishment of love and the substitution of lust (the Worm's disease). Occasionally, glimpses of a free and innocent existence akin to the pristine state of man and the gods in "Elegy on Dead Fashion" and "Metamorphosis" provide an instant of relief. An association with images of the sea, of voyages, of great distances and infinite spaces separates this ideal life from the relentless pursuits of our present civilization:

> How far is our innocent paradise,
> The blue-striped sand,
> Bull-bellowing band
> Of waves, and the great gold suns made wise
> By the dead days and the horizons grand.

Like Baudelaire in his famous cry, Dame Edith seeks a way out of this savage world to a new land, rich and exotic and pure—a fresh human start—but these romantic dreams slowly fade away. Still, the passages which offer this vision touch a nearly invisible vein of hope that will become more prominent at the poem's conclusion.

Following a section which treats the deterioration of a young girl into a prostitute through the economic dilemmas created by Lady Bamburgher and the other wizards of high finance and commerce, the poem changes suddenly and the poet's voice assumes a different tone. Dame Edith speaks again out of the *mélange* of voices, but not in the first person as she had done before. Instead, a voice—anonymous yet unmistakably hers— interrupts the general movement of the poem, a voice that chants its judgment of the modern world in exalted manner and uses rich biblical figures:

> Rich man Judas,
> Brother Cain,
> The rich men are your worms that gain
> The air through seething from your brain;
> Judas, mouldering in your old
> Coffin body, still undying
> As the Worm, where you are lying
> With no flesh for warmth, but gold
> For flesh, for warmth, for sheet:
> Now you are fleshless, too, as these
> That starve and freeze,
> Is your gold hard as Hell's huge polar street,
> Is the universal blackness of Hell's day so cold?

This passage alters greatly the direction of the poem and completes the definition of the poet's role within it. Thus far Dame Edith has moved along her original path downward into the hell lying at the core of our society and its mores; now, having experienced the journey, faced the diabolical frenzy of those who feast on the lives of others, she can reasonably judge this world. Her role of judge is won only at the cost of the journey. In classical litera-ture, mythology, and in Dante, the traveler to the underworld earns the reward of vision and wisdom for his undertaking; and Dame Edith as the protagonist of her own poem approaches a similar goal. Perhaps we can see in this journey and its achievement a justification and support for the role Dame Edith introduces here and develops more elaborately in later vol-umes. That is the combined role of poet and prophet, the wise old woman who reveals the hidden processes of creation, relates the myth of its cycles, and praises the Divine Spirit latent in it.

With the close of "Gold Coast Customs," Dame Edith's writing changes even more noticeably, and this must depend at least in part on the disclo-sure of religious convictions there. The early poems, it seems, all share a rather desperate laughter, which fails, at times, to cover the poet's despair, her grim stoicism—though she no longer keeps up this front in "Metamor-phosis" or the "Elegy." The latter exhibit a nostalgia for the sacred, for a divine mythology, but "Gold Coast Customs" at last asserts belief. One may feel sure that it is a shaky note of religious affirmation considering the ter-rible experience of the poem, yet it provides at least a tentative resolution to the questions of time, death, and the malicious futility of contemporary life raised in Dame Edith's poems from the outset of her career:

> Yet the time will come
> To the heart's dark slum
> When the rich man's gold and the rich man's wheat
> Will grow in the street, that the starved may eat,—
> And the sea of the rich will give up its dead—
> And the last blood and fire from my side will be shed.
> For the fires of God go marching on.

Until 1942, when *Street Songs* makes its appearance, Dame Edith adds no more to this ending with its promised redemption, but probably searches for the reality within herself and without, which could sustain and nourish this vision. And with her intuition of that reality, when it comes, she acquires an increase in poetic power and a new poetic style, a view which spans the whole of existence. The satirical impulse as we have seen it disappears from her work, and the judge's role is for the most part assimilated to that of the sage, whose joy of a metaphysical cast transcends the vicissitudes of living in our, or any other, time.

III

The Pentecostal Poet

During the 1930s, Dame Edith slows her writing of poetry almost to a halt. She does not, however, remain silent but uses her talents in prose and in the editing of several anthologies. Her return to poetry with the war years brings major changes in style, though these are based to a degree upon the themes and manner of the "Elegy," "Metamorphosis," and "Gold Coast Customs." The unity of her writing that Yeats noticed in 1935 is even more pronounced after *Street Songs*. Though her art always runs in its own course and maintains its distinctive qualities, these new poems introduce a style, a tone, and a use of forms quite foreign to contemporary British literature. Dame Edith often seems close to baroque poets like Crashaw, as Horace Gregory says, and sometimes to Shelley and Blake. In this late period of prophetic poems, the bond with those poets is strengthened, and she shows a kinship with such writers as the Paul Claudel of the *Cinq Grandes Odes* and with St.-Jean Perse, whose *Vents, Anabase*, and *Amers* have an epic range and are also dramatic and lyrical. Northrop Frye, grouping Dame Edith's later poems with those of Pound and Eliot, calls them examples of the "miniature epic"; that is, they contain in little, and by means of their symbolism, the suggested expansiveness of theme, event, and figure associated with more traditional forms of the epic.

The role and beliefs which Dame Edith claims for herself in these odes and songs draw together various strands from her previous poems and give to her writing a finality and completeness. Her attitudes, broadly hinted at the finish of "Gold Coast Customs," are those of a Christian (in 1955 she was received into the Roman Catholic Church), but we must not think they will manifest themselves poetically in a fashion identical with those of, say, T. S. Eliot or W. H. Auden, who express their Christian convictions in individual ways. While Dame Edith most certainly recognizes evil as it erupts constantly in human desires and actions, she seldom insists on original sin, human guilt and damnation as *ultimate* threats to man. Her role of judge and Jeremiah, played so effectively in "Gold Coast Customs," appears again in the war poems, the pieces on the atomic bombings of Hiroshima and Nagasaki—"Dirge for a New Sunrise"—and others, such as "Street Acrobat" and "The Shadow of Cain," contain severely critical valuations of man and the destructive waste he has called down on himself. In general, however, moral defection seems a less significant part of a much greater plan which absorbs evil in fulfilling its appointed destiny. Dame Edith's characterization of herself as the "old Woman," a prophet and poet who has learned the

secrets of the living and the dead, who enjoys a knowledge of the hidden
operations and spiritual resources of the universe, places her in a position to
survey the past, look forward into the future, and yet be, in a sense, beyond
both by virtue of this role and the wisdom assigned it. She sees in all things
now the signs of renewal, indeed, at moments, of the Day of Resurrection.

Both poetically and spiritually, this role is a bold one to carry off; but
Dame Edith gives it substance. As Dante does in *The Divine Comedy*, she
enters the precincts of her poems as observer, commentator, and spiritual
traveler. Defining herself as one who has lived to a great age, has experienced the extremes of moral torment over the human condition, Dame
Edith qualifies also as spiritual guide for the reader; she is, then, Virgil, Dante,
and Beatrice combined. In the poem "Invocation" she presents herself in
the new role:

> I who was once a golden woman like those who walk
> In the dark heavens—but am now grown old
> And sit by the fire, and see the fire grow cold,
> Watch the dark fields for a rebirth of faith and of wonder.

From this novel perspective in the poem, which opens the lengthy series of
odes and songs in her *Collected Poems*, she can speak with familiarity of the
"ultimate Darkness falling" and "the fly-like whispering of small hopes, small
fears, / The gossips of mean Death" that announce the world's disappearance
into the bleakness of "winter." The experience of death and the underworld, prominent in her poetry before, is here repeated, but as part of a
cycle, both natural and supernatural, which leads toward rebirth. Without
the earlier poetic journey through the hell of "Gold Coast Customs," the
apocalyptic tone and vision of these poems would lack some of their justification. But Dame Edith's role is earned and supported; and her identification with reborn vegetation goddesses, with Eurydice, depends partially upon
the metaphorical scheme of descent and ascent implied in the movement
from "Gold Coast Customs" to these prophetic poems. This is another reason why her writing is best looked at as an organic whole.

The belief on which most of the apocalyptic poems rest is that creation
itself is in a mysterious way divine because God continually declares Himself through it. With such a belief, Dame Edith has been able to incorporate
into her work primitive religious attachments to the seasonal cycle, as well
as the attitudes of Christian mystical writers and the theories of alchemy.
Her role as prophet, her affiliations with the seasonal goddesses, place her
at the heart of a poetic universe she brings into being:

> But I, a golden woman like the corn goddess
> Watch the dark fields, and know when spring begins

> To the sound of the heart and the planetary rhythm,
> Fires in the heavens and in the hearts of men,
> Young people and young flowers come out in the darkness.

And so she can foretell the seasonal changes, the return of spring with its renewed vitality, the surge of love and fertility, the new growth in field and hill and tree. But the literal spring is not her sole concern, for these poems do more than hymn that season's promise and the abundance of summer; their intention is also to relate the moments of human life to the eternal round of the year, to the earth, and, finally, to the divine harmonies manifesting themselves in and through the world. The second part of the poem "An Old Woman," called "Harvest," suggests the kind of symbolic elaboration Dame Edith gives to the correspondences reconciling man, nature, and God. Here is a long passage that demonstrates some of the metaphorical pattern:

> Then came the Pentecostal Rushing of Flames, God in the wind
>   that comes to the wheat,
> Returned from the Dead for the guilty hands of Caesar
> Like the rose at morning shouting of red joys
> And redder sorrows fallen from young veins and heart-springs,
> Come back for the wrong and the right, the wise and the foolish
> Who like the rose care not for our philosophies
> Of life and death, knowing the earth's forgiveness
> And the great dews that come to the sick rose:
> For those who build great mornings for the world
> From Edens of lost light seen in each other's eyes,
> Yet soon must wear no more the light of the Sun,
> But say farewell among the morning sorrows.
> The universal language of the Bread—
> (O Thou who art not broken, or divided—
> Thou who art eaten, but like the Burning Bush
> Art not consumed—Thou Bread of Men and Angels)—
> The Seraphim rank on rank of the ripe wheat—
> Gold-bearded thunders and hierarchies of heaven
> Roar from the earth: 'Our Christ is arisen, He comes to give a
>   sign from the Dead.'

Clearly, this poem, like most of Dame Edith's work, is written to be read aloud; and the necessity of understanding these later poems as chants and odes is crucial. The recurrent images and figures—the rose, the sun, Dives, Lazarus, the old woman, the lovers, the fools, Adam, Cain, Christ, the lion, gold, and so forth—accumulate their burden of meaning and value by that very repetition. Of course, this is not a new technique with Dame Edith, but it becomes more important at this last stage of her writing. Together with the exalted tones of her speech, these repeated images fill out her symbolism and lend the poems a feeling of the revelation of sacred knowledge of man and the world. Thus it would be a mistake to read the odes in the same fashion as one might read tight, witty metaphysical lyrics; they are closely interwoven but with a larger weave. Often the poems seem sections of a long book of prophecy.

The sort of revelation Dame Edith takes as her subject matter needs a language of substantial proportion and richness; and this means, more than a suitable diction, a vocabulary of symbols into which she can compress her thought. In the way of so many modern poets—Rilke with his angels, his mythological figures, his borrowings from the Christian story; Wallace Stevens with his private use of biblical characters and texts; D. H. Lawrence and his pagan deities—she has turned to familiar symbols and legends, old as time and heavy with the weight of human experience, to which she adds some fresh meanings. Many of these symbols we have already encountered in her poetry: the sun, gods and goddesses, the four elements which compose man and the universe, the heat and cold, the worm, the dust, angels, and others mentioned above. But the sun dominates all of them, and we do not read too far before we sense that Dame Edith has constructed a kind of solar myth or cosmology as the center of most of the odes. As it does in our own universe, everything circles about the sun, and each of the various symbols operates in conjunction with that fiery body. The first major statement of the sun's place is given in the second stanza of "An Old Woman":

> For the sun is the first lover of the world,
> Blessing all humble creatures, all life-giving,
> Blessing the end of life and the work done,
> The clean and the unclean, ores in earth, and splendours
> Within the heart of man, that second sun.

An entire set of symbolic correspondence to the sun is developed by the poet; for the sun, as this stanza indicates, is not only to be taken literally but has its metaphorical counterpart in the human heart—that which nourishes the life of the microcosm, the single person. Beyond this, the sun is an antique object of worship as the source of life and of the earth's annual renewal of fecundity; it is also a symbol for the Christian God, and for His Son, Jesus Christ, as Dame Edith reminds us by referring in a footnote to Thomas Aquinas's statement that "God is Intelligible Light." These are some of the affirmative meanings with which she endows the sun symbol, though the sun has further the capacity to sear man with its terrible heat and to bestow upon him the sign of his mortality. The earth's motion around the sun puts all the correspondences in play.

By using the sun as a central and controlling symbol for her poetic macrocosm, and viewing it as a redemptive power at work upon the earth, Dame Edith has had recourse to the main ideas of alchemy, as well as to the procedures and expectations of that arcane science. In his book *Anatomy of Criticism* Northrop Frye has a passage describing the alchemistic symbols which might almost be read as a gloss on a number of Dame Edith's late poems:

> The symbolism of alchemy is apocalyptic symbolism . . . the center of nature, the gold and jewels hidden in the earth, is eventually to be united to its circumference in the sun, moon, and stars of the heavens; the center of the spiritual world, the soul of man, is united to its circumference in God. Hence there is a close association between the purifying of the human soul and the transmuting of earth to gold, not only literal gold but the fiery quintessential gold of which the heavenly bodies are made.

The interest Dame Edith takes in this process of alchemy fastens on the belief in purification and renewal. On a literal plane, the sun's rays restore the vegetable life of the earth in spring; on a symbolic plane, they penetrate the earth's surface to activate the restorative forces latent in its ore and gold, and to bring life to the bodies of the dead buried there. History, as we saw in "Said King Pompey," is scattered in the layers of soil, and this past can be undone, as it were, with the release of time's victims (the dead) through the sun's miraculous powers. This purification and transmutation of the earth to gold, in which the sun seems to be no less than the instrument of God's will, brings about the banishment of evil and guilt. Judgment of human misdeeds or virtues is a matter of little significance when the world itself is being made over. "The secret of how Spring began / In the young world before the Fall of Man" is the revelation that orders the poems. In the days of apocalypse, we learn in "Green Song," the sun

                    comes to bless
        Immortal things in their poor earthly dress——
        The blind of life beneath the frost of their great winter
        And those for whom the winter breaks in flower
        And summer grows from a long-shadowed kiss.
        And Love is the vernal equinox in the veins
        When the sun crosses the marrow and pith of the heart
        Among the viridian smells, the green rejoicing.
        All names, sounds, faiths, delights, and duties lost
        Return to the hearts of men, those households of
            high heaven.

What occurs, then, in these heightened moments of Dame Edith's vision is no less than an abolition of the world as it presently exists and a restoration of the prelapsarian unity of man, earth, and God. As the prophet and singer of these "things to come," Dame Edith scans the mutations of human fortune with aloofness, though not without sympathy. Tragedies of war, greed, and death given expression in some of the later poems are erased by the fierce, energetic light of the sun in others. Ultimately, the world will be paved with the gold of the sun, not the gold of Dives, whom the poet employs to symbolize commercial gain and the lust for perishable riches:

> And he [the sun] who blessed the fox with a golden fleece,
> And covered earth with ears of corn like the planets
> Bearded with thick ripe gold,
> For the holy bread of mankind, blessed my clay:
> For the sun cares not that I am a simple woman,
> To him, laughing, the veins in my arms and the wrinkles
> From work on my nursing hands are sacred as branches
> And furrows of harvest . . . to him, the heat of the earth
> And beat of the heart are one,—
> Born from the energy of the world, the love
> That keeps the Golden Ones in their place above,
> And hearts and blood of beasts ever in motion,—
> Without which comets, sun, plants, and all living beings
> And warmth in the inward parts of the earth would freeze.
> And the sun does not care if I live in holiness,
> To him, my mortal dress
> Is sacred, part of the earth, a lump of the world
> With my splendours, ores, impurities, and harvest,
> Over which shines my heart, that ripening sun.
>
>   ("An Old Woman")

The Christianity of Dame Edith is a natural Christianity, mixed with elements of pagan religions, and its emphasis falls upon the final goodness of existence in a world transformed rather than upon the ascetic denial of earthly life. The prophetic and scriptural nature of these poems springs from the poet's faith in, her meditation on, a divinely ordained scheme for the world, its origins, character, and purpose. With Paul Claudel, Dame Edith sees in the physical creation the order implanted there by God; and in the fulness of time each particle of this creation, together with man, will receive the proper magnitude. The sun is the agent of transformation. The long lines in her late poetry with their endless celebration and vindication of life, their enumeration of created things, show a certitude of vision comparable to Claudel's in passages of "L'Espirit et L'Eau" and

"Magnificat." And, after the Whitman she admires, Dame Edith becomes a microcosmic figure in whom the objects and events of the larger cosmos resound. Because of the profound attachment to the earth she feels, the poet believes the destiny of man and of the concrete world are indissolubly bound.

The faith which Dame Edith places symbolically in the regenerative force of the sun augments her natural Christianity because the sun belongs in part to the symbolism of the Christian tradition; yet the belief she proposes, we are told quite explicitly in "An Old Woman," leans far outside doctrinal issues or structures:

> For though the soundless wrinkles fall like snow
> On many a golden cheek, and creeds grow old
> And change,—man's heart, that sun,
> Outlives all terrors shaking the old night . . .

Although Dame Edith's vision in these poems surpasses the bounds of logic and the modern insistence on empirical data, it is really of the simplest kind. With Gerard Manley Hopkins, she holds faith in "the dearest freshness deep down things," but her journey to that conviction is a long and troublesome one. While she was not delayed in her recognition of the vacuity of existence in the present-day world, the poet did not readily come by any belief to compensate for this overwhelming knowledge of human affairs. Her religious views developed in secret, only disclosing themselves gradually in her writings; there are no poems about conversion. But the effects of this spiritual growth permeate the odes.

In Dame Edith's new and affirmative regard the world radiates its original brilliance, which is the illumination of a Divine being, of a creation holy and good in its conception. Her odes rise from the death-bed of winter, the "Cold," and sing from the ripening grain and wheat, from light and air, from the revived heart of man a hymn of love for the Maker and for a fruitful earth. In spite of this dominant mood of optimism and praise, Dame Edith devotes a number of late pieces to the dictatorship of technology, the diabolical concern of man for inventing weapons, the human will to rule the cosmos and the moral regression that sets in when man thinks himself a god. So it is that the world we presently know is shaken by conflict and is bereft of spiritual considerations, as "Poor Young Simpleton" shows:

> We watched the somnambulists, rope-walkers, argonauts,
> Avatars, tamers of steel-birds and fugitives

> From dream and reality, emigrants, mourners,
> And each with his Shadow, (to prove that Man lives!)
>
> And with them come gaps into listening Darkness:
> The gun-men, the molochs, the matadors, man-eaters,
> Hiding in islands of loneliness, each one
> Infections of hatred, and greed-plague, and fear.

But everywhere in her poetry of the last years the promise of change directs the reader's sight out of the darkness of a world that appears doomed to perpetual night; faint streaks of light foretell, in Dame Edith's echo of Shelley's phrase, "great mornings of the world." In "Eurydice" the goddess, with whom the poet identifies herself, dies and enters the underworld, but there Dame Edith's version departs sharply from the legend, for Eurydice returns— "as if a lump of gold had changed to corn, / So did my Life rise from my Death." Her continuing metamorphosis from birth and youth to premature death, and then to rebirth, creates by analogy the pattern of all life as the poet now understands it; and the essential qualities of this pattern place it closer to comedy than tragedy. The concluding lines of "Eurydice" make this clear: though they present the goddess once more at the edge of death, our attention is already drawn toward resurrection. The singer Orpheus bears the healing, revivifying powers of the sun; his is the kiss of life:

> I with the other young who were born from darkness,
> Returning to darkness, stood at the mouth of the Tomb
> With one who had come glittering like the wind
> To meet me—Orpheus with the golden mouth,
> You—like Adonis born from the young myrrh-tree, you, the
>   vine-branch
> Broken by the wind of love . . . I turned to greet you—
> And when I touched your mouth, it was the Sun.

So, while death is a constant theme in the odes and songs, the Divine manifests itself through creation and with it always comes new life. Dame Edith's religious vision shares with Whitman, Blake, D. H. Lawrence, Dylan Thomas, and Theodore Roethke a firm grasp of sense experience and tangible reality. While she never confuses God with the processes of nature or the things that compose it, the poet still finds the sacredness and durability of the spirit in a fundamental bond with the sacredness of created matter.

The fate of the poor, the alienated from society, all who are reduced to rabble by the industrial machine, exploited by their fellows, victimized by war, is met by the full measure of Dame Edith's compassion. Korean war orphans or lonely scarecrow figures are introduced into late pieces from the *Collected Poems* and *The Outcasts* (1962). In "Tattered Serenade: Beggar to Shadow," for example, the poet testifies to their plight:

> These are the nations of the Dead, their million-year-old
> Rags about them,—these, the eternally cold,
> Misery's worlds, with Hunger, their long sun
> Shut in by polar worlds of ice, known to no other,
> Without a name, without a brother,
> Though their skin shows that they yet are men . . .

But the sun, with its blazing face turned on all men, will at last alleviate the pains of these living dead whose spirits and flesh have been scourged by society and by life itself. "The Bee Keepers," one of the greatest of the late poems, repeats choruses from the *Brihadaranyaka Upanishad* to indicate the joining of the elements of the universe one to another, and to the recreating energy of Divine love. The golden honey in the honeycomb becomes the golden ore of alchemy, transmuted by the sun and drawn back to its celestial source. By the same solar process, whatever wounds and scars the world has given to men vanish in the healing light:

> 'For the Sun is the Ardent Belief
> That sees life in the aridities of the dust,
> In the seed and the base excrement and the world's fevers . . .
>
> He loves alike, the common dust of the streets
> And the lovers' lips like the gold fires burning Troy.
> The Sun kisses the loveless,
> The mouth of the condemned by Man, the dog-mouth
> and the lion-fang
> Deep in the heart. . . . He comes to the criminal whose nature
> Was crippled before his birth by a new gravitation
> That changed the solar system of the heart
> To a universe reigned over by deformation. . . .
> None is condemned. . . . Then why should we lie loveless?
> He will clothe us again in gold and a little love.'

The ragged, maimed, and destitute are thus made whole; and in poem after poem we watch as these figures are cast in the pure gold of the sun, and we see the dead beneath the earth arise through the warmth of its penetrating rays, the soil push forth new grass and flowers. Young people and lovers are perhaps the most representative for the poet of this springtime of earth. Youth, we are told in "Out of School," pays no heed to the warnings of age and death passed on by the elders; the young rush forward to embrace life in a revived world, a world they in fact symbolize. What Dame Edith envisages in the apocalyptic moments of her poetry is the creation of a human community with the universe; and the odes comprise an effort, a deeply moving one, to show us glimpses of how this might be.

The beginning of "How Many Heavens . . ." consists of an ecstatic vision of the cosmos through which the realm of the spirit makes itself known to the poet. Each part of the physical world, no matter how grand or small, attains its separate splendor by disclosing a spiritual essence. Yet no division exists among the parts; their individual voices speak a common tongue of praise:

> The emeralds are singing on the grasses
> And in the trees the bells of the long cold are ringing,—
> My blood seems changed to emeralds like the spears
> Of grass beneath the earth piercing and singing.
>
> The flame of the first blade
> Is an angel piercing through the earth to sing
> 'God is everything!
> The grass within the grass, the angel in the angel, flame
> Within the flame, and He is the green shade that came
> To be the heart of shade.'
>
> The grey-beard angel of the stone,
> Who has grown wise with age, cried 'Not alone
> Am I within my silence,—God is the stone in the still stone, the
>   silence laid
> In the heart of silence'. . .

Right through her last poems Dame Edith held her role of visionary and prophet, of the poet who has the gift of final truths about man and the universe. This kind of oracular speech is not usually a popular one, and Dame Edith suffered her share of criticism for it. Yet those who were harshest in judging her were either poets of excessively modest ambition in their work or critics who had a vested interest in narrowing down modern literature to the accomplishments of one or two writers and denying worth to all the rest. For Dame Edith there was necessity in taking such tone and command in the language of poetry; it was the single way in which she could realize her imaginative vision. Certainly, understatement and irony and the witty conceit could hardly convey her kind of knowledge. And, of course, Dame Edith worked through a range of ironical techniques before putting herself in the distinguished tradition of Blake's mythological works, Whitman's hymns to man and the earth, and Shelley's and Claudel's philosophical poems. Like

her magnificent predecessors, she sought in the farthest reaches of her being an emblematic language through which the imagination could express
the reconciliation of human life, the physical world, and the Divine Nature
that moves within them. In her poetic achievement she closely resembles
the figure of one of the "earthly Gods" celebrated in her "Praise We Great
Men":

> Praise with our last breath
> These earthly Gods who bring
> All sounds, all faiths, delights and splendours lost
> Beneath the winter's frost
> Back to the hearts, the hearths and homes of men.

(1966)

4

The Visionary Poetry of
Kathleen Raine

*After all, I doubt not but there must be the study of this creation as well as art
and vision; tho' I cannot think it other than the veil of Heaven, through which her
divine features are dimly smiling; the setting of the table before the feast; the
symphony before the tune; the prologue of the drama; a dream, and antepast,
and proscenium of eternity.*
> —SAMUEL PALMER, letter to John Linnell,
> 21 December 1828

> *The poem I know, and the wisdom*
> *That is not mine, the poem that can never be written.*
> —KATHLEEN RAINE

"THE POETIC PROCESS IN WHICH HE EXCELLED WAS NEITHER VERBAL NOR VISUAL,"
Kathleen Raine writes in a monograph on William Blake, "it was symbolic
and mythological. He was a creator not of pictures, not of verbal rhetoric,
but of symbols, whose potency does not depend solely on the medium through
which they are expressed." The interpretation of Blake's achievement offered in this passage should be of interest not only to students of his work
but to those concerned with the poetry composed by the author of these
critical observations. Miss Raine, who has been writing and publishing her
poems since the 1930s, has certain spiritual affinities with Blake, regards
him as one of her mentors, and has spent a number of years in the study of
his symbolism, culminating in the A. W. Mellon lectures for 1962. She
places Blake in a tradition of symbolic and mythological poets which includes, among others, Milton, Coleridge, Shelley, Yeats, and Edwin Muir.

For Miss Raine it seems that the whole question of her art and its practice has been bound up from the beginning with what is clearly a profound kind of visionary knowledge and religious experience. This experience is of the sort which renders the search for a language commensurate with it difficult. She is, first of all, gifted with an intuitive sense of the relationship existing between human beings and the surrounding world of nature, a relationship so foreign to our habitual modern ways of thinking about ourselves and the urbanized, technological environment in which most of us live that its very simplicity jars us:

> A bird sings on a matin tree
> 'Once such a bird was I.'
>
> The sky's gaze says
> 'Remember your mother.'
>
> Seas, trees and voices cry
> 'Nature is your nature.'
>
> I reply
> 'I am what is not what I was.
> Seas, trees, and bird, alas!
> Sea, tree, and bird was I.'

This poem, unpretentiously called "Lyric," stands at the opening of *Stone and Flower* (1943), Miss Raine's first collection. It bears little if any trace—and this holds true for all of her writing—of the radical experimental techniques of the modernist movement; its plain and direct character, its literalness of a kind, set it to the side of that literary mainstream. In a recent essay, "The Poetic Symbol," she remarks, "It has taken me half a lifetime to discover the extent and depth of differences that I sensed from an early age between myself and the most widely read poets of my generation; with, of course, a few exceptions, like David Gascoyne and Edwin Muir." Thus the poem "Lyric" means exactly what it says: nature is not used as a metaphorical device to express inner moods of unrest or alienation, psychic maladies, as it is, say, in poems of Auden's; nor is it used to connote a free and wholly natural type of existence as it does in some of Spender's verse. Feelings of alienation or exile are, of course, evoked here, but the dialogue form, as well as what is said and the tone selected for saying it, implies a deep and true spiritual affinity of the speaker with nature. This affinity and the mysterious, unnamed but highly suggestive dislocation which has occurred within it convince the reader that they have an existence beyond the poetic event describing them; and they ask to be accepted as objectively real (though discernible only by the powers of imagination) in order for us fully to understand the poem and the poignant sensation of loss conveyed there. Looking further in Miss Raine's work, that loss is rather obviously connected with the primordial Fall of man and with the divisions which have taken place in creation as a result of it. Such a theme is archetypal, perennial, and authentically poetic in her view; it appears often in her poems and we shall come upon it again.

These comments about "Lyric" bring us to some consideration of Kathleen Raine's idea and use of symbolism, which we shall call here Platonic because she frequently invokes the names of Plato and Plotinus. That is, the symbols she employs refer to and partake of a metaphysical reality; and so she not only believes in them as valid linguistic and imagistic counters for her poetry, but also sees them as the means for disclosing a transcendent wisdom and knowledge which is both pre- and post-poetic. A true poem is an imaginative organization of these symbols and thus is a revelation in "a language of analogy, of images taken from the sensible world" of this higher nature, "which cannot be described, or evoked otherwise than by analogy." So Miss Raine says, "All symbolic poetry seeks to communicate, through the many, knowledge of the one."

The source of such images and symbols is within, part of a buried knowledge or awareness of transcendent reality which can be recognized through them. In various studies of Blake and Coleridge, and in her more recent essays on "The Poetic Symbol" and "The Use of the Beautiful," Miss Raine has discussed matters of symbolism. Blake's "Eden" and "Jesus or Imagination," Coleridge's "Secondary Imagination," and Yeats's "Anima Mundi" (borrowed from the seventeenth-century English neo-Platonist Henry More), as well as Jung's Collective Unconscious are, she says, names for the same source of imagery on which all valid poets draw. She cuts short what would surely be the modern temptation to account for this symbolism solely on the grounds of psychological explanation by her repeated quotation from Coleridge's definition of Plato's reason: *"something in which we are, not which is in us"*—a universal mind. Poetry depends, then, as we have already noted, on the "language of symbolic analogy," which "is only possible upon the assumption that . . . multiple planes of reality do in fact exist. Those for whom the material world is the only plane of the real are unable to understand that the symbol—and poetry, in the full sense of the word, is symbolic discourse, discourse by analogy—has as its primary purpose the evocation of one plane in terms of another." The appearance and persistence of archetypal images in the poet's imagination, whether in dream or vision or contemplation, tends to pull "into its symbolic field—to take an analogy from magnetic and other fields of force—memories of childhood, of things read or seen or heard," thus providing focal centers in the inward or spiritual life for the events of outer experience.

The sight of the outward eye Miss Raine does not find so consistently visionary or evocative in her sense. Nonetheless, in her own poems she has very often found through a deep, undistracted attentiveness to the material world in its unspoiled state the required language of symbolic analogy. She writes in "The Poetic Symbol":

> We may see, with our physical eye, without the experience being a form of knowledge, an epiphany; physical sense-perception may sometimes be a vehicle of imaginative vision but not necessarily so. A tree, a light over the sea, a mountain or a garden or animal or bird or a human face may seem to speak to us from beyond itself, but this is rare. But it is impossible to experience some inward and archetypal vision without at the same time experiencing it qualitatively, as an epiphany of knowledge. For these images are themselves the vehicles of that knowledge; only as such do they arise, or exist. Their meaning is their only reality, the content of their forms.

It is quite obvious from even a casual perusal of her poetry that Kathleen Raine has allied herself through the most fundamental spiritual and artistic inclination with the literary tradition and its practice of which she speaks. That tradition in English literature is the Romantic one, and Miss Raine has remarked that her "idea of what poetry was derived from the English Romantic poets"; but it also, in its emphasis on correspondences to be opened between earthly and spiritual reality by means of poetic images, and in its conception of the poet as medium as well as maker, has affinities with the line of French Symbolist poets from Baudelaire through Rimbaud and Mallarmé. Yet in choosing to work in the tradition she so strongly admires, Miss Raine has never overstepped the bounds of the most becoming modesty. While it would be inaccurate to rank her with the major poets of her tradition, such as Yeats or Shelley, the collected edition of her poetry (1956), with its careful pruning away of weak and, unfortunately, some good poems, and her new book, The Hollow Hill (1965), reserve a unique place for her in contemporary British poetry and in the small group of fine English women poets of our century, which includes Edith Sitwell, Ruth Pitter, Anne Ridler, and Elizabeth Jennings. The unrelenting manner in which she has committed herself to a vision of reality and the labor she has exacted of herself in shaping that vision poetically deserve closer attention and wider appreciation than they have usually received.

In an age which heavily stresses craftsmanship and innovation in the composition of poetry and has generally, though not always, looked askance at "inspirational" theories of creation, Kathleen Raine may appear as a vocal member of a dissenting minority. She sees poetry "primarily as a way of experiencing and not as a craft, or an aptitude for conceptual acrostics." And thus it is "that lyrical form, no less than a certain kind of imagery, is

archetypal, and emerges when a certain level of consciousness is attained."
The "advocates of craftsmanship" are measured against Miss Raine's symbolist notion of the poem and come out "mere imitators of the forms of
life."

One of the best of her early poems is "Invocation," where she treats the
theme of poetic inspiration in a terrifying way: the gestation of a poem
involves its author in the most excruciating mental and physical torments:

> There is a poem on the way,
> there is a poem all round me,
> the poem is in the near future,
> the poem is in the upper air
> above the foggy atmosphere
> it hovers, a spirit
> that I would make incarnate.
> Let my body sweat
> let snakes torment my breast
> my eyes be blind, ears deaf, hands distraught
> mouth parched, uterus cut out,
> belly slashed, back lashed,
> tongue slivered into thongs of leather
> rain stones inserted in my breasts,
> head severed,
>
> if only the lips may speak,
> if only the god will come.

Like Rimbaud, Miss Raine feels that "I is an other" ("Je est un autre"), that
poetry, its images and substance, is created *through* her rather than merely
made by her. In "Invocation" the poem awaited is transcendent; its revelation or utterance demands a submission which turns the poet into a sacrificial victim who must suffer the agonies of bringing it to birth. Yet Miss
Raine's reliance on what can perhaps best be called visionary experience,
and on what she has termed "archetypal epiphanies" (that is, images rising
into consciousness which can be compared to her definition of Blake's vision of the Last Judgment: "a vision" of "what eternally exists") never leads
to poor or careless writing; her whole career as a poet aims at an increasing
economy and purity of style—frequently the target of her detractors. And,
remarkably enough, the rigorous eye she bends to her art does not defeat
the experience of dictation or inspiration but helps to shape and clarify it.

These two attributes of seer and self-critic have their roots deep in Kathleen
Raine's personal history, and she has traced her life briefly in an autobiographical sketch written for *Twentieth Century Authors, First Supplement*
(1955). Born in 1908, her childhood was largely a country one, spent with

maternal grandparents, who were Scots, and a schoolmistress aunt in a Northumberland village. "The noble country and dignified way of life among the still feudal community of farmers and shepherds of Northumberland was then, and has since remained for me, the epitome of all that I have ever loved," she writes. In its effect on her poetic imagination this period of life resembles the pastoral childhoods of Edwin Muir and Herbert Read, so movingly recounted in their autobiographies, and the days which Dylan Thomas passed as a boy at the farm of Fern Hill. The wild, primitive country of Northumberland, Cumberland, and Scotland have kept for her the near-sacred aspect of a lost center, a touchstone world to which she seeks a final return. On these places she is dependent as an artist, for there alone, she notes, "I am able to feel myself anything other than an exile or a caged wild creature." This northern landscape appears in poems from her first book to her latest, but more recently, in the "Ten Italian Poems" from *The Hollow Hill*, she has found very different places rich sources for the imagination's work, too.

When she was still a child, Miss Raine was removed from this beloved and haunting northern environment to the London Suburbs and later went to Girton College, Cambridge, to study natural sciences, "specializing in botany and zoology." At that time I. A. Richards was riding an enormous wave of popularity, and many of Miss Raine's friends were among his students. Here she published her first poems in the undergraduate magazine *Experiment*, edited by William Empson, J. Bronowski, and Humphrey Jennings. In her autobiographical sketch she remarks about the intermingling of students from different disciplines. "There was no sharp distinction at that time in Cambridge between scientists and students in the humanities, and I believe that even the least of us . . . preserved to this day a certain dispassionate clarity of thought, or, at all events, a respect for such thought." The reader of Miss Raine's writings will observe in both poetry and prose the results of such training and habits of mind; there is directness of statement and a crystalline purity of image in all of her poems, as well as an occasional use of scientific names which recalls the years of her training.

While the knowledge and discipline of her studies in botany and zoology have quite evidently left their mark on her work, it appears also as though they brought Miss Raine to a crucial event or series of events in the inner life that issued in a profound alteration in her view of human existence and the physical reality about her in the world. The basis for my remarks, though they must inevitably be somewhat speculative, is an essay called "Flowers," published by Miss Raine in *Poetry London* close to the time her first collection of poems came out. She meditates there in so convincing a manner on the detrimental consequences of protracted scientific analysis for her perception of the world that I cannot but think she underwent some kind of spiritual crisis, which concluded—perhaps only after some duration—in a religious attitude. Discussing what happens if one looks too long and too hard at things in a scientific fashion, if one knows too much of biological construction, she records the disappearance for the observer of distinguishing human traits:

> But what, then, is it in the assembly of organs of special sense, at one end of the central nervous system, that makes a face, that has recognisable unity, entity, person? To think too far this way leads to that madness for which there are no faces in the streets; and in the trains and buses, not people, but collections of organs, topping a spine, whose upper bones are stretched and twisted a little—but no faces, any more than the fringed circle of the holothurian or the medusa.

What began, Miss Raine tells us, in her loss of relationship with nature grew until the most familiar things fell apart, and meaning and identity disintegrated with them. "Only long after the faces of the world had dissolved for me, did they begin to return," she writes. "Not in flower only, but in the leaf, the root, and the branch were latent faces." Her poetry is the surest testimony we have that these nightmares of hallucination were followed by developing powers of visionary perception. We ought to remember as we read her poems the warning and advice she offers in the essay: "Knowing too much is always to lose the object; knowledge dissolves contours, but only faith creates them."

This belief in the "contours" of objects is attested to by a concentration on the particularity and shape of trees, rocks, and stones, streams and waterfalls, fish, birds, and flowers in her poems. The north country of England and Scotland likewise etches all its forms upon her mind, and she draws upon it freely for images and locations. A considerable proportion of her best work, as we would expect, keeps to these resources:

> The rock is written with the sign
> In geometric diamond prison,
> Prism, cube and rhomboid, mineral grain,
> The frozen world of rigid form
> Inexorable in line and plane
> At every point where meet and part
> The cross-ways of the enduring world
> ("The Hollow Hill")

The imaginative world which unfolds poem by poem in *Stone and Flower* is, at first encounter, strange and various, sometimes confusing; but it is also clearly the product of a singular poetic mind with its own full store of imagery and its own mode of vision. In this book Miss Raine assumes a number of roles, yet manages to remain herself. We are aware of her as seer and transmitter and poet at the same time. On occasion she speaks in a kind of oracular first person:

> The moon is my eye
> smiling only at night,
> with my traveling eye I see
> the world that cast it out.
> ("Cattle Dream")

At other moments she claims the objective voice of prophecy or of sacred revelation:

> At the focus of thought there is no face,
> the focus of the sun is in crystal with no shadow.
> Death of the victim is the power of the god.
> ("The Crystal Skull")

While it is perhaps difficult to discern the individual personality of the poet in either of these excerpts, or for that matter in the full texts of the two poems, Miss Raine is still maintaining a fidelity to her experience. When she speaks in the first person, the voice in fact often seems to emerge from *woman herself* rather than a specific individual. This effect, which is especially noticeable in such poems as "Maternal Grief," "The Messengers," "The Red Light," and "The Hands," fulfills the poet's intention: poetry should surpass the transitoriness of personality and its fleeting, protean aspect in favor of an apprehension of a deeper and more permanent selfhood bound to creation and to the Divine. In many of the later poems, particularly those from *The Pythoness* (1949) and *The Year One* (1954), the first person has a prophetic tone; and the function of the first-person speaker is that of a "medium," to apply the word Hazard Adams has used with reference to Miss Raine, for her notion of the symbolic poem continues to demand the abdication of the superficial "I."

The role of woman in the more universal or fundamental sense mentioned is quite effective in certain of the love poems where the beloved appears in the complementary role. In treating her own very personal emotions and her close relationships with others, Miss Raine tends at times to be awkward and the verses fail to ring true. When she achieves distance, however, and imagines a relationship or perceives the wider symbolic implications of one instead of writing out her immediate involvement with it, any artistic hesitation or faltering vanishes; a timeless speech flows forth, merging together in love, man, and the world, with a strength of language and imagery arising from the farthest reaches of inwardness:

> Yours is the face that the earth turns to me.
> Continuous beyond its human features lie
> The mountain forms that rest against the sky.
> With your eyes, the reflecting rainbow, the sun's light
> Sees me; forest and flowers, bird and beast
> Know and hold me for ever in the world's thought,
> Creation's deep untroubled retrospect.
>
> ("Love Poem")

The love expressed here is surely unconventional, and in a very real sense it is not personal at all; it is rather suprapersonal. The anonymous figures and the generalized title make the impersonality of the poem at once obvious. But these characteristics of the piece do not for a moment suggest that the author lacks human feeling, for the emotion is profound, intense. We do, though, perceive from reading the poem that personal regard really means (even if we aren't totally aware of it) more than the affection of one individual for another. Because of man's make-up, because he shares in the life of creation, such a relationship becomes a manifestation of love for the entire world through one person, a beloved who is—like the lover—an integral part of the physical universe, "the deep grass, / And rocks and rivers." And through this attachment to creation by means of the beloved there comes also an intuition of the Divine from whom it and the lovers emanate:

> When your hand touches mine, it is the earth
> That takes me—the deep grass,
> And rocks and rivers; the green graves,
> And children still unborn, and ancestors,
> In love passed down from hand to hand from God.
> Your love comes from the creation of the world,
> From those paternal fingers, streaming through the clouds
> That break with light the surface of the sea.

A cosmology is implied in "Love Poem," though it derives from an inspiration, an inner perception the sources of which are not readily apparent but must be guessed from an experience of the poem itself. Miss Raine does not set forth her vision systematically because it does not present itself to her in that way. We have, however, in addition to certain poems, the help afforded by her prose. In the introductory remarks to her *Collected Poems* she indicates how "for the poet when he begins to write there is no poem, in the sense of a construction of words; and the concentration of the mind is upon something else, that precedes words, and by which the words, as they are written, must constantly be checked and rectified," as evidence of what she calls both "imaginative vision" and "platonic idea." In his book, *Inspiration* and *Poetry*, C. M. Bowra has stated that the "ideal poem" is hard, even impossible to make concrete: "The poet works with words, and words have many foibles and defects. They can hardly ever do all that is asked of them. . . ." But Kathleen Raine's tough self-criticism chastens her art and drives her toward the realization of this difficult poetic goal. Any failures seem the natural outcome of an inability to discover words and images completely adequate to the illumination with which her mind is suddenly filled. In *Living in Time* (1946), the effort to employ Catholic canonical symbolism collapses, by her own admission, because the symbols cannot bear the weight of meaning she wishes, though recently she has suggested that this fault is a personal artistic one and is not inherent in this body of symbolism, the amplitude of which she now acknowledges. Of course, a poetry dependent on visionary revelation or intuition faces many individual defeats, but by the same token its successes are the more valuable in extending the range of human consciousness or in awakening it to what seemingly has been forgotten. Miss Raine has accomplished in her best poems the recovery of a vein of symbolism and imagery which discloses a vision essentially religious and metaphysical; and so, as in "Love Poem," the plane of experience toward which we are directed lies beyond its imagistic reflections.

The spiritual realities she makes known are first perceived in many instances through the forms of nature, since, as we have noted, she finds that her visionary apprehensions frequently have originated in them. A considerable number of poems point up Miss Raine's belief that the world of nature is integrated, at one with itself, and does not know man's lacerating inner divisions. The hauntingly beautiful poem, "The Speech of Birds," is one of the finest statements of the human separation from the order of nature; and its concluding stanza comments on the weaknesses of man's language when compared with the open intervention of Divine speech in mundane affairs:

> It is not birds that speak, but men learn silence;
> They know and need no language; leaf-wise
> In shadowy flight, threading the leafy trees,
> Expressive only of the world's long thoughts,
> Absolute rises their one-pointed song,
> Not from a heart divided, and in pain.
>
> The sweet-eyed, unregarding beasts
> Waking and sleeping wear the natural grace.
> The innocent order of the stars and tides
> An impulse in the blood-stream circulates.
> Obedient to one living pulse,
> With them, at heart, converse the saints.

> We, ignorant and outcast, stand
> Wondering at the swallow's flight
> Gazing it the open hand,
> Questioning the lines of fate—
> Each individual destiny
> Preying on an exiled mind.
>
> Our words, our concepts, only name
> A world of shadows; for the truth is plain
> That visited Jacob in a dream,
> And Moses, from the burning desert heard,
> Or angels in annunciation bring.

The dreams and events which are manifestations of the Divine in the world become in the course of time, like other comparable images, symbols, or forms, inward and archetypal, ascending to the surface of the mind in meditation and trance or exhibiting themselves vividly in sleep. In the psychological thought of Jung they belong to the collective unconscious and are as old as human memory. It is precisely the force and currency of such symbolism that Miss Raine seeks in her art, whether in some traditional image like the Tree of Life or the fountain, or the spiritual resonance she frees in the contemplation of things in nature. Yet she realizes this poetic aim neither by craft alone nor by any act of the will, but through the timeless processes of imagination working within the self, though mysteriously independent of it.

Thus the use of nature and its forms could be classified only by the most careless reader of Miss Raine's work as simple description, though she obviously takes pleasure in its details. Like Blake, Wordsworth, and Coleridge, she is concerned with deciphering the secret hints of the larger scheme of being embodied in the visible surface of the natural world. And with most of the Romantics she favors a life lived close to the rugged simplicities of earth, sky, and water. Contemplation of the patterns shaped by the elements can lead to revelation. Physical appearances are clearly not the end of perceiving but the beginning; they stir in the beholder's imagination that inner world of correspondences of which we have spoken:

> Not upon earth, as you suppose
> tower these rocks that turn the wind,
> for on their summits angels stand.
>
> Not from the earth these waters rise—
> to quench not thirst, but ecstasy
> the waterfall leaps from the sky.

> Those nameless clouds that storm and swirl
> about the mountain are the veil
> that from these sightless eyes shall fall
>
> when senses faint into the ground,
> and time and place go down the wind.
>   ("Tu non sé in terra, si come tu credi")

As usual, directness and conviction characterize Miss Raine's presentation of intuitive vision, which pierces the outward appearances of landscape here by placing it in a further and different dimension, a dimension of which the physical is only one, and perhaps the least important, attribute. So this poem and many others do the same—carries implications of the cosmology inherent in moments of poetic inspiration we mentioned in connection with "Love Poem." For this singular way of seeing the material objects of what we might call our daily or common-sense reality (what we like to call the ordinary world), objects we credit with a reassuring solidity and durability that promise security in our routine activities, are frighteningly transparent, as we gather in the poem "Ex Nihilo":

> Out of nothing we are made,
> our cities rise upon the void,
>
> And in chromium-plated bars,
> Shadows drink their fill of tears,
>
> Women's transient fingers pass
> Over silks and flowers and glass,
>
> Cameras and motor-cars
> Spin on the hub of nothingness
> On which revolve the years and Stars.

In the stanzas that follow creation is again understood as spreading out in the layers and multitudinous particulars which compose the physical cosmos from a Divine center endowing all with its sustaining presence:

> Beyond the houses and the fields
> Rise the forest-shrouded hills,
> And upon each leaf is traced
> The pattern of the eternal mind
> That summons kingdoms from the dust.

> Above the forests lie the clouds,
> White fields where the soaring sight
> Rests on the air's circumference,
>
> And distant constellations move
> About the centre of a thought
> By the flat of that love
>
> Whose being is the breath of life,
> The terra firma that we tread,
> The divine body that we eat,
> The incarnation that we live.

Miss Raine holds, in general, a perspective at wide variance with our day-to-day smug one, and from its radical viewpoint the concrete world we take for granted becomes a geography of signs translating the sacred and eternal reality that sustains it. The true poet, I think Miss Raine would say, has the imaginative ability to perform this translation by means of the correspondence existing between the symbols he uses and the transcendent planes of being they evoke. In the poem "Formulation," she recalls in the figure of Blake a famous precedent for her poetic attitude:

> And once in Lambeth a hidden grain of sand
> Held all the world that vision can command,
> The great eternity within a poet's mind.

Still, the authenticity of her perceptions does not force us to conclude that an otherwise plain and empty landscape suddenly bustles with angels and shows itself balanced on the brink of a void, but that the landscape has always been so, only we have not known how to see it. English visionary painters from Blake through Samuel Palmer to Stanley Spencer and Paul Nash have testified in their pictures to a transformation of the eye not unlike the one Miss Raine proposes in her poems. The opening of the little poem "In Time" provides a moving example of spiritual reality present in the world but utterly unnoticed:

> The beautiful rain falls, the unheeded angel
> lies in the street, spreadeagled under the footfall
> that from the divine face wears away the smile . . .

The normally accepted evidence of the senses, as well as the rational constructions built upon such evidence, gives way to images of things or processes of nature disclosing themselves from within, as it were, and exposing an infinite prospect: we see them and, simultaneously, by the powers of imaginative suggestion see through them into a kind of indefinite or extended inner space which is in itself an enlargement of the mind and spirit. Time and space in our ordinary use of the terms, though real enough in the sense that we are slowly worn to death by the erosion of one and separated by the other, begin to crumble as categorical dimensions for the convenient arrangement of objects and experience. In her poetry Miss Raine shifts back and forth between different ideas of time. The poem "In Time," from which we quoted above, presents it as throwing a veil of illusion over the eternal realities that remain unseen and are yet so close to us. "The Wind of Time" dramatizes it as a destructive turbulence that carries all before it:

> Time blows a tempest—how the days run high,
> Deep graves are opened between hour and hour,
> A current sweeps the streets and houses by
> Too fast to board them.

When the storm is finished with its wrecking and "drowning" (this poem, it might be said, almost certainly reflects obliquely in some of its details—the phrase "Cities are wrecked by night," for instance—the air war on England), individual persons are left with the residue of their lives in broken images and ghostly places touched only with the remoteness of dying associations: "Fragments of past delight, and of past selves, / Dead rooms and houses, with the strangled shells." This last phrase, with its unnatural, hallucinatory quality, brings the poem to an overwhelming conclusion.

Another poem, "Seen in a Glass," dispenses with human vanity and self-ishness, defines "living creatures" as composed of "images / And dreams" moved by "feelings" which are "inherent in our frames / Of mutable earth, air, and fire." The final stanza locates this precarious earthly self in a temporal dimension equally deceptive:

> Unwise we feel, but wise we know
> Living in time is but to seem—
> Like green leaves on a tree we grow,
> But each must fall and fade alone.

Finally, in her later "Two Invocations of Death" from *The Year One*, she desires to cast off body, brain, and personality, all of them, in the tradition of neo-Platonic thought followed here, encumbrances to the soul which has descended (Miss Raine elsewhere says that this descent can be interpreted as comparable to the primordial Fall of man) into the universe of matter. The physical world deludes and distracts; time confuses with its perpetual flux and change; the mind finds deception, the heart loses love in suffering. As in the poetry of Vaughan, Wordsworth, and Muir, the farther

an individual travels from childhood, the more lost be becomes in the laby-
rinthine complexities of a temporal-material dimension grounded in illusion. The way of the soul or the spirit describes an arc, leading away from its
transcendent or Divine origins down into mundane reality and then striving for ascent, for a return to its source of being in God. But this renewed
union can come only by entry through the door of death; and so the first of
the two poems, a kind of ritual divestiture and symbolic purification of the
dross of personal, physical existence, proceeds by the invocation of death
(as indicated in the title) and a mood of penance:

> Death, I repent
> Of these hands and feet
> That for forty years
> Have been my own
> And I repent
> Of flesh and bone,
> Of heart and liver,
> Of hair and skin—
> Rid me, death,
> Of face and form,
> Of all that I am.

If this initial stanza concentrates on discarding the body, the second one
rejects "the forms of thought" and feeling: the "heart crippled / By long-spent
pain." As these go, so must the "memory-traces" with their lingering attachments to persons and places; words and speech also have falsified what was
never correctly "seen / Or understood," and the poet asks death to dispose of
them. The concluding stanza of the first poem, intensifying the penitential
motif, starts with an admission of guilt, of faulty actions committed and of
malice and anguish witnessed. In the last lines Miss Raine hopes not only for
absolution and "release" but for her total disappearance from the world:

> Not this or that
> But all is amiss,
> That I have done,
> And I have seen
> Sin and sorrow
> Befoul the world—
> Release me, death,
> Forgive, remove
> From place and time
> The trace of all
> That I have been.

The next poem, while its implications are surely just as severe, is more
lyrical and affirmative in its opening statement of the origin and hoped-

for end of the cycle of existence. The essential "I" recalls and looks toward its "lost beginning":

> From a place I came
> That never was in time,
> From the beat of a heart
> That never was in pain.
> The sun and the moon,
> The wind and the world,
> The song and the bird
> Travelled my thought
> Time out of mind.
> Shall I know at last
> My lost delight?

That beginning is, of course, timeless and Divine, but it is manifest in creation, too, in nature. Yet when the poet has attempted to seize its presence there, her own fallen, alien state prevents her. Trees, stones, birds, and fish simply in being themselves exclude man from their domain; he stands a stranger, even an enemy, in their midst. And the barrier that, like a transparent screen, allows him to see into the world of nature but forbids his full participation in it, derives from his imperfection and dividedness. Thus Miss Raine speaks not for herself alone in the closing stanza, though she finishes by seeking again that annihilation of self which is but the prelude to an assumption of her "lost being" in the oneness of God:

> Oh my lost love
> I have seen you fly
> Away like a bird,
> As a fish elude me,
> A stone ignore me,
> In a tree's maze
> You have closed against me
> The spaces of earth,
> Prolonged to the stars'
> Infinite distances,
> With strange eyes
> You have not known me,
> Thorn you have wounded,
> Fire you have burned
> And talons torn me.
> How long must I bear
> Self and identity—
> Shall I find at last
> My lost being?

Time and appearance lose some of their hold on the individual when he can locate a meaningful spiritual reality beyond them which at least momentarily robs them of substance. Yet, as the titles of two of Miss Raine's books imply, there is no quick or simple escape from the limitations time imposes; she is aware, as Eliot is in *Four Quartets*, that knowledge or experience of the eternal does not free a person from the pain of completing his temporal, physical existence. But the direction of her poetic thought leads toward the edge of time and to a sense of the pristine state of nature as it existed on the seventh day of the first week in the biblical account of creation.

Space in Miss Raine's poetry includes the space of the natural world and also the immensity of space which is hidden in or behind things. The presence of this interior space is seldom thought of outside laboratories or theoretical essays; but for our poet it is not a scientific conception, but a metaphysical certainty that urges attention to the final emptiness, the vast nothingness without measure through which the pervasive Divine spirit moves. In "The Invisible Spectrum" the impressions of the external world received by the senses, if we can follow their course, draw us "Beyond sense, the spinning spheres, / Atoms and stars / That weave our lives." The beginning stanzas assert the "void" of space yawning just the other side of our fragile, evanescent sensory perceptions:

> Learn, if I dare, the order of the wind,
> Fire, tempest and the sea.
> Learn if I dare into what mode of being
> The leaf falls from the tree.
>
> Everywhere
> There are holes in the air,
> Graves open to receive us,
>
> After the seventh colour
> And before the first
> Lies darkness.

Again, the individual dwells in a personal space made his by the boundaries of the body, of human selfhood, as we learn in "Night Thought." This poem starts with its author lying alone, trapped in the confinements of her physical nature and of the living space she inhabits; outside is the world, what she can see of it composed of rainy skies and wind-tossed trees "filled with their own life." As before, we find the individual cut off from the essential life of creation and enclosed as the "Inmate and prisoner of human walls":

For out of life, no living creature falls.

But "desire" cannot be so restricted, and Miss Raine sends forth her "heart," a cup or grail which bears her "life," carrying it "Through walls, through houses, through the stone of London, / Through dreams and real places. . . ." What she seeks is beyond vision or thought, her "Loves' rest," which I think we must understand as the One where all her confused and scattered affections find their true object. The earlier admonition, quoted above, that the living cannot escape their lives enforces itself now, for desire and hope inevitably weaken: the "heart is lost, / And tired returns, empty and crying to [the poet's] breast." The ending lines focus on the agonizing contradictions of "human love"; the heart reaches out from its isolation toward the ultimate object on which to bestow its gift of love, but it is unable to see that desired end, for life restricts and imprisons it in the self:

> In my dark room I weep that human love is so,
> Blindly must go, and blindly still return,
> Lost in the self it knows, and lost in the unknown,
> Lost for beyond its life, no living heart may go.

In many poems a certain angle of vision creates a space from the interpenetration of the natural and supernatural spheres. An image or symbol under these circumstances, however sensuous or earth-bound it may be, contains as an integral part of itself aspects of the transcendental reality in which it also shares or to which it gives access, so that in the body of the poem the physical-temporal and the spiritual elements stand side by side, overlap, or emerge the one from the other. The supplication with which Miss Raine finishes her poem "Pas Perdus" affirms her recognition of these planes of being and the wish to come upon the higher through the lower:

> Dreamer, our father, we are your children too,
> Open your worlds within worlds,
> Nature, and the eternal present of your days
> To us, earth's disinherited generation.

In nature's forms and patterns, then, time and space coincide; and prolonged contemplation of these designs and configurations may release the mind to spiritual vision. Miss Raine often discovers in natural parts and details a language of ciphers: the further she mentally probes its characters the nearer she approaches knowledge of the Divine center of creation. This course is followed in "The Hyacinth," where she meditates on that flower and turns her imagination in ever-widening circles outward from a time-bound material reality toward the eternal, unchanging source whose ultimate impulse is love. She must return from this exalted level of perception; but her sight has been altered, for the world as it appears at the poem's finish is seen to disclose its spiritual significance through symbolic figures like those of the rose, the lily, and the dove. As the poem progresses, the boundaries of time and space gradually vanish; when they come back at the conclusion with "the world unfolding into flower," their meaning and substance for the reader have changed considerably:

> Time opens in a flower of bells
> the mysteries of its hidden bed,
> the altar of the ageless cells
> whose generations never have been dead.
>
> So flower angels from the holy head,
> so on the wand of darkness bright worlds hang.
> Love laid the elements at the vital root,
> unhindered out of love these flowers spring.
>
> The breath of life shapes darkness into leaves,
> each new-born cell
> drinks from the star-filled well
> the dark milk of the sky's peace.
>
> The hyacinth springs on a dark star—
> I see eternity give place to love.
> It is the world unfolding into flower
> the rose of life, the lily and the dove.

The poetic mind thus contemplates the objects and recurrent cycles of nature as analogies of or paths to the eternal, or as incarnate symbols of Divine love: the blossoming hyacinth which dies and is reborn seasonally bursts into time from an origin deeper than winter sleep. This flower, like Miss Raine's other images of lily and rose, recalls the archetypal mandala shape whose universal significance as a symbol of integration and harmony is well known to readers of Jung. She writes in a poem about the symbol, "the centre of the mandala is everywhere." Her interest in it is of course less psychological than mystical because she finds it an emblem of incarnation, an image of life radiating from a Divine and timeless center which is at once Christ and the infinite circumference of God. Without difficulty, she associates her image with the legendary axletree around which the earth revolves (one might compare some of the meanings here with Eliot's use of the axletree in "Burnt Norton"), the Tree of Life and the Tree of Knowledge. The poet also sees herself at the central point of the mandala figure, but it is a point where again selfhood is vanquished. The eternal circle of the sun at the poem's close would appear to be the Divine being in which "all selves" are subsumed. Such is the plan of the soul's last journey; its earthly counterpart is given in the first stanza: "Wherever the eye falls," there the mandala's sign may be seen; when it is, "in the brooding heart the wings stir / Of the bird whose flight is through a thousand skies." This image of the homing bird is analogous to that of the converging selves in the final stanza:

> The centre of the mandala is possibility
> Of incarnation, seed of the tree
> About whose beams the myriad stars turn.
> I the infinity where all selves converge
> Into the perennial circle of the sun.
> ("The Mandala")

One should also add that the poet-herself is once more depicted in these lines as a medium, the individual through whom this vision of incarnation passes into the world and is translated into language.

Thus in Miss Raine's poems nature and the energies supporting it are plainly subordinate to a superior reality, as are likewise the commonplace categories of time and space. Like the poetry of T. S. Eliot, Edwin Muir, Edith Sitwell, Vernon Watkins, and David Gascoyne, to name some prominent kindred figures, hers indicates a meaning outside the temporal flow for human existence in time, though its whole meaning remains of necessity mysterious.

Fully recognizing the pain, imperfection, and death that mark and, at last, destroy human life, Miss Raine interprets this world after Plato's allegory of the cave with its insistence on man's separation from the ideal; or as she says in her recent poem "Last Things":

> The perfect is not in time
> Where all is marred;
>
> But lucid forms
> Cast their images
> Upon our waters:
> Their faces, veiled or radiant, are always beautiful . . .

Water in neo-Platonic thought symbolizes the lowest level of the realm of matter and so is farthest from ultimate spiritual reality. Miss Raine employs this symbol with some frequency, for it is highly suggestive of the human situation. The individual, trapped and weighed down by matter, encumbered by flesh, can still discover in this physical dimension the "marred" mirror-images of perfection. The symbolic character of water and its reflections thus seems comparable to the shadows on the wall of the cave in Plato's allegory.

The implications of such practice have a religious aspect which is Christian in the sense that, as we have noted, the world of matter corresponds to the postlapsarian universe. Several poems explore nature in ways that keep to Miss Raine's general Platonic symbolism while at the same time they have an unspecified Christian significance. In "The Still Pool," for instance, the poet watches on the surface of a pond the reflections of trees and stars, leaves and sky; her thoughts fasten on these images as "quiet semblances" of reality, though they are not less real, she thinks, than the pools in which they are mirrored. But the reflections do not belong to the water as the fish or vegetation thriving there do. Miss Raine culminates her meditations by blending overtones of the Platonic conviction of a transcendent ideal reality with suggestions of the Christian belief in the perfect form bestowed by God on His creation at the beginning, a perfection which, in terms of the poem, is maintained eternally on a supernatural plane:

> The pool holds their images: to weed and fish not real
> They rest upon the surface, colour and form of things
> True, though not here as they to themselves elsewhere are.

This continuous symbolic reading of nature is possible only because of the poet's trust in the veracity of its transcendental counterpart: the ideal nature from which nature as we know it through our flawed perceptions has fallen. Speaking of Coleridge's poetry, Miss Raine says it is "profoundly Platonic," and what she observes about the figures of the Romantic poet's work applies with equal validity to her own:

> They [the figures] are supernatural in the precise meaning of the word— they come from *above nature*, that is, from those regions of the mind that find in merely natural forms the symbolic terms of an imaginative language: "In looking at the objects of Nature while I am thinking, as at yonder moon dim-glimmering through the dewy window-pane, I seem rather to be seeking, as it were *asking* for, a symbolical language for something within me that already and forever exists, than observing anything new. Even when that latter is the case, yet still I have always a feeling as if that new phenomenon were the dim awakening of a forgotten or hidden truth of my inner nature." For Coleridge, as for Plato, physical appearances are shadows of ideas, projected upon the transient flux of nature, that Penelope's web that is forever woven and undone.

We can gather from this passage of the introduction to her anthology of Coleridge's writings how Miss Raine likewise subscribes for her own poetry to the Platonic notion of the identity of perception and recollection. The discovery of truth, the coming to knowledge and awareness, means no more or less than realizing what we have always known but never recognized. Adherence to Platonic thought also accounts for an abiding fascination with the "contours" of things: the whorls of a sea shell, the outline of a leaf, or the petals of a flower. Through these forms she pursues a higher order traced in but finally existing beyond nature. According to the figures of Plato's myth of the cave, she wishes to proceed straight into the fiery light of the ideal; in Christian terms, toward God. But as we are aware Miss Raine well knows, man is immersed in material reality through his physical being and suffers the inner torments resulting from self-consciousness, imperfection, and guilt. His inner torments, I believe the poet would say, are further aggravated by the development of an urban, mechanized civilization which obscures knowledge of his true origin and destiny by burying the symbolic language available through creation beneath the artificial constructions of will and practical intelligence; he succumbs to appearances. Miss Raine speaks of what are for her the authentic implications of human incarnation in "The Tree of Heaven" from *Living in Time:*

> Heaven, simple like a seed, from its minute beginning
> Rooted in flesh and blood, instinct with death and pain
> Grows complex, manifold; grows great with living,
> With green and blossom and bough, sky-covering
> With world, where nothing was, until heaven's spring.

After creation and man's primordial defection, Miss Raine appears to be telling us, whatever spiritual perfection he may attain—in fact, it is implied, at last *will* attain—cannot be wholly separated from him as a physical creature, as a participant in the world of waters and hills and trees into which he was originally introduced, though it is the "seed" of heaven, the soul or spirit, that grows outward to redeem the self. His present distance from nature becomes a fair way of gauging how far he has come from an unfallen harmony, from the "Eden where the lonely rowan bends over the dark pool"; but so deep and essential a relationship cannot easily be severed, as one of the later poems, "The Wilderness," demonstrates. Miss Raine begins this poem with a certain attitude of regret: the childhood years she lived in the harsh, craggy north country were still years of the twentieth century, and so the old legends, ballads, and magical beliefs had been swept away by the passage of time and, presumably, the loss of faith in the supernatural. As "a child," she writes, "I ran in the wind on a withered moor / Crying out after those great presences who were not there. . . ." But if the general sense of spiritual reality like the "holy water" that once filled "the wells and springs" had "ebbed away," she could yet regard, as she does also in other poems, the landscape and its non-human inhabitants as reminders of a lost paradise:

> Only the archaic forms themselves could tell
> In sacred speech of hoodie on gray stone, or hawk in air,
> Of Eden where the lonely rowan bends over the dark pool.

The last stanza of the poem provides even further compensations for childhood's spiritual deprivations. Here Miss Raine apparently refers to later experiences of a visionary order. The "bright mountain behind the mountain" would seem to suggest the kind of sacred mountain described by Mircea Eliade in his *Patterns in Comparative Religion* as appearing universally. Such a mountain "is the meeting place of heaven and earth" and "is situated at the centre of the world." Thus, for example, "To Christians, Golgotha is the centre of the world, for it is the peak of the cosmic mountain and the spot where Adam was created and buried." Miss Raine's image, I think, carries a similar weight of meaning, for the other experiences associated with the mountain in this stanza surely link it with the forsaken Eden we have already seen. "Under the leaves," and seemingly at some point on the body of the mountain, the poet has fed upon the tart berries of the rowan tree and drunk water from a covert fountain, which is the source of the "dark pool" of the previous stanza. The tree unmistakably, I believe, symbolizes the Tree of Life, and the bitterness of its berries only serves to support that interpretation. The fountain is perhaps more difficult. In "The Poetic Symbol" Miss Raine mentions both of these images as having occurred to her as "archetypal epiphanies," the tree in a vision, the fountain in a dream; they were obviously, as she indicates, overlaid with multiple associations. But I think that in the present context it is "the fountain of vision" the image evokes: in other words, the "inexhaustible" source of spiritual knowledge and wisdom. Such an image is appropriately linked with the sacred geography of the mountain and Eden. We can observe, then, that this closing stanza constitutes simultaneously a statement about the store of metaphysical symbolism to which she has found access and a representation of the experience of those symbols:

> Yet I have glimpsed the bright mountain behind the mountain,
> Knowledge under the leaves, tasted the bitter berries red,
> Drunk water cold and clear from an inexhaustible hidden
>   fountain.

This same theme of the search for man's lost paradise runs through the work of a number of modern English poets like a stream from that forgotten but magical spring of which Miss Raine writes. We feel its presence constantly in the poetry of Edwin Muir, David Gascoyne, Vernon Watkins, in Herbert Read's beautiful *Moon's Farm* and the lyrics of Ruth Pitter, and of course in the later poems of Dylan Thomas. To a greater or lesser degree, such poets provide a vision of man and nature unified, or of the pressing need for this unity, which is at the same time a vision of self-integration or inward harmony—the state of Eden. In the poem "Isis Wanderer" Miss Raine reflects on the "dismembered world that once was the whole god / Whose broken fragments now lie dead." She is not lamenting here the abandonment of a species of pantheism but recording the loss of a human sense of the cosmos as a sacred totality. As the poem moves forward, Miss Raine adopts the role of the lonely, wandering goddess in her "black cloak" of mourning who seeks to piece together from meaningful things in the world the body of her beloved dead Osiris and so to prepare the way for his resurrection:

> I search the twofold desert of my solitude,
> The outward perished world, and the barren mind.

Images of war's destruction and sacrifice become in this context emblematic of the death of the god; but the correspondence must not be seen as purely figurative: Osiris (and of course throughout the poem we think of Christ, as doubtless we are meant to) really dies again in the last agonies of a soldier: "his blood flows from a dying soldier's wound." And in a subsequent stanza the journeying goddess perceives her lost god in a variety of things ranging from a cathedral to the refuse of the streets. This passage in which the rubble of the world reflects a Divine reality calls to mind David Gascoyne's poem "The Gravel-Pit Field," much admired by Miss Raine. In that piece the poet's meditation on discarded fragments from life brings him to the recognition that he stands in a middle-zone between the world of history and the realm of the spiritual. Miss Raine's stanza exhibits a similar type of awareness, only she keeps it in line with her theme:

> His skull is a dead cathedral and his crown's rays
> Glitter from worthless tins and broken glass.
> His blue eyes are reflected from pools in the gutter,
> And his strength is the desolate stone of fallen cities.

From these considerations of physical objects and the world of appearances the poem turns away in its closing stanzas and focuses instead on the interior self, the levels of consciousness and the symbolism of dreams. The poet/goddess wonders now if in the "kitchen-midden" of her dream imagery—that is to say, in an inner refuse heap of images, shards of remembrance and past experience—she can possibly "uncover" the "loved desecrated face" of the god, if his whole image lies buried within and waits to be awakened.

Perhaps through the terrors of sleep, "the maze of nightmare," she can come through the "menacing nether waters" of the unconscious upon "the fish king" (a reference to Osiris's death by drowning and probably obliquely to Christ). At the end of the poem she pictures herself engaged in her sacred mission, fitting together the parts of the god, which from another point of view is Miss Raine's appointed task as a poet. And that activity is enlarged upon here: the image of the mandala appears and is used to designate wholeness or integration and a corresponding series of images of Divine "creative power" extending from God and the sun to the energy of the electron. The last line with its allusions to beginning and renewal, birth and rebirth, Genesis and Apocalypse completes a cosmic cycle. It also—as does the entire poem—says a good deal on the theme of paradise lost and regained, which we remarked in a number of Miss Raine's contemporaries. The pursuit of reunion, reintegration, Eden, the lost god, and the center of the mandala are all one; and "Isis Wanderer" illustrates very well the fundamental connections that exist between them, connections which once again emphasize our poet's abiding intuition of the relations of spiritual and material reality.

From *The Pythoness* on, Miss Raine's work shows, if that seems possible, an increased austerity and self-discipline, though otherwise she makes no abrupt stylistic alterations in her verse, nor would we expect her to. But, as in "Isis Wanderer," she frequently lends her voice to many levels of life and to a multitude of things in nature. This practice is most obvious in such poems as "Air," "Water," "Fire," "Dust," and "The Pythoness"; and in her next book, *The Year One*, this sort of voice dominates. It is a voice given over to the universe, as it were, by means of which things speak through her and reveal not merely themselves but the larger pattern to which they belong. Hazard Adams, in his perceptive essay on Kathleen Raine, stresses her fulfilment of the conditions Robert Graves lays down for the woman poet and thinks of her function as that of sorceress. This view has its interest, but I personally believe that it undervalues the extremely important religious and Platonic aspects of the poetry. The magical and supernatural qualities in these later books by Miss Raine arise, it seems to me, from imaginative insight into the realm of nature and the reflection of Divine being to be interpreted there; she should not be understood as attempting to control or manipulate natural energies. Her basic attitude is contemplative.

In the three sequential poems on the elements mentioned above the speaker appears to possess the most intimate knowledge of air, water, and fire in their pure states—which also includes their mythic or transcendental meanings. (The poem "Dust," printed a few pages later, may be taken as a poem on the fourth element of earth.) I say "speaker" because Miss Raine employs in these pieces a voice even more strictly that of the seer or of one whose identity merges with the poetic object in order to make that object articulate. The same unusual kind of perspective we saw applied to time is brought to bear upon air in the poem of that title; the result is a type of double vision:

> Element that utters doves, angels and cleft flames,
> The bees of Helicon and the cloudy houses,
> Impulse of music and the word's equipoise,
>
> Dancer that never wearies of the dance
> That prints in the blown dust eternal wisdom
> Or carves its abstract sculptures in the snow,
> The wind unhindered passes beyond its trace.
>
> But from a high fell on a summer day
> Sometimes below you may see the air like water,
> The dazzle of the light upon its waves
> That flow unbroken to the end of the world.
>
> The bird of god descends between two moments
> Like silence into music, opening a way through time.

Such a perspective not only understands the air as a contributing element in the physical universe but simultaneously perceives it as part of the eternal scheme of creation. Yet there is even more to the poem than a reading of nature's symbolic language; it concludes with a complex image set off from the rest of the poem in which the invisible becomes visible, the supernatural unveils its operations, and the actualities of ordinary sense perception and imposed temporal patterns, already challenged, begin to disappear. Miss Raine surpasses her previous activity of attending to natural signs and translating their higher significance and now wins a close *rapport* with the elements that by tradition and legend compose the universe. Without ever losing hold of appearances entirely (for as a poet she has to rely on the vocabulary of images), she is capable of reaching toward the manifestation of Divine presence in each of the four elements and giving it word and substance in poems.

If the Holy Spirit appears as dove and wind and fire, as well as the breath of life, in "Air," the poem "Water" reveals Jesus (and perhaps by symbolic extension Osiris, just as Christ was implied in a similar fashion in "Isis Wanderer") as "the King of the Fishes" at the heart of that element in nature. "Water" must be read as a version of the story of the soul's journey. The poem divides itself into two stanzas, each presided over by a deity. In the first one the goddess of the world of matter, the "water-Venus," rules the "night-cities" of men with illusion and unfulfilled desire; her very title explains her function, for water, as we said previously, symbolizes the lowest, most burdensome realm of matter, while Venus represents the striving for satisfactory love under the mortal conditions which render it impossible of attainment. Her influence cannot be avoided entirely because "our veins" are "still tidal to her moon," but in the second stanza it is possible to get past her by the intervention of the true god:

> But in mid-ocean of desire
> The King of Fishes stands
> Upon the teeming seas, and to him rise
> Like salmon to the poacher's light
> Miraculous drafts of Venus' spawn
> As from her element we are drawn,
> From living waters into birth.

These "teeming seas" may well remind us of those we find in Yeats's "Sailing to Byzantium," which the poet rejects there so he can search out spiritual wisdom and the soul's salvation. For Miss Raine this "mid-ocean of desire" indicates the mortal cycle of birth, generation, and death: these, it will be remembered, are all the "facts" in Eliot's fragmentary "Sweeney Agonistes." Belief in or attachment to them involves a quest for deceptive and unreal ends. In the Platonic tradition to which Miss Raine so closely adheres the sea designates the mortal world of passion, emotions, and desires—all of them distractions to the spirit. Yet just as Yeats learns from immortal sages and saints the path to eternity, so our poet envisages the Divine figure of the King of Fishes drawing to Himself from the turbulent waters of generation and vain desire souls into that paradoxical birth which leaves the material universe and time behind. From a naturalistic, rather than a mythic, point of view the movement described here leads directly to death; but Miss Raine's vision, and that of the line of poets and thinkers with whom she associates her work, interprets this voyage as the return of the soul to its prenatal state of spiritual joy.

Fire, in the poem devoted to that element, is viewed as a more basic component of the cosmos than water. In the first line it is placed quite literally at the beginning and the end of things; and as the poem continues, water, in various forms of fountains, springs, and dew, is constantly absorbed by flame or the sun. At the conclusion we see that

> . . . in the hidden electron of the water
> Consumes the zeal of burning for the last day.

The second stanza proposes images of "the burning of desire," which starts in "darkness" (doubtless that of the self) and then realizes itself in "sight." It might seem that the reference in these lines is again to the kind of unsatisfied longings and emotions dealt with in "Water," but the imagery goes on to achieve an apocalyptic cast in the last half of this stanza. Thus the one burning with desire is united with the object of desire, "consuming in one light," and this union becomes a mere portion of a universal fire which both envelops and separates:

> When rocks melt in the sun, and mountains pour
> Into those flames that to the bound are hell
> But to the freed elements, pure delight.

The third, and final, stanza introduces Christian figures that are certainly more familiar and help to explain, if only by juxtaposition with them, the preceding passages. Miss Raine begins here with the theme of purgation, the purification and abandonment of selfhood or personality ubiquitous in her poetry, presented under its common symbol of fire. But she has more to offer us with respect to the significance of this element. The inner "dark of the heart" (in correspondence, it seems, with the "darkness" of the previous stanza) holds at its center "the candle of the soul" (another version of "the burning of desire") which "burns," that is, longs to be joined or merged with, "the bridegroom," who is, of course, the traditional figure for Christ. And then the two subsequent lines we have already quoted finish the poem on a cosmic pattern which parallels the relationship between the individual and Christ. The element of fire is a symbolic aspect of the Divine: as such, its presence underlies the creation which originated from it and in which it will be consumed; in the human soul exists the candle-flame of "desire" for God, whose love compels it toward ultimate absorption; finally, that fire of Divine love cleanses too:

> Our forms are fearful of the fires that burn away
> Self and identity, but in the dark of the heart
> The candle of the soul still for the bridegroom burns,
> And in the hidden electron of the water
> Consumes the zeal of burning for the last day.

The poem "Dust" ambitiously sketches the larger unity of the cosmos, its distance from "the first flash" of Divine creation which called it into being, and the universal "figures of a dance" whereby the particulars of the world are composed and undone. Whirling and shifting, forming and reforming, the myriad particles of earthly dust exhibit their obedience to the superior laws governing them; the shapes of appearance and material reality, of living creatures emerge, change, disappear, and undergo metamorphosis through their determining energies. Once again, as the poem opens, we are provided with a statement of the separation of soul, which is pre-existent, from physical body, which is a temporary coalescence of "dust" whose particles belong to creation so long as it lasts:

> Only my dust is never laid
> And only I must always die.
> This dust has travelled with the earth since suns made
> Yet never left eternity
>
> Whose rule is traced upon my hands that writes,
> That bears the seal of nature's forms and states;
> The stars obey that order, and the grass,
> The beautiful, the innocent, and the saints.

The speaker, we note, is true to the role we indicated, and her relationship to the poet merely suggested by the reference to a writing hand; thus Miss Raine permits herself to be the vehicle for the poetic statement of an experience which is humankind's. In succeeding stanzas we are told how her bones are built up from elements that were present at the formation of the earth from "solar fires" and how her "blood streams with the motion of the tides." One might say, then, that in a certain sense the whole history of the world and the plan it follows are written into the ephemeral construction of her (or anyone's) human body. But those elements, we learn in addition, are subservient to laws which the speaker claims to have "broken." In that line are contained the implications of a fallen spiritual nature that occupy subsequent stanzas where the symbols of the cross and the tree, and the meanings attached to them, are seen as incorporated in the very makeup of the cosmos. First,

> The shape of the cross is laid upon the void
> By the first flash that leaps between the poles.

I think that perhaps the usual thoughts associated with the Incarnation and the Crucifixion, with the measure of descent God takes to become flesh and the supreme agony exacted I redeem that human flesh, will give a sense of what Miss Raine is saying in the next stanza. There the Tree of Knowledge determines the "passion" of all men, who must, after their own fashion, live the Way of the Cross:

> Man's passion is predestined in the tree,
> The cross-beams of the heavens, vegetation,
> The thorns, the iron, and the organic thirst
> From the beginning raise his calvary.

Miss Raine returns specifically to her image of "dust" at the end of the poem in a beautiful and moving stanza picturing the cosmic "dance" (given similar significance in Eliot's "Burnt Norton" and in Charles Williams's novel *The Greater Trumps*) in which creation continuously remakes itself according to the guidance of its paradigmatic order. In the next to the last line we observe that the figures exemplified recall "the beautiful, the innocent, and the saints" of an earlier stanza:

> The dust sweeps through the figures of a dance,
> Moves in its ritual transit like a bride
> Imprinting shells and flowers with spiral forms that pass
> To fossil wastes and whirling nebulae,
> Weaving the rose, the lamb, and the world's darling child,
> And then unmakes again the world the dance has made.

As awareness of the transcendent or eternal meaning of material things and of existence grows more direct and unimpeded in Miss Raine's imagination, there is a corresponding gain in prophetic quality and tone in the poems. That self which the poet believes will disappear into the being or at least the ambiance of God at death comes closer, poetically speaking, to the character of a completely spiritual voice, capable of moving from place to place, of projecting itself outside the inexorable chronology of time's flow, and of articulating sacred truths, lending human speech to the Divine principles hidden in things. How should we be surprised, then, to discover her prophesying as "the Herm" or the Delphic Oracle? In "Self" she asks what that title word now signifies to her:

> Who am I, who
> Speaks from the dust,
> Who looks from the clay?
> Who hears
> For the mute stone,
> For fragile water feels
> With finger and bone?
>
> Who for the forest breathes the evening,
> Sees for the rose,
> Who knows
> What the bird sings?
>
> Who am I, who for the sun fears
> The demon dark,
> In order holds
> Atom and chaos?

Who out of nothingness has gazed
On the beloved face?

Here the self must be identified, it appears, as spirit inhabiting the realm
of matter and so providing consciousness of it; but this view would not
make very much sense unless we could discern a little more purpose. Such
purpose lies in the fact that the self in this poem is particularly the self of
the poet, as Miss Raine understands it; and she is therefore defining its
function: the translation and articulation of the various non-human languages of creation. Through her, the "mute stone" and the "fragile water,"
or the "rose" and the "bird," have their essential qualities, the languages in
which they communicate their being, rendered into the words of man, and
so at least partially comprehended.

By means of the gift of imaginative vision the poet can identify herself
with the forces and energies of the universe which have remained unchanged
since their creation, or at least have maintained a unity, a coherence of
purpose seemingly absent from our divided and tormented human state. To
give this perennial order full expression in poetry, Miss Raine must do more
than subdue the self to a superior kind of revelation; not only what is personal in subject matter but anything that is merely topical, ephemeral, or
incidental has to be winnowed from her verse. Her single duty as a writer, as
she conceives it, is to transmit the religious vision which has been granted
her, and the authentic handling of this insight precludes any details which
detract from it. In the introduction to her *Collected Poems*, Miss Raine offers some explanation:

> It was David Gascoyne who said to me that nature remains always in the
> Year One—the phrase that I used as the title for my last book of poems.
> The ever-recurring forms of nature mirror eternal reality; the never-recur-
> ring productions of human history reflect only fallen man, and are there-
> fore not suitable to become a symbolic vocabulary for the kind of poetry I
> have attempted to write.

While some readers will think this aesthetic position excessively harsh
or restrictive, no one can deny that the discipline and dedication evinced
by it are truly admirable. The result of this severity is a purging of dross and
idiosyncrasy which finally works through to what one might call a trans-
parency of the imagination. By this term I mean that Miss Raine brings the
whole universe, visible and invisible, into poetic existence with a fresh
clarity at once timeless and original. Nor does her poetry ever suffer from a
lack of human emotions: love and loss, joy and pain, ecstasy and vision, all
are rendered through a sensibility which, as Cyril Connolly remarked, is

profoundly feminine. The little poem "Triad," from her newest book, *The Hollow Hill*, confirms the intuitions of her previous work:

> To those who speak to the many deaf ears attend.
> To those who speak to one,
> In poet's song and voice of bird,
> Many listen; but the voice that speaks to none
> By all is heard:
> Sound of the wind, music of the stars, prophetic word.

As we know, it is just to this "prophetic word" of nature in the perspective of Divine creation that Miss Raine loans her poet's tongue. In the poems of *The Year One* it speaks through her in a language old as time, as it does also in many pieces from *The Hollow Hill*. Barren rocky landscapes, clumps of soil and grass, the outlines of leaves, the shape and surface of stone, the ripples in a stream are some of the parts of the world whose language she understands and makes available to us. The "I" of these later poems is generally the impersonal, prophetic self we have already discussed, who permits speech only to those things in the cosmos which possess a symbolic resonance. Poems dealing with the character of the spirit and with its journey, like the metaphysical lyrics of Walter de la Mare or Edwin Muir, share a similar austere anonymity. One recalls how Rilke praised Jules Supervielle once for a poem that seemed as if it had been written by "nobody." And Miss Raine's refusal as a writer to experiment with techniques in any radical fashion comes as a further consequence of this same fidelity to visionary knowledge and symbolic language, to what must reveal itself through her; and so we cannot seek a display of artistry in her poems, simply the appropriateness of diction, rhythm, and imagery to her inner perceptions or to the illuminations arising from the thing observed.

In *The Year One* Miss Raine bears witness to a timeless kingdom unaltered by history, for nature's ceaseless recurrence serves her as an analogue for the eternal circle, the symbolic figure for God. But she treats the origin and conclusion of human life as well as the details of nature. The "Northumbrian Sequence" consists of six poems which comprise a life cycle beginning before the soul assumes the burden of flesh and descends into the world ("Pure I was before the world began") and ending with death, the return of the soul to its source ("Dark into dark, spirit into spirit flies, / Home, with not one dear image in the heart"). The poems, which conform to the Platonic belief about the soul and the pattern of existence, are prefaced by an epigraph from the well-known portion of Bede's account of the conversion of Eadwine, King of Northumberland, describing man's mysterious origin and destiny by the simile of a sparrow's passage through the banquet hall on a winter night. Between the first and the last poems, dealing respectively with the soul and with death, come four others occupied by considerations of the powers of nature and the powers of spirit. Miss Raine adopts for the initial poem of the sequence the voice heard throughout and relates an experience of the soul which places its being prior to the founding of the universe:

> Pure I was before the world began,
> I was the violence of wind and wave.
> I was the bird before bird ever sang.
>
> I was never still,
> I turned upon the axis of my joy,
> I was the lonely dancer on the hill,
>
> The rain upon the mountainside,
> The rising mist,
> The sea's unrest.

This experience also includes a knowledge of death before it became a universal condition; and the poem finishes with a paradoxical presentation of a pristine spiritual purity and an involvement in the physical cosmos:

> Before death's kingdom
> I passed through the grave.
>
> Times out of mind my journey
> Circles the universe
> And I remain
> Before the first day.

Certainly, these stanzas will remind us of parts of the Old Testament, such as the books of Proverbs and Ecclesiastes, but they are probably more intimately connected with the poet's Platonism, as noted before. Human life, the soul's incarnation, is created by a drop down into physical reality, as Hazard Adams likewise says, from a previous spiritual state; yet the soul retains its fundamental integrity "and is slowly drawn, through the span of earthly existence, back to paradise. Nonetheless, as Miss Raine's poems constantly tell us, changes occur in the transition to life in the world: the ties of the soul with its Divine source weaken in certain respects; innocence falls away as the adult struggles out of the cocoon of childhood; memories—the same that ran through the minds of the poets Vaughan and Traherne three centuries ago— deeply engraved upon the spirit, are obscured by the distractions of living. But we can, she writes in another poem, remember how we were conceived, even though the turbulence of modern civilization makes the task hard:

Now when nature's darkness seems strange to you,
And you walk, an alien, in the streets of cities,
Remember earth breathed you into her with the air, with the
    sun's rays,
Laid you in her waters asleep, to dream
With the brown trout among the milfoil roots,
From the same substance of star and ocean fashioned you,
At the same source conceived you
As sun and foliage, fish and stream.

                          ("Message from Home")

Whoever does recall this profound attachment to nature—and the poet's work is "remembrance"—has momentarily glimpsed life as it was intended to be at the Creation. That is what the lines, "seas, trees and voices cry / 'Nature is your nature,'" quoted at the start of this essay mean: in nature man finds that part of the created universe which has not been corrupted by the Fall, and so it becomes a book of symbols through which he can learn of his lost heritage, of Eden and the soul's true destiny. In the third poem of "Northumbrian Sequence" Miss Raine takes birds, their instinctive pursuit of patterns of being, as symbolic of spirit following its path through the world of matter:

Shining travellers from another dimension
Whose heaven-sent flight homes to the green earth,
What gossamer desire floats out to guide
Spirit ascending and descending between grave and sky?

Along with poems on illusion, death, landscape and creatures in *The Year One*, there are a number of "spells." These primitive poetic forms, magical in origin, are quite in keeping with the mood of the book and apparently engage Miss Raine's interest because, through them, she can evoke nature in the purest, most incantatory way, for the spell enables her to recreate the image of nature's unity by naming the particulars composing it. The distinctive "contours" of things are envisaged precisely and, grouped together, their combination suggests something of the spiritual force underlying them. The magical powers supposedly awakened by such recitations are grounded in the notion that everything in the universe participates in the being of everything else and that words are as real and frequently command an energy greater than the objects or things they name. The French poet Paul Claudel's phrase, "each thing in an infinite communion with all others" ("chaque chose dans un rapport infini avec les autres"), surely finds its realization in Miss Raine's "Spell of Creation":

Within the flower there lies a seed,
Within the seed there springs a tree,
Within the tree there spreads a wood.

In the wood there burns a fire,
And in the fire there melts a stone,
Within the stone a ring of iron.

Within the ring there lies an O
Within the O there looks an eye,
In the eye there swims a sea,

And in the sea reflected sky,
And in the sky there shines the sun,
Within the sun the bird of gold.

Within the bird there beats a heart,
And from the heart there flows a song,
And in the song there sings a word.

In the word there speaks a world,
A word of joy, a world of grief,
From joy and grief there springs my love.

Oh love, my love, there springs a world,
And on the world there shines a sun
And in the sun there burns a fire,

Within the fire consumes my heart
And in my heart there beats a bird,
And in the bird there wakes an eye,

Within the eye, earth, sea and sky,
Earth, sky and sea within an O
Lie like the seed within the flower.

This type of poem accumulates image upon image of an imaginative world stark and magnificent in its chasteness, and achieves by its visionary strength and construction the experience of reality as Miss Raine sees it. The hypnotic power of the words vividly depicts each particular, until we so feel their marvelous ability to call up whatever they represent that things seem to be discovered and identified anew. And the effect both of the naming and of the metamorphosis of elements, objects, and emotions engenders a paradoxical dreamlike sense of strangeness and familiarity with regard to this interchangeably inner and outer cosmos in process in the poem, as though, having been dimly conscious of it for some time, we suddenly turned to face it directly. No longer dead to perception, no longer simply the objects of scientific analysis, the life of nature and human life endlessly interchange in Miss Raine's vision.

Because the human person lives, in a sense, two separate existences—
one in time and nature, the other transcending it in the soul alone—he or
she should inevitably realize that the goal of life is the abandonment of the
world, its ties and images, and the return of the spirit to beginnings. "In my
end is my beginning," Eliot writes at the close of "East Coker"; and for Miss
Raine the soul belongs to earth only as a visitor. Spiritual vision, however it
arrives, in dream or rapt contemplation, can dissolve the barriers between
the planes of being. "The Hollow Hill," a sequence of poems about death
which derives its title from barrows or burial mounds, ends in a dream-
vision of the poet Edwin Muir, who leads Miss Raine to the threshold of a
landscape only the dead may cross:

> One night in a dream
> The poet who had died a year ago
> Led me up the ancient stair
> Of an ancestral tower of stone.
> Towards us out of the dark blew such sweet air
> It was the warm breath of the spirit, I knew,
> Fragrant with the wild thyme that grew
> In childhood's fields; he led me on,
> Touched a thin partition, and was gone.
> Beyond the fallen barrier
> Bright over sweet meadows rose the sun.

The symbolic implications of these images are, in Miss Raine's definition,
traditional; they are evident in the poetry of Yeats or in Muir himself. The
ascent of the winding stair in the "ancestral tower" signals the movement
upward toward spiritual reality; and the return to that higher level, announced by "the warm breath of the spirit," becomes the return to a symbolic childhood, the condition of the soul's innocence. The landscape, referred to as "childhood's fields" and "sweet meadows," is clearly that of Eden,
over which the morning sun, suggestive of God, rises to herald rebirth.

So just as one may be touched with an intuition of kinship with the rest
of creation, he can also be seized by a knowledge of his place in an order
superior to it. That is what Miss Raine urges on us (this time without benefit of visionary dream) in a little poem called "Message." Here the poet
asks a child to observe its own reflection in her eyes. The self "mirrored" in
their "living water" becomes an image of the way in which each individual
is held permanently in God's loving sight:

> Look, beloved child, into my eyes, see there
> Your self, mirrored in that living water
> From whose deep pools all images of earth are born.
> See, in the gaze that holds you dear

All that you were, are, and shall be for ever.
In recognition beyond time and seeming
Love knows the face that each soul turns towards heaven.

The individual, who dwells so short a period within the physical geography of the world, is an extension into space and time of a spiritual being
who exists, as we saw, both before and after that earthly excursion. "Perhaps
soul only puts out a hand," Miss Raine says in "The Instrument," the second
of her "Three Poems on Illusion":

> Antenna or pseudopodium, an extended touch
> To receive the spectrum of colour, and the lower octave of pain,
> Reaches down into the waves of nature
> As a child dips an arm into the sea,
> And death is the withdrawal of attention
> That has discovered all it needs to know,
> Or, if not all, enough for now,
> If not enough, something to bear in mind.

Life's movement once again takes the aspect of a journey in and out of time
and nature, a voyage of preparation, through knowledge and suffering, for
the final deliverance of the spirit to Divine love. Poems, of course, except
in imaginative vision, cannot bring about the reconciliations, the harmony
of man, nature, and the Divine, for which the inward self or spirit secretly
yearns. Yet there is no doubt that poetry like Miss Raine's (and that of the
poets she reveres) brings to consciousness an unnoticed dimension of our
lives, or the true life (which is one) behind our lives. In *An Autobiography*
(1954) Edwin Muir calls this dimension "the fable" and offers a statement
about it with which I am sure Miss Raine would essentially agree:

> It is clear that no autobiography can begin with a man's birth, that we
> extend far beyond any boundary line which we can set for ourselves in the
> past or the future, and that the life of every man is an endlessly repeated
> performance of the life of man. It is clear for the same reason that no auto-
> biography can confine itself to conscious life, and that sleep, in which we
> pass a third of our existence, is a mode of experience, and our dreams a part
> of reality. In themselves our conscious lives may not be particularly inter-
> esting. But what we are not and can never be, our fable, seems to me in-
> conceivably interesting. I should like to write that fable, but I cannot even
> live it; and all I could do if I related the outward course of my life would be
> to show how I have deviated from it; though even that is impossible, since
> I do not know the fable or anybody who knows it. One or two stages in it I
> can recognize: the age of innocence and the Fall and all the dramatic con-
> sequences which issue from the Fall. But these lie behind experience, not
> on its surface; they are not historical events; they are stages in the fable.

Another stage in "the fable," not mentioned in this passage but evident in much of Muir's later poetry, is the return journey to Eden, the quest for man's lost paradise. But though he approaches the gate to that abandoned world in various poems, he must halt there; he can merely gaze nostalgically, and we with him, on the distant landscape. The road remains barred for Miss Raine as well, for "everywhere the substance of earth is the gate we cannot pass"; she writes in "The Locked Gates":

> Seek in Hebridean isles lost paradise,
> There is yet the heaviness of water, the heaviness of stone
> And the heaviness of the body I bring to this inviolate place.
> Foot sinks in the bog as I gather white water-lilies in the tarn,
> The knee is bruised on rock, and the wind is always blowing.
> The locked gates of the world are the world's elements,
> For the rocks of the beautiful hills hurt, and the silver seas drown,
> Wind scores deep record of time on the weathered boulders,
> The bird's hot heart consumes the soaring life to feather and bone,
> And heather and asphodel crumble to peat that smolders on
>   crofters' fires.

The restraint upon the spirit's instinct to fly home like the winging birds of other poems lies in the burden of matter. The poet's portrayal of herself trapped by heavy mud as she reaches out to pick the water-lilies—surely symbolic of spirituality and purity—sufficiently illustrates the difficulties of the earthly condition. To unlock the elements means to deliver oneself back to the purity of union with Divine being; yet this is impossible until death parts all the strands of illusion from which our ordinary experience is woven and we relinquish our material bodies. But the visionary moment, and its embodiment in poetry, is for Miss Raine a glimpse through the locked gates. At best, she can provide hints of that ultimate journey in which the soul draws toward the center of Divine reality, the heart of the rose and the mandala, the fountain of love. The acquaintance she has with this final phase of things, impossible to grasp by normal processes of ratiocination and unyielding to the forms of language, presents itself in her poetry as the negation of sensate experience, the violation of appearances. Nature's fabric splits apart in visions of this kind:

> No, I have seen the mirage tremble, seen how thin
> The veil stretched over apparent time and space
> To make the habitable earth, the enclosed garden.
> I saw on a bare hillside an ash-tree stand
> And all its intricate branches suddenly
> Failed, as I gazed, to be a tree,
> And road and hillside failed to make a world.

> Hill, tree, sky, distance, only seemed to be
> And I saw nothing I could give a name,
> Not any name known to the heart.

By the end of this poem, "The Mirage" (the first of "Three Poems on Illusion"), the landscape is restored, things have become again what we so confidently like to think they are; but the revelation of the poem shatters preconceptions of the durability of the physical universe. The reality the senses know, Miss Raine keeps saying, consists of no more than endless series of waves or vibrations, which, running together in a vast tide from the Divine mind, create the illusory surfaces of the world we inhabit.

Eden, on the other hand, can appear to the imagination in an instant's vision unsullied and unchanged: the first reflection of the love that brought us into being. Though the estate of Eden is lost to man in general, he does experience it briefly as a child. (Eliot's "Burnt Norton," Muir's "The Gate," and Dylan Thomas's "Fern Hill" are poems founded on the same awareness.) Childhood is lived spiritually in the "garden"; and Miss Raine's poems often try to renew the innocent eye of that period of life, though combined with the sense of life's pattern which maturity brings. The recent "Childhood Memory" with its recollection of the poet's wish as a small girl to "look into the sun" because "it is golden, it is mine," and the adults' response that one cannot stare into the fiery orb, is exemplary of this childish wisdom, especially when we apply the obvious Platonic symbolism. And in the fourth of her "Soliloquies Upon Love" the meeting with a "dear companion" out of the past generates memories of a mutual experience of nature which now assumes, with dramatic immediacy, the character of Eden:

> In that remembered world, had body ever been,
> Or had we, thinking we were on bodily ground, walked in the
>   eternal mind?
> Together, as once there, we forgot that Paradise was lost,
> Whose times and places, in the world we travelled now, no longer
>   were.
> In that moment out of time all was as it had been;
> Innocence did not seem strange to us, but our simple selves.
> Then on those infinite skies and seas of light, and living voices,
> The grave closed again.

With extreme discipline and skill, in addition to a study of symbols and the grace of vision, Miss Raine has created the poetic speech which corresponds with her aims; and through her gifts as seer she has allowed the elements of nature to regain voice and image. Because the source of everything "is one, / Simple, single as love," she sees man unfolding into the dream of the world in the same fashion as bird or dragonfly, fern or flower. But man, whose nature and soul make him more complicated than any other living thing, has "farther to travel from his simplicity" due to the Fall, and thus has farther to go to regain it. If he searches the recesses of memory, the poem "Message from Home" implies, he will come upon the images of that simplicity, which are those of a familiar reality viewed in a new relation to him:

> As you leave Eden behind you, remember your home,
> For as you remember back into your own being
> You will not be alone; the first to greet you
> Will be those children playing by the burn,
> The otters will swim up to you in the bay,
> The wild deer on the moor will run beside you.
> Recollect more deeply, and the birds will come,
> Fish rise to meet you in their silver shoals,
> And darker, stranger, more mysterious lives
> Will throng about you at the source
> Where the tree's deepest roots drink at the abyss.
>
> Nothing in that abyss is alien to you.
> Sleep at the tree's root, where the night is spun
> Into the stuff of worlds, listen to the winds,
> The tides, and the nighfs harmonies, and know
> All that you knew before you began to forget,
> Before you had too long parted from those other
> More simple children, who have stayed at home
> In meadow and island and forest, in sea and river.
> Earth sends a mother's love after her exiled son,
> Entrusting her message to the light and the air,
> The wind and the waves that carry your ship, the rain that falls,
> The birds that call to you, and all the shoals
> That swim in the natal waters of her ocean.

Keeping these lovely lines in mind, I believe we can say that for Miss Raine the reading of nature's profound language, the pursuit of our memories of Eden, the tracing of the soul's journey through the universe, go far beyond the artifice of the printed word. When the world opens up to us as a place known and yet unknown, when it speaks to us from the face of every stone, the call of each bird, to tell us what we are, then the poems Kathleen Raine has written will have fulfilled their intentions: our experience of the world will itself be poetry.

(1967)

Two

5

Stanley Kunitz

LITERARY REPUTATIONS ARE CURIOUS AND UNSETTLING PHANTOMS; THEY COME and go like restless spirits, blown by dark winds of chance and influence. Quiet attention to craft, long and careful research into experience and the methods of expressing it, devotion to craft before fame—these are indeed rare virtues at any time and frequently they receive small reward. Such distinguishing marks have been evident for more than three decades in the poetry of Stanley Kunitz, and it is one of the disturbing facts of our contemporary literary life that this poet only recently began to gain the reception and the following he had so long deserved. Robert Lowell could say very truthfully that the appearance of Kunitz's *Selected Poems* in 1958 made him "the poet of the hour," for it brought belated recognition to one of the strongest and most energetic talents in American poetry.

Kunitz's output has not been large; the selected volume which covers thirty years, numbers only 116 pages. Before this book he had published just two other collections of verse: *Intellectual Things* (1931) and *Passport to the War* (1944). The table of contents of *Selected Poems* shows the scrupulous process of screening to which the author has characteristically submitted his work. An ample portion of the first book has been discarded—was, in fact, discarded in the second half of *Passport to the War*, where he included the earlier poems he apparently wished to preserve. One may readily lament this perhaps unduly harsh self-criticism, but it is the poet's right and is fully in keeping with the demands of perfection Kunitz so obviously makes upon himself. Again, in *Selected Poems* Kunitz has shuffled poems around and has grouped them under thematic headings. However, his themes have changed with time and his later manner has relaxed a little, so our approach to him in the following pages will occasionally justify chronological comments.

A reading of only a few scattered poems might lead one to believe that Kunitz is a writer of complicated occasional verse, a poetry dictated by outside occurrences, given over to capturing the isolated and particular moods or responses they evoke, and bound together by a uniform complexity of language. But this sort of reading would miss the forceful impression of a singular artistic mind on the raw material of these poems and the consequent realization that their main theme is the struggle of that very mind with the experience it comes up against. Having read the bulk of Kunitz's work, we recognize that his poetic intelligence and imaginative strength are not subservient to external occasions, but that, on the contrary, the poem is itself an occasion resulting from the tremendous pressures of the writer's psyche and his passionate feelings in contact with the processes of life. Although his later poetry more often takes in the public world of our time, it too is cast in the mirror-images of an interior state.

In "The Science of the Night," Kunitz begins with a conventional domestic or amatory circumstance, and with the diction and tone appropriate to gentle affections; but this intimacy merely spurs him to depart into more daring speculation. The poet, awake in the middle of the night, muses on the comfort of the woman beside him, until the adjectives of the poem's third line break off the emotion in a sudden reversal of intention which carries carries everything in another direction:

> I touch you in the night, whose gift was you,
> My careless sprawler,
> And I touch you cold, unstirring, star-bemused,
> That are become the land of your self-strangeness.

The lines that follow view sleep as an escape from the reality of self and personality in one closely known. The dreaming beloved turns into an explorer of vast and distant spaces; and the poet has forced upon him an understanding of the irrational, fleeting character of the individual, who slips uncontrollably away to hidden places, there to partake of other lives, to inhabit other worlds:

> And even should I track you to your birth
> Through all the cities of your mortal trial,
> As in my jealous thought I try to do,
> You would escape me—from the brink of earth
> Take off to where the lawless auroras run,
> You with your wild and metaphysic heart.
> My touch is on you, who are light years gone.
> We are not souls but systems, and we move
> In clouds of our unknowing
>   like great nebulae.

Science and psychology, both prominent and influential in Kunitz's writing, replace the outward considerations of conjugal love. Next, the poet proceeds to examine mythical analogy. Like Adam, from whose rib God formed Eve, he feels a profound connection with the woman who lies by him (the physical juxtaposition of their bodies in the poem creates a metaphorical identification) but is nevertheless remote; and by virtue of this bond he calls her back from sleep. Some lines near the end request her awakening and gifts from her journeys. Then the poet discloses his position as the opposite of hers:

> My whirling hands stay at the noon,
> Each cell within my body holds a heart
> And all my hearts in unison strike twelve.

Noon and midnight, male and female, reason and unreason: these are the contrasting poles about which the poem takes shape. An extreme tension results from the simultaneous pull toward order and disorder, and is noticeable in the straining energy of the language, which tries to loosen itself from formal restrictions but is guided by the poet's steady purposiveness of thought. He seems more interested in where that thought will ultimately lead him than in the situation with which it all began. Since what he has written is not really a love poem so much as a meditation on the unknowable in even the closest relations, we are inclined to think of the domestic scene at the beginning as initiating a train of images and thoughts of which it is simply an appropriate vehicle. This does not mean that the poem lacks unity, but that its strength and aims are inward.

This poem, a rather recent one, indicates, as many earlier pieces do, the manner in which Kunitz very commonly utilizes an experience or event as the starting point for poetic reflection. His intelligence and imagination inform the material; diction, tone, and the movement of characteristic rhythms help to fashion Kunitz's own voice. We discover in his work a true poetic personality which, T. S. Eliot's distinction aside, both suffers and creates in the same act of composition. Kunitz is not committed to epistemological problems as Wallace Stevens was, and though there are sometimes faint traces of Yeats's influence in a turn of phrase or a rhythm here or there, he does not write under the protection of a mythological scheme as that great Irish poet did. Rather he reminds us of the secular Donne, occasionally of Marvell, and in certain ways of Baudelaire and Dylan Thomas. Jean Hagstrum in a fine essay on Kunitz in *Poets in Progress* has shown the consistent employment of anatomical imagery, of surgical and destructive metaphors. The human body is forever being dismembered, dissolved, or shrivelled up in Kunitz's poems, and he has himself remarked that "the hard and inescapable phenomenon to be faced is that we are living and

dying at once" (*New World Writing*, 20). Here is a representative passage
from "Postscript," an early poem. The poet, trying to flee the inexorable
"progress" of things, is still caught on "time's acute / And bitter needle."
The end is not an enviable one:

> Crueler than a spine
> It penetrates the body till it pricks
> The bubbling brain, exploding life's gray tumor
> Together with its iridescent world.

Kunitz exposes himself without benefit of philosophical theory, firm religious convictions, or any other strict system of absolute beliefs to the furious onslaught of experience, "a bewildering density," he calls it, "an overlay
of episodes and images, both public and private," and to the awful loneliness and guilt that accompanies knowledge in the twentieth century. A
poem for him appears to be an enforced reconciliation of his own basic
emotions with his extremely sensitive perception of the realities he meets.
He brings the strongest instruments to his disposal—reason and stoicism—
to order these realities within himself. To the instruments named should be
added love and its symbol, the poet's heart:

> O child,
> From my angry side
> Tumbles this agate heart,
> Your prize veined with the root
> Of guilty life,
> From which flow love and art.
>   (" 'What Have You Done?' ")

Knowledge and perception can defeat the natural attempts to view experience reasonably; and logic fails to withstand the passionate responses which
well up in the poet. The tragic element in Kunitz's art often emerges from
the collapse of reason before overwhelming odds. Such is the matter of another early poem, "Geometry of Moods," in which he traces the failure and
destruction of a cosmological view, orderly and rational in its makeup through
a fantastic pattern of imagery. The poem begins with a narrator who sees
himself at the center of a number of universal spheres:

> Concentrical, the universe and I
> Rotated on God's crystal axletree,
>
> So perfectly adjusted in suspense
> I could not mark our split circumference,

> But sphere in sphere, devotion in devotion,
> Was a thing of folding air, a windy motion.

Purposely enough, it would seem, this cosmology of traditional origins grows more and more difficult to visualize; and we note that the tense in these lines is past: a previous state is being described. "Split circumference" likewise suggests the cracks and divisions in this whole to become evident later on. As the poem continues, the narrator outlines the essential features of man's spiritual anatomy which connect him—"My spinal pole, tipped with a globe of light"—with a world beyond the reaches of time—"Stretched long as time into the infinite." From his elevated position be looks back at earth, "love's incarnate form," which acts as a base and rest for the spirit in its exercise of comprehending the universe. Earth appears finally to be a transparent circle with man at its middle (this image is undoubtedly derived by Kunitz from the Ptolemaic system), but such spareness and purity of construction bring it dangerously close to the great emptiness of space in which it floats:

> I core of the world, a bead in a ball of glass
> So pure that only nothing could be less.

In the last two stanzas the security of this universal plan has very obviously become a thing of the past and exists now only in memory, for the poem has shifted abruptly into the present tense, dispersing the whole cosmic arrangement and leaving a lame, fragmentary residue still in operation:

> Oh how the earth ensphered me, liberal and warm
> When the curve of heaven was her sleeping arm.
>
> Now cubical upon a fractured pole
> It creaks, scraping the circle of my soul.

What has actually happened to cause this failure we are never told; but the change from faith in a universal system founded and supported by God, with man in its highest place, to the experience of disbelief and of a disordered universe occurs in the transition from past to present marked by the two stanzas above. Yet we must not overlook the fact that in this representative poem of Kunitz's something does survive the general ruin—"the circle of my soul." And this soul may be said to harbor those qualities we have already mentioned as this poet's essential equipment, that is, his reason, conscience, heart, individual integrity, and imagination. Together they raise a constant bulwark of stoicism and affirm the notion of a self that prevails

even after the conflagration of experience; a self tormented by the desire to
discover a truth underlying the vicissitudes of life.

This self is the primary object of focus in the poems of *Intellectual Things*.
Armed with few presuppositions, it is purged and toughened in the heated
ovens of existence but never burned away. Its chief means of resistance is
the making of poems that aim to lend form and significance to the arduousness of events, psychic or physical, by transforming them into words. In one
way or another this process so intrigues Kunitz and is so much a part of his
mode of self-preservation that he treats it as the subject or partial subject of
some of his poems, for example, "'What Have You Done?'," "Night Letter,"
and "Hermetic Poem." The last demonstrates the open concern for his art
that Kunitz has long shared with his contemporaries:

> The secret my heart keeps
> Flows into cracked cups.
>
> No saucer can contain
> This overplus of mine:
>
> It glisters to the floor,
> Lashing like lizard fire
>
> And ramps upon the walls
> Crazy with ruby ills.
>
> Who enters by my door
> Is drowned, burned, stung, and starred.

The secret of the heart referred to consists primarily of all the images and
feelings stored up and mixed together in the poet as the result of his encounters with the external world. Fermented by the imagination, these are
poured into the forms of art which do not entirely subdue them, so that
they leap forth to ravish the reader. Kunitz's poem is a practical application
of its thesis, and my account must therefore remain an oversimplification of
the creative activity, though it does sketch, I believe, the poet's main idea.
Poetic language under the conditions implied by this poem is stretched to
the snapping point by the surge of emotions pressing against it. What Jean
Hagstrum speaks of as Kunitz's "imagistic surrealism" accurately describes
this phenomenon. Let us quote one more poem, "Open the Gates," with its
more obvious nightmare effects, to exhibit the precision of Hagstrum's term
in the "overplus" of feeling aroused by this short, bizarre narrative with its
hauntingly suggestive words and images:

> Within the city of the burning cloud,
> Dragging my life behind me in a sack,

Naked I prowl, scourged by the black
Temptation of the blood grown proud.

Here at the monumental door,
Carved with the curious legend of my youth,
I brandish the great bone of my death,
Beat once therewith and beat no more.

The hinges groan: a rush of forms
Shivers my name, wrenched out of me.
I stand on the terrible threshold, and I see
The end and the beginning in each other's arms.

From his lonely kernel of *conscience* (to use the French word which means both "conscience" and "consciousness") Kunitz must try to develop a way of approaching life, a source of authority, for he has little else on which to rely. The figure of a woman in many poems helps to sustain him from without; and in "Father and Son" he searches through a dream landscape for his gentle but long dead father. But the end of his pursuit leaves him stunned with his terrifying independence:

At the water's edge, where the smothering ferns lifted
Their arms, "Father," I cried, "Return! You know
The way. I'll wipe the mudstains from your clothes;
No trace, I promise, will remain. Instruct
Your son, whirling between two wars,
In the Gemara of your gentleness,
For I would be a child to those who mourn
And brother to the foundlings of the field
And friend of innocence and all bright eyes.
O teach me how to work and keep me kind."

Among the turtles and the lilies he turned to me
The white ignorant hollow of his face.

Kunitz's skepticism and agnosticism are familiar attitudes in modern writing; and he is not graced with the persistent heterodox mystical intuitions of Theodore Roethke or Richard Eberhart. His vision at its deepest is generally a revelation of death and apocalypse with neither explanation nor promise, though there are moments of rebirth to a new plane of being within the self. But every venture to the outer rim of human existence—see, for example "For the Word Is Flesh" and "Father and Son"—hurls him back to the tumultuous core of that existence; there he has to seek his answers. These are not the only limitations under which he works, for the self is

incessantly stricken by its own pangs of guilt, or what Kunitz metaphorically calls the "wound." Affliction of this kind may be partially redeemed
(it is, however, recurrent) through continuous self-examination and the
assertion of a few fundamental beliefs: in the value of art and of human
relationships, in love and moral courage. Yet even these are challenged in
his brilliant and terrible poem "The Surgeons," where Kunitz personifies in
the figures operating surgeons the diabolical powers of the modern world
threatening human individuality and freedom. Once again a poem assumes
the aspect of a horrible but inescapable dream, populated with men of "medi-
cine" who cut away the living substance of their patients:

> My surgeons are a savage band,
> Surely their patient is ill-fated.
> Their tricks are coarse: the small sweet hand
> I seized was wax, or amputated.
> With the humiliated swollen-footed
> And the lost persecuted their traps are baited.
>
> Deftly they opened the brain of a child,
> And it was full of flying dreams;
> Father was prowling in a field
> With speckled tongue and a collar of flame.
> They labeled it "Polluted Streams,"
> The body floating with the name.

The victims are ambiguous: sometimes they seem to be identified with
the poet, sometimes they are separate; this coalescence and diffusion resembles the dream-work of the mind. The helpless and crippled, the innocent and kindly, are chief among these victims. In the midst of this nightmare the poet undergoes with them their anguish and deprivation. Here, as
elsewhere, Kunitz's position is something like that of a Christian without
theology or supernatural faith whose sympathy and love dictate an outraged dramatic speech. Toward the close of the poem he too falls victim to
the final stage of the surgeons' dissection:

> Lastly they squeezed out of my veins
> The bright liquor of sympathy;
> I lost the touch of souls, the reins
> On white revenge, and I was free
> Of pity, a solid man of snow.
> But in the night to whom could I go?

The crushing irony of these lines resides in the victim's fate: he is not killed
but, worse, spiritually and emotionally maimed. In the encompassing darkness

of the world that this poem evokes, human ties are severed and the person anaesthetized into a cipher of mute passions, frozen sensibilities, and ravaged intelligence. Kunitz's only answer, if it can be called as much, is a tiny wedge of hope and rebellion thrust between the closing doors of this monstrous world:

> Lie down with me, dear girl, before
> My butcher boys begin to rave.
> "No hope for persons any more,"
> They cry, "on either side of the grave."
> Tell them I say the heart forgives
> The world. Yes, I believe. In love.

Who is the girl? Her precise identity is not important. The first line of the stanza should be understood in part at least as metaphorical rather than completely literal, for sexuality as Kunitz uses it here covers the full range of feeling that exists in the communion of two individuals. The sexual act symbolizes any act of defiance toward the surgeons' decree that persons *as* persons are to be vanquished. And the last line of the stanza in effect echoes the first, supports it without equivocation or disguise. Nothing could prove more convincingly, I think, the humanizing element in Kunitz's poetry and his ability to employ it dramatically at the right moment to astonishing purpose.

Kunitz's early poems, as I have said, show a tendency to turn inward in the course of meditation. The mind itself is an enclosure or space for dramatic events: speakers and actors are introduced; imaginary scenes light up and disappear; biological investigations disclose the progress of corruption and decay in the human organism. A firm poetic intelligence probes these characters, situations, and images within its province in relentless quest of lasting answers and truths. The ultimate discoveries are usually tragic, but they inevitably throw Kunitz back on, and increase his awareness of, his own spiritual resources.

The later poetry changes this approach somewhat. While there is no lessening of intensity, Kunitz appears interested in moving his vision outside the arena of the mind. The result in many instances is an overt moral concern, a severe but compassionate dialogue with the world and its ways based on careful observation tempered by strong emotions. No doubt the growing political confusion and violence of the 1930s, culminating in World War II, distracted Kunitz from some of his previous artistic directions. "The Last Picnic," "Careless Love," "Night Letter," "Reflections by a Mailbox," "This Day This World," and "The Economist's Song" are among the best poems of this new type. Even when the poet now speaks of himself or takes himself and his art as the subject of a poem, there is in evidence a certain change of emphasis. Kunitz looks upon his vocation as a poet within a given time and place in history too. The closing lines of his poem "The Summing-Up" boldly define his later view: "I carve again on the lintel of the year / My sign: Mobility—and damn the cost!"

"Night Letter" presents Kunitz's new themes and outgoing tendencies in an arresting way. Like many of his poems it is composed in the form of a monologue, and the added epistolary technique of direct address involves the reader at once in the things described. The poet begins with himself, his failures and uncertainty; against personal dissatisfaction and a sense of guilt he puts the necessity of writing this letter (i.e., the poem). The recipient of the letter remains mysteriously obscure, though it is most likely the beloved woman whose guidance and understanding he needs. But the poem quickly passes beyond its initial mood of quiet nocturnal thought, and the poet is nearly overcome by the hallucinatory images that burst upon him when he requests her aid:

> Where is your ministry? I thought I heard
> A piece of laughter break upon the stair
> Like glass, but when I wheeled around I saw
> Disorder, in a tall magician's hat,
> Keeping his rabbit-madness crouched inside,
> Sit at my desk and scramble all the news.
> The strangest things are happening. Christ! the dead,
> Pushing the membrane from their face, salute
> The dead and scribble slogans on our walls;
> Phantoms and phobias mobilize, thronging
> The roads; and in the Bitch's streets the men
> Are lying down, great crowds with fractured wills
> Dumping the shapeless burden of their lives
> Into the rivers where the motors flowed.

The once peaceful night has become a dark well issuing an apocalyptic imagery of public life which possesses the poet's mind. "Disorder" does less to "scramble all the news" than to expose in its grotesque, surreal details the underlying meanings and outcome of our modern civilization. Among Kunitz's contemporaries, Randall Jarrell, John Berryman, and Karl Shapiro have devised, in their own distinctive manners, patterns of irrational imagery to display the frightening dream of the public world. "Night Letter" makes a suitable companion-piece to "The Surgeons," but goes even further in specifying the infectious diseases of the spirit in the present age. Kunitz does not, however, simply halt with destructive images, ones which recall *The Dunciad* and *The Waste Land* in the severity of their judgment; in the next stanza certain ghosts, the tattered remnants of industrial society, its aims and methods, loom out of the shadows as Disorder continues to play his tricks:

> Of those that stood in my doorway, self-accused,
> Besmeared with failure in the swamps of trade,
> One put a gun in his examiner's hand,
> Making the judgment loud; another squats
> Upon the asylum floor and plays with toys,
> Like the spiral of a soul balanced on a stone,
> Or a new gadget for slicing off the thumb;
> The rest whirl in the torment of our time.
> What have we done to them that what they are
> Shrinks from the touch of what they hoped to be?

The air in which these lost, suicidal figures move about and show themselves reminds us most of that bleak rushing wind of Dante's spirits of the Futile in the *Inferno*. But the hell of Kunitz's poem is a hell of our own invention, wherein we lock ourselves with greed, exploitation, and hatred of self and others. Is this not another picture of the same living death that Joyce and Eliot and Lawrence, to choose obvious examples, have drawn for us before? I make these allusions not to charge Kunitz with a mere repetition of his elders' work—his poem is original and forceful—but to indicate the common ground of the modern artistic conscience.

Though he denies many of the values and desires of this society in the poem and vividly depicts their negative effects, Kunitz realizes he cannot just shrug them off. He must, instead, endure their deceit and baseness within himself in order to chasten his poetic vision. Furthermore, he refuses to accept any idea of a lasting human defeat. Written in anguish and doubt, this poem, like his others, still testifies to a love that binds persons together in true community. The message of history Kunitz urges on us is a recognition of this first and final potentiality of men rising from the ashes of society or state. Beyond the general evil, he insists, that one value can be preserved:

> I suffer the twentieth century,
> The nerves of commerce wither in my arm;
> Violence shakes my dreams, I am so cold,
> Chilled by the persecuting wind abroad,
> The oratory of the rodent's tooth,
> The slaughter of the blue-eyed open towns,
> And principle disgraced, and art denied.
> My dear, is it too late for peace, too late
> For men to gather at the wells to drink
> The sweet water; too late for fellowship

And laughter at the forge; too late for us
To say, "Let us be good unto each other"?
The lamps go singly out; the valley sleeps;
I tend the last light shining on the farms
And keep for you the thought of love alive,
As scholars dungeoned in an ignorant age
Tended the embers of the Trojan fire.
Cities shall suffer siege and some shall fall,
But man's not taken. What the deep heart means,
Its message of the big, round, childish hand,
Its wonder, its simple lonely cry,
The bloodied envelope addressed to you,
Is history, that wide and mortal pang.

Kunitz lays the bulk of moral responsibility on the individual, and he
speaks as an individual acutely conscious of his own responsibilities. We
can see just how conscious he is if we notice the self-involvement in his
poems, his willing exposure there to the blows of experience; "I suffer the
twentieth century" sums up Kunitz's imaginative and moral effort. From
inner conflicts and reflections as well as from the larger external forces at
war with man's dignity and freedom, Kunitz has created a poetry that talks
to us by turns lyrically and savagely, and with disturbing honesty; his is a
voice that has long needed to be heard.

(1965)

6

Theodore Roethke

LOOKING BACK TO THE EARLY POETRY OF THEODORE ROETHKE, WHOSE PREMATURE death in August 1963 was an incalculable loss to American literature, we can see there the source of many of his constant thematic interests and of the restless exploratory impulse in technique that resulted from them. Roethke wished continually to plumb new areas of experience and to alter his style to match his discoveries. This impulse and his considerable lyric gifts give to the body of his writing a strong cumulative effect, for each successive stage of the work grows quite naturally from its predecessors. Reading his late poems, we feel the weight of earlier ones as an actual presence. By means of this closely woven pattern there is built up a universe of discourse. a poetic world of recurring themes and preoccupations into which the individual poems fit and within which they are comprehended.

Roethke's first book, *Open House* (1941), impresses the reader at the start with this poet's ability to sing, with his sharp, compact lines and his fundamental rhythmic sense. One is sure after seeing the best of these short lyrics and descriptive poems that Roethke could never have stopped with them; flexibility and the promise of real development lurk everywhere under the surface of his language and in the materials of his experience. In the title poem he announces the major theme that will influence nearly all of his future work and the artistic personality inseparable from it:

> My secrets cry aloud.
> I have no need for tongue.
> My heart keeps open house,
> My doors are widely swung.

An epic of the eyes
My love, with no disguise.

My truths are all foreknown,
This anguish self-revealed.
I'm naked to the bone,
With nakedness my shield.
Myself is what I wear:
I keep the spirit spare.

The anger will endure,
The deed will speak the truth
In language strict and pure.
I stop my lying mouth:
Rage warps my clearest cry
To witless agony.

The art proposed in these stanzas is peculiarly personal, "naked to the bone," and, we might say, resembles a journal, kept with great pain, which traces the path of a sensitive mind from bondage to freedom. Such is the course Roethke follows through a substantial part of his poetry. It appears too that this interest in the self as poetic theme evolves from a kind of curative effort by the poet—the exorcism of a demon, T. S. Eliot would call it. A progressive movement that takes place in his writing falls into stages ranging from the psychological to the visionary and mystical. This classification necessarily slights some excellent light verse and children's poems that are peripheral to the poet's main purposes and so will not be discussed here. Roethke sets out upon a journey in his work, a research into the bidden corners of the psyche; through his labors he seeks to secure the liberation and integration of the self. The poet must relive his own personal history and once more find his way back into the world in order to discover himself and his ties with creation anew. The developing body of Roethke's poetry over the length of his career creates a record of the self's mutations, its final relationship to nature, and the expansion into love and illumination, its last, anagogical disposition.

The series of brief poems opening *The Lost Son* (1948), Roethke's second collection, serves as an introduction to longer and more radical pieces in the same book. Roethke has stressed the eye as the most important organ (see his "Prayer," from *Open House*); and it is an eye of microscopic powers trained on the minute, thriving vegetable and mineral realms of the earth that determines the character of sensibility here. These poems remind us somewhat of Rimbaud's *Illuminations* and Whitman's *Leaves of Grass*, not so much in subject matter or method as in their bold affront to our habitual forms of perception. We are forced to see things differently, or to reject the poetry altogether. We are urged to strip away those winding cloths of cat-egory and convention in which we bury our sense of life, and to regain a simplicity of vision, a belief in human possibility. Lying flat on the soil, as we appear to do while reading these poems, our eyes level with the ground, we begin again with the elements of the natural world. Our origins are linked by correspondences with those elements. If this procedure of close addition to budding plants and tiny creatures clashes with our pretensions to adult dignity, Roethke shows us in "Cuttings *(Later)*" that such observation has a surprising relevance to our own estate:

> This urge, wrestle, resurrection of dry sticks,
> Cut stems struggling to put down feet,
> What saint strained so much,
> Rose on such lopped limbs to new life?

Should we disclaim recognition of this struggle, we either have failed to admit to ourselves the truth or have not risen to meet life. Roethke always succeeds in putting before us the images of grace and defection.

As he often remarked in commenting upon his writing Roethke spent his youth around the greenhouses in Michigan owned by his father and uncle, who had a large flower business, and he absorbed the atmosphere and the minutiae of plant life with an intensity of interest and a sympathy that transformed them into both literal facts and dominant metaphors of his poetry. Early influenced by his reading of Wordsworth, John Clare, and Whitman, and later by Léonie Adams, be quickly found poetic examples to spur his personal fascination with the details and processes of nature. There is a human lesson to be learned that starts with a humble attitude toward the lower orders of creation and the knowledge of our connections with them. True growth requires us to return along the way we came and to touch once more the roots from which we sprang:

> When sprouts break out,
> Slippery as fish,
> I quail, lean to beginnings, sheath-wet.

Such imagery identifies man with a process in the natural world and relates him to its stubborn fecundity. This assertion of existence is evident in a poem such as "Root Cellar," where

> Nothing would give up life:
> Even the dirt kept breathing a small breath.

The shorter poems of this period are generally devoted to what Roethke calls "the minimal." Their repeated themes and metaphors furnish a basis for more ambitious efforts and point to new departures. In a poem entitled "Transplanting" we watch young plants being set down in fresh soil and, as if through the lens of a camera equipped with a timing device, we see them unfurl and bloom:

> Watching hands transplanting,
> Turning and tamping,
> Lifting the young plants with two fingers,
> Sifting in a palm-full of fresh loam,—
> One swift movement,—
> Then plumping in the bunched roots,
> A single twist of the thumbs, a tamping and turning,
> All in one,
> Quick on the wooden bench,
> A shaking down while the stem stays straight,
> Once, twice, and a faint third thump,—
> Into the flat-box it goes,
> Ready for the long days under the sloped glass:
>
> The sun warming the fine loam,
> The young horns winding and unwinding,
> Creaking their thin spines,
> The underleaves, the smallest buds
> Breaking into nakedness,
> The blossoms extending
> Out into the sweet air,
> The whole flower extending outward,
> Stretching and reaching.

Roethke has realized how the same striving upward into life (suggested by the continuous movement of participles in the second stanza of this one-sentence poem) is an essential activity of the human spirit. His perception leads him to examine in a series of longer poems the relationships between the developing inner world of the self and the objects and forces of physical nature. What is merely a proposed analogy between psychic and natural processes in earlier poems approaches an identification of the two in work that follows.

The longer poems, which extend and deepen Roethke's previous concerns, finally appear as a full sequence in *The Waking* (1953). In a feat of imaginative re-creation and poetic skill be dramatizes, by means of a technique that sometimes seems close to the novelist's method of interior monologue, the borderline regions of the conscious and the preconscious in a child as he slowly, and often painfully, ascends from the mysterious center of his origins toward selfhood and a communion with the external cosmos. As the body grows the spirit grows with it, and the exchange between them, with the added consideration of lives and things outside which impose upon the forming self, creates the drama of these poems. Intimate attachments to the animal, vegetable, and mineral levels of creation are disclosed, and along with them, a tension in the child-protagonist between the desire for his whole existence and a contrary attraction for death and the inanimate. In order to embody the immediacy of this evolution of self in the poems, Roethke turns away from the stricter conventions of his previous work to looser and more eclectic forms suitable for rendering this complicated interior drama. The poems register the impression of sensations from without on a rapidly shifting psychic life until we sense a dialectical arrangement between them. Passages contain abrupt changes:

> Tell me, great lords of sting,
> Is it time to think?
> When I say things fond,
> I hear singing.
> ("O Lull Me, Lull Me")

conflict and isolation:

> A worm has a mouth.
> Who keeps me last?
> Fish me out.
> Please.
> ("Where Knock Is Open Wide")

and unexpected juxtapositions everywhere:

> Such music in a skin!
> A bird sings in the bush of your bones.
> Tufty, the water's loose.
> Bring me a finger. This dirt's lonesome for grass.
> ("Give Way, Ye Gates")

In spite of the difficulties caused by such associative and prelogical techniques, some of which should disappear once the reader surrenders himself to the purpose and rhythm of the poet's undertaking, we still find the same precise diction and familiar musical ease that distinguish Roethke's art. If the poems lack the rational order we found in *Open House*, this lack must be attributed to the fluid reality the poet tries to capture here. The

adjustments demanded of us are more extreme than before. Entering the
child-protagonist's mind, we must adopt a literalness of apprehension and
discard the adult's acquired skepticism—though we must not, on the other
hand, forget the sophisticated craftsmanship in these poems. The world,
from the new point of view Roethke provides, is transformed into a densely
populated, because animistic, universe where normal distinctions of subject and object, consciousness and unconsciousness, will and instinct are
abolished, and synesthesia is an accepted mode of perception. Perhaps the
license for such a departure in poetry can best be explained by a remark
the poet made in a recent essay (*Poetry*, October 1960). "We must permit
poetry to extend consciousness," Roethke says "as far, as deeply, as particularly as it can, to recapture, in Stanley Kunitz's phrase, what it has lost
to some extent in prose. We must realize, I think, that the writer in freer
forms must have an even greater fidelity to his subject matter than the
poet who has the support of form." Roethke, as a reading of his collected
verse will prove, has worked in both manners; many of his late poems
display his wish to experiment with "freer forms," as do the poems of the
childhood sequence.

These poems are, then, composed on a rationale wholly their own, a logic
nearer that of the dream or some ellipsis of thought and sensation than the
calculating intelligence. We can say of them, as T. S. Eliot says in the preface to his translation of St.-John Perse's *Anabase*, that "there is a logic of
the imagination as well as a logic of concepts." Individually, the poems constitute portions of a journey into the psyche, the memories and experiences
beneath everyday conscious thought, and so they participate in different
temporal dimensions by disturbing the dormant past within the self.
Roethke's poetic enterprise at this juncture involves him in something resembling the interpretation of the many layers of writing on a palimpsest;
each one draws him further back in time and into more obscure circumstances. But the journey is made with direction and, we feel, even with
urgency. It is an attempt to win a perspective on the general plan of personal existence from its remote beginnings by finding the "lost son" and
recovering the moments of that life already lived. Only a simple-minded
view would discount these poems as clinical materials or the raw stuff of
psychoanalysis; they are nothing of the sort. However private the resources
on which Roethke has called, the problem of understanding details of separate poems seldom comes from faults of privacy. The problem may be our
own carelessness or impatience. A statement Roethke wrote for *Twentieth
Century Authors* helps to clarify his intentions:

> I have tried to transmute and purify my "life," the sense of being defiled by
> it, in both small and formal and somewhat blunt short poems, and latterly,

in longer poems which try in their rhythms to catch the very movement of the mind itself, to trace the spiritual history of a protagonist (not "I," personally), of all haunted and harried men; to make in this series a true and not arbitrary order which will permit many ranges of feeling, including humor.

The universal character of Roethke's protagonist compels our participation in these inner travels. By association we are turned into partial actors of the drama his poems relate.

The journey back into childhood exposes old sores; and anxiety over questions about death, God, isolation, sexuality, and parental bonds looms large in the sequence. A desire to get out of the morass of such disturbances is the most pronounced feature of the protagonist, but he can attain his release only by facing directly all the hazards and powers—usually psychic ones— that endanger the gradually developing self. "The Lost Son" is probably the most representative poem of the group for our purposes because it holds within its careful design the prominent themes of the other poems. And so forms a paradigm of the interior journey. The plan of the poem falls into several sections tracing the narrator/protagonist's progress: the setting forth, the quest (with its accompanying ordeals), the discovery of a new harmony and integrity, the protagonist's expectation of another phase, and his speculation on what has occurred.

"The Lost Son" follows the trials and decided advance of the self or, to use a Jungian term, charts a process of individuation. Beginning, ominously enough, with suggestions of death, gloom, and ugliness, the poem drops us into the middle of the child-protagonist's pursuit of freedom and singular identity, a pursuit frustrated by the shocks experience continues to administer to the frail equilibrium of his psychic life:

> At Woodlawn I heard the dead cry:
> I was lulled by the slamming of iron,
> A slow drip over stones,
> Toads brooding in wells.

The proximity of destruction and the riddle of his own nature lure the protagonist into action, and he engages himself in the search for liberation:

> Which is the way I take;
> Out of what door do I go,
> Where and to whom?

But confusion dogs his tracks, for the animistic universe where each thing has an independent and ambiguous character is nothing if not deceptive;

like the magical forests of fairy tales it presents more false leads than true paths. The creatures, plants, and other entities filling this world, even the friendliest ones, haunt him, and yet he must inquire of them the way out. He looks among the smallest creatures for some reliable guides, though not always with happy results:

> All the leaves stuck out their tongues;
> I shook the softening chalk of my bones,
> Saying, Snail, snail, glister me forward,
> Bird, soft-sigh me home.

Under prevailing conditions movement offers the sole relief to the agonized protagonist, who is also heir to complaints of the flesh. His search brings him at last to "the pit," in the section of that title, and there he reaches the lowest and most dangerous point in the journey. In fact, the pit—clearly a female symbol—signifies the womb or place of his origins, and return to it indicates the risk of defeat, even of death. As the protagonist nears there to ask a fundamental question about life— "Who stunned the dirt into noise?"—he is answered with images of the womb and birth, "the slime of a wet nest." A harsh music of warning jangles his nerves, accompanied in section three, "Thee Gibber," by further alienation from his surroundings, sexual dilemmas, and shrill discord:

> Dogs of the groin
> Barked and howled,
> The sun was against me,
> The moon would not have me.
>
> The weeds whined,
> The snakes cried,
> The cows and briars
> Said to me: Die.

At the edge of annihilation the protagonist passes through the "storm's heart" and glides beyond it into a state of calm, another plane of being. The self, having survived the threats to its growth, breaks forth in a mood of spiritual exultation at the sheer pleasure of its attainment:

> These sweeps of light undo me.
> Look, look, the ditch is running white!
> I've more veins than a tree!
> Kiss me, ashes, I'm falling through a dark swirl.

Body and spirit revel in their newly won harmony. The freed self, no longer desperately struggling for independence, dissolves its conflicts with the physical world and, indeed, brings the things of that world into communion with it. The greenhouse, with its rich store of life, to which the young protagonist comes home after the quest within himself, becomes a scene of revelation and symbolizes both the unity and the potentiality of existence. This regenerative cycle is caught in the images of flowers:

> The rose, the chrysanthemum turned toward the light.
> Even the hushed forms, the bent yellowy weeds
> Moved in a slow up-sway.

In the poem's last section the protagonist meditates on his experience. This is "an in-between time" when he can merely await further motions of the spirit. The imagery of the passage recalls T. S. Eliot's "Ash Wednesday" and *Four Quartets*, and the resemblance is doubtless intentional, as it is also in the later "Meditations of an Old Woman." But Eliot's poems treat spiritual development as the product of individual effort in prayer and contemplation and faith, whereas Roethke sees it as the outcome of a natural process. The latter's religious vision is intuitive and remains far from orthodox Christianity. The narrator of "The Lost Son" hesitates to classify his experience; he will admit of no more than a strange visitation:

> Was it light?
> Was it light within?
> Was it light within light?
> Stillness becoming alive,
> Yet still?

The allusion to Eliot's "still point of the turning world" may be obvious, but the meaning in Roethke's poem should prevent us from taking it as a literal echo. Whatever generates the spiritual odyssey in "The Lost Son" derives from within the protagonist himself and is not based upon a definite external creed:

> A lively understandable spirit
> Once entertained you.
> It will come again.
> Be still
> Wait.

That spirit does "come again" in Roethke's writings. Though he will long be occupied with the progress of the self, the conclusion of this poetic sequence enables him to proceed in different directions.

Roethke's love poems, which began to appear in *The Waking* and have their own section in *Words for the Wind* (1958), manifest certain sharp deviations from earlier self-examination. The amatory verse blends considerations of self with qualities of eroticism and sensuality; but more importantly, the poems introduce and maintain a fascination with something beyond the self, that is, with the figure of the other, or the beloved woman.

The beloved woman of these poems takes various forms. Sometimes she assumes the figure of a wraith, an entrancing specter; sometimes she is purely physical. Her role in the poems can be called that of the female principle or the opposite or the other and frequently involves metamorphosis. Observation of her beauties by the poet leads him to rapport with creation:

> The breath of a long root,
> The shy perimeter
> Of the unfolding rose,
> The green, the altered leaf,
> The oyster's weeping foot,
> And the incipient star—
> Are part of what she is.
> She wakes the ends of life.
> ("Words for the Wind")

In some way this loved one possesses the elusive secrets of life and its potentialities; she partakes of all that is. The style of the love poems returns to a more formal order after the experimentation of the sequence pieces, but Roethke has obviously learned a new disciplined richness of language and music from that venture.

Fulfillment in love is the theme of a quartet of lyrics, "Four for Sir John Davies," which extends the search for unity and harmony so visible in "The Lost Son" from an internal, psychological probing to a vision of the relationship between the self and the beloved. Drawing its basic metaphor of dancing from Davies's sixteenth-century poem *Orchestra*, which explains the hierarchical plan of the universe through that figure, and from Yeats, who saw in the dance an image of sexual and spiritual reconciliation, the poem leaves the poet's isolated dance at the beginning to discover a transcendent completion in which both lover and beloved share. At the start the poet celebrates the vital energies of the cosmos and of his own rhythmic movements, but the latter are occasionally humorous and lack agility and purpose:

> I tried to fling my shadow at the moon,
> The while my blood leaped with a wordless song.

> Though dancing needs a master, I had none
> To teach my toes to listen to my tongue.

In spite of the pleasures of his single dance, which gives him the feeling of kinship with *things*, the poet seeks a deeper human bond. Attraction to his newly found partner begins between "animal and human heat," but we soon realize that the meeting of the lovers physically has created a corresponding spiritual engagement:

> Incomprehensible gaiety and dread
> Attended all we did. Behind, before,
> Lay all the lonely pastures of the dead;
> The spirit and the flesh cried out for more.
> We two, together, on a darkening day
> Took arms against our own obscurity.

As traditionally befits such lovers, they receive, in the poem's third part, one identity. They recall that pair in Donne's "The Canonization" whose pure devotion to one another divorces them from the profane public world and invests them with a sacred or mystical quality, for here also, Roethke writes, "the flesh can make the spirit visible." So this dance, though it originates in human love, is anything but simply ordinary and mundane. The vertical motion of these dancers and the successive alterations they undergo in their ascent establish something close to a religious dimension in this experience. We cannot fail to see how love at its most intense, which the poems portray, is described by the poet as a spiritual event of such magnitude and significance that the lovers' connection with the universe is completely revised. In "The Vigil," the concluding poem, Dante's paradisaical vision is introduced to set off Roethke's own version of an encounter with the eternal; but this moment seems, as it did in "The Lost Son," a condition of inner blessedness the cause of which—outside of human love—is not fully known. Yet there is no doubt that the moment is one of visionary perception rendering creation, as it were, transparent and mysteriously transfiguring the couple:

> The world is for the living. Who are they?
> We dared the dark to reach the white and warm.
> She was the wind when wind was in my way;
> Alive at noon, I perished in her form.
> Who rise from flesh to spirit know the fall:
> The word outleaps the world, and light is all.

Roethke dedicates himself much of the time, particularly in his later work, to the accomplishment of poetic moments such as the one above, and in his

Sequence, Sometimes Metaphysical (1963) openly searches for God in poems clearly written from a firsthand knowledge of the soul's dark night. But neither the ecstatic assertions of being nor the often tormented mystical visions hide from Roethke the realities of human life, indeed they are seen as the expression of that life at its zenith, when the self reaches in every direction to the heart of things. The concluding "Meditations of an Old Woman" from *Words for the Wind*, the visionary pieces of *Sequence, Sometimes Metaphysical*, and many other poems that have been published in various journals and are collected in *The Far Field* (1964) amply demonstrate the poet's repeated realization of these moments and his contemplation of the extremes of mortal experience.

"Meditations of an Old Woman," the group of five poems at the end of *Words for the Wind*, is a noteworthy achievement looking toward more recent experiments with a long, prose-style line in "Meditation at Oyster River," "The Rose," and other poems. Composed freely, the "Meditations" are sometimes said to be derivative from *Four Quartets*, but actually they owe, as Roethke confirmed, a larger debt to Whitman in both style and attitude, a debt that becomes even more plain in work that follows. Yet a limited confusion is understandable when we acknowledge that the poems are to a degree an answer to Eliot's mature view. The old woman who is the speaker of these reflective monologues serves as an opposite to Eliot, whose voice we hear throughout *Four Quartets*; and the conclusions at which she arrives in the course of the meditations about herself and the meaning of her existence have little in common with Eliot's. In fact, some passages like the following from "What Can I Tell My Bones?" can only be read as a direct reply to him—with slight overtones of parody:

> It is difficult to say all things are well,
> When the worst is about to arrive;
> It is fatal to woo yourself,
> However graceful the posture.
> Loved heart, what can I say?
> When I was a lark, I sang;
> When I was a worm, I devoured.
>
> The self says, I am;
> The heart says, I am less;
> The spirit says, you are nothing.

Old age, a retrospective look at life, and the approach of death are themes of both Roethke's and Eliot's poems, though their final visions diverge widely.

In contrast to the prayer and asceticism and renunciation of the world on which *Four Quartets* is founded Roethke's elderly lady embraces in memory and imagination the entire spectrum of her experience, its joys and delights, its sufferings and disappointments included. These meditations at last do more than just affirm the precious unevenness of life; they celebrate with religious exaltation its multitude of beauties and the horizons of possibility in evidence even at its close.

While the narrator of the poems was inspired by Roethke's mother, she is a mask for the poet too. The poems move with the changes of her, thought, touching on incidents and ideas of a long lifetime that revolve in her mind with many of Roethke's favorite images and metaphors from the natural world: the sun, the wind, the tiny creatures of earth, flowers and seeds and grass, water, and so on. But the poems turn to other matters as well; there is a brilliant and savage passage on modern forms of self-destruction in women, which leads also to suffering or destruction in those about them:

> I think of the self-involved:
> The ritualists of the mirror, the lonely drinkers,
> The minions of benzedrine and paraldehyde,
> And those who submerge themselves deliberately in trivia,
> Women who become their possessions,
> Shapes stiffening into metal,
> Match-makers, arrangers of picnics—
> What do their lives mean,
> And the lives of their children?—
> The young, brow-beaten early into a baleful silence,
> Frozen by a father's lip, a mother's failure to answer.
> Have they seen, ever, the sharp bones of the poor?
> Or known, once, the soul's authentic hunger,
> Those cat-like immaculate creatures
> For whom the world works?

These lines expose graphically the failure of the self to rise toward completion, a warping and perversion that contrast with the stalwart openness to surrounding reality so noticeable in the old woman. Though she is not always serene and knows fear, hesitation, and loneliness at certain times, the narrator can declare, in the last two stanzas of the final poem, her faith in the durable splendor of the world and in the miraculous transformation or rebirth the spirit works in the individual:

> The sun! The sun! And all we can become!
> And the time ripe for running to the moon!

In the long fields, I leave my father's eye;
And shake the secrets from my deepest bones;
My spirit rises with the rising wind;
I'm thick with leaves and tender as a dove,
I take the liberties a short life permits—
I seek my own meekness;
I recover my tenderness by long looking.
By midnight I love everything alive.
Who took the darkness from the air?
I'm wet with another life.
Yea, I have gone and stayed.

What came to me vaguely is now clear,
As if released by a spirit,
Or agency outside me.
Unprayed-for,
And final.

Though Roethke again chooses to keep his ultimate view somewhat indefinite, his later poetry has in general become more religious and mystical. In other poems from *Words for the Wind,* as well as in his last writings, he addresses himself solely to the presentation of his visionary experience. Some of these poems focus on the negative aspects of this experience, on the dilemmas in which the self is trapped, on psychic and spiritual torments, in a style that is musical but also terse and epigrammatic, with rapidly changing imagery. Roethke's concerns have progressed from those of the earlier childhood sequence poems, but we can still observe his extremely moving evocations of irrational, dreamlike perception. "The Exorcism" is a poem of spiritual pursuit and of the agony of purification that is the necessary preparation for experience or knowledge of the Divine. The poet is brought face to face with his soul's imperfections and must undergo the pain of being parted from them:

1
The gray sheep came. I ran,
My body half in flame.
(Father of flowers, who
Dares face the thing he is?)

As if pure being woke,
The dust rose and spoke;
A shape cried from a cloud,
Cried to my flesh out loud.

(And yet I was not there,
But down long corridors,
My own, my secret lips
Babbling in urinals.)

2
In a dark wood I saw—
I saw my several selves
Come running from the leaves,
Lewd, tiny, careless lives
That scuttled under stones,
Or broke, but would not go.
I turned upon my spine,
I turned and turned again,
A cold God-furious man
Writhing until the last
Forms of his secret life
Lay with the dross of death.

I was myself, alone.

I broke from that low place
Breathing a slower breath,
Cold, in my own dead salt.

Two lines from another poem, "Elegy," might serve as a helpful gloss on the theme of "The Exorcism":

I have myself, and bear its weight of woe
That God that God leans down His heart to bear.

Yet "The Exorcism" and "Elegy" show us only the darker side of Roethke's religious imagination, which is more than counterbalanced by his positive insight, the gift of a sudden and joyful revelation:

Dry bones! Dry bones! I find my loving heart,
Illumination brought to such a pitch
I see the rubblestones begin to stretch
As if reality had split apart
And the whole motion of the soul lay bare:
I find that love, and I am everywhere.
                                        ("The Renewal")

Here the poet, at the peak of vision, feels himself entering into the very essence of created things: knower and known are no longer separated by barriers of physical solidity or by appearances. The ordinary rubblestones that break open and disclose their hidden being to the poet do so only as he sees himself in the same undisguised way. Extraordinary as such a revelation is, and it is merely one of a number, we find, especially in some of Roethke's newest and most unusual poems, a profound sense of communion with this reality, though it is set forth in a more relaxed and detailed manner. These poems are freed of regular meters, and use long lines and an approach to reality previously seen in the "Meditations of an Old Woman." Roethke says (*Poetry*, October 1960); "There are areas of experience in modern life that simply cannot be rendered by either the formal lyric or straight prose. We need the catalogue in our time. We need the eye close on the object, and the poem about the single incident—the animal, the child." That is precisely what we get from Roethke—"the catalogue," "the eye close on the object"—in "Meditation at Oyster River," "Journey to the Interior," "The Rose," "The Long Waters," and other poems. He has named for us, one way or another, his predecessors in this mode as he went along; they are Christopher Smart, Walt Whitman, and D. H. Lawrence. To catch the feeling of this sort of poem, so rare in modern literature, we have to read more than two or three lines; here, then, are sections four and five of "The Long Waters":

IV

In the vaporous gray of early morning,
Over the thin, feathery ripples breaking lightly against the
    irregular shoreline—
Feathers of the long swell, burnished, almost oily—
A single wave comes in like the neck of a great swan
Swimming slowly, its back ruffled by the light cross-winds,
To a tree lying flat, its crown half broken.

I remember a stone breaking the eddying current,
Neither white nor red, in the dead middle way,
Where impulse no longer dictates, nor the darkening shadow,
A vulnerable place,
Surrounded by sand, broken shells, the wreckage of water.

V

As light reflects from a lake, in late evening,
When bats fly, close to slightly tilting brownish water,
And the low ripples run over a pebbly shoreline,
As a fire, seemingly long dead, flares up from a downdraft of air in
    a chimney,
Or the breeze moves over the knees from a low hill,
So the sea wind wakes desire.

My body shimmers with a light flame.

I see in the advancing and retreating waters
The shape that came from my sleep, weeping:
The eternal one, the child, the swaying vine branch,
The numinous ring around the opening flower,
The friend that runs before me on the windy headlands,
Neither voice nor vision.

I, who came back from the depths laughing too loudly,
Become another thing;
My eyes extend beyond the farthest bloom of the waves;
I lose and find myself in the long waters;
I am gathered together once more;
I embrace the world.

This poem, like the other "catalogue" poems of this last phase of Roethke's work, enumerates objects and details of the world fondly remembered and treasured as parts of the poet's spiritual odyssey. Thus the contemplation of external details in the universe never takes complete precedence over the consciousness of the poet; a relationship always exists between what has been seen in nature and the interior state of the observer. It seems clear from the end of "The Long Waters" that Roethke experiences a cycle of dispersal and reunification somewhat similar to the pattern in "The Exorcism" or "The Renewal," though the "embrace" of the final line here does not come with a blinding flash of mystical intuition but rather as a condition of the poet's soul gradually reached through the entire slow movement of the poem.

"The Long Waters" and the visionary lyrics of *Sequence, Sometimes Metaphysical* exemplify the last stage in the long metamorphosis of the self that Roethke attained in his poetry. This fundamental theme gave his work unity and yet never restricted the astonishing variety, invention, and artistry of which he was capable. Other modern poets have taken the self as theme, but no one has so fruitfully sounded his own subjective depths. Nor have any of his contemporaries been granted such an intimate communion with nature. (Eberhart grows ecstatic over the mystical suggestiveness of natural things on occasion, but he does not penetrate so deeply into it as Roethke, and he does not have the latter's vision of a profound evolutionary pattern.) Roethke's uncanny sensibilities led him to comprehend and to incorporate in his writing the continuous but nearly imperceptible communication that goes on among all living things, as well as to know moments of heightened awareness in which his relation and that of the created world to the Divine were suggested. He once said (in *New World Writing* 4) that the poet "may be lucky enough, on occasion, to create a complete reality in a single poem." Few poets of modern times have known this luck as often as Theodore Roethke.

(1965)

7

Brother Antoninus
(William Everson)

CATHOLIC POETRY, IN THE PERIOD OF TIME THIS GROUP OF STUDIES ATTEMPTS roughly to cover, originally saw its most unique and accomplished practitioner in the person of Robert Lowell. His first books, *Land of Unlikeness* and, particularly, *Lord Weary's Castle*, revitalized orthodox religious verse in this country, where one finds fewer poets committed to such matters in their work than one does in England. With its national church England continues to produce, even in an age of diminishing faith and widespread agnosticism, poets who write, and write well, from a firm core of Christian belief and thought. America, on its side, has no persevering tradition of orthodox Christian poetry, though a heterodox religious strain and a fierce moral sense are characteristic of American literature. In the twentieth century various experiments have been tried with religious poetry that involve formal artistic innovation as well. T. S. Eliot epitomizes this kind of experimentalist, but he has had no successful imitators; and Lowell, as the separate discussion of him will show, travels away from the apocalyptic religious vision of his early poems to look more closely at human life considered in itself, within a completely historical and natural context. Of the Catholic poets who arrived in the same generation as Lowell, or a later one, only a limited number have made their Catholicism a central issue in their art or have evolved a specifically religious vision of experience as the distinctive source of poetic inspiration. Some of the best of them—John Frederick Nims, Ned O'Gorman, John Logan, Ernest Sandeen, Samuel Hazo—are identifiable as Catholics on those occasions when they do bring their poems to bear on the joys and vicissitudes of faith. The poems of Thomas Merton, a Trappist monk, tend to be projected outward and now chiefly to embrace, sometimes very forcefully and movingly, public and social dilemmas with

their moral implications. By way of difference, the poetry of Brother
Antoninus builds its foundations in the problems and conditions of his own
life as an individual, both before and after his conversion to the Catholic
church.

Only a portion of Brother Antoninus's career as a writer has been devoted to religious, specifically Catholic, poetry. His earlier reputation was
created under his actual name of William Everson, and in examining this
first part of his work we shall call him by that name, which appears on his
books of those years. He made his debut with a small pamphlet of poems,
These Are the Ravens (1935), and this secular half of his poetic career culminated in the representative volume of selected poems, *The Residual Years*
(1948), published in his thirty-sixth year. Everson was born in Sacramento,
California; his poetic vocation is undeniably associated with the Western
states, where he has continued to live, to hold a variety of jobs, and to write.
There also, for the past fifteen years, he has pursued his monastic vocation.
After sporadic studying and a period of employment as a young man with
the C.C.C. he returned to Fresno State College in the autumn of 1934 and
was introduced to Robinson Jeffers's poetry, an encounter that signalled the
beginning of his own poetic efforts. In a passage from a letter quoted by the
publisher in his preface to *These Are the Ravens*, Everson says of his work:

> I like to feel that these poems are, with two or three exceptions, inherently
> of Fresno County. Although it was never my purpose to write of Fresno
> County, and although most of these poems could have been written in any
> section of the country, nevertheless the luxuriant vineyards, the heavy or-
> chards, the miles of desolate pasture-lands, and back of it all the tremen-
> dous mountains heaved against the east, hold for me an appeal that I hope
> has crept into my verse.

Without any doubt this "appeal" is obvious in the early poems, and all to
their advantage. In fact we should note here that many of the finest poems
from both the secular and the religious parts of Everson's writing owe a
great deal to their author's fondness for place and to his constant apprehension of what is involved in creation outside of man—in other words, the
existence of birds, animals, trees; of soil and rock; of the behavior of the
elements. His startling sensitivity to the created world may suddenly in-
trude upon the imagery of poems not otherwise concerned with such things,
and yet what intrudes will seem at once to authenticate and support the less
tangible regions of experience the poet is investigating. Probably this lesson was learned from Jeffers, though there exist similarities in this technique to two other poets with whom Everson has some affinity, Walt
Whitman and D. H. Lawrence, who frequently interrupt the abstract and
speculative with the concrete and descriptive. The beginning pieces, already

metrically loose, display a feeling for location, a responsiveness to nature, through the poet's occupation as a worker on the land. "Winter Plowing" is a lyrical evocation of his tasks and surroundings:

> Before my feet the plowshare rolls the earth,
> Up and over,
> Splitting the loam with a soft, tearing sound.
> Between the horses I can see the red blur of a far peach orchard,
> Half obscured in drifting sheets of morning fog.
> A score of blackbirds circles around me on shining wings.
> They alight beside me and scramble almost under my feet
> In search of upturned grubs.
> The fragrance of the earth rises like a tule-pond mist,
> Shrouding me in impalpable folds of sweet, cool smell,
> Lulling my senses to the rhythm of the running plow,
> The jingle of the harness,
> And the thin cries of the gleaming, bent-winged birds.

Critics of Everson often speak of the presence of a species of pantheism in his early work. While the regard for earth, for the natural rhythms of life, or for the biological cycle of birth, maturation, and death are especially plain, there appears to be very little mysticism in the treatment of these themes. That is to say, the poet does not venerate the physical universe and its processes, or human physical life and its processes, as if they were something divine, but rather brings them into the midst of his poetic vocabulary because they comprise the essential reality with which he is involved and, at this point, indicate the extent of the reality he knows and believes in. Poetry, for, Everson, should delineate his experience of this natural existence in all of its required instinctive will and strength. The poet has at his disposal for the artistic labor the spiritual energies of consciousness, imagination, and conscience; thus a poem turns into the occasion for an exchange between the spiritual and the natural in himself. This exchange is maintained but intensified in the later religious poems, where the spiritual takes on the added force of the supernatural, of Divine grace and command.

The dramatic tension arising from the interplay of these powers, first in the poet and then in the poem, doubtless accounts for the forcefully articulated quality of speech we meet everywhere in his writings. This poetic speech bears considerable weight, a weight derived from the utmost sincerity and a passionate desire for exactitude; Everson attempts to grasp the ultimate truth his language may be capable of yielding. But, we should understand, his motives on that side are not primarily aesthetic; and so his poetic manner is rough, sometimes even awkward or in poor taste. Words twist, surge, and lash out in his poems or, in other cases, they are formed

into massive, hewn blocks. At times Everson introduces unfamiliar words
or coins them, not out of pedantry nor with the idea of linguistic play we
see in Wallace Stevens; instead he resembles an existential philosopher, a
Heidegger or Sartre, who tries to wrest new and difficult meanings from his
experience. In a poem entitled "The Roots" from his third collection, *The
Masculine Dead* (1942), he contemplates the history of the English tongue
from its origins. His attention fixes on the life that has given shape and
weight to the language through centuries, invested it with untold emotions
and significance. As the poem unfolds, his own relationship as a writer to
that language becomes apparent, and he finishes by defining his understanding of what a poem's effect ought to be in the music of its words:

> And I, not English, in a level valley of the last great west,
> Watch from a room in the solstice weather,
> And feel back of me trial and error,
> The blunt sounds forming,
> The importunate utterance of millions of men
> Surge up for my ears,
> The shape and color of all their awareness
> Sung for my mind in the gust of their words.
>
> A poem is alive, we take it with wonder,
> Hardly aware of the roots of compulsion
> Quickening the timbre of native sounds;
> The ancient passion called up to being,
> Slow and intense, haunting the rhythms of those spoken words.

In the body of his own art Everson has given us what he calls in this same
poem "the core of existence caught on the tongue," though we should add
that it is his own existence he puts into his work, the persistent, uninhibited investigation of himself as a man. To be sure, such poems—and we
come across them in his religious as well as his secular writings—are precursors, with many of Kenneth Rexroth's, of the autobiographical tendencies
prominent recently in the poetry of Robert Lowell or Anne Sexton or Gary
Snyder; but there is an objectification of most of the admittedly personal
elements in Everson's verse that sets it part from the confessional bias of
some later poets, and especially from the nearly hysterical ravings of a number of San Francisco Beat poets with whom he was later—under the name
of Brother Antoninus—linked. Then we must also acknowledge the fact
that Everson did not occupy a position from which to influence other writers; he has always belonged to the company of writers who had nothing to
do with Metaphysical wit, Laforguean irony, or with Symbolism and the use
of mythology. His is a poetry of open statement, tortured and driven by the
poet's exhaustive probing of himself.

In the later poems from *The Residual Years*, Everson includes a long sequence, "Chronicle of Division," which is his most intimate piece of writing if we are thinking of personal or private detail. This sequence covers his
marriage, the separation imposed on the couple by the poet's imprisonment
as a conscientious objector during World War II, an attempted reunion following his release, and then a final separation. Painful, haunting, and abso-
lutely authentic, these poems resemble a diary in which are recorded the
torments and self-searchings, the brief moments of pleasure, the slow destruction of a relationship: in other words, they provide a lengthy account
of the inner man attempting to create a balance with his external circumstances. Yet the poems are not apologies for their author but serve instead as
the means by which Everson can take hold of his experience in all honesty
and give it form. He does not depart from this aesthetic strategy in his religious poetry. In place of such subjects as his marriage and separation we
discover in *The Crooked Lines of God* (1959) that he has taken his personal
spiritual condition as material for poetry or that he seeks an equivalent for
this condition in biblical and religious story. The same may be said in general for his latest volume, *The Hazards of Holiness* (1961), where, in a "Foreword," he clarifies some of his views on the act of writing. "A poem," he
says, "like a dream, is 'whole' to the extent that it registers the mystery of
the psychic complex which produced it. My poem can never be 'perfect'
because I cannot be. If I ever achieve a 'victory over language' it can only be
partial, and only to the extent that I have achieved a 'victory over myself.'"
Whatever we may think of this notion—which seems to me to identify
mistakenly the formal aesthetic perfection of a poem with the difficult, im-
probable spiritual perfection of the poet's life—it states boldly the moral
and therapeutic character of the creative process as Everson sees it. And so
we are not surprised when aesthetic criteria are also rejected a little further
on. "Thus," he continues, "I can say truthfully that I have no interest in the
conquest of language, as understood by those who seek to achieve a hy-
postatized aesthetic object. The victories I seek, those of 'appeasement and
absolution, and something very near to annihilation,' are one and all victories over myself, the unremitting attempt to exorcize the demon."

These convictions about the motives and processes of poetic creation
have only recently been formulated; therefore they need adjustment in our
minds when we consider the earlier, and secular, poems of William Everson
with their emphasis on the biological nature of human existence, the compulsive sexuality, the loneliness and frustration of individual endeavor un-
relieved by any religious hope. Those themes echo throughout *The Residual
Years*, and in the title poem of *The Masculine Dead*, not later reprinted, they
are strongly combined. The speakers in the passage I shall quote are "the
masculine dead," men who, prematurely deprived of life, lie underground

like the dead of some Hardy or Housman poem dreaming on their past and
on earthly existence as a whole. The device is highly artificial and purely
poetical, for we are not meant to assume that these souls of the dead really
survive in a spiritual realm by the will of a God. Everson has not yet settled
on his Christian outlook and the position he takes here is fundamentally
naturalistic. In the stanzas below he summarizes the entire cycle of mortal
life as he envisages it during the first phase of his poetic career:

> And there rises before us the childhood moment
> When, staring out of wondering eyes,
> We saw the pattern open its folds,
> Show us the wide land lonely and broad between the oceans,
> The little towns on the high plateaus,
> Making so tiny a light in the dark,
> We saw the forest of earth, and the long streets:
> We saw the wind in the frozen tomb of the north,
> And those tidal forces under the sea that alter the future;
> And knew in the flare of that opening glimpse
> The sudden awareness of what we were.
>
> And it comes, it rises.
> We see ourselves in the good strength,
> Arrogant, loving our quick limbs and our wit,
> Ignorant, singing our bawdy-songs,
> Shouting with pride and assurance in the plenty of our health.
> Till over us crowded the load of darkness,
> Slipping like shadow across the sun.
> There was one long look of the turning sky
> And our knees caved, the spring-tight nerves
> And the strained thews snapping and fraying,
> And we fell, urine burned on our legs,
> The broken lights and fragments of our dreams
> Raced on our eyes;
> Then only the night, shoreless,
> The sea without sound,
> Voiceless and soft.
>
> We lay for a time on the edges of death
> And watched the flesh slip into the earth.
> We watched the eyes loosen their holds,
> The brain that had hungered,
> Known fury and pride,
> Burned with lust and trembled with terror.
> We saw our sex vanish, the passionate sperm,
> All the future children of our loins

> Be nothing, make mud,
> A fertile place for the roots to plunder.
> After a time the bones were chalk,
> And the banded rings we wore on our fingers,
> Corroded and green.

The distance from this vision of existence to the one brought forward in the poems Everson began to write after his conversion to Catholicism in 1949 is great in some respects, and yet a decided continuity exists between the dilemmas posed by "Chronicle of Division," the ultimate pessimism of "The Masculine Dead," and their resolution in a new way of life (fourteen months with the Catholic Worker movement in 1950-51 and entrance into the Dominican Order following that) and the poetry that grows out of it. Nonetheless, we should not minimize the radical difference his changed beliefs do make in his poetic themes and his human concerns; if strains of somberness and of pain continue to show themselves, they do so for altered reasons and against an eternal rather than a temporal background.

The remarks quoted previously from *The Hazards of Holiness* indicate that Brother Antoninus (as we shall hereafter call him in correspondence with his newer books and his monastic vocation) does not aim at formal innovation or aesthetic polish. In fact his poems frequently introduce materials that would seem to have outlived their poetic—which is not to say theological or moral—value except in the hands of an ambitious innovator and formalist. The materials I refer to are Biblical story and incident, and the lives of the saints. Yet Brother Antoninus has given them new poetic spirit and force without sliding into the traps of banality and cheap piety. The reason for his success is that behind the retelling of familiar stories of the Wise Men and the shepherds, the birth of Jesus, the Flight in the Desert, the agony of Gethsemane, and the Massacre of the Holy Innocents there stands the poet's own inner or spiritual circumstance which has, as he says, its peculiar relation to each of these stories and the poems be has fashioned from them. This relation can only become clear to us through a quality in the poems themselves, for there we meet the same intense voice which marks the earlier work speaking with an urgency vividness, and singularity that give the stories a sudden life. Though certain of the poems articulate the sufferings and conflicts of a religious vocation devoutly obeyed, we still sense a deep and pervasive joy not present in *The Residual Years*.

Brother Antoninus writes poems that derive openly from his experience of the natural world as well as those dependent upon sacred history. In his love for the California coast and landscape there is no change except in perspective; he admires and marvels at the unspoiled life of creation, just as he did under the spell of Robinson Jeffers. But in a later poem such as "A Canticle to the Waterbirds," his new religious or supernatural perspective is surely alien to Jeffers's. This poem was "written for the Feast of Saint Francis of Assisi, 1950," and it is filled with the vitality and ecstasy we associate with Catholic visionary poets as different in other ways as Gerard Manley Hopkins, Paul Claudel, Edith Sitwell, and Ned O'Gorman, each of whom celebrates the particulars of God's creation:

> Clack your beaks you cormorants and kittiwakes,
> North on those rock-croppings finger-jutted into the rough
>   Pacific surge;
> You migratory terns and pipers who leave but the temporal
>   clawtrack written on sandbars there of your presence;
> Grebes and pelicans; you comber-picking scoters and you
>   shorelong gulls;
> All you keepers of the coastline north of here to the Mendocino
>   beaches;
> All you beyond upon the cliff-face thwarting the surf at Hecate
>   Head;
> Hovering the under-surge where the cold Columbia grapples at
>   the bar;
> North yet to the Sound, whose islands float like a sown flurry of
>   chips upon the sea:
> Break wide your harsh and salt-encrusted beaks unmade for song
> And say a praise up to the Lord.

An awareness of nature as the actuality surrounding crucial events and actions in sacred history appears in those poems which treat aspects of the Christian story and also, according to the poet's prefatory notes in *The Crooked Lines of God*, obliquely reflect in their arrangement the developing stages of his own faith and monastic vocation. Natural detail is used in such a way as to create the impression of contemporaneousness in what is being described. In "The Flight in the Desert," for instance, the setting with which the poem starts is, strangely enough, some part of the American West; yet Brother Antoninus allows the figures of Mary, Joseph, and the infant Jesus to journey through this landscape without a hint of incongruity or falsity. The poem, in fact, gains substance and an atmosphere of reality from this unusual transposition:

> The last settlement scraggled out with a barbed wire fence
> And fell from sight. They crossed the coyote country:
> Mesquite, sage, the bunchgrass knotted in patches;
> And there the prairie dog yapped in the valley;
> And on the high plateau the short-armed badger
> Delved his clay. But beyond that desert,
> Raw, unslakable, its perjured dominion wholly contained

In the sun's remorseless mandate, where the dim trail
Died ahead in the watery horizon: God knows where.

That is the first stanza. The poem progresses slowly, the long lines drawing each other on, reaches a section which portrays the fleeing family, and
then proceeds to consider the effects suggested by the narrative. Once again
the religious perspective reveals itself. Here the supernatural or Divine dimension of the story of the Flight, which contains its full meaning and
importance, opens out beyond the human reality of the three travelers on
their difficult journey and returns to it, for that, the poet seems to be telling
us, is the manner of our understanding. The landscape of these later stanzas
is still curiously modern and American, and the events that take place, like
those involved in them, appear both to be historical and somehow to defeat
history by coming to life over and over again and in different locations—or,
it may be, everywhere and always. Brother Antoninus's other poems based
on sacred story leave the same odd sensation.

But they, the man and the anxious woman,
Who stared pinch-eyed into the setting sun,
They went forward into its denseness
All apprehensive, and would many a time have turned
But for what they carried. That brought them on.
In the gritty blanket they bore the world's great risk,
And knew it; and kept it covered, near to the blind heart,
That hugs in a bad hour its sweetest need,
Possessed against the drawn night
That comes now, over the dead arroyos.
Cold and acrid and black.
This was the first of his goings forth into the wilderness of the world
There was much to follow: much of portent, much of dread.
But what was so meek then and so mere, so slight and strengthless,
(Too tender, almost, to be touched)—what they nervously guarded
Guarded them. As we, each day, from the lifted chalice
That strengthless Bread the mildest tongue subsumes,
To be taken out in the blatant kingdom,
Where Herod sweats, and his deft henchmen
Riffle the tabloids—that keeps us.

Over the campfire the desert moon
Slivers the west, too chaste and cleanly
To mean hard luck. The man rattles the skillet
To take the raw edge off the silence;
The woman lifts up her heart; the Infant
Knuckles the generous breast, and feeds.

Several poems in *The Crooked Lines of God* look to the poet's private or inner experience rather than to the life of Christ and the commemoration of saints as a fertile area for imaginative concentration. "The Screed of the Flesh," "The Encounter," "A Penitential Psalm," "Hospice of the Word," "A Canticle to the Christ in the Holy Eucharist," "Annul Me in My Manhood," and "Out of the Ash" focus on a variety of spiritual problems in the poet himself. Some of these poems, as well as a few addressed to saints, are heavily indebted to what Brother Antoninus terms in his foreword "the erotic religious psychology of the Spanish Baroque," an overripe combination of sensuality and mysticism in which the approach to God and the symbols of that approach are boldly ambiguous. The better poems are, I believe, those favoring austere renunciation and self-denial in a style that is accordingly sparse and wiry. The erotic and baroque poems appear heavy-banded and dull by contrast, bearing a foreign element that remains alien and unassimilated. The harsh, lacerating speech of such a poem as "Annul Me in My Manhood," or of "Sleep-Tossed I Lie" (from *The Hazards of Holiness*) proves the inappropriateness of the baroque pieces:

> Sleep-tossed I lie,
> Midnight stemmed under,
> And the bloat moon
> Shut in its sky.
>
> Lord, Lord of these tangled sheets!
> My wrestling's witnesses
> Certify my heat.
>
> I have lain long, lain long,
> Long in thy grasp am lain,
> Lord of the midnight watchings,
> The monk's tongue-shuttered groan
> And the hermit's heart-ripped cry.
>
> Somewhere the wanton lovers keep
> Vigils of fecklessness,
> Their hearts
> Bursted on passion
> And the body's blade
> Plunged deep.
> And in that death find sleep.
>
> But I? Long have I lain,
> Long lain, and in the longing
> Fry.

Sleep-smooth this brow.
Bless with thy rippling breath
These anguish-awkward limbs.

Grant thy surcease.
Toy me no more, Lord.
Lord of the midnight wrestlings
Keep the peace!

This poem in its unabashed severity discloses the self-scrutiny and the inward battles that generate some of the best poems in Brother Antoninus's latest book. There is also a very obvious infusion of violence in the new poetry, a violence the poet has defended in a "Dialogue on Holy Violence" with Albert Fowler in the magazine *Approach* (Fall 1963), remarking that his religious experience has involved him in it, and that he has consequently transferred it to his poems. This defense seems to me perfectly legitimate in most cases, though a few poems, and "The Hazards of Holiness" in particular, are pointlessly sadistic in detail. However, the largest part of Brother Antoninus's recent work attempts to objectify in word and image the poet's inner world where the struggle for his faith is carried out. Internal division, the endless demands imposed by the flesh, the desire for union with God and the equally powerful instinct to escape Him, self-assertion versus self-effacement: these are the themes that inspire the most durable poems here. Biblical subjects do appear a few times (in "Jacob and the Angel," "The Conversion of St. Paul," and "The Hazards of Holiness"), but this vein was generally exhausted by the previous book and now has a slight air of irrelevance. The chief accomplishment in the most recent volume is not to be found in the longer poems, nor in a continued reliance on sacred story, but in those brief, taut poems—"I Am Long Weaned" is a good example—torn by suffering, self-doubt, and the pangs induced by true religious belief:

I am long weaned.

My mouth, puckered on gall,
Sucks dry curd.

My thoughts, those sterile watercourses
Scarring a desert.

My throat is lean meat.
In my belly no substance is,
Nor water moves.

> My gut goes down
> A straight drop to my groin.
>
> My cod is withered string,
> My seed, two flints in a sack
>
> Some, day, in some other place,
> Will come a rain;
> Will come water out of deep wells,
> Will come melons sweet from the vine.
>
> I will know God.
>
> *Sophia*, deep wisdom,
> The splendid unquenchable fount:
>
> Unbind those breasts.

These bare, tormented lines give full voice to Brother Antoninus's existence and to the faith he embraces; with the honesty characteristic of his
poetry from its inception, he faces the realities in which he finds himself
situated and those others, supernatural ones, which he hopes for and trusts
in. His road as a Catholic poet has not been very easy, but his achievement
must make us grateful that he chose it.

(1965)

8

Karl Shapiro

KARL SHAPIRO, AND MOST OTHER AMERICAN POETS WHO BEGAN TO PUBLISH AND make themselves known in the late 1930s and early 1940s, could not help but be influenced by the example and practice of such English writers, just barely their seniors, as W. H. Auden, Stephen Spender, C. Day Lewis, and Louis MacNeice. Not only did Auden, in particular, wield influence in idiom and style, but also in his merciless psychological analysis and moral criticism of capitalistic society, reflected in his writings during the Depression, the Spanish Civil War, and the rise of Nazi Germany. Though a wide current of private meanings and covert references flows through his early verse— also picked up by some younger poets but seldom handled with anything approaching Auden's skill and dexterity—the elements of social revolution, satire, and moral judgment remain prominent.

Auden's ideas may seem to be confused in his first books between psychoanalysis, Marxist theory of history, and a personal belief in love and individual integrity as the means of defeating human sickness; yet the reader can never doubt for a minute that this poet is committed to the realities of his situation in time and place. Though Eliot and Pound had few direct imitators among the poets of this generation, Auden and his friends had them in plenty. Again, it is the open involvement of these English poets with the actual world of institutions, ideologies, technology, and urbanization that seemed bold and attractive to other writers. American poets of this period Muriel Rukeyser, Delmore Schwartz, John Berryman, Weldon Kees, Shapiro himself, to name a few—who began to struggle one way or another in their art with the life of contemporary society, were surely indebted to the English poets named, but such influences merely served, in their case, for an apprenticeship from which they graduated to independent and variegated poetic speech.

A second influence worth noting depends upon individual participation in the war. World War II was sensed in advance by many writers such as Yeats, Auden, Kunitz, Berryman, and others, who expressed the growing mood of tension and foreboding in their verse, frequently supplementing it with visions of cosmic disaster. These premonitions of war, rumors of collapse in Western society, and murmurs and threats of social revolution became integral to most poets' perceptions of reality. Poetry, by the fusion of imagination and conscience into a poem's moral imperative, actually became a mode of acting in the world. This literary atmosphere is the one in which Karl Shapiro's poetic talent came to birth and was nourished. Out of this literary and social situation his first collection appeared in 1942, published while its author was on active military duty in the Pacific. (I leave out of account an earlier book, privately printed.) After *Person, Place and Thing* he was to write and publish two more books, *V-Letter* (1944) and *Essay on Rime* (1945), before his return to the United States and his discharge. He fell heir to the two influences discussed above, and yet he was not mastered by them. Shapiro has always shown the power of imagination and will to seek his own desired goals as a poet; the latest phase of his work, beginning with *Poems of a Jew* (1958) and continuing to his recent *The Bourgeois Poet* (1964), proves his ability to travel alone and to reject his literary past.

But Shapiro's initial book gives us little cause to think that he would veer so radically in this later direction. In these poems he operates very smoothly and compellingly within an idiom that was in some part the creation of Auden; and he makes this idiom his own, lends it a personal finish. As the title *Person, Place and Thing* implies, Shapiro takes a poetic stance in the midst of the very definite everyday world. His manner is straightforward— with no unusual difficulties of symbolism or learned reference, no oddities of style. The poems are clearly statements of an alert, intelligent, and humane person who unabashedly concentrates on things as they are; that is, they reflect the knowledge and experience of a man thoroughly aware of his time and his surroundings. Through his perceivings; and discriminations in each poem, a precise picture of the world takes shape. We cannot fail to notice either, with the very first poem in the book, that the cast of Shapiro's mind can be critical and ironic; the opening lines of "Scyros" are sufficiently convincing:

> The doctor punched my vein
> The captain called me Cain
> Upon my belly sat the sow of fear
> With coins on either eye
> The President came by
> And whispered to the braid what none could hear

Self-revelation and self-characterization of the poet when they appear in Shapiro's poems are not, as they are in Robert Lowell's *Life Studies*, the center of interest, though perhaps we need to except a few pieces from *The Bourgeois Poet*; rather, the poet occupies a position of dramatic convenience, a route of access to the primary material of the poem, whatever that happens to be. If there is biographical disclosure in Shapiro's work, it aims to be representative rather than merely subjective. Movement is very often outward from the speaker to external reality; or a poem may have that reality impose itself upon the speaker, who is a representative individual or conscience. This should not, however, suggest that the speaker's voice lacks particular identity, but that it does not usually take such identity as a subject or a theme. We discover Shapiro assuming, not his own part, but the *human* one in his poems; in this he recalls the later Kunitz, whose voice is often prompted to speech on *man's* behalf. Thus, to pick a single instance, the title poem of *V-Letter*, while it surely contains details from its author's own life and relationships, becomes more than a love poem from one certain individual to another; we see it at last as the statement of almost any soldier in such circumstances. Yet Shapiro never sacrifices the concreteness that properly belongs to the poem, nor does he employ gimmicks to give it a spurious universality.

The concern with external reality or the public world in Shapiro's writing fastens with some frequency on different aspects of American life. The titles of his poems quickly illustrate this preoccupation: "Buick," "The Dome of Sunday," "Property," "Washington Cathedral," "Alexandria," "Hollywood," "Drug Store." Poets such as Eliot and Pound included particulars of environment in some of their poems, but these were used to enhance a general atmosphere. In Shapiro, as in Auden and MacNeice, these particulars are often brought into the foreground of the poem, where they are looked at for themselves or as inseparable, if not always desirable, ingredients of modern experience. The attitude required of a poet undertaking such observation and assessment is, I suppose, basically a moral one, though not moral in any trite or platitudinous sense. Other requirements, which Shapiro easily fulfills, are a gift for the satirical and a lightness of manner. His temperament is relaxed as a rule, even in many of his polemics, with genuine sympathy for what is natural and human in experience. He distrusts "The Intellectual," as he says so bluntly in the poem of that title: "I'd rather be a barber and cut hair / Than walk with you in gilt museum halls. . . ." So we should have no trouble understanding this poet's distaste for pretense, his resigned but ironical appraisal of the privileged and the poor as he envisages them buried together in "Necropolis":

Even in death they prosper; even in the death
Where lust lies senseless and pride fallow
The mouldering owners of rents and labor
Prosper and improve the high hill.

For theirs is the stone whose name is deepest cut;
Theirs the facsimile temple, theirs
The iron acanthus and the hackneyed Latin,
The boxwood rows and all the birds.

And even in death the poor are thickly herded
In intimate congestion under streets and alleys.
Look at the standard sculpture, the cheap
Synonymous slabs, the machined crosses.

Yes, even in death the cities are unplanned.
The heirs govern from the old centers;
They will not remove. And the ludicrous angels,
Remains of the poor, will never fly
But only multiply in the green grass.

Many of the poets of the generation preceding Shapiro's (and Auden's), poets of the post-Symbolist period, thoroughly lamented the growth of urban and technological society with its spiritual deficit and looked back longingly to an idealized past, the classical world of Greece or the mediæval Christian world of Dante. Although some of Shapiro's contemporaries, such as Roethke and Eberhart, show religious and mystical inclinations in parts of their work, none has expressed a historical nostalgia in the manner of Yeats, Pound, and Eliot. Shapiro is obviously historically aware, and not merely in his poems about military life—which are not so numerous in his work as in Jarrell's—but in most poems whose subjects have an historical dimension that hecan meaningfully explore. Yet this historical dimension does not lead to contrasts between the past and the present that ignore the imperfections of the former and discredit the latter altogether. I believe Shapiro would say that such an effort is, in any case, not a poet's business, though it might be a historian's or a philosopher's. A poet's business is not with culture either, he has insisted in his prose works, *Beyond Criticism* (1953) and in *In Defense of Ignorance* (1960); the poet's true affair is only with poetry. Shapiro introduces history into a poem as it helps to explain the present, whether his aim is praise or criticism; and he supplies those historical details which bear specifically on his subject. His poem "University" exemplifies this approach and also demonstrates the author's capacity for tough moral criticism and barbed satirical jabs:

To hurt the Negro and avoid the Jew
Is the curriculum. In mid-September
The entering boys, identified by hats,
Wander in a maze of mannered brick
    Where boxwood and magnolia brood
    And columns with imperious stance
    Like rows of ante-bellum girls
        Eye them, outlanders.

In whited cells, on lawns equipped for peace,
Under the arch, and lofty banister,
Equals shake bands, unequals blankly pass;
The exemplary weather whispers, "Quiet, quiet"
    And visitors on tiptoe leave
    For the raw North, the unfinished West,
    As the young, detecting an advantage,
        Practice a face.

Where, on their separate hill, the colleges,
Like manor houses of an older law,
Gaze down embankments on a land in fee,
The Deans, dry spinsters over family plate,
    Ring out the English name like coin,
    Humor the snob and lure the lout.
    Within the precincts of this world
        Poise is a club.

But on the neighboring range, misty and high,
The past is absolute: some luckless race
Dull with inbreeding and conformity
Wears out its heart and comes barefoot and bad
    For charity or jail. The scholar
    Sanctions their obsolete disease;
    The gentleman revolts with shame
        At his ancestor.

And the true nobleman, once a democrat,
Sleeps on his private mountain. He was one
Whose thought was shapely and whose dream was broad;
This school he held his art and epitaph.
    But now it takes from him his name,
    Falls open like a dishonest look
    And shows us, rotted and endowed,
        Its senile pleasure.

Here the present and past are juxtaposed, but not, as it might look at a
glance, for the purpose of contrasting the splendor of former times with the

ethical weakness and social corruption of the modern age. Though Jefferson's "dream" is shown to have come to a different end than he planned, it is still only with reference to his life, thought, and character that the poet can discover any ideals in the past. Otherwise, the implication seems to be, historical conditions, customs, prejudices, have formed this university as it is today, with its instinctive contempt for racial minorities, its neglect of the poor whites (the "luckless race" of hill people), its morally neutral scholarship, its continuation of pre-Civil War attitudes and the active transmission of them to its members and students, its encouragement of hypocrisy and falsity in those it teaches by means of sanctioned but reprehensible traditions ("the young, detecting an advantage, / Practice a face").

Shapiro likes to use poetically what presents itself in the course of daily experience, and thus to achieve that representativeness of which we have spoken. He scrutinizes intensely, though not without humor and sympathy, the places lie visits, whether Melbourne, Australia, or Washington, D. C. American customs and institutions fall beneath this steady gaze, and so do a great variety of type-figures, whom he examines with care in as many ways as he has subjects. Some of these figures permit him to indulge a talent for the grotesque and the irrational, qualities that come into prominence later in *The Bourgeois Poet* but which appear earlier in, "'The Glutton," "The Fly," "The Gun," and other poems. The beginning stanzas of "The Glutton," from *Person, Place and Thing* prove his early desire to try this talent for the monstrous caricature:

> The jowls of his belly crawl and swell like the sea
> When his mandibles oily with lust clamp and go wide;
> Eternal, the springs of his spittle leak at the lips
> Suspending the tongue like a whale that rolls on the tide.
> His hands are as rotten fruit. His teeth are as corn.
> Deep are the wells of his eyes and like navels, blind
> Dough is the brain that supplies his passion with bread
> Dough is the loose-slung sack of his great behind.

In Shapiro's recent prose poems the technique of the grotesque becomes a practical one for conveying something of the enormity of contemporary urban existence and the business corporation milieu without confinement to a single figure as the center of focus. The following poem, number 8 from *The Bourgeois Poet*, attempts to depict the character of this life, its vulgarity and horror and artificiality, through attention to pertinent and revealing details or objects, fragments of the general experience, and a semi-surrealistic mode of presentation. The result may call to mind Chaplin's *Modern Times* and Kafka's fiction in the mixture of feelings—satirical laughter and moral revulsion—it arouses, but it is still very much Shapiro's vision; the reality it explores belongs to this country at this moment in time. We can estimate the distance Shapiro has covered, stylistically, from his previous work by comparing this prose poem with "The Glutton."

> Office love, love of money and fight, love of calculated sex. The offices reek with thin volcanic metal. Tears fall in typewriters like drops of solder. Brimstone of brassieres, low voices, the whirr of dead-serious play. From the tropical tree and the Rothko in the Board Room to the ungrammatical broom closet fragrant with waxes, to the vast typing-pool where coffee is being served by dainty waitresses maneuvering their handtrucks, music almost unnoticeable falls. The very telephones are hard and kissable, the electric water-cooler sweetly sweats. Gold simmers to a boil in braceleted arms and sunburned cheeks. What ritual politeness nevertheless, what subtlety of clothing. And if glances meet, if shoulders graze, there's no harm done. Flowers, celebrations, pregnancy leave, how the little diamonds sparkle under the psychologically soft-colored ceilings. It's an elegant windowless world of soft pressures and efficiency joys, of civilized mishaps—mere runs in the stocking, papercuts.

> Where the big boys sit the language is rougher. Phone calls to China and a private shower. No paper visible anywhere. Policy is decided by word of mouth like gangsters. There the power lies and is sexless.

Grotesque effects are created in this piece with less aesthetic self-consciousness, which is to say, with less obvious care for the artistic surface as something to be regarded for itself, and with more commitment to the actuality of the life disclosed, than they are in "The Glutton." The earlier poem attracts us in part because of its dazzling linguistic and musical performance; the later one forsakes the opportunity for such a display in order to try out subtler devices and rhythms and to allow concentration on the thing presented without much distraction. As satire, the prose poem thrusts deeper and is, in its surrealistic perceptions, the more realistic of the two.

Discussion of the satirical and grotesque elements in Shapiro's writing should not blind us to the personal attitude manifest in those other poems which formulate the values and temper the emotions underlying the criticisms he does make. That attitude is the one I indicated when I said that Shapiro always takes the *human* part or role in his poems—and does it in the teeth of the same world that he faces in his satires. "Auto Wreck," which is again one of his early, but also one of his best, poems, illustrates the meaning of this human part. The poem starts after the wreck has occurred, and its opening disarms us with a wonderfully lyrical description of the ambulance coming from afar toward the scene of the accident:

> Its quick soft silver bell beating, beating,
> And down the dark one ruby flare
> Pulsing out red light like an artery,
> The ambulance at top speed floating down
> Past beacons and illuminated clocks
> Wings in a heavy curve, dips down,
> And breaks speed, entering the crowd.

These lines are effective, to be sure, yet they remain on what I shall call, for lack of a better phrase, a purely lyrical plane, a level at which we can enjoy the imagery for its sheer beauty because we have still to be acquainted with the connected events. Shapiro has so far withheld details of the disaster. And as the stanza continues with its muted account of the efficiency of the ambulance and its crew we are not brought much closer to the accident; only two words stand out as startling indicators of the occasion's horror: "mangled" and "terrible." In them we can see something of the human depths stirred by what has taken place. Shapiro has, of course, used these words to awaken our expectations and to prepare us for what really interests him but won't appear until the second stanza—the accident's aftermath. With that stanza, point of view in the poem is also clarified. While Shapiro is plainly the speaker, he employs the collective "we," thus implying that he speaks for the other bystanders as well as for himself, and that he is articulating what they merely feel and think. Such an implication adds considerable force and range to his own voice. Furthermore, it gives a full human resonance to the awe, the terror, and the questioning of poet and spectators alike:

> We are deranged, walking among the cops
> Who sweep glass and are large and composed.
> One is still making notes under the light.
> One with a bucket douches ponds of blood
> Into the street and gutter.
> One hangs lanterns on the wrecks that cling,
> Empty husks of locusts, to iron poles.
>
> Our throats were tight as tourniquets,
> Our feet were bound with splints, but now,
> Like convalescents intimate and gauche,
> We speak through sickly smiles and warn
> With the stubborn saw of common sense,
> The grim joke and the banal resolution.

The traffic moves around with care,
But we remain, touching a wound
That opens to our richest horror.
Already old, the question Who shall die?
Becomes unspoken Who is innocent?
For death in war is done by hands;
Suicide has cause and still birth, logic;
And cancer, simple as a flower, blooms.
But this invites the occult mind,
Cancels our physics with a sneer,
And spatters all we know of denouement
Across the expedient and wicked stones.

The poem moves through these two stanzas to its climactic point—the question about violent and chance death, death that strikes suddenly and without any discernible reason. It is characteristic of Shapiro to proceed toward some larger theme beyond his immediate poetic subject. The unexpected auto crash, the pain and death, are not directly shown; emphasis is put, less sensationally, on the aftermath, from which we are easily able to reconstruct as much of the catastrophe itself as is necessary. Shapiro has no wish to render the victims' experience. More subtly, he wants to investigate the *second* collision—the impact of this apparently senseless accident on the logical operations of the spectators' minds, and the emotions aroused by that impact. The knowledge urged on those at the scene, the poet believes, defeats any reasoning and invites darker speculations, which even hint at ideas of innocence, guilt, and retribution. Reason and knowledge are destroyed in the very event ("And spatters all we know of denouement / Across the expedient and wicked stones"). The significance of the poem lies in the discovery of the inexplicable that the auto wreck makes possible. Shapiro's bafflement is the same as the other witnesses', and so he proffers no conclusions to comfort us. Since he refuses to turn to any metaphysical or religious explanations, he can only register a shrewd but perfectly human admission of the inadequacy of our minds before such tragic facts.

A similar condition of pain and loss, though not of death, attracts Shapiro's efforts in another of his best poems, "The Leg." Again the poet as speaker gives over his voice to another individual's thoughts and feelings; this time, however, he identifies himself with the situation of the victim, a soldier who awakens in a hospital to find that his leg has been amputated. But if Shapiro is imaginatively capable of entering the life of this young soldier, he also wants to keep his own voice distinguishable and a part of his separate identity, so that it can emerge to speak for him in the closing meditative stanza. Therefore Shapiro uses the third person as a narrative device and yet can make himself seem to be a kind of presence absorbed in the soldier's inner experience, a sympathetic and vocal consciousness which momentarily inhabits the soldier's world of suffering and adjustment.

At the start of the poem the wounded soldier floats slowly upward to awareness, but still in "twilight sleep" he knows that he has lost something. Between the first and second stanzas there is an indefinite passage of time which permits the patient, in the latter one, to arrive at the stage of recognizing his deprivation: ". . . he will know it's gone, / O where! and begin to tremble and cry." In the next stanza he has begun to live with his injury, to come to terms with his own altered shape in a curiously—but how necessarily!—amiable way:

> He learns a shape
> That is comfortable and tucked in like a sock.
> This has a sense of humor, this can despise
> The finest surgical limb, the dignity of limping,
> The nonsense of wheel-chairs. Now he smiles to the wall.
> The amputation becomes an acquisition.

There follows a reversal of the established manner of thinking about this injury. Shapiro changes briefly to the point of view of the severed leg itself and sees it as "wondering where he [the soldier] is. . . ." The man who has endured this loss is not the only victim in the light of the reversal; the soldier is transformed into the leg's "injury," and "the leg is the orphan." A notion of the profound organic unity of the self, of the physical and the spiritual, arises in the last half of this stanza and becomes a vision of the fundamental nature of reality, religious in character and requiring our devotion. Babette Deutsch, in her *Poetry in Our Time*, has remarked with reference to another of Shapiro's poems that it exhibits a strain of thought probably influenced by Rilke; this view holds, in the German poet's words (as translated by Miss Deutsch), that "all life is lived" by all creatures and things, which means, as Shapiro is saying in "The Leg," that the lost leg has its own life, is not simply a dead, cast-off appendage, though it exists properly in relation to the whole self, the body and spirit of the soldier. As the poem progresses toward its finish, Shapiro first recommends that the crippled soldier "pray for its [the leg's] safety, / And after a little it will die quietly"; then in the closing stanza lie offers his own prayer, which submits an interpretation of the body as a reminder of the spiritual, a token of God's creative power as the origin of our being:

> The body, what is it, Father, but a sign
> To love the force that grows in us, to give back
> What in Thy palm is senselessness and mud?
> Knead, knead the substance of our understanding

> Which must be beautiful in flesh to walk
> That if Thou take me angrily in hand
> And hurl me to the shark, I shall not die!

Unlike "Auto Wreck," this poem finds a resolution in the transcendent Divine "force that grows in us" and explains the purpose of suffering as a means of recalling our attention to that force. The ending lines of religious supplication, very moving in themselves, express an attitude we seldom come across in any such overt form in Shapiro's writing. This poet is not too explicit, as he does not have to be, about his ultimate beliefs, but I think it is fair to say that he generally displays a strong aversion to religious doctrines and institutions (in spite of a few poems that testify to a momentary attraction to Catholicism). In the closest he has ventured to straight autobiographical poetry until *The Bourgeois Poet*, a group of lyrics called "Recapitulations," published in their entirety in *Trial of a Poet* (1947), he describes his wedding, and the beliefs of his bride and himself:

> The atheist bride is dressed in blue,
> The heretic groom in olive-drab,
> The rabbi, of more somber hue,
> Arrives upon the scene by cab.

Shapiro's later essays plainly state their distaste for the orthodoxy of Eliot and the homemade philosophy of Yeats's *A Vision*. It is probably best to think of him as a poet whose particular attitudes or positions depend upon the ordering of an individual experience that the composition of each poem demands. Thus he remains true to the feeling of terrified puzzlement resulting from the events of "Auto Wreck"; and in "The Leg" his thought leads him from contemplation of a single physical injury to a vision of the bond between material bodies and spiritual nature. Both poems are dictated by an emotional honesty and an understanding that belong to their separate occasions. Shapiro's quest for accurate and unhindered perception is the implicit justification for this poetic method. And so his is the way of sympathetic identification, though he manages to keep a certain valuable detachment through irony. Shapiro matured in a period when myth, due to the influence of Yeats, Eliot, and others, was all the rage, but he avoided the imitation of these predecessors. His one "mythological" work did not appear in a book until the publication of his selected *Poems 1940-1953*. This cycle of poems, entitled "Adam and Eve," he writes in a note in *Poem of a Jew* (1958), where it is reprinted, consists of pieces that "are not symbolic but literal interpretations. That is, I wrote them according to my own interpretation of the lines in Genesis, where they are first presented." We are supposed to read these poems just as we do his others, as direct interpretations of an experience—in this case, not an auto wreck or an amputation, but the experience of reading Genesis.

Ultimately, Shapiro refuses everything but fidelity to his own experience, his perceptions and ideas. His writing over the past few years is the best illustration. In his volume of polemical essays, *In Defense of Ignorance*, and his latest book of prose poems, *The Bourgeois Poet*, he vigorously severs most of his past allegiances and associations. He washes his hands of the dominant tradition in modernist poetry, particularly the work of Eliot and Pound. Though some of his judgments appear arbitrary, there is courage and frankness in his manner. And some of his opinions have a freshness and an incisive quality that are positively healthy. Shapiro's rebelliousness actually stems from a greater about-face than he bothers to admit. If he now praises D. H. Lawrence as a poet—and we can agree with much of the praise—he doesn't trouble to remind us of his scathing poem "D.H.L." from *V-Letter*, which censures the English writer for his lack of humanity. Likewise, the debt to Auden in his early poems goes further than his confession of it in *In Defense of Ignorance* suggests.

This change assumes tangible artistic form in *The Bourgeois Poet*. As Lowell does in some of the pieces in his *Life Studies*, Shapiro breaks with accepted metrical patterns to attempt a stark poetry of direct speech. But Shapiro goes beyond the experiments of Lowell, and those of Robert Bly, James Wright, John Ashbery, or Frank O'Hara; he tackles the difficult form of the prose poem, composed not in broken lines or irregular stanzas, but in prose paragraphs. If we look for a precedent in his earlier writing, we will come upon two prose poems, "The New Ring" and "The Dirty Word," in *Trial of a Poet*. We can estimate Shapiro's seriousness in turning completely in that direction by noticing how he has chosen "The Dirty Word" for inclusion as his favorite piece of work in Paul Engle's and Joseph Langland's anthology *Poet's Choice* (1963). Commenting on his selection, Shapiro says:

> Why must grown people listen to rhymes? Why must meters be tapped out on nursery drums? Why hasn't America won the battle of Iambic Five? When are we going to grow up?
> I wrote "The Dirty Word" almost twenty years ago and others in the same vein, yet it has taken me a lifetime to wear this form like my own coat. In those days I was just trying it on. Now I feel ashamed when I write meter and rhyme, or dirty, as if I were wearing a dress.

The extremity of this statement may understandably prevent a number of readers from accepting it objectively, but there is no doubt in my mind that it springs from Shapiro's most fundamental emotions with respect to his art. We should, then, view it as a statement of personal intention, rather than a

judgment having widespread validity. But for Shapiro it is an aesthetic declaration; after twenty years the prose poem has come to be for him a more
genuine and natural artistic form. In a recent paper that asks, "Is Poetry an
American Art?" (*College English*, March 1964), he decides it is not. For
Americans, "trying to write poetry in the old manner is murder," and we are
treated to his version of the struggles, apparently judged unsuccessful, of
Cummings, Jeffers, Roethke, Marianne Moore, and others, to "produce a
poetry of sensibility." The alternative is "the heaven of prose," which Shapiro
says we do contribute to. Here are some of his summary remarks:

> I am in earnest when I argue that American poetry is yet to be born and
> that what we have optimistically called our poetry is only a garden of chemi-
> cal flowers. I share the responsibility with Whitman, who laid it on the
> line when he denied the possibility of a formal poetics in America. I elicit
> the support of Eliot who shrewdly named Whitman a great prose writer.
> Pound who demonstrated how the Old World forms might be broken.
> Williams who struggled so long to locate in language the rhythm of Ameri-
> can life at its worst.

In applying himself to the form of the prose poem, which has only occasionally been tried by American poets, Shapiro is mapping one possible
road to follow. Not only is he drawing on the support of Eliot, Pound,
Whitman, and Williams, but he is coming close to the solid French tradition of the prose poem and is perhaps learning something from poets like
Baudelaire, Leon-Paul Fargue, Max Jacob, St.-John Perse, Henri Michaux,
and René Char who have added so much to its development. Given the
plastic nature of the prose poem (which doesn't make it any easier to write),
it provides certain opportunities to handle experience differently, with less
sacrifice to the demands of poetic formality and convention. Baudelaire, in
the preface to his *Le Spleen de Paris*, points out some of the advantages to be
gained in the prose poem. "Which one of us," he writes, addressing himself
to the problem, "has not, on his ambitious days, dreamed of the miracle of a
poetic prose, musical without rhyme or rhythm, supple enough and striking
enough to adapt itself to the lyrical movements of the soul, to the undulations of revery, to the surge of consciousness?" It is just these sorts of advantages that Shapiro seeks, and has won for himself to a degree in *The Bourgeois Poet*: a literary technique that combines the freedom of prose with the
brevity, the attention to word, image, and music associated with poetry.

The Bourgeois Poet definitely has about it the air of a new imaginative
release. Irony and social criticism are still there, but autobiography, invective, heavy doses of sexuality, often dominated by an atmosphere of the
dream and of irrationality, and an occasional prophetic note are now blended
together. Unquestionably, an energy and a frankness that were formerly

constrained have become primary agents of this altered poetry. Because of their length—and they are ruined by presentation in bits and fragments—the prose poems must be sparingly quoted here; besides, The Bourgeois Poet has to be read through as a book, even though it contains no strong narrative thread. It is not a uniformly good book, but the pieces that make it up belong together and give a cumulative impression. Then again it is a book we should not try to decide about at once; it will take some getting used to.

But I would like to include another of these prose poems by way of ending—though with Shapiro it is a beginning—and as an illustration of the effects he can create. In this poem Shapiro is once more identified with what happens, but he also remains the observer and commentator. The paragraphs of the prose poem allow for the juxtaposition of different but related elements, so there is not always an obvious line of narration or of logical continuity. The treatment of the material itself within the paragraphs likewise differs from ordinary straightforward prose in being more compressed and highly charged with feeling, more abrupt and elliptical. The aim is to present rather than to explain. The subtleties and nuances are those of a more conventional poetry but arranged within another framework. Beyond such remarks we will have to let Shapiro's prose poems speak for themselves. To close, here is poem 23 from The Bourgeois Poet, in which the narrator evocatively describes an experience but leaves it without comment to our own feeling for its peculiar suggestiveness:

> From the top floor of the Tulsa hotel I gaze at the night beauty of the cracking-plant. Candlelit city of small gas flames by the thousands, what a lovely anachronism dancing below like an adolescent's dream of the 1880s, the holy gas redeemed from Baudelaire's mustachioed curses. Elsewhere are the white lights of the age, but here, like a millionaire who frowns on electricity, the opulence of flame. Descending on Rome from the air at night, a similar beauty: the weak Italian bulbs like faulty rheostats yellowly outline the baroque curves of the Tiber, the semicircles of the monstrous Vatican, endless broken parabolas.
>
> The cracking-plant is equally palatial. Those oil men in the silent elevator, like princes with their voices of natural volume, their soft hats and their name-drops (like the balloons of words in the mouths of caricatures in political cartoons), men of many mansions. The doors of the room are mahogany. Through one which adjoins and is locked I hear the guttural laughter of undress, neither leisurely nor quick, indistinct wording, and all is silent but a woman's moan. Now it rises like the grip of pain; it is almost loud; it is certainly sincere, like the pent-up grief of deep relief; now it is round, now vibrant, now it is scaly as it grows. (Then it steps off into nothingness.)

I stand awed in my stocking-feet and move respectfully toward the window, as a man in an art gallery moves toward a more distant masterpiece to avoid the musical chatter of intruders. The cracking-plant sails on through the delicate Oklahoma night, flying the thousand hot flags of Laputa.

(1965)

9

Isabella Gardner

"Writing poetry," Isabella Gardner says in the title of a recent poem that leads right into its opening lines, "is a game that no one quits while he or she's ahead. The / stakes are steep." And though she, like Elizabeth Bishop, has been slow to publish, Miss Gardner is still, to keep to her metaphor, running ahead of the game. In the first of her two books, *Birthdays from the Ocean* (1955), she established her indisputable claim to natural gifts any poet would be proud to possess. The most obvious of these are her love for words—the ability to use them freely and unself-consciously, and with a gay vitality that recalls Dylan Thomas and e. e. cummings—and her innate rhythmic sense. Of the women poets who are her approximate contemporaries only a few, such as Muriel Rukeyser, Jean Garrigue, and the late Sylvia Plath in her final poems, could rival her energy in handling words. In Miss Gardner's work the rhythmic movement and the richness of language merge to fashion a sturdy but flexible musical idiom completely her own; and the poet is not afraid to permit it the utmost liberty of sensuous play. Her short poem "Cadenza" even borrows its title from a light musical flourish:

> Conjure away the blue and the dim and the dark cloths
> I am no longer in the night or the half light
> I want a shout of white and an aria of fire
> and a paean of green and a coral carillon
> not Cinderella's slippers not the Emperor's new clothes
> not the skull behind the flower but the bone that is the rose.

The absence of punctuation here—it is occasionally very sparse in Miss Gardner's poetry—is worth noticing because it leaves the task of ordering the flow of the poem at least partially up to the reader, who is, by this tactic, fully engaged with its language and rhythm. Reading these poems requires an active participation that truly recreates them in the mind. "Summers Ago," a later poem dedicated to Edith Sitwell, herself an expert at musical wordplay in verse, illustrates in just a few of its lines the persistence of the author's musical talents:

> Children I told you I tell you our sun was a hail of gold!
> I say that sun stoned, that sun stormed our tranquil, our blue bay
> bellsweet saltfresh water (bluer than tongue-can-tell, daughter)
> and dazed us, darlings, and dazzled us. . . .

The exuberant voice that resounds throughout Isabella Gardner's poetry has its origins in these musical propensities, and they endow her work with a refreshing buoyancy. But the inclinations carry their own dangers; too great a facility can damage poems by letting them become excuses for mere stylistic exercise, brilliant perhaps, and fanciful, but weak in meaning. Such chances are courageously taken by Miss Gardner, and her lapses are surprisingly rare, particularly when measured by the risks. Even more important, she can think concretely in the words and images she disposes, a habit that allows her to try always to increase the capacity of her language, to enlarge the range of suggestiveness and connotation in a poem. Miss Gardner seems at certain times to wish that her words could break all bonds and confinements, soar beyond restriction, but she knows too the impossibility of such freedom, which can quickly transform itself into a kind of captivity. In his collection of essays *The Dyer's Hand*, W. H. Auden discusses this problem: "It is both the glory and the shame of poetry that its medium is not its private property, that a poet cannot invent his words and that words are products, not of nature, but of a human society which uses them for a thousand different purposes. In modern societies where language is continually being debased and reduced to nonspeech, the poet is in constant danger of having his ear corrupted. . . ." Isabella Gardner has easily avoided that corruption, though she has surely felt her language pulled in contrary directions by the personal significance and emotion she attaches to the words she selects and arranges in poems, and by the limiting definitions and standards—to say nothing of deflations and perversions—imposed on them in society-at-large. Her poetry attains its distinctive quality by the conjunction of lyricism with a penetrating vision of life.

The poem "At the Zoo" demonstrates Miss Gardner's imaginative activity with all restraints cast aside. Though it is ostensibly a poem of at least partial lamentation, an infectious mood of joy and boundless energy dominates it from beginning to end. The poet starts by lodging her fundamental complaint against the loss of colorful mythological creatures who once captured man's fancy but now exist only in memory—presumably the memory of poets alone. Next she expresses in a lively way her devotion to various members of the animal kingdom, an affection quite plain in other poems as well; but her enthusiasm is dampened because these creatures are imprisoned in their zoos. The fourth, and last, stanza proposes freedom and renewal, a kind of paradisaical image, which begins with the creatures already named at the poem's outset but now, through its emotional resonance, tries to implicate everything in its burst of new life:

> O the phoenix is gone and the unicorn
> and the Chinese Nightingale.
> No White Whale blows
> nor Persian rose,
> the buffalo is robe and dust.
>
> I have a headlong leaping lust
> for zig and zag and hues and cries,
> for the paradox of the musky ox
> and the mute giraffe's embarrassed eyes.
>
> One should not (in this zoo) throw down a glove.
> It is the bars that shame a zebra out of love
> and flinch the tender faces of giraffes
> who stick their necks out and are good for laughs.
> The beautiful the gentle the enraged
> the strange the pitiful are shooed and caged
> the preying cats and the shy kine who browse
> on treetops. Peanuts are not thrown to cows.
>
> If the buffalo quicken in his hide
> and the phoenix rise and the virgin bride
> lie with the unicorn
> Roland's born and Omar's rose and Moby Dick will blow
> and every piper will be pied and cages will be never,
> giraffes will wink and zebras prink and spring come on forever.

This last stanza works toward a remarkable rhythmical climax, analogous to its meaning, which builds up through lines of moderate length and then through unusually long ones. Miss Gardner exhibits here and elsewhere great skill in manipulating with so much case lengthy lines that ordinarily might be cumbersome and wooden. The rhythmical climax is also the high point of her vision, reflecting an attitude of compassion for captive life that is characteristic of her fundamental assertion of liberty and regeneration. In "To Thoreau on Rereading Walden" she praises that writer for his "taut and

tender gaze" at "herds of birds and fishes, stars in droves," but nevertheless
uncovers in him a terrible lack, a narrowness of love:

> You loved the faces in the fire, Thoreau,
> the goldgreen pickerel, the huddling snow.
> I too love these, and O love you, fierceheart,
> and yet were you, like Lazarus, to rise,
> you would look everywhere but in my eyes.

Thoreau stands accused in her mind of a failure to seek or win any human
love, and in the final line is seen to have "dried safely" in his "shroud" as a
result. The poet's censure is, of course, not total; she loves what he loved
but knows her emotion must go further. Isolation is no virtue in Miss
Gardner's poetry, which constantly puts before us the imagery of relationships, the patterns of sympathy and understanding.

Prominence is given to the question of relationships at the very beginning of *Birthdays from the Ocean* in the form of an introductory poem called
"That 'Craning of the Neck'" and two quotations from the Jewish philosopher Martin Buber, one of which is an epigraph to the book, the other an
epigraph to the poem. The first epigraph provides the title for the introductory poem and may have been the inspiration for it:

> Believe in the simple magic of life, in service in the universe, and the
> meaning of that waiting, that alertness, that "craning of the neck" in crea-
> tures will dawn upon you.

This brief but amazing piece of advice is really accepted by Miss Gardner as
more than an epigraph or the source of a poem's title; it serves her as a
moral and artistic credo. This poet is in her work "a conjurer, a believer," as
Richard Eberhart says; and her poems are "in service in the universe" as
celebration and commemoration of the mysterious variety and beauty of
life in its changing but recurring moments. And so Miss Gardner commits
her self poetically to a complicated network of relations with the living
cosmos.

One of the finest formulations of this commitment in both theme and
the actual substance and texture of the writing occurs in her poem "Of
Flesh and Bone." Here again are many of the long, opulent lines we have
already mentioned. The poem gets underway in childhood recollections
which first affirm the amplitude of human existence and next adopt a stead-
fast rejection of death:

> Child and girl each morning summer winter or dis-
> may my eyes saw waterfalls my ears heard madrigals

> I tasted strawberries touched moss smelt hay and roses, and through
>   the blue
> the bright sky I with my first and once-love flew
> Willow-boned sun-marrowed and air-skinned,
> sea-water in my veins, I drank wine and the southwest wind.
> The noun death and the verb to die were exiled
> from vocabulary, and when the salty boys and sun-burned girls I
> mooned with on the honeysuckled porch through locust-
> loud and sigh-soft summer nights did speculate upon the
>   disposition of my dust
> I said to them I am a girl of flesh and bone, my shift's no shroud,
> and d-e-a-t-h is the word I do not say out loud.
> That is the word I said that I will not admit.

While the others assume the usual adolescent postures that declare a wish
to die young, the poet, like Yeats in "A Dialogue of Self and Soul," would be
"content to live it all again / And yet again":

> I vowed that eyeless earless, loinless lonely,
> I would refuse to die; that even if only
> one sense was left me, touch or smell or taste,
> I would choose to live; that in a sewer of waste
> a thicket of pain a mountain of fear or the sea-
> wrack of sorrow I would beg, steal, and betray to be.

Her girlhood fear of death, she goes on to say, was of "the releasing / of the
I," the loss of self-identity, rather than by any terror of pain or suffering. As
she matured her anxiety shifted to the anticipation of an "engagement [with
death] some tomorrow." What she is so reluctant to abandon is her selfhood
and, through it, her communion with the abundance of the world. The
unknown element in death which most irritates her is, understandably, the
time of its arrival, for one is forced by this uncertainty always to keep the
end in mind. In the closing stanza Miss Gardner returns momentarily to the
pleasures of living, asserts a desire to appoint the hour of her own death so
as to escape the annoyance of expectation, and, at the last, restates her
basic attachment to her human, earthly nature. So strong is that tie that
she can envisage herself watching death face to face as it comes to claim her
from within. Through this image is "dead-certain" and the poet's "horror,"
that very fact sustains the special value she has placed on her life in opposition to the threat of a "coming nothingness":

> Now mornings are still miracles and my dear now love is my true
> love and we fly we fly ... O the sky was never once so bright and blue
> and I still wish to live with living's theft-
> ing and assault if even one sense will be left,

> but to escape the meals and miles of waiting
> I might elect the hour of my negating
> and sleep peacefully to death some winter night,
> cold finally to morning and to mourners and to fright.
> Still, flesh and bone is wilful, and this knowledge is dead-certain
> and my horror,
> that I shall not close my eyes when ITS eyes stare out of mine in
> every mirror.

The hidden fears and hesitancies we nourish in ourselves in a twisted effort to avoid encounters with the multifarious realities of the universe we inhabit are taken by Miss Gardner as the theme of another poem, "The Panic Vine." Botanical and biological details in the imagery suggest the primary character of this psychic malady which so ruthlessly circumscribes our outer existence too. But these details lead on to others that hint at something like, if not exactly the same as, the exposure of the psyche's secrets during the course of psychoanalysis. It is, however, a sort of auto-analysis the poet recommends; its goal is not simply a more durable self but also, once more, that attitude of openness to creation which unveils an otherwise neglected dimension of all human experience:

> The panic vine quickens on the spine with the rise
> and fall of every breath; and blooms inside the eyes.
> A cold fruit bulges from the veins of wrists and arms
> to bleed a virus juice into our sueded palms.
> We spread disease when our be-gloved infrequent rites
> of greeting are performed. If we exhume the roots
> That lie in nightsoil bedded with the lungs of crows
> roots watered by the coiled insistent garden hose
> cold-framed against the thorn the analytic wind
> the dazzling showers of the thundering sun bird blood
> the grey goose feather and the white mare-mother's end—
> if we expose these roots to weather and to wound
> they would survive and we could bear the scattered rose
> the spattered foal the honking flight and the sun's alms.

Miss Gardner's second collection, *The Looking Glass* (1961), reveals no particular alteration in her outlook. Though it contains some of her lightest verse—especially in "Saloon Suite," "Canzonetta," and "Summers Ago," the book also includes several elegies; in spite of the airiness of the pieces just mentioned, a vein of seriousness is apparent. The best of the elegies, I believe, is the one addressed to Dr. Louis Cholden and called, in the Yiddish phrase which means "farewell," "Zei Gesund." This poem does not deviate from the positive humanistic vision already indicated in the previous work; the dead man who is honored here is a person whose "life-spirit" was "robust past compare." As a medical man and a psychiatrist he had healed the sick and restored them to life. For himself, he did not fear death and came to accept it when he was confronted with the impossibility of recovery. So, Miss Gardner maintains, it is we, the living, who grieve at the loss of this man to ourselves; we do not mourn his suffering but our own deprivation. In "Of Flesh and Bone" the poet states her religious convictions, such as they are: "I am not faith-less but with those who see no future in eternity I do agree." Thus we find that her testimony to the deceased doctor's survival is kept within the mortal terms of those who will remember him and receive guidance from his example:

> It is not easy to remember that you died.
> Neither your funeral nor our tears persuade
> us, yet, that you have died. We shall confide
> to you in phantasy through years of need
> the flabby failure, shabby sin, and pride-
> fully, the high Hungarian deed.
> Our spirits shall by your quick soul be fed
> until our bodies, too, are dead.

Personal though her elegies and other poems in the book, such as "Nightmare" and the extremely moving "Widow's Yard" may be, the piece that gives its title to the entire collection is one of the most revealing, as well as one of the most fully achieved, to be found there. A type of stoicism, reminiscent of certain of the Elizabethan lyricists, is manifest in "Zei Gesund," and another version of it becomes apparent in "On Looking in the Looking Glass." Miss Gardner describes in this poem a pitiless inspection of her face in the mirror; her close and unsparing eye reads every line, interprets it; opens up past, present, and future to investigation; bares secret worries and inner deficiencies. A diversity of selves is laid bare and brought to consciousness and to the order of language, just as in this strange little colloquy of the interior life by Paul Valéry two apparently different voices below the mind's surface contribute to the poet's total self:

> —Who is there?
> —I.
> —Who is I?
> —Thou.
> And that is the awakening—the Thou and the I.

In "On Looking in the Looking Glass," as in her other poems from the more recent volume that strike a grave note, Miss Gardner exercises a new economy and restraint in diction and music to control nearly overpowering effects. Since those effects are weakened by piecemeal quotation, I give the poem here in its entirety:

> Your small embattled eyes dispute a face
> that middle-aging sags and creases.
> Besieged, your eyes protest and plead,
> your wild little eyes are bright, and bleed.
>
> And now in an instant's blink my stare
> seizes in your beleaguered glare
> the pristine gaze the blown-glass stance
> of your once
> total innocence.
> I see and dare the child you were.
>
> And for a wink's lasting, There
> Now in your blistered eyes dazzles the flare
> of Youth with years and love to swear
> the kindling enkindled fire
> heedless and sheer . . .
> I see and fear the girl you were.
>
> And now for a tie's lending, Now for the stint
> of a second's fission I light to the glint
> of your Daemon, that familiar whom you stint
> so prodigally. Shunting, shan't-
> ing, wincing fabricant
> I see the maker that you want
> and aren't.
>
> And now just now I closed your eyes
> your infant ancient naked eyes.
> Gaze glare and flare and glint are buried by
> my neutral eye-
> lids. These island citadels are now surrendered
> and with imagination's eye I see you dead.

Of course, Miss Gardner's fundamental wordplay has not disappeared in this poem, but it has been subordinated to her total vision. As the intensity of that vision increases with the progression of the poem toward considerations of her artistic vocation and the intuition of her own death, the language, in the second half of the fourth stanza, begins to loosen under the pressure of pent-up emotions.

It would be presumptuous to attempt a prediction of Miss Gardner's future poetry, but it appears as if the exuberance of *Birthdays from the Ocean* had been permanently tempered and controlled by more sober concerns. Her recent tendency is to make her language work for an experience, except in poems that are quite clearly no more than light exercises. The earlier poems often exist in part as experiences generated primarily by words, but Miss Gardner's newer poetry, while it shows no loss of linguistic power, embodies a deepening of insight and a firmer grounding of her attitudes. Her two distinguished books enable us to acquaint ourselves with the line of development of her truly lyrical art.

(1965)

10

Richard Wilbur

BY GENERAL AGREEMENT RICHARD WILBUR IS ONE OF THE MOST VERSATILE AND brilliant American poets to make his debut since World War II. His intelligence, imaginative agility, command of language, and flexibility of technique are awesome and frequently breathtaking. Yet he is not a poet who has put these gifts to the service of some obsessive theme or vision on which the ultimate significance of his work hangs. On the contrary, his inclinations have attracted him toward the tradition of English lyricism which maintains its center in formalism and wit and musical grace. Thus his natural predecessors can be found most easily not only among the Elizabethan, Metaphysical, and Cavalier poets, but also in Emily Dickinson and A. E. Housman. We should not, however, be misled by these affinities into believing that Wilbur lacks his own voice or that his voice is merely a tissue of other voices from the past. He is a very distinctive poet, and though he has undertaken no major stylistic change in his four volumes, there has been a gradual but quite noticeable sharpening of perception and a corresponding modification of manner. These subtle alterations become clearer in his two latest collections, *Things of This World* (1956) and *Advice to a Prophet* (1961). Throughout his poetry are qualities and characteristics that endow it with a particular identity and may help to account for its appeal.

To begin with, Wilbur is a poet of ceaseless celebrations. As Frederic E. Faverty has said in his essay on Wilbur in *Poets in Progress*, whereas the prevailing mood of much twentieth-century literature has been tragic or negative, this poet, who doesn't try to deny those elements in our experience, still chooses to bring his imagination into contact with other, now somewhat fashionably neglected, aspects of life. The subject, at least the main one, of Wilbur's poetic celebration is the world of things. I am certain he would agree in principle with Wallace Stevens's view in "Esthétique du Mal" (without adopting all of Stevens's philosophical ideas) that "The greatest poverty is not to live / In a physical world." The things on which Wilbur lavishes his artistic care are not limited to any specific category, no more than are his techniques for treating them poetically. Two poems, one early, one late, will show something of the variety of these things that catch his alert interest. The first poem, "Poplar, Sycamore," from *The Beautiful Changes* (1947), is a rich, though brief, descriptive piece on those trees. What we are aware of at once is the wealth of implication his language and rhythm give to the objects of his attention. The poplar seems to gather into its wind-blown motions and its relationships with earth, air, and sky a meaning extracted from the very heart of existence, a meaning of which it is the untranslatable embodiment:

> Poplar, absolute danseuse,
> Wind-wed and faithless to wind, trowelling air
> Tinily everywhere faster than air can fill,
> Here whitely rising, there
> Winding, there
> Feinting to earth with a greener spill,
> Never be still, whose pure mobility
> Can hold up crowding heaven with a tree.

The sycamore is granted by the poet its own peculiar importance in the next, and final, stanza. In the closing lines Wilbur speaks most explicitly about the meaning of this tree, for we learn suddenly that the theme underlying the observation of poplar and sycamore in all their sensual grandeur is the activity of imagination. Again we might note another similarity to Wallace Stevens, who spent his poetic career exploring the transformation of physical reality by the faculty of imagination. For Wilbur the body of the world perceived in its particulars (here the two trees) stirs the poet/observer's imagination to take up the possibilities for meditation inherent in them. What Wilbur is talking about in this stanza applies perhaps first of all to the poet, who goes further than meditation and creates a poem containing the implications his imagination has discovered—the "more" than what is seen of the last line. But surely he is not restricting this activity of mind to artists alone; it is a human potentiality. Here, then, is the sycamore:

> Sycamore, trawled by the tilt sun,
> Still scrawl your trunk with tattered lights, and keep
> The spotted toad upon your patchy bark,
> Baffle the sight to sleep,

> Be such a deep
> Rapids of lacing light and dark,
> My eye will never know the dry disease
> Of thinking things no more than what he sees.

Like Stevens and Roethke, Wilbur singles out the eye as the most prominent vehicle of imagination. In his recent *Advice to a Prophet*, the poem
"Stop" again exemplifies Wilbur's devotion to things in his verse. He bestows the same loving concern on what is frankly unpoetic, even beneath
ordinary regard or scrutiny, that he did on the much more promising and
conventionally artistic material of poplar and sycamore trees. In fact, "Stop"
surpasses the merely descriptive; it concludes on a different plane from the
one on which it begins. The imagination carries it over, through the device
of simile, into mythological suggestiveness, so that the ugly and the commonplace are redeemed by a hidden radiance:

> In grimy winter dusk
> We slowed for a concrete platform;
> The pillars passed more slowly;
> A paper bag leapt up.
>
> The train banged to a standstill.
> Brake-steam rose and parted.
> Three chipped-at blocks of ice
> Sprawled on a baggage-truck.
>
> Out in that glum, cold air
> The broken ice lay glintless,
> But the truck was painted blue
> On side, wheels, and tongue.
>
> A purple, glowering blue
> Like the phosphorus of Lethe
> Or Queen Persephone's gaze
> In the numb fields of the dark.

Among these dreary objects, under a leaden sky, the poet's eye is caught
by the odd, luminous color of a painted baggage-truck and an imaginative
transformation occurs. The consequence of this apparently aimless glance
is a new vision of things usually looked at without being seen.

In another poem from the same book entitled "Junk," Wilbur, borrowing
his form from the Anglo-Saxon, carefully examines his "neighbor's ashcan."
Its contents are the discarded, broken, or worn-out shabby paraphernalia of
our lives; the list starts with a split axe handle:

> The shivered shaft
>   rises from a shellheap
> Of plastic playthings,
>   paper plates,
> And the sheer shards
>   of shattered tumblers
> That were not annealed
>   for the time needful.
> At the same curbside,
>   a cast-off cabinet
> Of wavily-warped
>   unseasoned wood
> Waits to be trundled
>   in the trash man's truck.

Looking on all these abandoned, useless, and cheaply made objects the poet first yields to the natural tendency to be done with them completely, to have them removed from sight. But that very desire arouses its contrary, which is obviously a more genuine feeling, and is more complicated as well:

> Haul them off! Hide them!
>   The heart winces
> For junk and gimcrack
>   for jerrybuilt things
> And the men who make them
>   for a little money . . .

This feeling emerges fully a few lines later when Wilbur finds in these random, cast-off pieces a strange dignity, a self-possession and character which their dereliction only magnifies. From that discovery it is just one step further in the poem to a consideration of the basic materials of the "junk" objects in their pure state:

> Yet the things themselves
>   in thoughtless honor
> Have kept composure,
>   like captives who would not
> Talk under torture.
>   Tossed from a tailgate
> Where the dump displays
>   its random dolmens,
> Its black barrows
>   and blazing valleys,

They shall waste in the weather
                                        toward what they were.
The sun shall glory
                         in the glitter of glass-chips,
Foreseeing the salvage
                              of the prisoned sand,
And the blistering paint
                                  peel off in patches,
That the good grain
                           be discovered again.

Wilbur's admiration grows as he continues beyond the kinds of things these objects were, the shapes and uses men had given them, to a kind of rapt attention to their elemental properties, by means of which they participate in the life of the cosmos as a whole. We see in this part of the poem how Wilbur indicates through his imagery a cycle of death, disintegration, and renewal for the basic components of the material universe. Words such as "dolmens," "barrows," and "valleys" are more than reminiscent of death and burial. Indeed, the dump where these things finally will be tossed is their grave; and there a process of decomposition sets in which the poet records above with something exceeding simple accuracy. This process and what follows it begin to assume a symbolic design; things decompose, to be sure, but they do so in order to disclose their purest essence, to return to that essence in preparation for a new creation. Once more Wilbur completes his imaginative vision with mythological and legendary allusion:

Then burnt, bulldozed,
                              they shall all be buried
To the depth of diamonds
                                  in the making dark
Where halt Hephaestus
                               keeps his hammer
And Wayland's work
                          is worn away.

If these two poems succeed in illustrating Wilbur's preoccupation with and reverence for things, they may also begin to acquaint the reader with the spiritual atmosphere of this poet's writing. In an early poem, the title of which is borrowed from the seventeenth-century poet and meditational writer Thomas Traherne, "'A World without Objects is a Sensible Emptiness,'" Wilbur makes it unmistakably clear that those who seek spiritual reality cannot properly do so by denying the physical:

O connoisseurs of thirst,
  Beasts of my soul who long to learn to drink
Of pure mirage, those prosperous islands are accurst
    That shimmer on the brink

Of absence; auras, lusters,
  And all shinings need to be shaped and borne.
Think of those painted saints, capped by the early masters
    With bright, jauntily-worn

Aureate plates, or even
Merry-go-round rings.

And at the poem's conclusion we are admonished "wisely" to "watch" for
"the spirit's right / Oasis, light incarnate"; the emphasis, of course, falls on
that last word. So it is that while Wilbur often journeys to the region of
the spiritual—"Junk" and "Poplar, Sycamore" are good evidence of it—he
renders his experience with a profusion of language and imagery that fills
out the supposedly remote reaches of the spirit with mass and weight and
color.

   Though there is little of the ascetic mystic in Wilbur's temperament, he
is—at least some of the time—a religious poet. But he is not religious in
any strict or doctrinal sense of the word; rather, he is deeply concerned
with an experience of life and of the universe as sacramental—as possessing a spiritual worth that shines on surfaces but also hides in recesses. His
best critics, Frederic Faverty for one, have brought notice to the considerable number of poems that, in one way or another, have to do with painters
or painting, and a few others that have sculpture for their subject. The eye,
which we said was the chief instrument of imagination for Wilbur, must be
understood as very close in its perceivings to the painter's eye as it attends
to the reality it will transmute into a picture. In the poem "Objects," he
writes of the artist's responsibility to the things that populate our earthly
habitation, and of what must be done for them through the power of imagination that they are incapable of doing for themselves. Their inner nature
is released for our observation: "Guard and gild what's common, and forget
/ Uses and prices and names; have objects speak." Then Wilbur becomes
specific and selects the kind of painter who can excellently represent his
aesthetic point:

There's classic and there's quaint,
And then there is that devout intransitive eye
Of Pieter de Hooch: see feinting from his plot of paint
The trench of light on boards, the much-mended dry

Courtyard wall of brick,
And sun submerged in beer, and streaming in glasses,
The weave of a sleeve, the careful and undulant tile.

The religious aspect of Wilbur's verse is created through the work of this same "intransitive eye" he praises in Pieter de Hooch, for that eye concentrates the poet's amazing sensitiveness to the phenomenal world, to every fluctuation and nuance in his surroundings, and to the incredible beauty he sees there. His perceptions lead him to discern spiritual threads woven into the texture of what his sight finds out, while his impressive learning, which he carries effortlessly, helps him to articulate his discoveries by metaphor. The poem "October Maples, Portland" gets started with lyrical description, introduces a religious theme, and ends in a Christian legend that illuminates everything that has preceded it:

The leaves, though little time they have to live,
Were never so unfallen as today,
And seem to yield us through a rustled sieve
The very light from which time fell away.

A showered fire we thought forever lost
Redeems the air. Where friends in passing meet,
They parley in the tongues of Pentecost.
Cold ranks of temples flank the dazzled street.

It is a light of maples, and will go;
But not before it washes eye and brain
With such a tincture, such a sanguine glow
As cannot fail to leave a lasting stain.

So Mary's laundered mantle (in the tale
Which like all pretty tales, may still be true)
Spread on the rosemary-bush, so drenched the pale
Slight blooms in its irradiated hue,
They could not choose but to return in blue.

The natural world in its particular season and through its lovely brightness of detail is changed in the poet's eye, and through his deft use of analogy and allusion, into a sacramental reality: the zones of the spiritual and the material draw together momentarily in the poem, there to be experienced again and again. But this instant of fusion also delineates a boundary for Wilbur's vision; his poems do not cross it in search of a more direct mystical communion. He always keeps to his insistence in "Objects" on the necessity of a bond with physical reality.

As Robert Herrick—whom he resembles somewhat in the ease and perfection with which he writes—employed fixed forms, and instinctively picked the right tone and phrase, so Wilbur is essentially a poet of the sensible world and of its implications. But one should add that he is not so attracted to the composition of erotic and amatory verse as Herrick was. His sense of the comic and his ability to produce it in poetry are, however, great—as his successful translations of Molière's *Misanthrope* and *Tartuffe*, his lyrics for the Lillian Hellman-Leonard Bernstein comic-opera version of Voltaire's *Candide*, and some of his shorter poems amply witness. Wilbur ranges in these different works from the barbed wit of Molière to the whimsical feeling of "Epistemology," which consists of just two couplets:

I

Kick at the rock, Sam Johnson, break your bones:
But cloudy, cloudy is the stuff of stones.

II

We milk the cow of the world, and as we do
We whisper in her ear, "You are not true."

Wilbur's talent for the comic takes marvelous form in the elegant bawdiness of "Pangloss's Song: A Comic-Opera Lyric" from *Candide*. Pangloss, wasting away with venereal disease, still contrives to offer a universal hymn of praise to sexual love. These first three stanzas give an adequate impression of the whole piece:

Dear boy, you will not hear me speak
    With sorrow or with rancor
Of what has paled my rosy cheek
    And blasted it with canker;
'Twas Love, great Love, that did the deed
    Through Nature's gentle laws,
And how should ill effects proceed
    From so divine a cause?

Sweet honey comes from bees that sting,
        As you are well aware;
To one adept in reasoning,
        Whatever pains disease may bring
Are but the tangy seasoning
        To Love's delicious fare.

Columbus and his men, they say,
        Conveyed my virus hither
Whereby my features rot away
        And vital powers wither;

Yet had they not traversed the seas
And come infected back,
Why think of all the luxuries
That modern life would lack!

Wilbur has demonstrated skill and beauty in his translations of lyric poetry from the French, Spanish, and Italian, as well as in his versions of Molière. Lyrics by Francis Jammes, Jorge Guillén, Quasimodo, Valéry, Baudelaire, and others, stand firmly in Wilbur's translations as fine poems in English. Each of them seems chosen because of a certain kinship of spirit between the foreign poem and the artistic personality of the translator. In other words, they are poems of a kind Wilbur himself might conceivably have written; in the act of translating he has apparently entered so intimately into an experience of the original that a new poem has been born of it in another language. The watchfulness, the notation of detail, and the final realization of an underlying or symbolic meaning in what is being looked at that we find in his lovely treatment of Guillén's "The Horses" are features of Wilbur's own art:

Shaggy and heavily natural, they stand
Immobile under their thick and cumbrous manes,
Pent in a barbed enclosure which contains,
By way of compensation, grazing-land.

Nothing disturbs them now. In slow increase
They fatten like the grass. Doomed to be idle,
To haul no cart or wagon, wear no bridle,
They grow into a vegetable peace.

Soul is the issue of so strict a fate.
They harbor visions in their waking eyes,
And with their quiet ears participate
In heaven's pure serenity which lies
So near all things—yet from the beasts concealed.
Serene now, superhuman, they crop their field.

The poems discussed in these pages should warn us that Richard Wilbur is not the sort of poet from whom we can abstract a systematic view of life after the fashion of Yeats, Eliot, or many another modern poet. He is probably better called an occasional poet of the finest kind. "What is in a poem is essentially the same as that which is in one's own life," Goethe says; and this little dictum applies nicely to Wilbur and his poems, which so often have their foundation in the chance occasion of a thought or a visual observation. Take the poem called, "A Hole in the Floor," dedicated to the French Surrealist artist René Magritte, who has painted precise images of dreams and the subconscious:

The carpenter's made a hole
In the parlor floor, and I'm standing
Staring down into it now,
At four o'clock in the evening,
As Schliemann stood when his shovel
Knocked on the crowns of Troy.

A clean-cut sawdust sparkles
On the grey, shaggy laths,
And here is a cluster of shavings
From the time when the floor was laid.
They are silvery-gold, the color
Of Hesperian apple-parings.

Kneeling, I look in under
Where the joists go into hiding.
A pure street, faintly littered
With bits and strokes of light,
Enters the long darkness
Where its parallels will meet.

The radiator-pipe
Rises in middle distance
Like a shuttered kiosk, standing
Where the only news is night.
Here it's not painted green,
As it is in the visible world.

For God's sake, what am I after?
Some treasure, or tiny garden?
Or that untrodden place,
The house's very soul,
Where time has stored our footbeats
And the long skein of our voices?

Not these, but the buried strangeness
Which nourishes the known:
That spring from which the floor-lamp
Drinks now a wilder bloom,
Inflaming the damask love-seat
And the whole dangerous room.

Wilbur makes his poem resemble a surrealist painting (but not a surrealist poem): the objects of everyday reality—here, in this case, parts of a house— are transformed almost magically into counters for an unseen psychic world. Things that are perfectly commonplace threaten, under these circumstances, to become something much more mysterious. But, characteristically, Wilbur does not linger in this subterranean place; in the final stanza he comments to his reader on the value of a descent below the surface of the quotidian. His valuation rests on the knowledge that the familiar and visible are enriched by the unknown that lies just under their surface.

Perhaps because of the urbanity and sophistication of his poetic manner, critics have seldom noted the moral element informing a considerable portion of Wilbur's writing. I do not, of course, imply that he is addicted to the platitude or to easy moral generalizations; rather, he tends to handle the poetic events he creates in a way that involves his own deepest instincts and considered judgments. Sometimes judgment inheres in a disarming lightness of touch; sometimes, as in his poem "Advice to a Prophet," it is expanded into a more comprehensive imaginative vision. In that poem—one of Wilbur's best —he advises a prophet how he may convince men of their folly by an appropriate illustration of the type of penalty they can expect to bring upon themselves. This poem may likewise be said to be an occasional one, arising from the hostility and terror of the world's present condition, but the importance of its theme might be felt under any such situation. As we read through the opening stanzas we find the poet enumerating, then discarding, various threats to the continued existence of man on this earth as insufficiently strong to deter him:

> Spare us all word of weapons, their force and range,
> The long numbers that rocket the mind;
> Our slow, unreckoning hearts will be left behind,
> Unable to fear what is too strange.

> Nor shall you scare us with talk of the death of the race.
> How should we dream of this place without us?

Alternatively, the poet tells the prophet, "Speak of the world's own change"; and in the stanzas that follow Wilbur proceeds to show us, through a fullness of imagery and metaphor, how the natural world—trees and rivers, birds and beasts—could alienate itself, voluntarily, from man, leaving him alone in a universe that has robbed him of the meanings for himself and his life he had once found reflected there:

> Ask us, prophet, how we shall call
> Our natures forth when that live tongue is all
> Dispelled, that glass obscured or broken

> In which we have said the rose of our love and the clean
> Horse of our courage, in which beheld

The singing locust of the soul unshelled,
And all we mean or wish to mean.

Ask us, ask us whether with the worldless rose
Our hearts shall fail us; come demanding
Whether there shall be lofty or longstanding
When the bronze annals of the oak-tree close.

If, after four volumes, Richard Wilbur has undertaken no radical over-
throw of his earlier manner, has sought no new and different forms simply
for the sake of novelty, we should hardly criticize him for that. From the
outset of his career his art has embodied the highest lyrical qualities, demanded the strictest standards of craftsmanship, and proposed a compassionate and reverential attitude toward life that has grown into a constant,
mature spiritual outlook. One cannot ask for much more.

(1965)

11

Denise Levertov

AMERICAN POETRY AT THE PRESENT TIME SUSTAINS TWO EXTREMES, WITH A WIDE range of practice in between in which the best—as well as the most truly advanced—writing is usually done. One extreme is represented by the academic poets. The term does not necessarily apply to all poets who happen to teach in universities for their living, but denotes those writers whose materials are often selected from the history of literature and culture, and whose methods are dictated by the critical theories of what poetry ought to be. At the opposite extreme, the Hip writers mistake the exhibition of hysteria and the release of invective, unhindered by the requirements of craft, for poetry. Whitman and Rimbaud, the "true gods" the Hip writers claim for their masters, had both the genius and the strength to navigate the rapids of emotion and vision in which these self-styled successors capsize and drown.

At the same moment—around 1957—that such figures as Ginsberg and Kerouac began to make news, a number of other, previously little-known, poets also published their own books and caused a less sensational but more worthy stir. Some of them may even have been loosely the minds of their audience with the Hip associated in writers next to whom they were occasionally printed; but there is little resemblance except in their mutual rejection of the ruling literary and critical modes. And these poets differ greatly among one another as well. All of them, however—and I include here poets such as Robert Creeley, Paul Carroll, Frank O'Hara, John Ashbery, Barbara Guest, Gary Snyder, David Ignatow, Brother Antoninus, Galway Kinnell, and John Logan, in addition to Denise Levertov—aim at an expression of the most personal kind of experience, an authentic statement about themselves, what they see and know, suffer and love; their responses to the things, relationships, and heightened instants of their lives. The tendencies of these poets lead them to the repudiation of Eliot's belief in an "objective correlative" that screens the artist from his work and maintains the privacy of his life as an individual. The idea of masks that explains so much modern poetry of the post-Symbolist generation has no value for these younger poets, who really walk naked, as Yeats said poets should.

We have considered in a previous chapter how the poetry of Robert Lowell moves into this same area of the highly personal or confessional, though he comes from a very different corner of the literary map than does Denise Levertov or Robert Creeley or David Ignatow. The latter have steeped themselves for a long time in that tradition of modern writing whose pioneers are William Carlos Williams, Ezra Pound, and H. D.

Among her fellow-poets in this tradition, Denise Levertov stands out as one whose art, fresh and compelling, convinces us of her genuine rapport with the reality she presents as its core. Her poetry is frequently a tour through the familiar and the mundane until their unfamiliarity and otherworldliness suddenly strike us. Her imaginative gaze feasts on the small objects we usually treat as insignificant appendages to our lives, or pauses with affectionate interest on the seemingly trivial activities in which we spend so much of those lives. Thus she engages very naturally in a persistent investigation of the events of her own life—inner and outer—in the language of her own time and place, and completes that investigation in the forms emerging from what she discovers as it is translated into words. Miss Levertov shares the spirit of Martin Buber, for she always says "thou" to the persons, occasions, and objects she encounters; that is her imagination's essential humanizing gesture toward every aspect of existence.

As I have already indicated, Miss Levertov, along with a variety of other poets, departs sharply from the poetic and critical line passing down through Yeats, Eliot, Auden, and the critics who have developed aesthetic views from their initiative. In the introduction to his anthology *Contemporary American Poetry*, Donald Hall offers a good summary description of qualities emphasized by the poets working in the opposing tradition, with its foundation in the example of William Carlos Williams. "This poetry," Hall tells us, "is no mere restriction of one's vocabulary. It wants to use the language with the intimacy acquired in unrehearsed unliterary speech. But it has other characteristics which are not linguistic. It is a poetry of experiences more than of ideas. The experience is presented often without comment, and the words of the description must supply the emotion which the experience generates, without generalization or summary."

In allying herself with this movement, Miss Levertov had to grapple with prevailing literary modes and, finally, to discard them. A struggle of this

sort, the purpose of which is to open a way for poetic development, normally makes or breaks a writer—that is, if he or she dares to undertake it, as
many do not—and it is a real sign of Miss Levertov's abilities that she has
returned victorious. But the effort to win a voice of one's own amounts to
nothing or becomes artificial unless it has been prompted by the conditions
of human experience itself, by all that is cast into the poet's field of vision
in the course of living. Poetry, if it will earn its name, must never begin with
experience at second hand, but with a steady eye on what surrounds us
everywhere. As the French philosopher Jacques Maritain says in his *Art and
Scholasticism*, "Our art does not derive from itself alone what it imparts to
things; it spreads over them a secret which it first discovered in them, in
their invisible substance or in their endless exchanges and correspondences."
Miss Levertov has learned this lesson well, and it is identical to the one her
art teaches us. The conclusion of her "Note on the Work of the Imagination" (*New Directions* 17, edited by James Laughlin) adds to the quotation
from Maritain a consideration of this spiritual faculty which makes the poetic object possible; she writes, "What joy to be reminded . . . that the
Imagination does not arise from the environment but has the power to create it!"

Some poets make their published poems the battleground for style and
individuality, and the reader can witness the spectacle, and its success or
failure. In Denise Levertov there is an unseen conflict which occurred somewhere in the eleven-year span between her first book, *The Double Image*
(1946), published in England before she came to the United States, and her
next, *Here and Now* (1957), issued by Lawrence Ferlinghetti's City Lights
Bookshop in San Francisco. Kenneth Rexroth, who anthologized her work
some years ago in his *New British Poets*, placed her then as one of the most
promising neo-romantics of the war period; but his later statements about
her writing, collected in *Assays* (1961), indicate that he believes—as I do—
Miss Levertov's full powers as a poet began to unleash themselves only after
she bad been in America awhile and, as Rexroth says, had come "to talk
like a mildly internationalized young woman living in New York but alive
to all the life of speech in the country."

The poems included in *The Double Image* give evidence of a true poetic
gift in their author, though they are not marked with those characteristics
of thought and rhythm and speech that would insure them as her handi-
work, and hers alone. I don't mean that the poems are imitations; on the
other band, they seem to partake of a general mood in English poetry of the
time, owing, no doubt, to the war. Here is world-weariness, disenchant-
ment, a flirtatiousness with death and the twilight regions of the spirit.
Somehow a vein of uncertainty runs through these pieces, as if the poet
almost suspected her self in what she was doing. I am sure, however, that I

could never gain such an impression if Miss Levertov had published only
that single volume or if she had continued in her initial style. She served
her poetic apprenticeship in works suffused with vague emotion, filled with
whispers of mortality and unrest, the damp vegetation of England, and
murmurs of perishable love. I will quote just a few lines from one of these
early poems, "Five Aspects of Fear," before approaching her more central
productions:

> In fear of floods, long quenched, waves fallen,
> shattered mirrors darken with old cries;
> where no shot sounds the frightened birds go flying
> over heights of autumn soft as honey:
> each country left is full of our own ghosts
> in fear of floods quenched, waves fallen.
> Rags of childhood flutter in the woods
> and each deserted post has sentinels;
> bright eyes in wells watch for the sun's assassin:
> the regions bereft of our desires are haunted,
> rags of childhood flutter in the woods.

Something of the Georgians lingers on in this passage with its rural
withdrawal from contemporary affairs, but the strongest and most obvious pull is toward Surrealism, which had crossed the channel in the 1930s
and was still a strong influence during the war. Miss Levertov tries, by
means of dreamlike associations and indefiniteness of imagery, to articulate as nearly as possible the purity of her emotions, unsoiled by the concrete or the particular. That vagueness is far removed from what we have
come to know as the essential poet in her, the poet whose sleeves are
rolled and who wrestles up to her elbows in the dust of a common world.
In this poem the effects are atmospheric; the words, I believe, are supposed to bear a cumulative weight of feeling apart from any denotation.
How different from the present Denise Levertov, who senses her materials as a Giacometti or a David Hare senses the materials of his sculpture.
Her "Pleasures," as she calls them in the title of a later poem, are now
quite altered:

> I like to find
> what's not found
> at once, but lies
>
> within something of another nature,
> in repose, distinct.
> Gull feathers of glass, hidden

> in white pulp: the bones of a squid
> which I pull out and lay
> blade by blade on the draining board—
>
> > tapered as if for swiftness, to pierce
> > the heart, but fragile, substance
> > belying design. Or a fruit, *mamey,*
>
> cased in tough brown peel, the flesh
> rose-amber, and the seed:
> the seed a stone of wood, carved and
>
> polished, walnut-colored, formed
> like a brazilnut, but large,
> large enough to fill
> the hungry palm of a hand.

The reader will not be wrong, I think, if he sees in this poem, behind its fascination with the beauty of small objects and concealed things, an allegorical statement of the poet's own concern with material reality. In forcing tangible things to disclose their truths and felicities, she urges human reality to yield some of its secrets—and its covert analogies and predilections too.

The change that takes place between her first and second books—in a decade that saw Miss Levertov leave England, travel in Europe, meet the American novelist Mitchell Goodman, marry him, and settle in this country—is remarkable and must have demanded no less than a complete renovation of her poetic values. But this revolution of the heart, the head, the senses, how worthwhile it all was! She was compelled to start from scratch, and that meant for Miss Levertov a confrontation of the happenings of her life. What she so shrewdly observed was that the ordinary is extraordinarily unusual:

> What a sweet smell rises
> when you lay the dust—
> bucket after bucket of water thrown
> on the yellow grass.
> > > The water
> flashes
> each time you
> make it leap—
> > > > arching its glittering back.
> The sound of
> > > more water
> pouring into the pail

almost quenches my thirst.
Surely when flowers
grow here, they'll not
smell sweeter than this
              wet ground, suddenly black.

Of course, as Kenneth Rexroth further noted, Miss Levertov came under
novel influences in America that were quite unlike any English ones. He
names as a chief influence the poet we have already mentioned, the writer
whose lessons she must have learned well, though without sacrificing her
own intentions and capacities. That poet is the late William Carlos Williams. It is likely that she also learned from Rexroth's own poetry, and from
the Imagists; in her moving tribute to H. D. entitled "Summer 1961," she
records some of her debts to Williams, Pound, and H. D.:

They have told us
the road leads to the sea,
and given

the language into our hands.

Perhaps if we look at a brief but fairly representative poem by Williams to
remind ourselves of certain qualities in his work we will be able to determine, by comparison with Miss Levertov's "Laying the Dust" above, some
of their similarities. Williams's poem is called "Between Walls":

the back wings
of the

hospital where
nothing

will grow lie
cinders

in which shine
the broken

pieces of a green
bottle

Clearly, this poem has little relation to the kind of poetry in the ascendency
during the first half of the twentieth century; the poetry of the French Symbolists has had no bearing on what we read in these lines. Again, if we try to
apply the sort of exegesis to Williams's poetry—or to Miss Levertov's, for

that matter—that is used on Eliot's or Rilke's or Valéry's, we shall miss the point and look foolish. Ingenious explication is beside the point here and will bury the meaning of both poems; we should do better to contemplate them as we would a painting. Williams's attraction to the *disjecta membra* of the physical world, particularly of the modern urban setting, set a firm precedent for Miss Levertov's own poetic venture. We should not forget, either, Williams's insistence that the moral responsibility of the American poet lies in using his native tongue "to represent what his mind perceives directly about him," because this endeavor is, to a degree, Miss Levertov's. Yet there is also a gradual inward turning in her latest poetry and an increasing preoccupation with parable, dream, and interior illumination that are foreign to Williams's imagination.

Williams was for years a champion of younger writers in the United States and, further, was a stalwart foe of the post-Symbolist literature of Yeats and Eliot, as well as an opponent of what he thought was an outworn tradition of English verse forms and meters. It is hardly by accident, then, that young poets, in search of a way past the official poetic idiom, looked to Williams's writings and his viewpoint for guidance. The rejection of conventional for organic form; the repudiation of established metrical patterns in favor of what Williams called "the variable foot"; the return to the spoken language, the American spoken language—these are some of the most prominent results of the senior poet's influence. These younger poets likewise avoid in general the habit of making their work a repository of intellectual history, learning, and fragments of the European cultural heritage. I should like to call the poetry of Miss Levertov, and that of a number of her contemporaries, "poetry of the immediate."

My term requires some explanation. I do not mean by "the immediate" an art without craftsmanship, an art that fixes on the disorder of sheer impulse or emotional notation. Miss Levertov has never allowed her poetry to become even slightly vulnerable to that kind of charge—a glance at any one of her poems will prove it. Moreover, we need only cite the comment she supplies for Donald Allen's anthology *The New American Poetry 1945-1960*, where there is no mistaking her distaste for sloppy composition: "I long for poems," she writes, "of an inner harmony in utter contrast to the chaos in which they exist." Poetry must not be a shapeless replica of external things but an organically formed transfiguration of them in which the transfiguration, rather than poetic convention, dictates the form. What I call "the immediate," then, signifies the complex of relationships existing between the poet and the elements that are close at hand in her personal experience. The things, the happenings, the thoughts and dreams that are subjective events in themselves—everything that falls within the circumference of the poet's life as an individual—become the matter of poetry. The author's private circumstance is explored, its potentialities drawn out; but however far her speculations lead her, Miss Levertov never oversteps that circumference. Instead, she creates from within herself an attitude with which to face her environment, as in her poem "Something to Wear":

> To sit and sit like the cat
> and think my thoughts through—
> that might be a deep pleasure:
>
> to learn what news
> persistence might discover,
> and like a woman knitting
>
> make something from the
> skein unwinding, unwinding,
> something I could wear
>
> or something you could wear
> when at length I rose to meet you
> outside the quiet sitting-room
>
> (the room of thinking and knitting
> the room of cats and women)
> among the clamor of
>
> cars and people,
> the stars drumming and poems
> leaping from shattered windows.

This poem grows around the mind's self-reflective activity. While poems about poetry, the act of composition, or the mind contemplating its own powers and processes are common in the literary history of the past 170 years—Mallamé and Wallace Stevens, for example, expended much of their artistic energy on these themes—Denise Levertov treats such matters in a more personal, autobiographical way than most previous poets have done. Mallarmé, in his famous sonnet, "La vierge, le vivace et le bel aujourd'hui," depicts the poet's failure of imagination through the remote but lovely symbolic image of a swan trapped in ice and earthbound:

> Un cygne d'autrefois se souvient que c'est lui
> Magnifique mais qui sans espoir se délivre
> Pour n'avoir pas chanté le région où vivre
> Quand du stérile hiver a resplendi l'ennui.

> (A swan of former times remembers it is he
> Magnificent but who without hope gives himself up
> For not having sung of the region where he should have been
> When the boredom of sterile winter was resplendent.)
>   (Translation by Wallace Fowlie, from *Mallarmé*, 1953.)

But however acutely the poet has felt the anguish of impotence in his art, he has removed those feelings from the sphere of his own life and incorporated them into the symbolic universe of his poetry. Stevens is less divided; indeed, his notebooks indicate that he wished to have his theory of the imagination become a cosmic view that could be shared by all men. Nonetheless, Stevens's poetry is generally impersonal and almost totally divorced from the important details of his existence as a man. Miss Levertov does not recognize such separations and refuses to hide her life from her imagination. Yet she may have learned from Stevens—as well as from her own thoughts or from other poets' work—that poetry can be involved in the mind's activity as an individual goes about his daily business of registering and interpreting and responding to surrounding reality. The poem "Something to Wear" describes in part the preparations the mind or self makes to encounter this reality ("the clamor of / cars and people . . .") and to elicit from it the substance of art and beauty ("the stars drumming and poems / leaping from shattered windows"). The contemplating self of the poem's beginning does not keep to solitude but, as in "Matins," goes out to meet the world and come upon the stuff of poetry there:

> vii
> Marvelous Truth, confront us
> at every turn,
> in every guise, iron ball,
> egg, dark horse, shadow,
> cloud
> of breath on the air,
>
> dwell
> in our crowded hearts
> our steaming bathrooms, kitchens full of
> things to be done, the
> ordinary streets.
>
> Thrust close your smile
> that we know you, terrible joy.

Thus for Denise Levertov, as for certain other poets, it is proper, even imperative, for the literary enterprise to concentrate on assigning judgment and value, on finding the marvelous, within the particular range of personal observation and knowledge. If such writing is criticized for a lack of ambitious scope, one might reply that it compensates by a penetrating and scrupulous honesty, by a fundamental human resonance that is anything but restricted, and by a fidelity to the experience of contemporary life. Younger writers today, of almost every allegiance or group, have withdrawn their efforts from the elaboration of symbolic systems and mythologies; the *Cantos, The Waste Land, The Duino Elegies,* although they are still widely admired, apparently are looked upon as distant accomplishments. Now the poet believes he must use his art to define the space he inhabits as a person—if I may be permitted the figure—the space in which he exists, chooses and asserts value, loves and hates and dies. And so for Miss Levertov the poem is an instrument of personal measure, of tests and balances, estimating and preserving the valuable in the teeth of a public actuality that day by day magnifies its impersonality, falsity, and unreality. A poem such as "The Instant" rises out of personal experience and the depth of genuine emotion and significance attached to it by the author. As Miss Levertov's own testament the poem cannot be refuted or denied, for it stands well inside the space her poetic imagination circumscribes about her life as she lives it. Here is the complete poem, taken from her third book *Overland to the Islands* (1958); to cut it would be to destroy the form of an experience as she has realized it:

> "We'll go out before breakfast, and get
> some mushrooms," says my mother.
>
> Early, early: the sun
> risen, but hidden in mist
>
> the square house left behind
> sleeping, filled with sleepers;
>
> up the dewy hill, quietly with baskets.
> Mushrooms firm, cold; tussocks of dark grass, gleam of webs,
> turf soft and cropped. Quiet and early. And no valley
>
> no hills: clouds about our knees, tendrils
> of cloud in our hair. Wet scrags
> of wool caught in barbed wire, gorse
> looming, without scent.
>   Then ah! suddenly
>
> the lifting of it, the mist rolls
> quickly away, and far, far—

       "Look!" she grips me, "It is
           Eryri!
                It's Snowdon, fifty
       miles away!"—the voice
       a wave rising to Eryri,
       falling.

              Snowdon, home
       of eagles, resting-place of
       Merlin, core of Wales.

                  Light
       graces the mountainhead
       for a lifetime's look, before the mist
           draws in again.

This poem is both an abbreviated narrative, dramatic in character (in this it resembles many poems by Robert Creeley, Paul Carroll, and others), and a spiritual adventure of a neatly ineffable sort. Within the tradition of post-Symbolist literature such a private illumination as the poet has here would be objectified into the order of a larger metaphorical universe—which is not to say that its value would be sacrificed, but that the value would be transmuted. But in the present poem the experience remains unchanged, is viewed in its own terms. Miss Levertov molds the event into art without abandoning the quality of direct utterance or leaving the domain of her life. The instant to which the poem's title refers is the moment of enlightenment that occurs when mist and clouds part to expose the far-off mountain peak shining in the early light of day and richly endowed with legendary meaning. Still, the poem retains its status as a poem of fact, so to speak, emerging from ordinary circumstances and immediate life, and returning there. We are acquainted with this kind of illumination in Blake or Rilke, though for them it confirms the basis of a whole mythological scheme: the world of things ablaze with the eternal Being they mirror. But to find any metaphysical revelation in Miss Levertov's art we must enter the precincts of the poet's own existence, for she justifies her art through that existence, as well as her existence through her artistic perception.

Miss Levertov's primary intention as a poet has not been the statement of visionary experiences but rather the dogged probing of all the routine business of life in search of what she calls "the authentic" in its rhythms and its details. Her marriage may be a subject for investigation:

       I want to speak to you.
       To whom else should I speak?
       It is you who make

a world to speak of.
In your warmth the
fruits ripen—all the
apples and pears that grow
on the south wall of my
head. If you listen
it rains for them, then
they drink. If you
speak in response
the seeds
jump into the ground.
Speak or be silent: your silence
will speak to me.
          ("The Marriage, II")

or the city's winter streets and the snatches of conversation overheard there:

As the stores close, a winter light
  opens air to iris blue,
  glint of frost through the smoke,
  grains of mica, salt of the sidewalk.

As the buildings closed, released autonomous
  feet pattern the streets
  in hurry and stroll; balloon heads
  drift and dive above them;
  the bodies aren't really there.

As the lights brightens, as the sky darkens,
  a woman with crooked heels says to another woman
  while they step along at a fair pace,

  "You know, I'm telling you, what I love best
  is life. I love life! Even if I ever get
  to be old and wheezy—or limp! You know?

  Limping along?—I'd still . . ." Out of hearing.

To the multiple disordered tones
  of gears changing, a dance
  to the compass points, out, a four-way river.

Prospect of sky
  wedged into avenues, left at the ends of streets,
  west sky, east sky: more life tonight! A range
  of open time at winter's outskirts.
          ("February Evening in New York")

This delighted involvement with what most of us continually neglect as trivia or noise, and the ability to carry out, as Marianne Moore and William Carlos Williams do, poetic conquests in the categories of the prosaic, are so natural to Miss Levertov's temperament that she seems scarcely to think of them. She is totally alive to each fluctuation, each breath and vibration of the atmosphere through which she moves with watchful case. Poetry speaks to her with the innocent tongues of children:

> Martha, 5, scrawling a drawing, murmurs
> "These are two angels. These are two bombs. They
> are in the sunshine. Magic
> is dropping from the angels' wings."
>
> Nik, at 4, called
>   over the stubblefield, "Look
> the flowers are dancing underneath the
> tree, and the tree
>   is looking down with all its apple-eyes."
>
> Without hesitation or debate, words
> used and at once forgotten.
>   ("The Lesson")

Even though I find it hard to picture Miss Levertov as an aesthetic theorist musing abstractly upon the rightful function of poetry in a hyper-industrialized society, I am sure that in practice poetry is for her an integral part of the acts, thoughts, and gestures of living. In many of her poems we cross into a world very like our own, with the same ornaments and refuse, commonplaces and strokes of grace, but it is also a world made splendid and different by this poet's wise and clear apprehension of it, her abundant imagination. Poems do more than leap from windows; they appear in the humblest, most mundane things, such as this image, seized from a minute's glance out of the poet's kitchen window over the city at sunset:

> On the kitchen wall a flash
> of shadow:
>   swift pilgrimage
> of pigeons, a spiral
> celebration of air, of sky-deserts.
> And on tenement windows
> a blaze
>   of lustred watermelon:
> stain of the sun
> westering somewhere back of Hoboken.
>   ("The World Outside," I)

The quotidian reality we ignore or try to escape, Denise Levertov revels in, carves and hammers into lyric poems of precise beauty. As celebrations and rituals lifted from the midst of contemporary life in its actual concreteness, her poems are unsurpassed; they open to us aspects of object and situation that but for them we should never have known. And that is no mean achievement for any poet, though it is not the only one Miss Levertov can boast. Another side of her work has slowly asserted itself in two later books, *With Eyes at the Back of Our Heads* (1959) and *The Jacob's Ladder* (1961). I have already alluded to this visionary disposition in discussing "The Instant," but the subsequent pieces rely much more on dream, mystical imagery, and meditation than they do on external conditions that are suddenly transfigured. Some of these poems reflect on the sources of art and imagination and are developments in the line of "Something to Wear," though they find their materials in a deeper layer of consciousness. "The Goddess," "The Well," and "The Illustration," from *The Jacob's Ladder*, are excellent representatives of this category. Other poems press forward on a spiritual journey whose purpose is to uncover the nature of self and its destiny. Miss Levertov's father was a Russian Jew who later became an Anglican clergyman; something of this combination, plus her reading in biblical, Hasidic, and other mystical writings, undoubtedly has had a decisive influence on these poems.

An example of her meditational poetry is the title poem "With Eyes at the Back of Our Heads"; here Miss Levertov brings to focus two planes of reality that seem to be distant but somehow border one another. The problem is how to get front the first into the second, and the poet addresses herself to it:

> With eyes at the back of our heads
> we see a mountain
> not obstructed with woods but laced
> here and there with feathery groves.
>
> The doors before us in a façade
> that perhaps has no house in back of it
> are too narrow, and one is set too high
> with no doorsill. The architect sees
>
> the imperfect proposition and
> turns eagerly to the knitter.
> Set it to rights!
> The knitter begins to knit.
>
> For we want
> to enter the house, if there is a house,

to pass through the doors at least
into whatever lies beyond them,

we want to enter the arms
of the knitted garment. As one
is re-formed, so the other,
in proportion.

When the doors widen
when the sleeves admit us
the way to the mountain will clear,
the mountain we see with
eyes at the back of our heads, mountain

green, mountain
cut of limestone, echoing
with hidden rivers, mountain
of short grass and subtle shadows.

Miss Levertov gives us here a parable of the inner life, a metaphorical presentation of spiritual pilgrimage in the individual heart of the poem appears paradoxical because the mountain, which is an image of paradisiacal proportions, a depiction of the Great Good Place, is seen only within, by intuition (the "eyes at the back of our heads"), while the obstacles to be overcome and those to which we have to accommodate ourselves lie before us. Yet, as in Heraclitus and Eliot's *Four Quartets*, the way forward and the way back are one and the same. Thus movement ahead, with the alterations of the self it requires, will be completed in a reconciliation of the inner image of a desired goal with a personal condition of life. Perhaps what we are being told is, "The Kingdom of God is within you." In this, as in her other remarkable poems, Miss Levertov subtly points the way to see with our whole sight.

(1965)

12

James Wright

WITH THE PUBLICATION OF HIS FIRST COLLECTION OF POEMS IN 1957 IT WAS ALREADY clear that James Wright would establish himself as a poet of independence who pursued his artistic goals without regard for the changeable market of literary fashions. From the start of his career to the present time he has dedicated himself single-mindedly to the demands of his art. This independence in Wright's early poetry made him stand out noticeably during a period that produced a plethora of slick and elegant verse sadly lacking in human substance. In the years following it has been encouraging to see the emergence of a resolute poet who has, all along, taken a harder and lonelier course than he might have done. The consequence is impressive: a body of poetry that has grown and matured with its author, increasing in depth and range, expanding in its means of execution.

In *The Green Wall*, chosen by W. H. Auden as an award-winning volume for the Yale Series of Younger Poets, Wright announced that be had "tried very hard to write in the mode of Robert Frost and Edwin Arlington Robinson," and that he "wanted to make the poems say something humanly important instead of just showing off with language." In that initial book, and in his second one, *Saint Judas* (1959), the poet sets himself to this task through poems that are meditations on his own experience, observations of other lives, dramatic situations; his speech is direct, his sympathy and judgment are undisguised. The world called up by his imagination in poetry is unmistakably the one we know, in which people are born, endure pain, discover love, encounter success or defeat in their efforts, and go down to death. It is not a symbolic world or a self-contained poetic cosmos, but a reality composed of men and women, of animals and birds, of stones and trees, and is usually located in the American Midwest, in Ohio and Minnesota where

Wright has spent so much time. As a poet he is always able to bring us into contact with the physical details of this reality that is so familiar to him and yet distinct and independent too:

> The stone turns over slowly,
> Under the side one sees
> The pale flint covered wholly
> With whorls and prints of leaf.
> After the moss rubs off
> It gleams beneath the trees,
> Till all the birds lie down.
> Hand, you have held that stone.
>   ("A Fit Against the Country")

A number of poems touch on persons or events and are conceived in the same terms of intimate acquaintance and objective existence. Though he looks closely at experience, Wright never tries to maneuver it to his own ends. Frequently, he pauses to study the most ordinary things, which his imagination lifts at last from the limbo of the routine and unworthy in an attempt to search out the meanings lying dormant in them. Each thing has its shadow or hidden life disclosed by the poet.

In the poem "A Girl in the Window," for example, we learn how Wright can take a commonplace occurrence—his casual view, as he sits outside in the evening, of a girl's attractive silhouette in a lighted window—and from it obtain gentle nuances of feeling, in this case the warm but not lustful affection of flesh for flesh. It is also worth remarking how this literal shadow of a girl exemplifies in a poem the shadow of implication I mentioned metaphorically above. "A Girl in a Window" is, in a certain sense, really about the significance of what would ordinarily seem rather insignificant.

> Now she will lean away to fold
> The window blind and curtain back,
> The yellow arms, the hips of gold,
> The supple outline fading black,
> Bosom availing nothing now,
> And rounded shadow of long thighs.
> How can she care for us, allow
> The shade to blind imagined eyes?
>
> Behind us, where we sit by trees,
> Blundering autos lurch and swerve
> On gravel, crawling on their knees
> Around the unfamiliar curve;
> Further behind, a passing train

Ignores our lost identity;
So, reassured, we turn again
To see her vanish under sky.

Soon we must leave her scene to-night,
To stars, or the indiscriminate
Pale accidents of lantern light,
A watchman walking by too late.
Let us return her now, my friends,
Her love, her body to the grave
Fancy of dreams where love depends.
She gave, and did not know she gave.

The collective "we" makes of Wright the self-appointed speaker for what are probably other men, anonymous figures who also enjoy the evening air and in their fancy take this girl for their own. Her appearance at the window inspires these lonely watchers to join their lives with hers briefly in imagination.

The tone of Wright's early poetry is conversational and quiet, which helps in preserving the atmosphere of familiarity already noted; but there are poems—primarily those treating what Auden calls in his introduction to *The Green Wall* "social outsiders"—in which an intensification of vision, prophetic of more recent work, occurs. Such poems look toward the frank self-exposure of Saint Judas. In the figures of those whose actions have transgressed the conventions of the community, and who, as a result, are converted into scapegoats of society, the poet can discover no guilt greater than the culpability that hides itself behind the masks of their respectable persecutors. "Sappho," a monologue spoken by a lesbian who has carried on an affair with a married woman and has now to suffer the social and moral disapproval of her fellow citizens, concludes with an acceptance of pain, of the body's demands that purges the speaker and elevates her to a position of spiritual dignity far surpassing the one her accusers occupy:

For I know that I am asked to hate myself
For their sweet sake
Who sow the world with child.
I am given to burn on the dark fire they make
With their sly voices.
But I have burned already down to the bone.
There is a fire that burns beyond the names
Of sludge and filth of which the world is made.
Agony scars the dark flesh of the body,
And lifts me higher than the smoke, to rise

> Above the earth, above the sacrifice;
> Until my soul flares outward like a blue
> Blossom of gas fire dancing in mid-air:
> Free of the body's work of twisted iron.

In another poem, "To a Fugitive," Wright identifies himself with the desperate grasping for freedom and life of an escaped convict. He dreams of the escape, its violence, and a nightmare of pursuit by dogs and police. The final lines direct the fleeing criminal past every barrier and into a transcendental realm of absolute liberty: "Strip run for it, break the last law, unfold, / Dart down the alley, race between the stars." With other modern poets, as dissimilar as e. e. cummings and Stanley Kunitz, Wright takes the side of the alienated individual, the hunted and persecuted, and opposes the impersonal majority or the monolithic state.

Other poems approach alternate extremities of human experience. Death, to which Wright turns frequently in all of his books, is considered variously through elegies and meditations, and also by means of vision or dream. His religious attitudes cannot be fully determined from such poems, though they are rather obviously heterodox and private. While we sometimes come upon allusions to Christ, to resurrection, and to other religious phenomena in Wright's poetry, a consistent relationship is maintained between the dying or the dead, both human at animal, and the earth whereon they passed their lives. Even the poem "Come Forth," which presents Lazarus's awakening from the sleep of death, unquestionably stresses the ritual reassembling of his body in a celebration of human, earthly existence rather than Christ's miraculous deed. To be sure, a miracle is performed, but the exclamatory closing line focuses on the desired world to which the dead man has been restored: "O blessed fire, O harsh and loving air."

At times Wright lets the imagination confer its own speculative fate upon the dead, but in these cases the view of things underlying the mental reflections is fundamentally one of stoical resignation. The fine "On the Skeleton of a Hound" is a poem of this sort. Here the poet, walking by moonlight, accidentally comes across the skeleton of his old dog and sees that the remains have not been disturbed but have kept an arrangement suggesting orderly repose. The earth, we are told, "nurses him now," sending its life branching through and around these bones:

> Flies would love to leap
> Between his eyes and hum away the space
> Between his cars, the hollow where a hare
> Could hide; another jealous dog would tumble
> The bones apart, angry, the shining crumble

> Of a great body gleaming in the air;
> Quivering pigeons foul his broken face.

The poet then muses on what a group of primitive believers would do with the skeleton. He imagines them practicing magic in the vain endeavor to revive life:

> I can imagine men who search the earth
> For handy resurrections, overturn
> The body of a beetle in its grave;
> Whispering men digging for gods might delve
> A pocket for these bones, then slowly burn
> Twigs in the leaves, pray for another birth.

Having entertained the contrary images of dissolution and rebirth, Wright dismisses both of them and turns away from this "ruin of summer, collapse of fur and bone."

In the remainder of the poem the author seeks resolution in the subjective area of his individual consciousness, where memory and imagination can write their own finish to the dog's story. So the memory of a life is forged into private legend in the poet's mind, finally becoming fixed in the more permanent form of his art:

> For once a white hare huddled up the grass,
> The sparrows flocked away to see the race.
> I stood on darkness, clinging to a stone,
> I saw the two leaping alive on ice,
> On earth, on leaf, humus and withered vine:
> The rabbit splendid in a shroud of shade,
> The dog carved on the sunlight, on the air,
> Fierce and magnificent his rippled hair,
> The cockleburs shaking around his head.
> Then, suddenly, the hare leaped beyond pain
> Out of the open meadow, and the hound
> Followed the voiceless dancer to the moon,
> To dark, to death, to other meadows where
> Singing young women dance around a fire,
> Where love reveres the living.

The closing image of the circle of dancing women (a similar image occurs in a much later poem, "A Message Hidden in an Empty Wine Bottle . . .") hints at a kind of symbolic eternity, a perpetual ring that is the world of the dead but is still plainly linked to life and the physical universe. More than a meditation on death, this poem illustrates the technique of making the personally meaningful, through the power of imagination, into something bearing a more general significance. The latest of Wright's poetry is in some ways an extension of the process in this piece, but radical changes in style intervene. Scattering the bones of the bound to earth in the last few lines, the poet accompanies his actions with a prophecy, one quite in keeping with his vision of the attachment of the dead for the living in the preceding stanza.

> Strewn to the woods, now may that spirit sleep
> That flamed over the ground a year ago.
> I know the mole will heave a shinbone over,
> The earthworm snuggle for a nap on paws,
> The honest bees build honey in the head;
> The earth knows bow to handle the great dead
> Who lived the body out, and broke its laws,
> Knocked down a fence, tore up a field of clover.

Saint Judas continues most of the interests of Wright's first book, but a more penetrating insight into the poet's own person is apparent in many of these poems. The injurious and tragic aspects of existence are examined freely, and the quality of Wright's poetic speech becomes even more direct and terse as he attempts relentlessly to locate and state the human truths that matter to him. "The Morality of Poetry," a dramatic monologue in which the poet starts out to formulate a rather strict aesthetic and ends with a different poetic outlook, is one of the most arresting pieces in the collection. At the beginning the poet walks by the sea—just as Wallace Stevens does in his famous monologue on the activity of poetry, "The Idea of Order at Key West"—thinking over some words of Whitman on the relation between art and reality ("Would you the undulation of one wave, its trick to me transfer . . ."), and at the same time watching in the scene before him the kind of brute material facts from which his literary predecessor had wished to wrest artistic secrets:

> I stood above the sown and generous sea
> Late in the day, to muse about your words:
> Your human images come to pray for bands
> To wipe your vision clear, your human voice
> Flinging the poem forward into sound.
> Below me, roaring elegies to birds,
> Intricate, cold, the waters crawled the sands,
> Heaving and groaning, casting up a tree,
> A shell, a can to clamber over the ground:
> Slow celebration, cluttering ripple on wave.

At the start of the second stanza the poet enumerates the profusion of things in the natural surroundings be gazes upon. The "sheer outrage" of the sea makes it appear to be "hammering itself to death," while "hundreds of gulls" descend into the waves but without any particular sense for the writer who views them carefully ("Counting those images, I meant to say / A hundred gulls decline to nothingness . . ."). This absence of discernible meaning in seemingly random motion and energy, and also in an undifferentiated mass of creatures, proves to be the turning point in Wright's thinking, for he next places against those first impressions the image of an isolated particular, in this case a lone gull:

> . . . high in a cloud, a single naked gull
> Shadows a depth in heaven for the eye.

And the ear, the other organ of sensory perception indispensable to poetry, learns an order of sound from the chaos of received sensations:

> And, for the ear, under the wail and snarl
> Of groping foghorns and the winds grown old,
> A single human word for love of air
> Gathers the tangled discords up to song.

In subsequent lines a statement of aesthetics of a sort not strange to readers of contemporary literature is offered. This notion of the poem is based on a belief in rigorous economy of expression, the exact relationship of part to part, and part to whole; it demands as well, "the rare word for the rare desire." Wright holds to his dominant sea imagery, demonstrating his aesthetic outlook as he presents it; the gull is changed into his metaphor for the poem:

> Summon the rare word for the rare desire.
> It thrives on hunger, and it rises strong
> To live above the blindness and the noise
> Only as long as bones are clean and spare,
> The spine exactly set, the muscles lean.
> Before you let a single word escape,
> Starve it in darkness; lash it to the shape
> Of tense wing skimming on the sea alone . . .

From here on the poem moves in a direction somewhat different from the one it has taken thus far. The poet confesses that the "careful rules of song" he had certainly expected to compose and deliver to a friend (Gerald Enscoe, to whom the poem is addressed) with a "cold lucidity of heart" have not been completed, for he has been caught up and distracted by the ceaseless animation of the seascape. He seems to be saying that his ideas about poetry—its sources and craft, its connections with reality—must be modified in the face of reality. The moon rises, altering the scene and "flaunting to nothingness the rules" he intended to set forth. Reality now assumes the upper hand; it is not something the poet can simply shape to his own will and personal measurement but a dimension of things he must enter, to whose being he must submit himself ("Where the sea moves, the word moves, where the sea / Subsides, the slow word fades with lunar tides"). What he gives to his friend at the conclusion are "echoes of [his] voice" that apparently partake of the sea, the moon, and the restless interplay of elements that have so absorbed him. His poem, we guess, will be a poem of the reality that goes into its making; thus it will fulfill Whitman's wish by learning its essential patterns and laws from reality.

As he did in *The Green Wall*, Wright in *Saint Judas* devotes poems to persons whose lives have brought them to the far side of society's moral boundaries. "American Twilights," "At the Executed Murderer's Grave," and "Saint Judas" are outstanding demonstrations of this poet's obsession with themes of guilt and innocence, justice and punishment, moral right and hypocrisy. Furthermore, these poems show a distinct advance to a franker, more straightforward manner, which is linked, in turn, to the very evident involvement of the poet as an individual in the experience conveyed by the poem. Wright outspokenly blends his voice with that of Jesus' betrayer in the dramatic monologue of "Saint Judas." While this device might not seem any more intimate than is usual with our poet, we perceive quite suddenly that the radical twist he gives to the narrative and the tragic force of its conclusion are distinctively his own:

> When I went out to kill myself, I caught
> A pack of hoodlums beating up a man.
> Running to spare his suffering, I forgot
> My name, my number, how my day began,
> How soldiers milled around the garden stone
> And sang amusing songs; how all that day
> Their javelins measured crowds; how I alone
> Bargained the proper coins, and slipped away.
>
> Banished from heaven, I found this victim beaten,
> Stripped, kneed, and left to cry. Dropping my rope
> Aside, I ran, ignored the uniforms:
> Then I remembered bread my flesh had eaten,
> The kiss that ate my flesh. Flayed without hope,
> I held the man for nothing in my arms.

From this sonnet we can understand, easily enough, Wright's strong feelings about the ambiguities of human motive and behavior, the differences—
in the story of Judas as told here—between design and impulse. Because
man is at one moment weak and treacherous, and at another moment brave
and selfless, it is implied that he should be more sparing in the judgment of
his fellows and freer with his mercy.

"At the Executed Murderer's Grave" strengthens our awareness of the
invisible bonds existing between people, outcasts and criminals included.
In this poem Wright puts himself at the center, engaged in the activity of
meditation. The poem begins with his self-declaration, but it goes on to
consider the figure of George Doty, executed Ohio murderer, whose life and
guilt are finally seen as unavoidably entangled with the poet's, for when
"the princes of the sea come down / To lay away their robes, to judge the
earth / And its dead" he, James Wright (and the rest of us with him), will
have our "sneaking crimes" revealed too. The tone is matter-of-fact, but
sharp; the lines, though rhyming, are blunt, at times rhythmically choppy.
A quality of undiluted directness prevails throughout the poem. The last
stanza serves as a climax to the poet's thoughts about the dead man and to
the harsh self-examination they have provoked:

> Doty, the rapist and the murderer,
> Sleeps in a ditch of fire, and cannot hear;
> And where, in earth or hell's unholy peace,
> Men's suicides will stop, God knows, not I.
> Angels and pebbles mock me under trees.
> Earth is a door I cannot even face.
> Order be damned, I do not want to die,
> Even to keep Belaire, Ohio, safe.
> The hackles on my neck are fear, not grief.
> (Open, dungeon! Open, roof of the ground!)
> I hear the last sea in the Ohio grass,
> Heaving a tide of gray disastrousness.
> Wrinkles of winter ditch the rotted face
> Of Doty, killer, imbecile, and thief:
> Dirt of my flesh, defeated, underground.

The emphasis on a mood close to dreamlike subjectivity which gradually
replaces argument and logical thought in the stanza above prepares the way
into James Wright's most recent poetry. That poetry is still regional in the
sense previously mentioned; and I think it would not be misleading to call
certain poems pastoral, for they do adopt the Minnesota countryside and
farmlands as the setting for a calm, reflective—if not perfectly idyllic—
mode of living. Shepherds may be missing, but animals are not; Wright has

created a haunting yet delicate poem about the kinship between men and horses in "A Blessing":

> Just off the highway to Rochester, Minnesota,
> Twilight bounds softly forth on the grass.
> And the eyes of those two Indian ponies
> Darken with kindness.
> They have come gladly out of the willows
> To welcome my friend and me.
> We step over the barbed wire into the pasture
> Where they have been grazing all day, alone.
> They ripple tensely, they can hardly contain their happiness
> That we have come.
> They bow shyly as wet swans. They love each other.
> There is no loneliness like theirs.
> At home once more,
> They begin munching the young tufts of spring in the darkness.
> I would like to hold the slenderer one in my arms,
> For she has walked over to me
> And nuzzled my left hand.
> She is black and white,
> Her mane falls wild on her forehead,
> And the light breeze moves me to caress her long ear
> That is delicate as the skin over a girl's wrist.
> Suddenly I realize
> That if I stepped out of my body I would break
> Into blossom.

This lovely poem from Wright's third collection, *The Branch Will Not Break* (1963), makes plain, as do the other poems in the book, his very decisive innovations in style, in concern and approach. In the first place, the music and rhythm of these new poems is noticeably different; as Lowell does so often in *Life Studies*, and Roethke in some of his later work, Wright employs extremely free lines of irregular length yet never loses his rhythmical coherence. This change helps to account for the gentle, thoughtful quality, the relaxed character so prominent in "A Blessing." But there is a second change that is perhaps more important, a change in the kind and arrangement of imagery. Wright is not alone in his new poetic practices. Robert Bly, with whom Wright has been in close association in the past few years, is a solid and vocal proponent of these changes too, both in his own poetry (*Silence in the Snowy Fields*, 1962) and in the critical pieces be has written for the journal he edits, *The Sixties*, and for John Logan's periodical of poetry, *Choice*. Another poet who has lately given proof of similar interests is Louis Simpson (*At the End of the Open Road*, 1963), though he lives in California, halfway across the country from the Minnesota residents Bly and Wright. Wright has not, to my knowledge, put down in print any of his ideas about his recent writing, except to say that "from now on [it] will be entirely different"; and so we must rely on Bly's prose for a little guidance. It should be trustworthy guidance, however, because his poems and Wright's are so obviously allied in spirit. In the introductory paragraphs of an omnibus poetry review published in *Choice* (2), Bly discusses the element of "inwardness" which, he feels, distinguishes the true modern poem and is so scarce in the English and American verse of our time:

> Poetry, by breaking up the stanza and moving toward inwardness, is creating for itself a way of expression open to new thought. It is creating for itself an instrument of knowledge, a poem, responsive entirely to the imagination. Poetry's purpose in growing is to advance deeper into the unknown country . . . . In order to penetrate into this country poetry must learn to sleep differently, to awake differently, to listen for new sounds, to walk differently.
>
> What is the unknown country? It is a change in inward life which corresponds to the recent changes in outward life. Let us consider some of the changes in outward life in the last hundred years: colonialism dies, engines are born, the religions lose power, business takes power. The change has been thorough. The change penetrates deeper than we believe. Poetry has been able to describe this inward change better than fiction has. Neruda tells us more about modern life than Faulkner; Rilke tells us more than Mann.
>
> All around us are huge reservoirs of bypassed emotions, ignored feelings, unexplained thoughts. As Rilke said to sculptors, there are hundreds of gestures being made which we are not aware of. The purpose of poetry is to awaken the half of us that has been asleep for many years—to express thoughts not yet thought. All expression of hidden feelings involves opposition to the existing order. Among the great poets of this century who sense this meaning of poetry most strongly Rainer Maria Rilke of Germany, Pablo Neruda of Chile, and Cesar Vallejo of Peru stand out. But there are strong American poets also.

Unfortunately, we are not told who these American poets are, for Bly proceeds to his business at hand in this essay, which is the review of a number of new books of verse. I do not wish to attribute all of Bly's ideas to James Wright, but I think we cannot avoid the fact that in practice both poets attempt to create a poetry of the type described above. Such a poetry relies to a considerable degree on sources below the level of consciousness or of rational thought ("thoughts not yet thought"). Of course, most poetry has always depended upon these well-springs in the preconscious and

the unconscious, but the question raised here is really aimed at the disposition of this material for poetic ends. Reading the recent poetry of Wright,
Simpson, Bly, Merwin, and also some of the poems of James Dickey, such
as "The Owl King" and "Drowning with Others," one notices how frequently they mold their work around a group of images deriving from sub-
liminal regions of the mind and joined by associations of an emotional,
symbolic, and lyrical kind. We must not mistake this enterprise for the
automatic writing and revolutionary philosophy of the French Surrealists,
even though Bly speaks of "hidden feelings" at odds with "the existing
order" in a manner slightly reminiscent of André Breton. To begin with,
we cannot for an instant doubt the intervention and exercise of conscious
craftsmanship upon the imagery of poems such is Wright's, a violation of
Surrealism's iron-clad laws of irrationality without interference. We might
indicate, too, that not all of the images used by these poets are dredged
from the subconscious. Second, I believe that the sort of opposition to the
existing state of things advocated by Bly, while it may involve politics, is
directed primarily toward a renewal of sensibilities, a more comprehensive
vision of the world.

What we do find very often in the poems of Wright or Bly is a fluid,
dreamlike construction; each poem seems to mirror a condition of intense
subjectivity, a moment of extreme perception personal to the poet and yet
capable of stirring subtle and profound responses in the reader. Donald Hall
adds something more to this point in the introduction to *Contemporary
American Poetry*. The writers we have been discussing, Hall maintains, have
put to work "a new kind of imagination" in their poetry. "This new imagination reveals through images a subjective life which is *general*, and which
corresponds to an old objective life of shared experience and knowledge."
Hall's italicized word *general* aids us further in understanding the appeal of
Wright's or Bly's or Simpson's imagery, for that imagery circumvents the
rational intelligence to strike far into the interior world of emotions and
memories, there to awaken forgotten portions of the affective life.

In the poem "Fear Is What Quickens Me," Wright investigates through
the web he fashions of irrational but carefully woven images themes of
human guilt and anxiety growing out of the ties between man and other
creatures, the conquest and urbanization of America (really the urbanization of the modern world), and man's own divided and frustrated nature.
The poem is arranged in three sections of sharply diminishing size, but
increasing force:

1

Many animals that our fathers killed in America
Had quick eyes.

They stared about wildly,
When the moon went dark.
The new moon falls into the freight yards
Of cities in the south,
But the loss of the moon to the dark hands of Chicago
Does not matter to the deer
In this northern field.

2

What is that tall woman doing
There, in the trees?
I can hear rabbits and mourning doves whispering together
In the dark grass, there
Under the trees.

3

I look about wildly.

Logical explication of such a poem will not be easy, nor will it necessarily be
to the point. The poet appears to discourage that conventional approach by
the very way he writes. An alternative is an absorbing of the poem which
will permit its images, their suggestiveness, to permeate the reader's mind
gradually.

In telling us how poems of inwardness voice their opposition to the status
quo, Bly implies, among other things, a love for the rural mode of existence
which both he and James Wright juxtapose with the urban environment
augmented by our contemporary technological and industrial gains. The
two settings are plain in the city images and in the pastoral qualities and
meditative lyricism of *The Branch Will Not Break*. Moral passion, which
generated an ample part of Wright's earlier writing, has been assimilated by
the new poetic method. His criticisms now submit themselves to the ruling
influence of the imagery rather than depend upon any declared moral purpose. The total effect of this imagery is slow and cumulative; it is in accord
with the actual movement of the poems, with their free but apt rhythms,
their shifting but calculated emphases.

Wright's later kind of political and moral criticism, in the poem
"Eisenhower's Visit to Franco, 1959," for example, embodies the same
lyrical and imagistic material we have in the less topical pieces, but here
the magnificently evocative imagery is tinged with irony. To make his
position perfectly clear, Wright draws into the middle of this poem about
state and military leaders and their powerful troops the lone figure of one
of the greatest twentieth-century Spanish poets, Antonio Machado, and
through him recalls not only the negative theme of exile but, more affir-
matively, the perennial life of Spain, unchanged by Franco's dictatorship.

The last stanza, however, again stresses the leaders of state and their force of arms. Wright's critical attitude upholds the ancient human patterns of Spain against the encroaching pressures of the abstract, impersonal state that bosses like Franco try to impose upon the country and its inhabitants. The poem's epigraph is borrowed from the Spanish philosopher and poet Miguel de Unamuno: ". . . we die of cold, and not of darkness."

> The American hero must triumph over
> The forces of darkness.
> He has flown through the very light of heaven
> And come down in the slow dusk
> Of Spain.
>
> Franco stands in a shining, circle of police.
> His arms open in welcome.
> He promises all dark things
> Will be hunted down.
>
> State police yawn in the prisons.
> Antonio Machado follows the moon
> Down a road of white dust,
> To a cave of silent children
> Under the Pyrenees.
> Wine darkens in stone jars in villages.
> Wine sleeps in the mouths of old men, it is a dark red color.
>
> Smiles glitter in Madrid.
> Eisenhower has touched hands with Franco, embracing
> In a glare of photographers.
> Clean new bombers from America muffle their engines
> And glide down now.
> Their wings shine in the searchlights
> Of bare fields,
> In Spain.

Personal perceptions begin many of Wright's new poems, as they did previous ones. In their own fashion Wright, Bly, Simpson, and Merwin are as autobiographical as the more explicitly confessional poets, Robert Lowell, Anne Sexton, W. D. Snodgrass, and Galway Kinnell. We are constantly aware of a particular active consciousness in Wright's work, a consciousness that sometimes dwells on its own history and that generally makes its presence felt as the single agent of what we see and know in any poem. Thus there are poems definitely inaugurated by moments in their author's life;

"Having Lost My Sons . . .," "Milkweed," "Mary Bly," "A Blessing," "I Was
Afraid of Dying," "Lying in a Hammock at William Duffy's Farm . . .," and
"A Dream of Burial" are among the finest of them. But even these pieces,
their specific details picked from Wright's living experience, from events in
his biography, assume, through the poetic means by which they are incar-
nated, the aspect of dream or of trancelike vision that is peculiar to *The
Branch Will Not Break*. In "A Dream of Burial" the poet foresees his own death,
the slow-motion (so true to the quality of dreams) of his dismemberment, and
the period of waiting the soul must be subjected to before beginning its last
journey to a final resting-place. Though the dream belongs to Wright's personal experience, it is doubtless a shared dream, including as it does archetypal images of imagined death in the whitened bones, the mausoleum building, the chorus of mourners, the corridor which is another place of burial
but also the way of exodus for the soul, the sea as symbol of eternity or God,
and the horse as vehicle for the journeying spirit:

> Nothing was left of me
> But my right foot
> And my left shoulder.
> They lay white as the skein of a spider floating
> In a field of snow toward a dark building
> Tilted and stained by wind.
> Inside the dream, I dreamed on.
>
> A parade of old women
> Sang softly above me,
> Faint mosquitos near still water.
>
> So I waited, in my corridor.
> I listened for the sea
> To call me.
> I knew that, somewhere outside, the horse
> Stood saddled, browsing in grass,
> Waiting for me

Poetry of this sort links James Wright to Roethke, Eberhart, and Kunitz in
their visionary and mystical moods. Yet Wright's later technique, which he
has partially in common with Bly and Simpson, has no parallel in the writing of his predecessors in America with the exception of Roethke, whose
sequence poems of psychic life in *The Lost Son* and *Praise to the End* are
similar in their scheme of juxtaposing images from the preconscious mind.
Yet one has to look elsewhere for the poets who have inspired Wright most
thoroughly. Some of them are named in the passage quoted from Robert
Bly—Rilke, Neruda, Vallejo—but there are others, Trakl, Jimenez, Machado,

Lorca, and Chinese poets among them. Both Wright and Bly have published translations from many of these writers, and their appearance is fresh and different and stimulating for American literature. It would be a serious mistake, though, to explain away Wright's newest poetry through his reading. In less than a decade he has reached the forefront of contemporary poets and by his own accomplishments he has advance our imaginative frontiers.

(1965)

Three

13

Char and Michaux:
Magicians of Insecurity

Never being, but always at the edge of Being. . . .
—STEPHEN SPENDER

I

RENÉ CHAR, IN HIS COLLECTION OF MEDITATIONS, *PARTAGE FORMEL*, CALLS THE poet by that name I have borrowed for a title—"magician of insecurity"—a name suggesting a good deal about the activity of the artist at the present time. The entire statement runs like this: "The poet, a magician of insecurity, can have only adopted satisfactions. A cinder never quite burned out."[1] "Insécurité": the French word and the English are nearly identical; and both have their usually unpleasant connotations of instability and vulnerability and lack of equilibrium translated into positive values by association with the poet's task. And that labor, in Char's aphorism, becomes hieratic and magical: the poet is a special being who turns our modern condition of insecurity—of human isolation and unbelief—into something else, his art. Still, we are warned that the poet will find no permanent refuge for himself in the realm of his poetry; his "satisfactions" are simply momentary releases from the "normal" state of shifting balances. This notion comes closer to Keats's "negative capability" than to any other well-known conception of the poet's role in England or America, but it is not the same because, for Char at this point in the twentieth century, the idea of the poem has altered almost completely. The metaphor of the cinder, though highly elliptical, seems to support a certain belief in inspiration through the wind or breath of the spirit which habitually restores life to the dying fire of imagination. "Draw without particular intention, scribble mechanically," says

Henri Michaux of his pictures—and he has made similar remarks about poetic composition, "faces nearly always appear on the paper."* Poems seem to arrive through their author, but neither Char nor Michaux would think the origins supernatural, as Rimbaud apparently did. Instead, they appear to be the result of impersonal forces at work in the depths of the poet's unconscious or operating upon his immediate circumstance.

These two French poets, neither of them young— Char was born in 1907, Michaux in 1899—represent in their separate accomplishments the latest phase in a romantic tradition of poetry which reaches through Lautréamont and Rimbaud in the late nineteenth century down to the Surrealist movement of the nineteen-twenties and thirties. Both Char and Michaux had loose connections with the Surrealist writers and painters, and they bear the residual signs of this affiliation in the compressed, irrational or dream-like quality of much of their imagery. Char, a native of Provence, led a group of the *maquis* there during the war and was a friend of the novelist Albert Camus. His poems and aphorisms show, in their emphasis on will, responsibility, and independence, a genuine affinity with the view of life expressed in *La Peste, Le Mythe de Sisyphe*, and *L'Homme Revolté*. A comparative study of their writings would reveal, I believe, a number of correspondences and the spiritual foundations of one aspect of the contemporary literary conscience.

Born in Belgium, Michaux went to sea as a young man and, later even composed some travel books. He commented briefly on this portion of his life in an introduction to *Peintures* (1939):

> North and South Atlantic. Repatriated ill. Later, voyages in the Amazon, in Ecuador, to the Indies, in China.

> He is and would wish himself elsewhere, essentially elsewhere, other.

> He imagines it. It is very necessary that he imagine it.*

As a painter and writer, Michaux has remained free of attachments and has contained his creative efforts primarily as explorations of the human self. Recently he has experimented with Mescalin and written about it, not in an attempt to force the imagination or fabricate mystical experience but to observe detachedly the effects upon his mind and senses. Char, with his poetic notations on guerilla life under the occupation and his constant reflections on "the poet's vocation,"[2] and Michaux, with his travels through inner spaces, his creation of bizarre worlds that rise like ghostly scenes from hidden layers of the mind, push the method of poetry into new territory. Literature, in their hands, is not a profession, but a condition of life: the indispensable signature of the human person. As Char writes in *Le Rempart de Brindilles* (1953):

Poems are those bits of incorruptible being we toss into the repugnant jaws of death, arching them high so that they ricochet and fall into the formative world of unity.

II

The disposition of much contemporary writing and painting—and this is particularly true in France—has been hostile towards the rigors of formal composition, and fascinated with the secret operations of the mind from which the work of art issues. If we think of the achievement of Paul Valéry, that magnificent poetic heir of Mallarmé and the Symbolist movement, our first recollections are of the classical purity of his verse. Yet this poet saw the production of his art as just one possible exercise of the mind, as one way of investigating the mysterious regulations and potentialities of language. In this insistence on poetry as the outcome of a complicated living situation, and not as the production of transcendental monuments, Valéry prefigured the attitudes of writers like Char and Michaux though his art is very different. He was, at the same time, mathematician, philosopher, essayist, and amateur scientist, as well as a poet. His Monsieur Teste, a creature of sheer intelligence, inhabitant of icy zones beyond human feelings, gives fictional form to the burden placed on the mind in a universe where God has been buried and man savors the headiness and the loneliness of his predicament. In an excerpt from some notes for a portrait of M. Teste we get an indication of Valéry's reflexive thought:

> Everything seemed to him a particular case of the functioning of his mind, a functioning that itself had become conscious, identical with the sense or idea he had of it.
> At the end of the mind, the body. But at the end of the body, the mind. Pain tried to invent a mechanism that would convert pain into knowledge—a process that mystics have glimpsed, vaguely. But the reverse was the beginning of this experiment.
> God is not far. He is what is closest.[3]

But what sort of God can we imagine in this laboratory of consciousness, a room constructed from a Cartesian and Manichean nightmare and filled with mirrors reflecting its own center? Indeed, Valéry writes a few lines after the quotation above: "The notion of external things is a restriction upon inner combinations." It is some version of an essential self which resides like a god in solitude here; the mind alone occupies the pivotal position in subsequent writing. In Valéry's work, fragments, notes, aphorisms, and journals—all the records of self-consciousness—swell out the bulk of his long research, an attempt to arrive, as Maurice Blanchot has said of this whole aspect of modern art, at the end of literature.[4]

From the Surrealists to the recent group of new novelists, including Claude Simon, Nathalie Sarraute, Samuel Beckett, and others, there has been a strong and conscious tendency to focus on subjective states of mind and to depart from the accepted forms and traditions of literature. The doctrines of the Surrealists, if not always their practice, aimed at a literature and painting of revolutionary intention which exalted the impulsive, the illogical, and the chance; they deliberately rejected the influence of the artist's choice or will, the interference of his control. André Breton, poet and leader of the movement, had early studied psychology, was influenced by Freudian theory and even carried on some correspondence with the Viennese psychologist. The goal of Surrealism was to uncover the sources of thought by admitting the subconscious contents of the mind into the world of consciousness, reason, and practical affairs. Though the beliefs and techniques of these artists are remote from those of Valéry, we see again that art is drawn by centripetal force towards the self; its main concern seems once more to be a research into the spirit or psyche. In line with this preoccupation, the development of writing during and after World War II has been away from formal literature and towards what Claude Mauriac has called "alittérature"[5]: an art which no longer wishes to resemble art; an art that divorces itself from the graces of an artistic style or one that purposely cultivates a neutral style; a kind of writing that removes itself from the Establishment of Literature. The novel and the poem withdraw to the opposite extremes of the single consciousness and the confession or to the quasi-journalistic account; they no longer support the arbitrary invention of elaborate fictional worlds and characters. The French veneration of the books of Henry Miller, all of them portions of an endless autobiography, is one of the signs of this antiliterary feeling. Like so much recent painting—Abstract Expressionism, *Tachisme*, and the like—which completely abandons the world of human faces and recognizable objects, replacing it with the painter's instinctive gesture, spiritual and physiological, unmediated by referential signs and images, this literature has assumed its own *informality*, an independence of the laws and expectations set up for poetry, fiction, and drama.

In the variety and unconventionality of his style, and in the momentary combinations of thought and emotion he wishes to discover through language, Char belongs—but in his own individual fashion—to this direction of modern writing. The poetry of Char is of several kinds, but these overlap; and such classification must not be taken as absolute. There are roughly three dominant classes: poems about poetry; poems dealing with the rural life and love he knows so well; poems treating man in extreme situations, especially those of war and death. The majority of his poems are prose poems or aphorisms, but even in these he experiments carefully with sounds and internal rhymes:

> Homme de la pluie et enfant du beau temps, vos mains de défaite et de progrès me sont également nécessaires.

> Man of rain and child of fine weather, I need your hands of defeat and hands of prosperity, equally.

A persistent element of the irrational can be found in Char's imagery. Some of his associations are so far-reaching and curious that a poem may assume the magical properties of a dream. "Le Visage Nuptial" exemplifies this strain in his work, one which shares characteristics of the Surrealist verse of Breton or Eluard: a startling juxtaposition of objects and qualities that defies the order of logical thinking; a mixture of visceral, sexual, and assorted psychological imagery; the sense of being witness to the fluid motions of the mind working loosely on an obsessive theme:

> The desert body, opposed to being mixed, yesterday came back
>   talking dark.
> Descent, do not change your mind; let fall your mallet of trances,
>   acrid sleep.
> Bareness diminishes the bones of your exile and swordplay.
> You refreshen slavery gnawing its own back;
> Snigger of night, stop this lugubrious hauling
> Of glazed voices, lapidated departures.

> Early snatched from the flux of creative lesions
> (The eagle's pickaxe spouts high the splayed blood)
> Beyond present destiny I have led my franchises
> Toward the multivalve sky, the dissidence of granite.

Clearly, this is not Char at his best; the passage—and translation into English only compounds the weaknesses—displays all the confusions and obfuscations of Surrealism at its worst. At any rate, these lines show the limit of Char's use of such techniques.

The basic tendency of Char's poetry leads just the other way from the exfoliation of unconscious images; that is, toward a tight, elliptical statement, an oracular utterance with its meanings compressed or suggested. I have already mentioned the aphorism with regard to Char, for so much of his prose takes that form. These aphorisms are both lyrical and dramatic in their intensity; and in spite of the riddling philosophical tone of many of them, they are fundamentally poems. Constituted of thoughts or emotions that appear to be struck off at the instant they occur, the aphorisms gain a terrible force and beauty through their spontaneity. As Char says, "Lucidity is the wound closest to the sun"; the poet needs to achieve a painful and shocking clarity, a lightning-stroke of vision. Whatever the subject matter of Char's works, and however densely metaphorical they might be, they always bear on man's position in the world. While he is without religious convictions of any sort, this poet possesses a humane and deeply moral imagination. His life in Provence has taught him a reverence for the things of earth: flowers, grass, bushes, streams, the various movements of wind and water, the routine of peasant and farmer. The order and simplicity of existence in these country regions provide the feeling of an ancient human pattern which serves as a framework for the values Char upholds. His sequence of little poems about legendary country vagabonds, "Les Transparents," fills the reader at once with an understanding of the pastoral background against which Char has created his poetic universe. A brief and lovely poem about a lark, "L'Alouette," renders his belief in freedom and the miraculous beauty that is natural only to life:

> Extreme ember of the sky and first glow of day,
> She stands, a jewel mounted in dawn, singing the shaken earth,
> A chime that is master of its breath and free to choose its way.
>
> To kill this enchantress, strike her with wonder.

The world, and the acts of the spirit within it, complete the province of human experience. Beyond that, there is annihilation and nothingness in Char's understanding. What happens here and now, within the physical and spiritual cosmos of man's mortal condition, counts for everything: "Eternity is not much longer than life."

Death, then, assumes the role of a hated antagonist for Char, and is a constant sinister presence in his poetry. The journal he kept while fighting with the *maquis* in 1943–44, *Feuillets d'Hypnos*, one of the most remarkable war documents of our time, reveals this presence at the margin of daily life. The book follows the same plan of aphorism and prose poem we find in *Partage Formel* and *Le Poème Pulverisé*. Here are jottings on events of the day; notes about the poet's companions; indications of peril and risk at every moment; severe self-examinations; incidents of heart-breaking tragedy; and a pervasive belief in the nobility of human life and freedom—with the poetic enterprise an essential part of that dignity. Poetry answers death because it arises from the details of living; it seizes in speech the mercurial transformations of experience and names them. In the face of annihilation, it gives substance to man's passing thought and emotion. The poetic act, if it is genuine, has a promethean air about it, involves danger but attains a zenith which the false poet will never know:

A poem is furious ascension; poetry, the sport of arid banks.

To Char's manner of thinking, literature erupts from the nature of things as
they are, is an act bound by moral implication and human concern, though
not in Sartre's more restricted sense of commitment. The writer effaces himself before his poems; these reach out to other men:

> Accumulate, then distribute. Be the densest part of the mirror of the uni-
> verse, the most useful and the least apparent.

The theme of fraternity runs like a current through all of Char's writings, not
just the war journals, and extends the feeling of community and companionship into the love poems, where the poet gains a more profound relationship
with creation through his adoration of a woman. In "La Chambre dans
L'Espace," one of his later pieces, he draws together these human and natural
lines of attachment. The mutual affection of the two lovers quite literally
creates a "room in space" which includes much more than themselves:

> Such is the wood-pigeon's song when the shower approaches—
>   the air is powdered with rain, with ghostly sunlight—
> I awake washed, I melt as I rise, I gather the tender sky.
>
> Lying beside you, I move your liberty.
> I am a block of earth reclaiming its flower.
>
> Is there a carved throat more radiant than yours? To ask is to die!
>
> The wing of your sigh spreads a film of down on the leaves.
>   The arrow of my love closes your fruit, drinks it.
>
> I am in the grace of your countenance which my darkness covers
>   with joy.
>
> How beautiful your cry that gives me your silence!

Lettera Amoroso, a longer prose poem in the form of a letter, traces the
filtration of love through all the poet's thoughts; his experiences and activities each day; his memories and observations. Love, like the loyalty and
comradeship of men, is one of those personal values on which this poet
relies for his moral outlook.

Though he has the skill of an accomplished craftsman, Char stands outside
the institutional and professional areas of the literary life; no one would ever
mistake him for a grand man of letters. His poetry itself, as I have already
suggested, makes its appearance at the edge of any living situation, on the

very fringe of human actions as they occur. Char might say that poetry is the whole manner of being, physical, moral, and imaginative, of a person immersed in a multifarious existence; poems are hieroglyphics or notations expressive of that life. As an admirer of the early Greek philosopher, Heraclitus, Char tries to obtain something of both the precision and the paradox of his fragmentary writings. The juxtaposition of apparently incongruous elements in Char's work reveals a mystery at its heart, and human experience is suddenly illumined by a light breaking from previously unseen affinities and tensions. Such truths do not allow paraphrase, which accounts for the difficulty of doing more for this poetry than indicating constant themes, subjects, attitudes; these poems, unlike Rilke's or Eliot's do not lend themselves to exegesis. The poetic act projects its author into the future by realizing his desire. But the contradictory nature of this risk lies in the dangerous freedom which the poet enjoys, for he has become the man who invents and tests possibility, the one who refuses to call upon any *external* reserves of belief or creed or dogma. He leaps in advance of his fellows, opening a space through his imagination in which man can see himself renewed and free:

> To escape the shameful constraint of choosing between obedience and madness, to dodge over and over again the stroke of the despot's axe against which we have no protection though we struggle without stay: that is the justification of our role, of our destination and our dawdling.

> We must jump the barrier of the worst, run the perilous race, hunt on even beyond, cut to pieces the wicked one, and finally disappear without too much paraphernalia. A faint thanks given or received, and nothing more.

Surely, this passage from "Le Rempart de Brindilles" is fixed upon the poet's function—really, his ordeal—and it is further charged with allusions to the traditional quest of the public hero of myth, legend, and epic. These references are contained in the assertion of personal freedom over tyranny; the series of perilous tasks; the slaying of the monster; with everything arranged in the climactic stages of the hero's separate labors and their accomplishment. Char views the poet as the spiritual protagonist of mankind:

> Recognize two kinds of the possible: the *daily* possible and the *forbidden* possible. Make the first, if you can, the equal of the second; put them on the princely way to the fascinating impossible, that highest degree of the comprehensible.

*   *   *

Every time proof collapses, the poet responds with a salvo of futures.

The poet of Char's aphorisms is, of course, primarily himself: he follows his own dicta, his own paradoxes by setting them on paper. In a world "faced with the destroyed god," as he believes, the solitary figure of the poet is transformed into the last priest, the final proprietor of value. Char's art does not partake of the fullness of a culture because that is fast dissolving all about him in mechanical utopias and international aggression; but the poems he writes, while they are the most personal statements, are still universal. They invest with significance, with love and care the objects or the moments of life, preserve and place them in a numinous circumference about man.

Char's true line of descent comes directly from Rimbaud, though he never enters that completely *other* spiritual dimension which was the adolescent poet's habitation. His poems do not fashion a whole universe suggesting the "true life" which in our ordinary lives is "absent." Instead, Char's poems are fragments, snatches of the difficult complex of existence at any moment, words in which such bursts of thought, feeling, and instinct receive a transfiguring power; they are—to use a French word appropriate to them—*témoinages*, testimonials to the perseverance and beauty and potentiality of the human estate. Char does not differ much from the Camus who so admired him: each supports the worth of life before the threat of death as absolute, yet each is also endowed with the same religious impulse, which has to seek its outlet within the limitations of the physical world and the meagre span of an individual existence. As Georges Mounin says in his excellent book, Char opposes his common materialist notion of death with the supreme moment of life: a sunlit Grecian noon from whose heights death can be surveyed with "an *objective* serenity."[6] In the prefatory comments to *Feuillets d'Hypnos*, Char speaks of the anonymity and impersonality of these notebooks: "A fire of dry grass might well have published them. . . . This notebook might well have belonged to no one, the meaning of a man's life being so subjacent, to his wanderings. . . ." Though he is most assuredly the author, in a more subtle way he is the mediator, for poetry comes into being through him, in a secret collaboration to which he remains just one party. Char's poems are the "elementary poetry," to use Mounin's phrase[7], of a time, a place, a web of ideas and emotions as these come to focus in language through the writer's presence and craft. The last entry in these diary "leaves" brings together in two brief sentences the entire spirit of his work— a fundamental wish to have his writings give voice to the happenings of life and the things surrounding us, extract their utmost possibility and make them ours:

> Within our darkness, there is not one place for Beauty. The whole place is for Beauty.

III

If Char celebrates man standing "upright" in the wind, the native of a world
dominated by a mortal beauty and a passion which resists, through poetry,
the encroachments of death and dispersal, Henri Michaux immediately
brings his reader into places where uncertainty and fear proliferate, places
ruled by savage ironies. Death would be a relief, one often thinks, in
Michaux's subterranean kingdoms, for it might halt the ceaseless parade of
tortures, the continual metamorphoses, the victimization of almost everyone—including the poet and his readers. Armand Hoog, who sees Michaux's
writings as closely akin to the productions of the primitive mentality, even
warns the reader of the prose poems: "First, you who cross the frontier, abandon all pride in existence or human structure."[8] Every journey on which
Michaux conducts us is an expedition to the interior, to "the space within,"
as he so aptly called his selected poems. Here the darkness falls away to
reveal a scene more familiar to us in our sleeping hours than in our waking
ones. Similar principles seem to apply to both writing and painting for
Michaux. His newest pictures are indebted to oriental calligraphy, are not
too different from some of Mark Tobey's paintings, but many of the others
show forms struggling to come into existence, to be realized. In an illustrated edition of his book of poems, *Exorcismes* (1943), the drawings appear
unfinished: half-figures, half-faces, half-buildings emerge from the empty
whiteness of the pages. The illustrations for an earlier volume, *Peintures*
(1939), are done, by contrast, on black paper. And what Michaux says of
this use of materials is equally applicable to his writings:

> Michaux paints curiously on black foundations,
> hermetically black. The blackness is his crystal
> ball. From blackness alone be sees life come forth.
> A life completely invented.*

The blackness which the poet remarks is comparable to the atmosphere
that first strikes us when we enter the inner world of the poems, a darkened
borderland of the mind where manifestations of a life we could hardly imagine elsewhere acquire visibility.

Events frequently have very matter-of-fact beginnings in Michaux's poetry. The protagonist—and there is nearly always one, even if it is the strange,
anonymous "I" that Michaux shares with us—is discovered pursuing some
ordinary course of affairs, like going to bed:

> I am accustomed to turn out the light at night long before fatigue obliges
> me to.

After a few minutes of hesitation and surprise, in the course of which I hope to be able perhaps to speak to some creature, or to have some creature come up to me, I see an enormous head about six feet across, which, after suddenly forming, dashes upon the obstacles which separate it from the open air.

From out of the debris of the wall which its power tunnels through, it appears (I feel it more than I see it), lacerated all over and bearing the marks of a painful struggle.

For months now it has come regularly with the darkness.

If I understand correctly, the cause of all this is my solitude which weighs on me these days, which I subconsciously strive to get away from, and which I squeeze out like this, finding great pleasure in it, especially in the hardest blows. This head is alive, of course. It possesses *its* life.[9]

And so on, until a few paragraphs later the protagonist, having smashed at everything about him in the attempt to unlock his solitude, finds that nothing is even slightly damaged, "the woodwork has not even squeaked." The quasi-psychoanalytic diagnosis of his state, while perhaps accurate in part, is rather beside the point. Interior and exterior conditions have merged; the spectral head comes alive at the expense of the protagonist—it possesses its life, he does not possess his. This instability of being colors most of Michaux's efforts.

A good number of the poems open with an ordinary observation or description—at least, that is what we first think—and then a change takes place as we alter our vision in accord with this new universe. The result of the change makes us spectators (and nearly participants) of an interior region where no law governs but that of the unexpected. The chance character of much of his writing depends upon the vestiges of Surrealism still clinging to Michaux's idea and practice of composition. In one part of a statement of method written for an anthology, he hints that his experience in creating the poem is not so distant from ours in reading it:

I write as I can, the first time after a bet or rather a rage. I was very surprised by the result of the explosion which was called a poem. That repeated itself. I am not used to it yet . . .

I do not know how to make poems, or regard myself as a poet, or find, particularly, poetry in my poems, and am not the first to say so. Poetry, whether it is transport, invention, or music is always an imponderable which can be found in no matter what genre—a sudden enlargement of the World.[10]

Enlargement is certainly the word; but which world does Michaux mean? The odd nations and peoples which the poet visits in *Voyage en Grande Garabagne* (1936) resemble only superficially the reality we like to think we know. Though Jonathan Swift's writings have sometimes been introduced as parallel to Michaux's, the comparison is a bit faulty. Michaux seldom relies on such devices as giants and midgets and intellectual horses with contrasting philosophies of life; nor can his prose poems be readily interpreted as allegories. Nonetheless, in Michaux's imaginary travels we never lose sight of many recognizable things, since the natives of the various countries—the Hacs, the Hivinizikis, the Emanglons, the inhabitants of the "land of magic"— and their customs always exhibit exaggerated human features or habits, and so thrust back at us an ironical, often horrifying image of our own mores. The Hacs, for example, spend most of their time watching fights, robberies, mobbings, and other acts of violence, which are thought of as games or kinds of mass entertainment by those who engineer them and those who witness them. These general activities are called "spectacles." Throughout the lengthy poem, Michaux—who acts as a traveler narrating his trip in all its detail— offers descriptions of various kinds of "spectacles," including their classification according to type and number. Here is one performance he comes across:

> I found cities where nobody is ever calm, because their appetite for certain spectacles dominates them too strongly. And young people lack the moderation of the old.
>
> It's easy to introduce some savage beasts into a city (there are plenty of them in the outskirts). From out of a traffic jam suddenly come three or four black panthers who, though beside themselves, can endure the most painful wounds. This is Spectacle Number 72. Oh, of course! Those who have organized this entertainment have done so without malice. But when you happen to come upon it, don't admire it too much; move fast, for the black panther comes to a decision very much faster, terribly fast, and not infrequently a woman or a child collapses under horrible wounds.
>
> The authorities undoubtedly make an effort to suppress these diversions, but good-humoredly. "Young people try experiments that are a little brutal," they say, "but there's a fine spirit in it. Besides, this spectacle pays the fine."

The "fine" is a monetary penalty placed by law on all spectacles classified above a certain number; but this is, of course, irrelevant to the brutality of the event and thus underscores Michaux's frightening irony.

It would, perhaps, be very tempting to unravel such a poem as "Chez les Hacs" and assign to its contents specific practices, attitudes, and objects in the contemporary world. Yet this habit would be as destructive of Michaux's writing as it would be of Rimbaud's *Illuminations*: the indefiniteness of

Michaux's meanings and the coherence of his fantastic countries and characters supply them with their power. His "enlargement of the World" creates a singular domain with a relation to ordinary reality—if we can believe there is such a thing after reading Michaux!—that is more effectively felt as a total experience than dissected into components and equations. Furthermore, this writer denies that he is a poet; his intention is not to make beautiful and finished artifacts but to explore the workings of his own mind as a means of relentlessly probing the human situation, the nature of the self. One of the chief effects of Michaux's literary method—and probably the most unsettling—is the reader's shocked awareness that he too has been probed and exposed to himself.

The self falls victim to Michaux but is frequently a humorous one—grimly humorous. His fictional character, Plume, whose partial likeness to Charlie Chaplin has been noticed, is forever trapped by a remorseless logic of events that have nothing to do with his own patterns of thought or behavior. In these pieces, Michaux displays his comic brilliance at the same time that he manages to convey, through the unfortunate matters that befall Plume, states of the inner being:

> Plume cannot say that people are excessively considerate of him on his travels. Some step on him without warning, others calmly wipe their hands on his coat. In the end he has accustomed himself to it. He prefers to travel inconspicuously. As far as possible, he will do so.

That is merely a start for Plume, who must endure misfortune after misfortune. Yet each calamity appears to us less as an occurrence of a tangible sort than a muffled explosion in the psyche. But Michaux carries his dissolution of the integral self even further in those poems devoted to metamorphosis. There is comedy and pathos—and a kind of terror beneath them—in the dilemma of his narrator, a dilemma in which both reader and poet also participate. "Encore des Changements" begins with an enigmatic loss of human identity that precipitates a series of alterations which the protagonist is compelled to undergo, with increasing rapidity and not without pain:

> By force of suffering I lost the limits of my body and irresistably gave up my shape.
>
> I was all things: ants especially, interminably in file, laborious and yet hesitating. It was a terrific moving about. I had to devote all my attention. I soon noticed that I was not only the ants, but also their path. And after being crumbly and dusty at first, it became hard and my suffering was horrible. I expected every moment that it would explode and be hurled into space. But it held firm.

> I rested as well as I could on another part of me, a softer one. This was a forest and the wind stirred it gently. But a storm blew up, and the roots, to resist the increasing wind, bored into me—a mere trifle—but went on to hook so deeply into me that it was worse than death.

> A sudden fall of earth made a beach enter into me, a pebbly beach. Then it began to ruminate inside me and that summoned the sea, the sea.

The poem finally ends, not with the protagonist's victory over his changing forms but with his delight at finding in a book some pictures of animals into whose shapes he has not yet been metamorphosed. He concludes with satisfaction, "Ah, peace." In the manner of the travel poems and other pieces on character or situation, those about the innocent victim or about the person deprived of all but a minimal permanent identity bear the sharpened barbs we quickly learn to spot as belonging peculiarly to Michaux. His nonsense wounds; his horror provokes laughter. By demolishing every rule of literature, the poet frees himself of the reader's demands, turns the tables on him, and confronts that reader with an unfamiliar poetic universe in which he is at the poet's mercy. But, as I indicated earlier, we are led to believe that even before his own creation, for it attacks him as well.

   Some of the themes and methods of Michaux's work suggest a marked similarity to those of Samuel Beckett, especially if we consider them in his trilogy of fictional narratives: *Molloy, Malone Dies*, and *The Unnamable*. Obviously, I do not infer anything like a literary influence one way or the other; each author has traveled his own distinct route for several decades, and each has his uniqueness of expression. Beckett's narrators and characters, however, suffer continual metamorphoses, as Michaux's often do, collapsing at last into the chimerical figure of the unnamable one, inventor of every story that has gone before in the trilogy, who can only be an extension, of the writer himself. So Michaux also makes a profession of alliance with the creatures of his imagination when he writes in the introduction to *Épreuves, Exorcismes* (1945):

> Into the very spot of suffering and obsession you introduce such exaltation, such magnificent violence, together with the hammering of words, that the pain, gradually dissolving, is replaced by an ethereal and demoniacal ball—wonderful state![11]

Thus Michaux's anonymous characters, as well as his humble Plume, are extracted from himself and escape into the cosmos of a poem. Language rather thin literary formalism is taken as the saving instrument by these writers, because through it they can assert, with whatever distortion and agony, the human "substance that prevails," to use a phrase of Wallace Stevens. Beckett's unnamable being finishes his string of tales by crying out into the misty void surrounding him both affirmations and denials of the very words he employs and the stories he tells for nothing. He questions the act of speaking itself, for it is his compulsive talk that prevents him from disappearing into the silence he desires, a blankness against which his last evidence of humanity—the ability to speak—revolts.

In the poems of Michaux and Char, just as in Beckett's novels, the radius of literature has shrunk. Writing has melted into the very moments of life: the moments of beauty and courage, or the ones of unknown conflicts and motives concealed from the examining eye of consciousness. In the confusion of our society, poetry is called into doubt; but, rebuffed as he is, the poet rediscovers within the bounds of his imagination and sympathy the sources of art and language—the words of his condition as a man undefiled by pretense and artifice, fed by the purity of his emotions: the quintessence of poetry.

(1961)

NOTES

[1]All translations of René Char, unless otherwise indicated, are taken from the standard edition: *Hypnos Waking, Poems and Prose by René Char*, selected and translated by Jackson Mathews, with the collaboration of W. C. Williams, R. Wilbur, W. J. Smith, B. Howes, W. S. Merwin, and J. Wright (New York Random House, 1956). Translations marked with asterisks are my own.

[2]See Wallace Fowlie: "René Char and the Poet's Vocation," *Yale French Studies* 21, Spring-Summer 1958, pp. 83-89; also Maurice Blanchot: "René Char" in *La Part du Feu* (Paris: Gallimard, 1949), pp. 105-117.

[3]Paul Valéry: *Monsieur Teste*, translated by Jackson Mathews (New York: Alfred A. Knopf, 1947), p. 80.

[4]See Maurice Blanchot: *Le Livre à Venir* (Paris: Gallimard, 1959).

[5]Claude Mauriac: *The New Literature*, translated by Samuel I. Stone (New York: George Braziller, 1959).

[6]Georges Mounin: *Avez-Vous Lu Char?* (Paris: Gallimard, 1946), p. 31.

[7]*Ibid.*, p. 33.

[8]Armand Hoog: "Henri Michaux, or Mythic Symbolism," *Yale French Studies*, 9, n.d., p. 145; also Wallace Fowlie: "Henri Michaux," *Poetry*, 81, 4, January 1953, pp. 265-268; Philip Toynbee: "Some Trends and Traditions in Modern French Literature," *Horizon*, XI, 65, May 1945, pp. 347-361.

[9]Quotations from Henri Michaux, unless otherwise indicated, are taken from the standard edition: *Selected Writings of Henri Michaux*, translated and with an introduction by Richard Ellmann (New York: New Directions, n.d.). Translations marked with asterisks are my own.

[10]Quoted in the introduction by Richard Ellmann to *Selected Writings of Henri Michaux*, p. xiii.

[11]*Ibid.*, p. xv.

14

Samuel Beckett's Man

"IF I COULD SPEAK AND YET SAY NOTHING, REALLY NOTHING!" THESE ARE WORDS from the torrential monologue comprising the third volume of Samuel Beckett's trilogy of fictional works: *Molloy, Malone Dies* and *The Unnamable*— one of the most remarkable achievements in modern European fiction. One is perhaps excusably hesitant in calling the books novels, for to read through them is to have almost all sense of reality destroyed, to be left at last with a solitary voice echoing its unbelievable torment in a blank, gray void. And the torture—which gradually insinuates itself into the reader's consciousness—is compounded by the speaker's inability to be born into life, or to extinguish the spark of existence with which he has unhappily been endowed.

He, the unnamable one who lends the last volume its title, remains trapped in a hell to which God, man or nature is alien, forced to utter the endless speech of a mysterious "they" that sounds within him. The single hope permitted him is that through the flow of words repeating themselves, deluding him, contradicting each other, occasionally erupting into stories or producing grotesque figures, he may—more by accident than plan—reveal himself, discover the elusive "I" and "me" of a personal identity. This accomplished, he might pass into sheer oblivion. But arriving at that point is apparently impossible; everything misleads and deceives: "I seem to speak, it is not I, about me, it is not about me." Since he cannot speak of himself, the unnamable narrator has vicariously experienced human existence by inhabiting various characters constructed out of his agonized but comic imagination. Who are these characters? They are, of course, the ones who populate the two preceding volumes and Beckett's earlier novels in English, *Murphy* (1938) and *Watt* (1953).

Both *Molloy* and *Malone Dies* are books about writers; that is, in each a chief character is engaged in recording the adventures of a physical odyssey (Molloy and Moran), or retelling in fragments certain portions of his life as if it were another's (Malone). Thus preparation is made for the Cartesian nightmare of The *Unnamable*, in which the speaker tries to forge an existence for himself through the creation of outrageous, crippled buffoons, all of whom collapse into one another and dissolve in the stream of language. *Molloy* opens with the character of that name settled in his mother's room, committing to paper the story of his strange journey to find his maternal parent. Reflecting on his situation before the tale begins, he views the act of writing as compulsive, as something to be done so he may "finish dying." Further, he furnishes us with premonitions of the books to come: an excruciating process that strips life of its flesh. Malone, likewise imprisoned in a tiny hospital or asylum room, writes stories to himself in a battered notebook and awaits his death. The unnamable one has, so far as we know, been deprived of the small comforts of paper and pencil; his narrative is vocal. Even Moran, the police agent who is assigned to capture Molloy, ends by composing a written report. Because the stories themselves are interrupted, doubted, terminated without actual conclusions and—finally denied altogether, we are forced to realize that the concept of fiction as an art is called into question. And this inquiry is closely linked to the themes of the trilogy.

I

Beckett hardly stands alone in his abrogation of the traditional novelistic forms. Joyce, Woolf, Gide, Kafka and Djuna Barnes set admirable precedents. But Beckett pushes writing to its extreme—the brink of silence. Born in Ireland, serving for a time as secretary to Joyce, he is well acquainted with and relies on the history of English literature, while his temperament, experimentalism and saturnine metaphysics belong to recent French art. He has adopted the French language successfully, and he is skilled at translating his work back into English. After the manner of many of his contemporaries, he responds to the conditions of the age with violence, pessimism and mordant humor. Suspiciously he eyes language, corrupted and twisted out of shape by advertising or politics, as an instrument no longer entirely trustworthy. And he looks with disdain at the profession of letters, at literature as an institution. For Beckett there is no solace, as apparently there was for Flaubert or Proust or Mann, in the manufacture of aesthetic monuments. Such monuments will not do in the shambles of our day; they demand a faith in art which cannot now be mustered. Though Beckett, like his characters, resents and disbelieves nearly every line, he continues to write out of

the poet's internal necessity. Words and the tales fashioned by their procession are distortions of the truth, if not open lies.

For the symbolists and post-symbolists of earlier generations, language
provided refuge from the hostile world and, often, a way of recovering a
spiritual realm or a lost absolute. Literature turned into a church of the
imagination; its fictions had a veracity which scientific and historical discourse could not tarnish. But with the advent of World War II and the
existentialist novel (Sartre's *Nausea*; Camus's *The Stranger*) man's responsibility was limited to concrete situations. Any possibility of fleeing this circumstance became cowardly. A new didacticism took root in the novel—a
didacticism which explored in dramatic terms the problems of human conduct in a world without appeal to anything higher than man, a world beset
with the tragic absurdity of death. Samuel Beckett, however, surpasses these
novelist-philosophers in his passionate reduction of the scope of human
activity. He does not ask how to order one's behavior in an irrational environment bounded by time and space, but why there is anything here at all.
Though the question is never answered, we come away from *The Unnamable*
knowing at least that there is something, if only a voice.

To make his quest plain Beckett dispenses with most conventional trap-
pings of the novel and employs a version of the *récit*, the short narrative in
which a single speaker reluctantly offers his experiences for consideration.
With other exponents of the form as diverse as Benjamin Constant and
Maurice Blanchot, Beckett wonders, through his narrators, why experiences
should be put down; but he feels they must. In a certain sense, he banishes
artistic refinements. Of Proust, Beckett once remarked that his book "takes
form in his mind"; and Molloy, ostensibly thinking of his story, says, "It's in
the head." In these works not much energy is expended in keeping up the
credibility of appearances. Along with Paul Valéry's fictive genius Monsieur Teste, Beckett seems to think that a work is irreparably damaged in
the transition from thought to language. In fact, he goes much further and
claims that "the myth of our imagination" and "the caricature furnished by
direct perception" are both distant from reality. Little wonder then that in
The Unnamable the events and figures of the two previous books are drained
off by their revelation as products of what amounts to solipsism: "All spins,
it's a head, I'm in a head."

II

While it is quite difficult to paraphrase with accuracy the occurrences in
the three volumes, a rough attempt should be made so we can follow the
progressive spiral of the narratives as they circle toward their source. In the

first volume *Molloy*, an aged and crippled hulk of a man, for reasons unknown sets out to visit his mother. Strangely, he cannot recall the town in which she resides and, equipped with a bicycle and crutches like a Mack Sennett clown, he pursues a haphazard course as, simultaneously, his physical afflictions increase. His peregrinations include an encounter with the law, a stay with a woman who takes him in and tries to domesticate him and an idyllic episode at the seashore, where he sits and sucks pebbles. Molloy's decrepitude reaches such a stage that when he goes from the beach into the forest he is compelled to lie flat on the ground and pull himself forward with his crutches. In the end he gains the farther edge of the wood and sees an open plain; beyond are the spires of a town—perhaps, though not likely, the one he seeks. There Beckett abandons him; the rest of the book takes up the pursuit of Molloy by the policeman Moran and his son. The assignment is given to Moran from remote authorities; curious preparations for the journey follow; after the two depart they undergo a process of alienation and decay. Though Moran kills a stranger—sometimes thought to be Molloy—he never comes in contact with his quarry. Finally he returns crippled like Molloy or his double.

In *Malone Dies* travels are restricted to mental operations. The invalid Malone makes up vague fables about a boy (Sapo), who later is metamorphosed into the older MacMann, a hospital inmate resembling the narrator. Between spasms of storytelling Malone occupies himself with a scrupulous survey of his room and his possessions. In the trivial pursuits of his characters Beckett continually depicts the emptiness of life: Molloy's game with stones; the abiding interest of Watt and MacMann in hats and overcoats; the concern of Vladimir and Estragon with boots (in *Waiting for Godot*). These preoccupations, Plus the recounting of stories, are distractions from the prospect of an existence which simply "goes on." Malone does die, just as he finishes off MacMann, his own creation; and, we are led to think, it would be well and good if this were the end. It isn't. Malone's tale is done, but the story, to use a word applicable to the whole trilogy, is ceaseless: a monologue that begins anew with the disclosure of another voice.

In more ways than one that voice is final in *The Unnamable*. It is clear that the actions of characters and the representation of external reality, abbreviated from the outset, dwindle as one proceeds from book to book. In the third volume the setting is a cloudy, indefinite space shot through with glimmerings of light. Seated on his haunches, a being without name fills the claustrophobic atmosphere with a speech containing shredded accounts of two other figures, Mahood and Worm, in whom the being looks vainly for himself. But this is a small part of the ever-changing scene imparted by the speech, which moves feverishly from despair to hope and back, from bawdy comedy to disgust and resignation. As Wallace Fowlie has noted, this creature has dropped out of life (evidenced through the disappearance of earlier characters who were somewhat in life) and cannot regain entrance. Though the unnamable denies validity to Murphy, Molloy and Malone, they were, his only ties with a tangible world, the unpleasantness of which is at worst preferable to present suffering. In confusion and fury he tries to locate his own image and abolishes all else:

> Ah yes, all lies, God and man, nature and the light of day, the heart's outpourings and the means of understanding, all invented, basely, by me alone, with the help of no one, since there is no one, to put off the hour when I must speak of me.

At the last page the unnamable's actual story is yet to be told. And because of the demonic pressure for self-identification he resolves—still lacking any assurance of victory—to carry on the embattled search.

He has no choice. Each of Beckett's works reflects the same dilemma—one of waiting. Only the form, the outward manifestation, varies. All the characters—in the plays as well as in the novels are one, a fact that deepens their loneliness and desolation. Godot will never really arrive; nor will the unnamable close his monologue. For Beckett the curse and the marvel of human existence are its tenacity. Characters run through a gamut of moods and attitudes toward their individual plights, but they assert themselves vigorously to the end. Even then, they are removed from our sight by the exigencies of literary or dramatic composition; in effect, they exist beyond the arbitrary conclusion of any single work. How should Beckett falsify this theme which haunts him by contriving novels in the ordinary sense, novels that probe the psychologies of contrived personages, novels that raise and resolve unreal conflicts? Such devices mean little to him. There is one story; it is his own, and perhaps ours. With Molloy, Moran and Malone—those characters so personal—he composes a testament to the passage through the world of that paradoxically heroic and insignificant presence, human consciousness. In the nothingness, that presence leaves a small trail that waits to be seen.

(1959)

15

Earth Hard:
David Ignatow's Poetry

Earth hard to my heels
bear me up like a child . . .
—DAVID IGNATOW

Multitude, solitude: identical
terms and interchangeable by the
active and fertile poet.
—BAUDELAIRE

DAVID IGNATOW IS A LATECOMER, A DARK HORSE IN, CONTEMPORARY AMERICAN
poetry, chiefly because he was never recognized nor did he think of himself
as a member of the poetic generation to which he properly belongs by age—
that is, the generation which includes, among others, Lowell, Berryman,
Nims, Schwartz, and Shapiro. He has written steadily in isolation and independence for several decades. His earliest books, *Poems* (1948) and *The
Gentle Weight Lifter* (1955), were published by small presses, one of them a
New York art gallery. Only with the appearance of three successive volumes
in the Wesleyan Poetry series, beginning with Say *Pardon* (1961) and culminating recently in a fourth, comprehensive collection of *Poems 1934-
1969* (1970), has Ignatow's work become generally known for its remarkable imaginative and stylistic accomplishment, and then among a younger
generation of poets and readers. A look at the developing course of his art
over thirty-five years discovers no abrupt changes in manner but rather an
extraordinary firmness of purpose and direction, the cultivation of a language and approach to experience that could derive only from the most
severe demands upon himself.

The reader can merely guess at the private cost of these demands, but he can discern their sources in Ignatow's work and his comments about it. First, there is his will to face himself squarely, to bear witness to every failure, weakness, destructive impulse, and to a nearly overwhelming feeling of guilt ("Guilt is my one attachment to reality," he writes in a much-quoted line). Ignatow constantly explores his inner life, carrying what he finds into the light, bearing whatever pain it may cause him. But such self-examination is just one side of the coin in his poetry; the second side involves him in the lives of others, for his aim, beyond the earliest poems, is to become a poet of the city—specifically, of New York—to make himself, as he says, "the metaphor of his community."[1] Awareness of identity and of self-integrity depend not simply upon the ability to scrutinize with honesty and care one's inward being, but also on the capacity for extending the self outward into immediately surrounding existence. "My kind of writing forces me to go out among people," Ignatow remarks. "I'm not a social poet. I'm a poet of individuality and I only know my individuality by interacting with others. I can't do less than respond as I'm made to respond by environment. Yet I'm conscious, as a poet, of exactly what's happened to me."[2] Precisely here, at the margin of daily existence, where the self encounters others or turns away to look within, the elements of his experience take the shape of a unique poetic articulation. The word "poetic" does not in this instance awaken any of the usual lyric connotations; the speech of Ignatow's poems, mined from the spoken language, earns its victory the hard way, by educating the reader's ear to realize and appreciate its marvelous flexibility and strength, its subtle beauty.

The creation of that poetic speech or voice which lends Ignatow's writing so much forceful singularity can be traced in part to influences avowedly decisive for him. These include, he tells us, Baudelaire, Whitman, William Carlos Williams, and the Bible.[3] For Ignatow the ideals and values of Whitman are questioned and counterbalanced by the sombre, pessimistic vision of urban life to be found in Baudelaire's poetry and prose poems. The former's optimistic view of America—to which the French poet might well reply, "Dreams! Always dreams! And the more ambitious and delicate the soul, all the more impossible the dreams" (translated by Louise Varèse)— are vigorously challenged, inverted, by the harsh realities of the twentieth-century America which Ignatow's poetry so stunningly captures. In "Communion'" Ignatow begins each of the poem's three stanzas with the same declaration of Whitman's desire for brotherhood, and proceeds to demolish it through the bitterly ironic disclosure of the fate of such hopes for America. Enmity and death pervade the poem's atmosphere, and a desolate prophecy of annihilation brings it to conclusion, thus simultaneously effacing Whitman's vision—though not, of course, his imaginative or poetic greatness which Ignatow surely admires. The delicate, unobtrusive way in which he uses the word "contended" in the first stanza, allowing it to accumulate a terrible suggestive power in terms of the spirit of free enterprise as the poem progresses inexorably toward its suicidal climax, is indicative of Ignatow's characteristic skill:

> Let us be friends, said Walt,
> and buildings sprang up
> quick as corn and people
> were born into them, stock
> brokers, admen, lawyers and doctors
> and they contended
>   among themselves
> that they might know
>   each other.
>
> Let us be friends, said Walt.
> We are one and occasionally two
> of which the one is made
> and cemeteries were laid out
> miles in all directions
> to fill the plots with the old
> and young, dead of murder, disease,
> rape, hatred, heartbreak and insanity
> to make way for the new
> and the cemeteries spread over the land
> their white scab monuments.
>
> Let us be friends, said Walt, and the graves
> were opened and coffins laid on top
> of one another for lack of space.
> It was then the gravediggers slit
> Their throats, being alone in the world,
> not a friend to bury.

When national and historical ideals are perverted, employed as tools for self-promotion or as weapons against others, Ignatow finds himself in the difficult situation of so many contemporary poets who also lack any kind of religious commitment, namely, that of possessing no ideological or meta-physical frame of reference from which to comprehend experience, derive values, and order imaginative vision. This condition assumes primary importance in Ignatow's case, for he turns this deprivation to positive account and develops from it his own notably anti-poetic "flat style," which likewise owes its inception to a close study of the abstract techniques of pioneer modern painters, as well as his wish to fashion a poetry utilizing the idiom of urban American speech. He comments:

The *flat* style is precisely the style of Picasso when he is working with urban images. The *flat* style is the style of Matisse for which he was condemned at the beginning. It is the cubist and abstract style divorcing itself from perspective. In fact, there no longer is perspective. There is the thing itself—that which we must concentrate on. We can no longer put anything or any idea in a context of references to other or more distant goals or larger perspectives in life. We must work with what we have, and what we have lived through—our sensibilities, and nothing else.

This is especially true in the arts where the authenticity or originality of the work derives from the uniqueness of the artist's expression. The fact of the matter is that I studied the flat style of Picasso and Matisse and Mondrian and saw its usefulness—let me say, significance—for poetry, and I began to use it. At that point, I abandoned the romantic rhetoric I was enjoying in myself so immensely, finding it inadequate to my experience. The work of William Carlos Williams confirmed the direction I began to take.[4]

It becomes evident from these remarks on the loss of perspective that the enterprise of religious and/or cultural allusion which does lend perspective to the work of Eliot and Pound—and, later, in varying degrees, to that of David Jones, Robert Duncan, Charles Olson, and Nathaniel Tarn, let us say—is for Ignatow, as man and poet, quite impossible to sustain without fabrication. Alternatively, he returns to the immediacies of existence, the particulars of here and now, "the thing itself," and concentrates single-mindedly upon them. Two brief poems, printed next to each other in *Figures of the Human* (1964), reflect this preoccupation. In "The Sky Is Blue," a recollection from childhood of his mother's angry command and his own view at that moment of the blank sky outside the window in which the sole thing visible is the contingent one of a neighboring roof, he obliquely challenges, through his boyish (but now pointed) query, her presumed belief in some kind of fixed order comprehending everything, with even a niche for his toy soldier:

> Put things in their place,
> my mother shouts. I am looking
> out the window, my plastic soldier
> at my feet. The sky is blue
> and empty. In it floats
> the roof across the street.
> What place, I ask her.

"The Song," which follows, emphasizes more directly and definitely the absence of transcendental meanings for existence. The "emptiness" to which the song is surrendered in the opening line Ignatow refers to elsewhere as "the emptiness of consolation"; he continues: "How do we console ourselves

in a world that can no longer be motivated by the ideals of the nineteenth
century? We haven't any ideals to speak of now and the spirituality is the
sense of defeat. For us it's a defeat that forces us into a kind of humble-
ness."[5] As the poem implies, in the appearance and disappearance of creatures and things in the universe, in the activities of men, whether recre-
ations, hobbies, or the writing of poetry, there is no further significance. For
Ignatow, nothing will be rescued from oblivion by the benevolence of a
Divine eye: living beings, the acts and gestures that occur within time and
space, are simply and finally themselves and are subject to the fate imposed
by the temporal order, which is to vanish, in the longer reaches of history,
without a trace:

> The song is to emptiness.
> One may come and go
> without a ripple. You see it
> among fish in the sea,
> in the woods among the silent
> running animals, in a plane
> overhead, gone; man
> bowling or collecting coins,
> writing about it.

Having taken these poems as representative of a fundamental attitude underlying Ignatow's work, a conviction of the severely reduced scope of possible beliefs or ideals for himself and contemporary man, one must still account for certain poems in the third section of *Say Pardon* in which the figure
of God appears, for they will help us to discern what values he struggles for
through his writing. Altogether, these poems at first create an effect of ambiguity and uncertainty. In "A Semblance" the poet, standing at his mother's
graveside, hears the rabbi's prayer for the dead with bewilderment and can
only "follow unsteadily / its meaning"; in conclusion he asserts: "You pray / to
the air." He wonders, in "Without Fear," if the "self-pity, / terror and love"
which comprise the constant ingredients of human feeling aren't in themselves sufficient "to preserve us" so we might affirm, in a phrase echoing Eliot's
in "Little Gidding" (in turn borrowed from the fourteenth-century mystic
Juliana of Norwich), that "all will be well," since it is through the rhythm of
these contrasting, recurrent states that the Divine becomes manifest: "Without fear of contradiction," he ends, I give you God in my life."

Two other poems, "I Felt" and "The Rightful One," come closest to estab-
lishing the kind of basic principle we grow conscious of as we read through
Ignatow's poetry. Here the Divine and the human belong to the same dimension of reality, which is earthly, mortal, and also profoundly Christian
in a certain sense, one might add, though completely devoid of ecclesiastical,

transcendental, or supernatural implications, thus once more confirming a belief in the closed perspective and the resulting necessary confrontation with existence as it is at each moment. An obligation is placed upon the poet in "I Felt" to authenticate his life, to make it his own by loving and caring for another. The poem plainly indicates that the poet must deliver his life from the Lord—which I understand as meaning to take it away from the realm of potential or idealized virtue and into the world of specific activity, turn it into the realized gesture of himself toward another person; in this manner alone can he win the attribute of selfless love ordinarily relegated to the Divine, and so enter also his own existence through the fulfillment of its inherent possibilities:

> I felt I had met the Lord.
> He calmed me, calling me
> to look into my child's room.
> He said, I am love,
> and you will win your life
> out of my hands
> by taking up your child.

"The Rightful One," a longer, more dramatic poem, begins with the poet's son announcing excitedly the presence of God in his room, arrived there because the boy, unlike his father, "had searched for Him." The appearance of the Divine figure is all too human: He is scarred by experience, worn with fatigue and the burden of too much knowledge, and comes to disclose the inevitability of weakness, the necessity of suffering, and, in spite of that, the need to bless, to bestow love and "forgiveness":

> He had come. I saw Him standing,
> his hair long, face exhausted, eyes sad
> and knowing, and I bent my knee,
> terrified at the reality,
> but he restrained me with a hand
> and said, I am a sufferer like yourself.
> I have come to let you know.
> And I arose, my heart swelling, and said,
> I have failed and bitterness is in me.
> And he replied, And forgiveness too.
> Bless your son. And I blessed him
> and his face brightened. And the Rightful One
> was gone and left a power to feel free.

Such freedom as is available here depends, I believe, on the acceptance of one's own life, which, as in "I Felt," achieves completeness only when it includes responsibility and love for others. (This freedom stands in absolute opposition to the negative or selfish state of being free from obligation to anyone but oneself which Ignatow countenances in the later "Ritual" poems and "Rescue the Dead.") In both poems blessedness, freedom, and integrity must be earned in terms of present existence; what value they might have elsewhere Ignatow does not know, for, as we have seen, he has no faith in the transcendent, in perspective, and admonishes us to recognize the "emptiness" beyond which we have already encountered. Value, when it does emerge, as in the poems just discussed, has been labored for and discovered within the context of the work, or rather in the difficult, complex process of transforming daily experience and perception into the language of poems. Ignatow repeatedly uses walking—frequently in the sense of a dogged persistence against the odds and of bearing the onus of pain and guilt—as a highly evocative metaphor for the slow, hard progression through a lifetime and, by implication, for the strenuous activity of writing poems along the way:

> I've got to have the things that hurt me.
> People want to deprive me of them in pity.
> It is they who are made miserable
> by my painful life, and I am sorry
> for them without weights upon their feet,
> walking.
>
> ("Walking")

With the realms of idealism scaled off for him in both the religious and socio-political sense, Ignatow abandons himself to the world of the actual, the day-to-day, and to the environment he inhabits. Ignatow grew up in Brooklyn, which, after he began to know New York as a city in his teens, he came to think of as suburban, "as that great part of America that lived under the trees and among the grasses";[6] subsequently, at the age of eighteen, he moved to the city. The earliest pieces in *Poems 1931-1969* do not reflect the deep impression resulting from his exposure to the city but are instead love poems; if they are not as yet revelatory of the dramatic interaction between the poet's self and his urban surroundings, certain of them, such as "Pardon Keeps the Sun," are notable for their candid self-scrutiny and careful delineation of the relationship of lover and beloved, both of which are important and enduring themes in Ignatow's writing. Other poems of the 1930s—"For a Friend," "Forks with Points Up," and "My Neighbor" are among the best—show an increasing preoccupation with rendering the complicated mode of life into which he had thrust himself, in other words, with "writing a poetry of New York." That attempt, to be successful, required the creation of a style, a form of language and rhythmic movement

avoiding the "poetical," through which his urban experience could be in-
carnated:

> I had to meet the city on its own terms if I was going to get it into my work.
> And that meant being overwhelmed by the city's life in order to emerge
> with all the facts. This is how language becomes transformed from one
> historical period to the next, through history or the individual. I was not
> going to write in the iambic pentameter when the very tone and pace of
> the city denied such a regular, predictable and comfortable style—com-
> fortable, of course, from long use and its acceptance, as style. I wanted the
> spirit of the city in my poems while I, as a city man, knew how to manipu-
> late the spirit in terms of its language. I was the city's artist and as its artist
> I could feel both in and out of the city at the same time.[7]

In these observations and aesthetic convictions Ignatow demonstrates
his affinity with William Carlos Williams, whose poetic career was dedicated to developing a new metric, a "measure" evolved from American speech
and liberated from the bond with traditional English rhythms and forms.
Williams immersed himself in his New Jersey environment of Rutherford
and Paterson and in the details of his life as a man and a practicing physi-
cian. In "The Wanderer," the opening piece in his *Collected Earlier Poems*,
he symbolizes his artistic ties with the immediacies of existence and its location by his leap into "the filthy Passaic" river, where he receives, as in an
initiation rite, new knowledge within himself, including even the "rotten-
ness" and "degradation" of the place and the lives closely surrounding his.
This poetry of location or environment, which may incorporate geography,
topography, and history as well, and puts the poet in the personal context
created by direct contacts in relationships with the past or the present or
both—that is, the milieu of his life—is visible in different ways in the writings of Charles Olson (its chief theoretician), Louis Zukofsky, Edward Dorn,
Gary Snyder, and Denise Levertov, to name the most prominent. For Ignatow,
who can be linked with them, though only in his own independent fashion,
the poetry which he sets out to write must be capable of embodying the joy,
terror, evil, shame, and tragedy discovered each day in himself and in the
lives of other city inhabitants, but it also demands a plain, unvarnished
language that can, in the interests of accuracy and truth to experience,
present those qualities in all of their intensity, drawing out their basic human implications while resolutely avoiding any kind of adornment. The
reader, abruptly greeted by these bare essentials, gradually realizes how much
poetry is in them. A strong, if partial, statement of the aesthetics of Ignatow's
type of poem can be found in the poetry itself, and in a variety of different
pieces. One of them, "Singers of Provence" from *The Gentle Weight Lifter*,
contains an unmistakable refusal to hide, beautify, or dissemble in writing.

Unlike the Provençal poets who, fearing for their safety, disguised the significance of their songs, the contemporary poet needs to bear testimony, to make known what he has seen:

> You made music
> to cover your guilt, you were all scared;
> and you sang to bring on the ecstasy of lies;
> while we with the door wide open
> on the scene of the crime face the day
> clearly with these words: We were here
> and we witnessed the deaths and drownings,
> the deeds too dark for words;
> they would rumble in the belly meaninglessly,
> but we speak our minds and the song sticks.
> The people sing it, the singer believes it,
> the air springs with a new song.

Evidence of this receptivity and honesty is inscribed on every page of Ignatow's poetry and stems directly from his dedication to the hard, often frightening and dangerous task of exposing himself to, even assimilating, the experiences and torments of others ("My life has been a seeking / to identify with pain and suffering . . ."), frequently reaching out to adopt their voices and identities so as to recognize them in himself, himself in them. Penetration of the existence of another person becomes simultaneously a means of self-knowledge. In "Day My Dream" Ignatow comprehends those unpleasant or destructive aspects of life which the majority of people like to ignore, content with themselves and their own well-being, or to protect themselves from, armored with conventions which proscribe sensibility and empathy. Startlingly, the poet acknowledges that he feels contradictory behavior is "normal" because he has intimate acquaintance with all sides of himself, the secret impulses toward pleasure or negation at work in the depths of the psyche when sleep loosens the control of reason and conscience. The dying fish, unnoticed by passersby, the "terror" of the stalked deer to which the hunters are insensitive, the slovenly, decrepit old woman who embarrasses the bus passengers by her reminder of the frailty of human dignity and poise Ignatow can fully understand, for he has uncovered the same fears, weaknesses, and incongruities in his own psyche:

> Fish tossed on sand,
> flopping for air; overhead
> two-legged people stride about.
> Such a scene is normal to me.
>
> Deer hunted through the woods,
> heads high in terror. Men train

> normal guns on them.
>   The explosive
> mouth that fragments the atmosphere;
> the old woman who drools on a bus
> crowded with intensely dressed salesmen.
> How they look away in disgust.
> All this is normal to me,
> as the face in my mirror each morning—
> lined by guilt of the night;
> lips relaxed from rightness, creases
> wider the eyes enfolding pleasure
> in dark folds.
>   Since the tunnel
> in which I have acted out my dreams
> has been lit with these passions,
> revealing my form, I converse with all,
> is if night were day and my dream.

In another poem, "Nocturne," from the same period (the 1940s) the poet puts himself clearly on view, again rejecting subterfuge or masquerade. He shows us himself "Sitting at [his] window" at night, with lights on and the shade up; and just as he willingly reveals himself in the interests of truth, so he may expect to

> look into the windows of others,
> giving warning to those
> who like to hide.

His admitted intention here is to probe degradation, to perceive "that moment when human passes / into beast," obviously not for sensational purposes or out of prurient motives but essentially "to distinguish the difference" and thus locate some groundwork for what is properly human. Once more, as in "Day My Dream" and many another poem, Ignatow has involved himself with the scale of man's behavior, sounding those subconscious layers of the mind that dictate our actions but which we usually prefer to forget since cognizance of them breaks down pride and self-esteem, opens a window on our fears, guilt, and covert energies. But the poet does not flinch from these realities and asks us to observe exactly those elements present in ourselves. How else shall we begin to try to live as humans, brought together in a mutually shared world?

> Ugly is the word
> and do not be scared of mirrors.
> The sewer runs through the neatest block,

the tide carrying crud and contraceptives,
and I have thoughts to make the hair
of strangers stand on end.
                    We are together
by contact of our hands on furniture,
books, plates and fruits of the corner peddler's
busiest intersection.

So, as he writes in another poem, "To say what has to be said here, / one must literally take off one's clothes," and proceeds to do it, finding in his nakedness a relationship: "I am / of my own kind / and my heart beats. / I have brothers." Self-exposure and vulnerability enable Ignatow to participate in the common life of humanity and bring to his poems revelations of moods and emotions otherwise unspoken. A second poem with the title "Communion" contains as much irony as the one already discussed but of a different sort:

In the subway I had the impulse to kill
and sat and stared straight ahead
to avoid the eyes of strangers
who might read my dread
and when finally I had the courage
to shift my gaze from the poster above
I saw to my dismay the eyes of others
turning away.

Ignatow's characteristically plain, conversational diction and his quiet tone lend this little poem an almost placid surface which is suddenly disturbed by words such as "kill" and "dread," as well as the phrase "eyes of strangers" that creates for a moment a spasm of paranoiac terror. The absence of any punctuation forces the reader more completely into the poem to find for himself its rhythmic flow, a movement which, because of its lack of ordinary guideposts, comes to seem synonymous with the felt time of the experience itself. The thematic implications remain purposely indefinite yet highly suggestive. The poet senses in himself a terrible initiative to destroy, not for a discernible reason but apparently from a concatenation of psychic causes whose motives are invisible. At the same time, he has enough self-possession to realize that this eruption of malevolent desire must be held in check, and here the poem pivots about the word "dread." "Dread" catches up the various ramifications of his condition: fear at what has announced itself within him, anxiety over the problem of maintaining self-control in a public place, and, of course, a kind of horror that what is going on inwardly—the struggle of will, the tumult of emotions—might be read on his face by the other passengers. With an effort, he fixes his gaze on an advertising

poster until the impulse passes, or is at least manageable. Only then is he
struck with another disclosure, more far-reaching than the first. With "dismay" he discovers that he has been watched during his bout with his feelings and, in addition, that those feelings have been interpreted, a fact which
draws him into a strange union (or "communion") with the passengers,
since they must also, at times, have known the same inspiration to murder
in order to perceive it and now look aside, abandoning to the poet a part of
themselves they should best like to forget. Through this haunting brief episode, Ignatow again forges the links of fraternity.

Living in New York, working at a variety of jobs to maintain himself and
his family, always under the threat of economic insecurity, the pressures of
his superiors, Ignatow has realized comprehensively the nature of modern
urban experience; it has formed the very substance of his existence for a
period of more than thirty years. As a result, his poetry abounds in instances
of closely rendered observation of individuals at their tasks, at lunch, in the
streets, during the working day. It is impossible in an essay to cover all such
poems, but "The Fisherwoman," as an example, with its extremely sensitive
description of mundane labor, manages to simulate, through the skillful progression of its lines, the actual physical feeling and pattern of this woman's
procedures, the movement of her body and the movement of her day:

> She took from her basket four fishes
> and carved each into four slices
> and scaled them with her long knife,
> this fisherwoman, and wrapped them;
> and took four more and worked
> in this rhythm through the day,
> each action ending on a package
> of old newspapers; and when it came
> to close, dark coming upon the streets,
> she had done one thing, she felt, well,
> making one complete day.

Occasionally, a poem of this kind may open a dimension beyond itself,
assume something of the quality of a parable, in which the activities of the
particular person depicted take on a more portentous aspect than mere facts
allow, as if, indeed, they signified in their peculiar fashion the larger configurations of life. Two poems, "'The Errand Boy I" and its sequel, among
others from Say Pardon, are representative; I quote only the first:

> To get quicker through the day
> and to bring on night as a blessing,
> to lie down in a sleep that is a dream
> of completion, he takes up his package

from the floor—he has been ordered
to do so, heavy as it is, his knees weakening
as he walks, one would never know
by his long stride—and carries it
to the other end of the room.

Readily enough, one can detect in these lines the sort of symbolic implications I've referred to: the burdensome task is not simply detailed for its own
sake, as in "The Fisherwoman," but tends, especially through the resonant,
allusive diction of the opening half of the poem, to suggest something of
the character of man's lot. The biblical overtones aroused here hardly need
mentioning, particularly those in which God, expelling Adam and Eve from
Eden, places upon them the requirements of hard labor. What Ignatow adds
is the notion of reward and fulfillment man finds for himself in doing the
things imposed upon him by implacable necessity, and doing them without
exhibiting their arduousness. Yet this "dream of completion" many also carry
connotations of death, the point at which rest occurs after a lifetime of such
days as the poem describes. If that is so, perhaps there is some irony in the
fact that a man tries "to get quicker through the day," that is, hurry through
the duration of his existence, in order to discover his only lasting refuge and
satisfaction in his demise.

If ordinary work brings on exhaustion, it further permits release of pressures and drives which otherwise might seek destructive outlets; that is the
idea behind "Sales Talk," where at first Ignatow appears to be defending the
frenzied pace of business life as a safety valve:

Better than to kill each other off
with our extra energy is to run after the bus,
though another be right behind. To run
and to explain to ourselves we have no time
to waste, when it is time that hangs
dangerously on our hands, so that the faster
we run the quicker the breezes rushing by
take time away.

But once more a thread of irony runs through the poem's fabric, and it is the
irony of a momentarily detached, appraising eye which views things as they
are, the demands of circumstance. Doubtless, this critical attitude tacitly
implies that our modern human situation should not be what it is, for to
avoid killing one another we are forced to kill ourselves, or at least to use up
time, our precious commodity. Moreover, as the latter part of the poem
indicates, the environment of the city breeds murderousness and enforces a
conformity beyond the limits of which exist isolation and danger. The business

"uniform" signifies membership in the ranks of regularity and normalcy, prohibits any close inspection of our nakedness, especially of the kind we have already seen Ignatow undertake for himself:

> For comfort we must work
> this way, because in the end we find
> fume-filled streets and murder headlines:
> one out of insanity breaks loose:
> he could not make that extra effort to
> keep connected with us. Loneliness
> like a wheeling condor was attracted
> to the particle that had strayed apart.
> The brief case we carry, the pressed trousers,
> the knotted tie under a white collar add up
> to unity and morale.

"The Business Life," in the poem of that title, offers a type of exposure to the hardness and antipathy of individuals at their jobs. In this instance it is the ethos of the office or white-collar job Ignatow attends to; thus the poem contrasts markedly with the sympathetic portraits of the much humbler positions on the economic ladder held by the errand boy and the fisherwoman or "The Gentle Weight Lifter," who achieves "love and honor by lifting barrels" and wins the poet's praise as opposed to those with "a soft job, pushing a pencil / or racketeering, the numbers game." The poem finally brings about a conditioning experience, a realization and acceptance of the brutal, intemperate terms for working fostered by a competitive system. The poet, if he will survive, must learn to "live" with the viciousness of others while retaining his own gentleness; gradually, the initial reaction of horror and dread will pass into a relatively stable feeling of illness—bearable illness—at this daily encounter with sheer malice:

> When someone hangs up, having said
> to you, "Don't come around again,"
> and you have never heard the phone
> banged down with such violence
> nor the voice vibrate with such venom,
> pick up your receiver gently and dial
> again, get the same reply; and dial
> again, until he threatens. You will
> then get used to it, be sick only
> instead of shocked. You will live,
> and have a pattern to go by, familiar
> to your ear, your senses and your dignity.

Ignatow has noted that "the one overriding experience we have had in this country and which we will probably continue to have [is] a sense of violence about ourselves."[8] This poem reveals such active animosity exercised routinely as part of making one's living. Yet the closing lines, if ironical, are not totally negative, bleak and desolate as they seem; for the poet remains sickened by this situation, a sign that be will not abandon his sensitivity to its evils. He finds, in the end, a means of surviving in extremely trying circumstances without being overwhelmed by them or relinquishing his own humanity and "dignity" to become himself a figure of violence and ruthlessness. In general, that is the moral history of Ignatow's art.

"Tenderness is our posture," he writes in another poem; and the cultivation of gentleness and love in the specific acts and practical affairs of daily living is Ignatow's mode of asserting value concretely in the midst of the dehumanizing "business life." But it is made unmistakable in this poem that love, when genuine, never wears the guise of some remote spiritual ideal, the "golden trophies or fair kisses" mentioned below; rather, it is a force working through the particulars of an individual's existence, a generative, driving energy that discriminates between the objects of experience and bestows worth as it goes. At last, love discards us, handing us over to death, but we are "racing" toward that conclusion in any event; "tenderness and waiting," with their air of attentiveness and gentle restraint, are, the poem insists, the true expression of love in a temporal, mortal world and provide the strength and integrity to stand "upright" in a valid, fulfilled selfhood:

> Be torn by lions of the day,
> love rends us. Or we must walk among our fellow men,
> at peace in our deaths, not knowing
> the difference between a flower and a spittoon,
> between sitting and walking, running and racing,
> and the panting breath at the far end
> of the field where nothing awaits us
> but a fence over which the ash heap lies:
> dumping grounds that someday shall become
> new racing fields. In our panted breath
> we shall expend ourselves, seeking no cause
> or climax: golden trophies or fair kisses,
> too tired, too happy in our weariness:
> loss of the heavy part of us, run
> to be rid of it: love forcing us, living us,
> wearing us. Finally, when we are useless
> to other needs, tearing us to pieces by lions
> before the crowd.
>   For love is when we are racing,
> expressed in tenderness and waiting.

> Wait always. Waiting we are racing.
> And tenderness is our posture, not crouched,
> not forward, nor leaning backwards but upright
> like a man in which love can recognize itself.

Again, in this passage, we encounter the type of spirituality noted previously in "I Felt," "The Rightful One," and other poems. Here, as specific allusions to the grim fate of early Christians in Rome vividly demonstrate, love is envisaged in terms of martyrdom. But obviously, for Ignatow,
life is not sacrificed to love in the expectation of gaining an extra-terres-
trial paradise; instead, it defines the right way to live out present existence. A paradox underlies this conception of the poet's, a religious paradox central to the teachings of the Gospels as well, namely, that selflessness opens the path to self-fulfillment. The "upright" figure at the poem's
conclusion has won that "posture" or stance of the spirit through "tenderness and waiting," which certainly require nothing less than self-abnega-
tion and a kind of humility, an intention of self toward others. In "The
Dream," a beautiful small poem from *Say Pardon*, Ignatow dramatizes the
same theme, using the simplest yet most evocative language and detail,
creating something which seems endowed with the clarity and luminosity
of a vision:

> Someone approaches to say his life is ruined
> and to fall down, at your feet
> and pound his head upon the sidewalk.
> Blood spreads in a puddle.
> And you, in a weak voice, plead
> with those nearby for help;
> your life takes on his desperation.
> He keeps pounding his head.
> It is you who are fated;
> and you fall down beside him.
> It is then you are awakened,
> the body gone, the blood washed from the ground,
> the stores lit up with their goods.

With a marvelous stroke of intuition, Ignatow employs the pronoun "you"
here so as to include both poet and reader, drawing the latter into the heart
of the situation the poem presents. Assuming another person's agony and
deprivation as he attempts to aid him, his life and the victim's merge until
his action redeems them both. It is worth observing that while the poem
shows some of the qualities of parable, Ignatow does not neglect to give it
an urban setting, as if to remind us that the drama belongs to daily experience. The closing line puts the events and figures in touch with material

reality, with city environment; at the same time, the details, particularly of light, contribute vitally to the aura of purification and renewal that characterizes the end.

The relation of self to others also demands acknowledgment of the individuality and integrity of each person, even under somewhat unlikely circumstances, as in the poem "Say Pardon," where Ignatow achieves a perfect mixture of humor and irony with the possibilities for humiliation to enforce the affirmation of identity and freedom in the final lines:

> Say pardon to a bum,
> brushing past him.
> He could lean back
> and spit
> and you would have to wipe it off.
> How would you explain
> that you have insulted
> this man's identity,
> of his own choosing;
> and others could only scratch
> their heads and advise you
> to move on
> and be quiet.
> Say pardon
> and follow your own will
> in the open spaces ahead.

The reference to space at the finish, and the suggestion of movement through it, put us in mind of Ignatow's recurrent metaphor of walking, mentioned before, which he introduces usually to designate some sort of progression of the self in the search for wholeness and completion. For the poet does not discover himself or the direction he needs to pursue solely through his exchanges with others; there are numerous poems in which he gazes inward or adopts a meditative attitude toward objects or elements of nature that become charged with significance for him. "And Step" is such a poem. In it Ignatow confronts reflectively his own physical nature and that of a stone. With this inanimate object he does share his material substance, but he wonders if he should think himself inferior because he lacks the hardness and durability of stone. On the other hand, he possesses a voice and a mind, the potentiality for thought, and he decides to stand on his merits, "proud / and fragile" as he is, and then respectfully move on. The "step" he proposes at the end is obviously kindred to the procedure indicated at the finish of "Say Pardon." In both poems an experience is concluded which enlightens and magnifies the poet's sense of identity, and his way lies clear to continue:

> I understand myself
> in relation to a stone,
> flesh and bone.
> Shall I bow down
> to stone? Mine
> is the voice
> I hear. I will
> stand up to stone.
> I will be proud
> and fragile, I will
> be personable
> and step over
> stone.

In an extremely short poem, "All Comes," Ignatow finds cause for celebration in the most ordinary combination of things, sunlight and the form of a bird in flight. If they appear to us commonplace, he implies, that is because we fail to see them as he now does, reading them as signs available in nature which conceal a message of hope in the brightness of air, in the lifting of wings, a direction to pursue mapped by the flying bird:

> All comes to sunlight.
> A bird stirring its wings.
> In the air it has the shape of a dream.
> It too is perfect off the ground,
> I follow its flight.

Ignatow can also withdraw into a silence that seeks self-integration and individual assurance which his life needs for its continuance. The wall, in "Blessing Myself," serves to symbolize both the isolation he has chosen and the blankness he faces in consequence. He speaks to it, wishing to obtain grace, but nothing miraculous occurs; he receives no answer from the wall, and the reader suspects that he never anticipated a reply. What this strange meeting with the wall effects is a dialogue within the poet which leads to a state of balance allowing him to bestow this desired grace or blessedness upon himself. Ignatow has been forced, then, into an examination of conscience, as it were, an inventory of his own being; only when he can approve himself in honest judgment with scrupulous standards can he win the exaltation of the poem's direct, moving conclusion:

> I believe in stillness,
> I close a door
> and surrender myself
> to a wall and converse

with it and ask it
to bless me.
The wall is silent.
I speak for it,
blessing myself.

Such poems represent a strong and important strain in Ignatow's work,
that of the personal meditation in which, turned away from the external
matters of urban life, he contemplates himself and his nature—both in a
personal fashion and as *human* nature, concentrating on his intimate problems, awareness of guilt and failures, the inevitable slow approach of death.
Closely related to these poems are the recent pieces, most of them included
in *Rescue the Dead* (1968), treating his marriage (other love and marriage
poems are, of course, scattered throughout his work), which similarly belongs to the sphere of his private emotions and intimate perceptions of
himself. One can say without exaggeration that the distinguishing feature
of Ignatow's poetry as his career lengthens out through the1960s is an increasing intensity in his approach to experience, a tendency to probe even
more boldly, thrusting himself forward so as to become as completely engaged as possible with aspects of pain and suffering, violence and death; as
he comes more completely to grips with his condition, he does so with man's
condition in mid-twentieth-century America as well. This intensity dominates the later poems of social and political affairs—"The Appointment
Card," "A First on TV," "My Native Land," "1965," "Emergency Clinic,"
"Play Again," and the brilliant prose poems, "The Cookout," "America
America," "Where There Is Life," and "A Political Cartoon"—to the same
degree it does the personal or inward pieces. Any reader of Ignatow knows
quite well the extent to which these elements pervade all of his writing, yet
now he makes us feel that he must enter more fully into contact with the
negative, terrifying forces which erupt everywhere in the modern world as a
means of validating not only his own individual existence but even existence as such. He undertakes, as a result, what might be called a descent into
the hell of contemporary experience which appears simultaneously as his
private inferno; there, divested of traditional spiritual values and with every human impulse and emotion, measure of good and evil, under question,
he must attempt to make his passage, literally, save his life.

Nowhere do we see these preoccupations more dramatically and powerfully articulated than in the poems of *Rescue the Dead* and a few others
written afterward and now included in the closing section of *Poems 1934-
1969*. Ignatow has supplied his own epigraph for *Rescue the Dead*, and its
three lines again recall the metaphor of the journey or walking with its
corresponding desire for a route away from confinement, toward freedom
and harmony. The phrase "edges of life," which occurs in the epigraph,

further suggests a tentative, often perilous testing of the perimeters and extremities of human experience that is so prominent a feature of much of the
ensuing poetry:

> I feel along the edges of life
> for a way
> that will lead to open land.

In several poems from the book's opening section Ignatow frankly countenances personal feelings of guilt, self-estrangement, and failure which en-
courage in him states of terror or despondency and, frequently, a longing for
death. "Nourish the Crops" begins with the poet standing in sunlight,
"warmed on body, face and hands," yet nonetheless desperate within himself, searching for his "life's goodness" before this solar source of nature's
fertility. In doubt of his own motives, accusing himself of an endeavor to
escape his guiltiness through self-deception, he quickly reaches a condition
of fear and trembling so severe that his very life seems momentarily threatened. But the seizure passes, permitting the poet to regain his mood of calm
reflection, which is almost pantheistic in its implications of an individual's
place in the natural order under the sun:

> True as I breathe, I tell myself.
> It is just as I say. Back to this understanding
> of myself, my breathing becomes normal.
> Guilty in the sun. My peace now is truthful,
> I am truthfully at peace. Oh sun,
> your kindness is a mystery to me.
> How dark I am to myself. How cold I am to myself.
> How close to death I bring myself.
> Because I see you shine on me, I am amazed
> at a loss about myself. I stop to reconsider
> my purpose. Whose death am I seeking?
> I feel myself inconsequential in your warmth
> as it descends on me and on birds, flowers
> and beasts. You give us life, no matter.
> I feel humiliated in my self-importance.
> My wish to die in retribution for my sins
> is laughable. I die in any case like a flower
> or bee or dog. Should I live then as you do
> in brightness and warmth, without question?
> Because I am a product of you to whom all life
> is equal. Do I not sin against you
> by staying dark to myself? You who have given
> the tiger and the snake life
> and nourish the crops?

The poem does not end here but its meditations do, leaving Ignatow with questions that may have answers, though he cannot be sure. His attack of guilt has abated, his thinking has traced a line of possibilities terminating in the notion of self-forgiveness as a virtue, which still remains only a query, a hypothesis brought forth from the situation of unbelief where the poet must try to read what truths he can from his surroundings. The closing stanza shows him persisting in his quest:

> Slowly I move over the field,
> one tired foot ahead of the other,
> feeling through my soles
> the rise and fall of the land.

This sensitive meeting of his feet with the earth as he proceeds, obviously reminiscent of the book's epigraph discussed above, indicates the poet's cautious, perhaps one should say empirical, approach to the events of life, at the same time implying, through the connotations of "rise and fall," the alternating highs and lows, periods of light and darkness, which characterize the climate of his inner being.

The very next poem in sequence, much briefer, confirms this pattern of ascent and decline as if by intentional design. Not surprisingly, since "Nourish the Crops" focuses upon the sun's life-giving rays which appear to the poet to demand the obliteration of darkness, anguish, and deathward inclinations, this poem is called "The Moon." In it Ignatow divides his perceivings between awareness of lunar (or cosmic) ignorance of and alienation from the concerns of men and a sharp cognizance of his own movements and frame of mind, which is bleak:

> I walk beneath it, seeing a stranger
> look down on my familiar state. I walk,
> and it does not know where or for what
> reason on the black surface of the earth.
> I hurry, it is late. I disappear
> into the dark shadow of a building,
> running, and ask of the moon
> what does it expect to discover,
> what does it do in the sky,
> staring down on the intimate
> despairing actions of a man?

The atmosphere of night, "the black surface of the earth," "the dark shadow" into which the poet hurries, as if in flight, combine to create an overall effect of both fear and desolation. The moon hangs over this scene like a blank, stone-faced god who continues to gaze at man's world in utter

incomprehension of it and the activities of the poet, caught up in the flux
of time ("I hurry, it is late"). One recalls other such "despairing," dead-end
poems of the night as Elizabeth Bishop's "The Man-Moth" and Eliot's "Rhap-
sody on a Windy Night." Whatever considerable differences exist between
these various pieces, they all share a common element in their use of fantasy and the irrational. Ignatow in his later work frequently establishes a
surrealist or dreamlike situation through which he can expose hidden aspects of thought or behavior. In "The Moon" the darkness that was contained within himself and, so to speak, neutralized by the energy of the sun
in "Nourish the Crops" achieves release; the shadowy realm of night becomes a vast projection of the poet's anxiety. Finally, the poem leaves us
with a firm impression of the mute indifference of the universe, quite opposite to the indiscriminate benevolence of the sun entertained by the poet in
thought in "Nourish the Crops," as the backdrop against which man makes
the futile, frustrated gestures of living.

Subsequently, Ignatow examines some of these gestures in even more personal fashion, moving relentlessly toward the book's terrible nadir of violence and suffering in the group of three "Rituals." The title poem, "Rescue
the Dead," starts the second section, and its somewhat generalized statements prepare for the particular, private pieces to come; it also raises fundamental questions of value with regard to human relationships.[9] The development of the poem depends upon an apparent alternating pair of choices:
to live or to love. The latter has the aura of sacrifice and is associated with
the incapacity for survival, while the former is clearly compounded of sheer
practicality, an attitude which, in sum, looks selfish and predatory. The first
stanza begins by relinquishing love without regret, and the initial lines point
a return to the state of nature, of primitive man who accepts and respects
the rules of rudimentary living, puts no ideal constructions on them in the
sense in which religions do, but then the poem shifts suddenly to reveal this
primitive type as modern urban man, the dweller in mass society who must
keep on his mettle in order to feed himself and stay alive in the jungle of his
cities:

> Finally, to forgo love is to kiss a leaf,
> is to let rain fall nakedly upon your head,
> is to respect fire,
> is to study man's eyes and his gestures
> as he talks,
> is to set bread upon the table
> and a knife discreetly by,
> is to pass through crowds
> like a crowd of oneself.
> Not to love is to live.

Of the poem's three remaining quatrains the next introduces the theme of love with exotic and romantic imagery, allusions to death and the unfathomable enigmas of existence, which are neither denied nor avoided but are indissolubly bound to the pursuit of love. In this stanza love appears magical, hypnotic perhaps, and ultimately quite perilous for the individual who follows its seductive course. The contrast between this reckless quest for the ideal or the absolute in love's terms and the wary role of self-protective pragmatism previously advocated for survival in the world could not be more deliberately defined:

> To love is to be led away
> into a forest where the secret grave
> is dug, singing, praising darkness
> under the trees.

Enchanted, rapturous, the believer in love, like an ecstatic mystic or visionary, willingly embraces death as part of the whole to which he has dedicated himself and leaves behind the concerns of mortality and ordinary existence in favor of the hidden principle that animates them. But the next stanza balances the scales on the opposite side:

> To live is to sign your name,
> is to ignore the dead,
> is to carry a wallet
> and shake hands.

These lines return us to mundane affairs, the practical and commercial life in which a person of necessity carefully preserves his surface identity (the assumption here must be, I think, that he never looks far within), faces always the present moment and its expediencies. To carry a wallet is to pay one's way, to be self-reliant, and again to hold those cards with signatures that indisputably prove identification, while shaking hands, in this context, is less an expression of friendship than a conventional act placing both parties on an equal but separate footing, poised to do business. Thus Ignatow has set up in the poem two irreconcilable attitudes or modes of being; and at least on one level, a very important one, he is scrutinizing approaches to life in modern society which are widespread, especially in the instance of the hard-headed, pragmatic view. The poem's conclusion finally brings the poet himself into sight, along with the title's implications, which now, as he has noted, carry ironic overtones:[10]

> To love is to be a fish.
> My boat wallows in the sea.
> You who are free,
> rescue the dead.

The first line above, which might at a glance seem merely odd, has direct relevance to what has gone before in the poem. The fish can survive only in its own element, not in the earth-and-air environment of men; the sea is linked in this stanza with the remote setting of forest and trees in the earlier quatrain on love. Yet the crucial image here remains that of the poet who, speaking about himself, says he "wallows in the sea," not quite a fish then (that is, presumably, committed to the vision of love), yet closer to that than to the ruthlessly self-seeking conduct of those "who are free" of such illusions and dreams, dealing only in the brute facts of existence. Ignatow's "boat" tips dangerously, for his position is still precarious and uncertain. Yet his command in the last line really constitutes a challenge to the liberated "realists" to deliver those trusting in love from the death to the world's actualities their faith imposes and guide them to the authentic life—if they can. The suggestion is that, in any event, they cannot.

Subsequently, Ignatow plunges into areas of experience where love is ne-gated, human sympathy and feeling denied, perverted, or corrupted into violence, whether that of war or individual criminal acts. "A Suite for Mar-riage," "Sediment," and "For Your Fear" probe with painful precision the dilemmas and agonies of the poet's relationship with his wife. In the first of these poems he envisages the abolition of his personality and identity, fi-nally, his life itself, within the circumscribed world of domesticity in which husband and wife, locked in their respective solitudes, struggle beneath the surface, almost like characters in Nathalie Sarraute's novels, to endure, even to dominate the situation:

> You keep eating and raising a family
> in an orderly, calm fashion
> for the sake of the child,
> but behind you at your heels
> in a humble mass
> lies a figure.
>
> Do you own me?
> I sense it in your nervous
> irritated talk, as for someone
> who has become a burden—
> when what is possessed
> becomes equally demanding
> for being possessed.
>
> I am not sure that you wish me to live.
> I am not sure that I can.
> We circle each other
> with the taut courtesy

of two respectful opponents.
Difficult to say what next,
this could be all,
to confront each other
in suspense.

Your eyes are so cold-looking,
rejecting me silently
as I talk in low, cultured tones
to convince you
of my superiority.

With the next stanza the child, Ignatow's daughter, enters the poem; in ignorance of her parents' conflict and misery "she stands between them / like a light of many colors, turning / and dancing." (One should read this poem together with "Steps for Three—A Prose Poem" which dramatizes the same problems.) Her appearance mediates to a degree the marital combat and urges the poet—he does not presume to speak for his wife, whose role with the girl must anyway be different—to partial resolutions, the effort to elicit benefits for his daughter's existence. We observe in this attempt something of the selflessness recommended in earlier poems as the means for achieving grace or spiritual welfare for another and so, at last, for oneself:

My daughter, I cry to you from my solitude.
I play the yea-sayer, most bitter,
to spare you with deeds I know can win
good from evil, my despair
a blessing for your life.

The poet's own suffering persists, however, without diminishing; though he is able to wrest value from it for someone else, his relations with his wife stay unchanged, as the powerful and strange concentration of imagery in "Sediment" proves. In the dream landscape of this poem Ignatow envisages himself as "a lake for you"—addressing his wife—"not to see you shrivel up," for she looks, in the opening lines, like "a well-rounded sponge / from head to foot." As the poem progresses, he adds further detail to the setting—trees, sky, a mountain—until it seems complete, a world in which their relationship is at the center. Since the sky is cloudless, the season dry, the sponge keeps absorbing the lake's unreplenished waters, and such is the odd vision of their mutual fate the poet entertains in the end. Apparently the bond between them precludes any other possibilities, and besides, the poem's events bear the inexorability of nightmare. The image of sediment in the closing line again indicates a sacrifice of self which is reductive for Ignatow, leaving him, in this instance, quite literally emptied out:

> No rain comes while you and I float together,
> your reflection in me, and then slowly
> you settle down, filled.
> I think you are going to drown
> and I will go dry, utterly absorbed in you,
> my mud and rock showing. I worry about us,
> you swollen and out of shape
> and I tasting of sediment.

Plainly enough, this situation works hardships and performs distortions on both parties involved, though our main interest naturally focuses on the poet since it is he who struggles in these domestic poems through the primal levels of his experience, staring hard at his "mud and rock showing." In "For Your Fear" he tries to strike a temporary balance that will be true to his uncertainties as well as responsive and fair to his wife. His most promising effort here is "to think / and keep open between us lines / which might someday carry messages / when it's with you as with me"; and he finishes with a request: "Love me for my desperation / that I may love you for your fear."

Desperation is a word increasingly appropriate to the poems of *Rescue the Dead*, as the reader proceeds through the book, page after page. "The Room," which immediately precedes the trio of "Ritual" poems, prepares an entrance of a sombre kind into the tortuous labyrinth of these pieces. Like the lonely, deprived figures of Samuel Becket's fiction and plays, the poet occupies a place of isolation, a room which is equivalent to the bare, reduced circumstances of his own existence. There he is left to confront the rudiments of his relationships and endeavors, the thinking and writing ("charts / and prescriptions and matches") with the aid of which he attempts to navigate the psyche's dark channels:

> There's a door to my name
> shutting me in, with a seat
> at a table behind the wall
> where I suck of the lemon seed.
> Farther in is the bed
> I have made of the fallen hairs
> of my love, naked, her head dry.
> I speak of the making of charts
> and prescriptions and matches
> that light tunnels
> under the sea.

Yet Ignatow can merely "speak of the making" of such guidelines and maps; when we reach the second stanza, we realize that the harsh conditions already described comprise only a beginning, which now gives way to frightening sensations of vertigo forcing the poet to cling to the form and density of ordinary objects to maintain his equilibrium:

> A chair, a table, a leg of a chair—
> I hold these with my eyes to keep from falling,
> my thoughts holding to these shapes,
> my breathing of them that make my body
> mine through the working of my eyes.
> All else is silence and falling.

In the extremity of this state only the most commonplace *things* suffice to keep the mind occupied and away from the storm of nerves and emotions, the eruptions of thought which send the self toppling into an abyss of disorder and madness. (Again one thinks of Beckett's characters, obsessed with object rituals like Molloy's pebble game and Malone's endless check on his meagre belongings, and of the young American novelist Rudolph Wurlitzer, who introduces similar figures that devote themselves to collecting and arranging cigarette packages, penknives, etc.—the debris of modern life.) The poem's last stanza finds visibility gone and the poet maneuvering in blackness. The void around him becomes alive with the movement of wings which he, in turn, emulates, circling about in the confines of his small space at the end:

> In the dark
> I hear wings beating
> and move my arms around
> and above
> to touch.
> My arms go up and down
> and around
> as I circle the room.

This conclusion leaves the poet intact, keeping himself going, but directionless and unsure of his bearings. The "dark" through which he flies seems purposefully to serve as a preliminary setting for "Ritual One." The latter begins in a theater, as if a curtain lifted in the darkness of "The Room" and the poet suddenly found himself on foot again, now at the threshold of his worst nightmares; for his "falling" has finished, but only in the sense that Ignatow has reached the depths and has no alternative to seeing through the imminent horrors to their completion. The play, already in performance when he arrives, appears composed of banal complaints and reports of mechanical breakdown uttered by a father and son. Yet, odd as this dialogue may be, our attention is suddenly caught by the poet's declaration of his own overwrought state and a startling announcement of the appalling drama that rapidly unfolds, not on the stage as might be expected, but in the audience, involving him completely:

> Tiptoeing down the aisle, I find my seat,
> edge my way in across a dozen kneecaps
> as I tremble for my sanity.
> I have heard doomed voices calling on god the electrode.
> Sure enough, as I start to sit
> a scream rises from beneath me.
> It is one of the players.
> If I come down, I'll break his neck,
> caught between the seat and the backrest.
> Now the audience and the players on stage,
> their heads turned towards me, are waiting
> for the sound of the break. Must I?
> Those in the aisle nod slowly, reading my mind,
> their eyes fixed on me, and I understand
> that each has done the same.
> Must I kill this man as the price of my admission
> to this play ? His screams continue loud and long.
> I am at a loss as to what to do,
> I panic, I freeze.

The stanza develops with the inescapable logic of a brutal dream, but one from which the poet is helpless to rouse himself. The demands upon him as the price of entrance to this play—a play which, incidentally, bears something of the negative aspects of everyday living with its pointless hagglings, its routine irritations—really take the form of an ordeal of initiation that severely tests his hardness, his willingness to look out for himself and secure his niche, and thus to have no qualms about taking another's life. At this point we should note how the present poem draws out to their conclusion the attitudes of those who "forgo love" in "Rescue the Dead." The appeal of the "doomed" like the player trapped in the poet's chair is made in vain; "god the electrode" certainly refers to a universe without a deity sensitive to man's dilemmas. Yet Ignatow himself is not lacking in human sympathy; to kill another person contradicts his basic impulses, though the entire audience has found it possible to do. Finally, we realize—there is no other way; he cannot turn back or simply depart; this theater *is* existence.

The second stanza starts with a mixture of memories which recount the growth of his feeling and affection for other humans through love for his father, but it likewise reveals his acquaintance with man's capacity for slaughtering animals. The first line indicates how the poet, whose heritage is Jewish, has been forced from the beginning to live according to the rules of a profane, even repugnant reality, to get used to it and to learn kindness and love in its midst. In spite of this backward glance, the actuality of the present reasserts itself, and the poet completes his initiation only under physical pressure:

> My training has been to eat the flesh of pig.
> I might even have been able to slit a throat.
> As a child I witnessed the dead chickens
> over a barrel of sawdust absorbing their blood.
> I then brought them in a bag to my father
> who sold them across his counter. Liking him,
> I learned to like people and enjoy their company too,
> which of course brought me to this play.
> But how angry I become.
> Now everybody is shouting at me to sit down,
> sit down or I'll be thrown out.
> The father and son have stepped off stage
> and come striding down the aisle side by side.
> They reach me, grab me by the shoulder
> and force me down. I scream, I scream,
> as if to cover the sound of the neck breaking.

Desirous of a participation in existence, he is unwillingly compelled to become a murderer like the other members of the audience and the players. His hysteria continues into the closing stanza, where at first he is treated as something of a celebrity—presumably because he has now been initiated—but then his mood changes to one of rage and he attacks the players with particular violence, which merely creates amusement. Finally, however, his reasoning prevails, eliciting its stark conclusions from the paradoxical nature of this theater and the behavior required of the occupants. Ignatow sits down to watch a new performance, a crude and ugly act with children as participants, which leads directly into "Ritual Two":

> All through the play I scream
> and am invited on stage to take a bow.
> I lose my senses and kick the actors in the teeth.
> There is more laughter
> and the actors acknowledge my performance with a bow.
> How should I understand this?
> is it to say that if I machine-gun the theatre
> from left to right they will respond with applause
> that would only gradually diminish with each death?
> I wonder then whether logically I should kill myself
> too out of admiration. A question indeed,
> as I return to my seat and observe a new act
> of children playfully aiming their kicks
> at each other's groins.

Clearly, the realm into which the poet has been introduced with so much reluctance on his part to pay the cost exists without benefit of any traditional convictions or creeds and apparently neither knows nor respects humanistic values; on the other hand, there is no indulgence in pretense here either. The picture Ignatow so shockingly sketches discloses a type of naked, primitivistic humanity whose primary concerns are the aggressive activities necessary to individual endurance. Violence and death constitute the ordinary practice rather than the exception, and variations on them provoke interest, even laughter (as in the poet's anger and physical assault upon the actors), for watching fights or other kinds of violent acts supplies the chief form of entertainment in this hellish auditorium.[11]

A poem from the same period which has affinities with these "Ritual" pieces and the atmosphere they generate is the equally excruciating "A First on TV," in which Ignatow openly announces his intention of portraying the unfeeling fascination and complicity with violence done to humans that characterizes our age:

> This is the twentieth century,
> you are there, preparing to skin
> a human being alive. Your part
> will be to remain calm
> and to participate with the flayer
> in his work as you follow his hand,
> the slow delicate way with the knife
> between the skin and flesh,
> and see the red meat emerge.
> Tiny rivulets of blood will flow
> from the naked flesh and over the hands
> of the flayer. Your eyes will waver
> and turn away but turn back to witness
> the unprecedented, the incredible,
> for you are there
> and your part will be to remain calm.

A second stanza brings out the watcher's reaction of indignation and fury, approximating the poet's in the theater, but, as Ignatow insists through his repetitions of the phrases "to remain calm" and "you are there," a person's response is incapable of altering the entire complex of his society and his time. In the end he is hopelessly enmeshed in a frightening network of events which appear immediately before him, yet his blows struck against these evils are wild flailings that cannot touch their object. The calmness which finally arrives—or is perhaps predicted with assurance—suggests both a kind of resignation to brutal actuality and an accommodation to it, or the first gradually becoming the second:

You will smash at the screen
with your fist and try to reach
this program on the phone, like a madman
gripping it by the neck
as it were the neck of the flayer
and you will scream into the receiver,
"Get me Station ZXY at once, at once,
do you hear!" But your part
will be to remain calm.

With "Ritual Two" the children kicking "at each other's groins" in the previous poem have regressed even further toward a savage state, lashing themselves into frenzied activity punctuated by their single nihilistic cry which echoes throughout:

The kids yell and paint their bodies
black and brown, their eyes bulging.
As they brush, they dance, weaving
contorted shapes. They drive each other
to the wall, to the floor, to the bed,
to the john, yelling, "Nothing!"

No reader can fail to recognize in this and the following stanzas a brilliant, though terrifying, dramatization of the purposeful reversion to the primitivistic by many young people in the midst of an increasingly streamlined technocratic society, a society which, to repeat, has taught them "to forgo love" or demanded false allegiances and now reaps the harvest of hypocrisy in frantic horror. As the poem continues, the kids tear up the stage "on which they stand" (literally, destroy the world in which they find themselves) with ferocious intentness until the poet himself arrives to stand among them, offering them with hand and mouth what would seem to be signs of his identity as a writer, then entering on a death dance which they surround him to watch with anticipation and pleasure. The progression of the dance involves Ignatow in the abandonment of the ordinary accoutrements of civilized Western man, his clothing and his bank account; all of these movements are accompanied by the kids' refrain of denial: "'Nothing, Nothing!'" The last stanza, however, finds the poet enacting what might at first appear to be a different drama but is actually a continuation of his fatal dance onto another phase, climaxed by his death and a rebirth as his own child:

I pretend to hold a child by the hand
and walk as though strolling up a street
with him and stoop to listen to this child
and talk to him, when suddenly I act

as if shot, slowly falling to the ground,
kissing the child goodby with my fingertips,
but I spring up and pretend to be the child,
lost, abandoned, bewildered, wanting to die,
crouching as the circle keeps chanting,
"Nothing, Nothing!"
I then rise slowly to my full height,
having grown up through my agony.
I throw my head back proudly
and join hands with others as they dance,
chanting their theme. We converge in the center,
bang against each other, scream and scatter.

In losing his parent the imagined child loses love, security, direction; worse than this, the elder person dies by senseless or gratuitous violence, and this death must be assumed to tell us something of the character of the world the two inhabit. The poet, having died, now mimes the boy's role and knows in himself the isolation, confusion, and suffering to which the youth is subject. But he passes beyond these pains to achieve a stature and independence of his own. This resolution still contains its ambiguities, however, for the pride and maturity lead to a freely chosen participation in the kids' dance and its ending in chaos, probable belligerence and terror—though it is difficult to be certain of the full implications of the final line except for its unequivocal statement of disorder. The poem should be read, I think, like its predecessor, as an initiation ritual; growing up through "agony" here does not possess the same redemptive connotations as we have observed in other poems but signifies instead a decision to proceed from pain and abandonment and to live, though that entails an acceptance of existence as founded upon "Nothing."

Such an interpretation may be further justified by the substance of the two reflective sections comprising the whole of "Ritual Three," a poem which penetrates to the very center of "the heart of darkness" Ignatow pursues in spite of everything. The poem has for preface a single sentence designating the matter on which the poet subsequently meditates, acts of an insane cruelty that defies rational comprehension or explanation: "In England, the slow methodical torture of two children was recorded on tape by the murderers." Ignatow's mood at the beginning might be described as one of somber exhaustion, for it appears that he has lived through, at the deepest levels of himself, the evil and horror of those children's murders (though he refers only to one of them), probably after reading a detailed account of what occurred, and has felt vicariously their agony and also the maiming of his own spirit at the realization of the unspeakable crimes perpetrated by these killers. The child's suffering is over, he admits at the outset, simultaneously recalling his own mortality; but as his thoughts turn to the offenders he veers dangerously toward a precipice, prepared for by the earlier initiations of the previous "Ritual" poems and by such other pieces as "Rescue the Dead" and "A First on TV." If at first he acknowledges the bond of humanity with the murderers, while adding that he has never shared their perverse and base impulses, yet, as he reflects, the savage creature latent in himself (and in all of us), devoid of reason or sympathy, awakens to action:

> Let me rest, let me rest from their mistakes.
> They were human like myself, somehow
> gone in a direction to a depth I've never known.
> I am not thinking,
> I am contemptuous of thought.
> I growl in my depths, I find blood flowing
> across my tongue and enjoy its taste.
> Call me man, I don't care.
> I am content with myself,
> I have a brain that gives me the pleasure.
> Come here and I will tear you to pieces,
> it'll be catch is catch can
> but I can throw you who are weakened with the horror
> of what I say, so surrender peacefully
> and let me take my first bite directly above your heart.
> I am a man, your life lost in feeling,
> I never knew what mercy meant,
> I am free.

We are witnesses in this disturbing passage to the poet in troubled dialogue with himself. For once he relinquishes his tormented thinking and emotional suffering over the killings and those involved, tries to find some respite from the state of mind he has come to, then immediately the predatory voice, a constant element in the human composition, dedicated only to the ends of self-gratification (in whatever form desire may dictate to the individual), rises up within him and, taking advantage of his spiritually exhausted condition, attempts to dominate. The last line of the stanza connects this poem directly with "Rescue the Dead," where at the conclusion Ignatow admonishes: "You who are free, / rescue the dead." The dead, we recall, are those who believe in love (in terms of the present poem, those with "life lost in feeling"), while the free "forgo love" in favor of self-seeking and survival, unencumbered by the moral baggage of feeling for others. The monstrous presence who announces his intentions above is merely a more completely defined—and thus more frightening—version of the "free" man of the earlier poem; as this voice echoes and elaborates in its speech the ending of "Rescue the Dead," we can see how cutting is the irony of the poet's final words there. The free will "rescue" no one: the act of rescuing implies a care for the welfare or the life of someone else, an idea totally alien to the free. The single thing they will do for persons of sensitivity, love, and mercy is destroy them, a literal fulfillment of the word by which the feeling are identified—"the dead."

The closing section of the poem, addressed to the murdered child, finishes the series of initiation rituals by confirming the poet in the attitudes of the free and unfeeling. Wishing for the guise of a crocodile, he commits himself, not to the nightmare of hideous criminal activities ("I will not run a knife across the skin / or cut off a nose or tear off the genitals, / as screams fade in exhaustion") but to the requisites of self-preservation:

> Child gone to a calm grave,
> I want to be a crocodile,
> opening the two blades of my mouth.
> I'll slide through swamp, taking in small fish and flies.

So he becomes convinced that while perverse extremities must be avoided and rejected as forms of behavior, given the circumstances of life as we find it men must accommodate themselves to living with the jaws and scaly armor of reptiles rather than aiming toward ideals or kinds of goodness beyond their capacities and the harsh rules of the world:

> . . . I dream I am sane, purposeful
> and on my course, dreaming that we no longer should trouble
> to live as human beings, that we should discuss this,
> putting aside our wives and children,
> for to live is to act in terms of death.

The group of "Ritual" poems comes full circle here, leading us back to the killing imposed upon the poet as the entrance fee to the theater of existence. If a man can win his life only at the expense of taking another's, then he surely cannot with honesty pretend to exist in accord with the ideals of humanism or Christianity, the spiritual legacy of the Western tradition. Struggling for survival within his own species, he paradoxically regresses on the evolutionary scale (at the same time he has been developing tremendous technical skills and powers), turned at last into a grim creature fending for himself in a swamp in the midst of an earth which is nothing but jungle. Ignatow's unflinching need for truthfulness brings him to the poem's sobering finish, where the vestments of aspiration and finer feeling have been discarded and the rude facts laid bare.

The anguish of this exposure for Ignatow—and it is obvious from the poems how he has proceeded personally step by step into these fearful depths

of thought and vision—manifests itself in the three pieces following the
"Rituals": "The Open Boat," "A Dialogue," and "From a Dream." The first
returns again to "Rescue the Dead" to pick up the image of the poet at sea in
a boat; in this instance his isolation and distraught emotions derive from
the enervating course of experience in the "Ritual" poems—or so its place-
ment suggests. But more is to be discovered here than the inevitable sense
of anguish, fatigue, and solitude which results from traveling perilously far
in pursuit of valid grounds for human existence. The poem ends with a
shocking confirmation of all the poet has realized, rendered the more frightful
because it occurs through the gesture of a supposedly lesser creature than
man and symbolizes the rejection of him by the remainder of living beings:

> With no place to lay my head
> beside a friend
> who could give peace,
> none to guard my door
> nor still my house,
> I am five miles out: the sea
> flexes its muscles
> and I have gulls for companions
> overhead—veering off,
> afraid, afraid
> of a human.

"A Dialogue" leaves no alternative to its speaker, who chooses suicide as
a way to "express sorrow in its pure form" but is prevented, declared "insane" and carried off to the hospital to "die there / in sorrow." Death provides the single resolution to the unspecified suffering in this poem, which
is another expression of Ignatow's despairing state or a momentary exorcism of it. And in "From a Dream" he vividly relates his feelings of frustration and terror during a dreamlike descent that takes him uncontrollably
further and further away from the ordinary amenities and habits of daily
life. Once more we see him walking, but now in a direction he cannot determine for himself, which elicits his nervous speculation at the close:

> I'm on a stair going down.
> I must get to a landing
> where I can order food
> and relax with a newspaper.
> I should retrace my steps to be sure,
> but the stairs above disappear into clouds.
> But down is where I want to go,
> these stairs were built to lead somewhere
> and I would find out.

> As I keep walking,
> ever more slowly,
> I leave notes such as this on the steps.
> There must be an end to them
> and I will get to it,
> just as did the builders,
> if only I were sure now
> that these stairs were built
> by human hands.

The concluding phrase, with "human" as the modifier, creates an extremely disturbing ambiguity in terms of the poems which have gone before. A first response, perhaps, is to experience a quick, conventional flash of hope, reassurance, and familiarity at the sight of this word. But once we recollect its fundamental implications, the uses to which it has been put, in Ignatow's dark imaginative vision through the poems leading up to this one, we are struck suddenly with the knowledge that the human may be something to arouse apprehension, that its designs possibly offer no more assurance than those of nonhuman hands.

The present section of the book, which began with "Ritual One," comes to an end with two poems of public violence. "East Bronx" discloses "two children" who "sharpen / knives against the curb," while parents and elders "leaning from the window" above this scene of mounting antagonism and viciousness not only make no effort to prevent it but even turn away as from a wearying commonplace, retreating into their bathrooms to read of exotic and nonhuman affairs: "of the happiness of two tortoises / on an island in the Pacific— / always alone and always / the sun shining." In "I See a Truck" a similar but more widespread spectacle of violence as an acceptable or routine part of everyday life assumes large, grotesque proportions. A truck goes wild in the city streets, running over citizens who are participants in some sort of parade; limping, the victims still alive rise up "to follow" the vehicle, while "a cop stands idly swinging his club" and, as if in a dream, "No one screams / or speaks." This enigmatic silence is interrupted by an ecclesiastical retinue who recite their prayers, perhaps blessing and condoning this bizarre yet clearly quotidian incident, in a carnival atmosphere, where the dispensation of money is intended to right all wrongs, heal all wounds, and brings about the mock joyous air of festivity with which Ignatow ironically finishes:

> From the tail end
> of the truck, a priest and a rabbi intone
> their prayers, a jazz band bringing up
> the rear, surrounded by dancers and lovers.

> A bell rings and a paymaster drives through,
> his wagon filled with pay envelopes
> he hands out, even to those lying dead
> or fornicating on the ground.
> It is a holiday called
> "Working for a Living."

Preoccupation with violence, cruelty, and injustice continues into the next group of poems. "All Quiet" and "An American Parable" are incisive attacks on the Vietnam war and the financial investments of American foreign policy; there are individual pieces about Medgar Evers, Churchill's death, and Christ, followed by a harsh retaliation to the brutalities of militarism in "Soldier." But in the midst of these poems is placed the extraordinary and crucial "A Meditation on Violence, which must be understood, in the structure of *Rescue the Dead,* as a pivotal point for Ignatow's attitudes, bringing him some measure beyond the torment and hopelessness that invest so many of the pieces we have discussed. Starting in broken lines, as if to simulate or catch the poet's mind in its first groping motions of thought on the subject, the poem then develops, from the rather general sense of violence done to others—and the potential we possess for it—in fragmented images, toward a second stanza where Ignatow reflects on specific news reports from the war:

> On my birthday
> they knocked out
> two bridges
> a fishing boat standing at anchor
> and a forest
> defoliated with a napalm bomb
> on my fifty-first year

After another stanza, which comments on the official rhetoric of "peace," he looks at himself in his room, relaxing in thought between the heat of the day and a breeze that tempers it; these physical conditions supply analogies for rumination on men's heedless passions and their desirable but neglected capacities for rationality as a substitute for force:

> Through an open window
> facing the river
> the wind blows this hot day
> while I sprawl upon a bed,
> my skin cooled. Would
> that this were the fate of the world.
> a stream of cool reason
> flow serenely between hot shores

into which steaming heads
could dip themselves

Then, pointedly, with the initial line of the subsequent stanza, Ignatow
both recollects and reverses his concluding statement from "Ritual Three,"
in which he had asserted that consideration for the welfare of women and
children must not prohibit us from thinking how, perhaps, "we should no
longer trouble/to live as human beings." Now, as he lies in his room enjoying the wind, it carries to his ear the sounds of children at play outside; in
their rapid shifts of mood, their emotional flexibility and resilience, a lesson in human comprehension is to be learned. Recognition of the children's
liberty and elation breaks in upon his brooding over the war and man's
inclination toward violence, begetting a renewed feeling of possibility. With
serious intentness he gives himself up to these young voices which seem
like a nourishing rainfall for an earth that urgently needs it:

> But the children, I think, should not be blotted out,
> as I sit listening to the rise and fall
> of their pleasures, the sudden change
> to bad temper quickly forgotten
> by the shift to joy,
> pleased with the world that lets them
> shout and jump and play at tantrums
> for this is freedom to understand
> until they wander off to bed.
> Shall I say their sounds are an intrusion
> when they show the meaning to my life
> is to celebrate, always to celebrate?
> I listen as I would to rain falling
> upon a field.

The potentiality for affirmation established in these lines does not weaken
again, though it can hardly avoid numerous challenges from other poems.
In the fifth section Ignatow starts out with a brief poem, "The Signal," in
which the intimations of forward movement to his life, contained in the
tacit message of the green traffic light he studies ("It is when the signal
turns red / that I lose interest"), lend it a redeeming quality; faults become
less significant when viewed against the new and changing:

> At night
> I am content to watch the blue-green
> come on again against the dark
> and I do not torture myself
> with my shortcomings.

This play of light in opposition to darkness occurs several times in the imagery of poems immediately subsequent to "The Signal." A number of the finest are love poems, beautiful, tender, and moving declarations of affection for his wife, Rose Graubart, the painter, and, of course, they more than offset the rigorous questionings of his marital relationship in those poems preceding the "Rituals." The central place she occupies in the pattern of Ignatow's life is unmistakable from the citation of a passage or two:

> She is my love for everyday
> and darkness is the absence of her;
> and so it is enough for any man
> that he may do as much in this world
> as to have a Rose for his woman.
>   ("Domestic Song")

> I need to see and touch
> and talk to you each day
> to assure myself
> I am not made happy with dreams.
> Then you become for me a tree
> of comforting shade, bellying
> where the branches bunch together
> full of leaves.
> I want a maternal world.
>   ("For Nobody Else")

Intimations of harmony and a revived purpose for existence, in spite of difficulties or obstacles which periodically loom up in forbidding aspect, emerge from these love poems and modify others following them. Meditating on books and reading in "Against the Evidence," Ignatow is compelled to examine his own mental habits and processes, then to think about his isolation:

> I use books
> almost apologetically. I believe
> I often think their thoughts for them.
> Reading, I never know where theirs leave off
> and mine begin. I am so much alone
> in the world, I can observe the stars
> or study the breeze, I can count the steps
> on a stair on the way up or down,
> and I can look at another human being
> and get a smile, knowing
> it is for the sake of politeness.

"Estrangement" and loneliness, he realizes, are basic ingredients of man's situation, and books offer no correctives, for the reader consults them only by himself. With a gesture which recalls his attempt to gain reassurance and stability from tangible objects in "The Room," though here in a calm, thoughtful rather than high-pitched, nervous mood, the poet reaches out to touch his writing desk and settles down to work within the confinements of the dilemma he has perceived. Separateness still exists; he cannot alter the fact but may exorcize the demons haunting his inner life, to borrow Eliot's metaphor from *The Three Voices of Poetry*. The final line makes a positive declaration which puts behind him the substance of Ignatow's ordeal with the forces of negation, inhumanity, and degradation. Obviously, I am not implying that he can now simply dismiss those forces because he has faced them in favor of an easy optimism. On the contrary, he must always bear the scars and sense the strain of that journey through agonized suffering, of trial by fire; but if he was not to succumb to its vicissitudes in a manner which, logically speaking, could very well issue in death, then he had to pass through a nihilistic underworld and seek the means to go on. This closing passage reveals an intention to do just that and the strength of will supporting him:

> I stroke my desk,
> its wood so smooth, so patient and still.
> I set a typewriter on its surface
> and begin to type
> to tell myself my troubles.
> Against the evidence, I live by choice.

The sixth and last section of *Rescue the Dead* resonates with the poet's newly won energy and enthusiasm for living, visible in each of the marvelous, vital poems to be found there. But in order to secure the imaginative power for affirmation he desires, Ignatow must countenance openly the contesting negation of death and, without the solutions orthodoxy contributes and he cannot accept, refuse to be ruled by its ubiquitous, unpredictable presence. Something of what this struggle to salvage the human, mortal character of existence entails can be seen in the brief poems, already mentioned, on Medgar Evers and Christ; both of these exemplary sacrificial figures form in death an alliance with earth and so with the true prevailing spirit of existence—with life as it should be. This theme receives elaboration and amplification in the lovely poem "Six Movements on a Theme," which inaugurates and sets the tone for the entire sixth section. The piece at once establishes itself as a poem of reverie or waking dream; but if it exhibits characteristics and properties familiar to, dreams, its progression can hardly be described as loose or random when, in fact, it moves increasingly in the direction of wakefulness and conscious aims.

The poem begins in the realm of Ignatow's consciousness, where desirable images of a temperate landscape and climate relax mind and body, drawing him toward sleep and actual dream. The dream itself is complex, consisting of several stages, the first of which discriminates between the poet's outward appearance—the way he looks to friends gathered round him as if to witness the end of his life—and the processes at work within him, or perhaps we should say, in his essential self or spirit:

> Thinking myself in a warm country
> of maternal trees under whose shade
> I lie and doze, I dream I am weightless.
> Magnified faces stare back at me—
> of friends wanting me to live
> to whom I am dying stretched out
> on the ground and barely breathing.
> Dead, they say as I hold my breath
> to close in and possess myself.

Reverie slides into dream, a dream of death which is neither feared nor resisted by the poet but seems deliberately sought, for he stops breathing by choice, so as to conclude the separation from his physical or bodily nature begun with his awareness of a levitated state, an airiness, in the third line. Whatever this death involves in terms of external reality, it does not bring extinction; instead, it precipitates or hastens that inward movement toward self-integration noted in the last line.

The dream continues with the second stanza, sinking deeper into the levels of creation, away from ordinary human concerns, and the poet experiences a corresponding transformation of a profound sort which locates him completely within the elemental context of the natural world:

> I dream my life to be a plant
> floating upon a quiet pool,
> gathering nourishment from water
> and the sun. I emerge
> of my own excess power, my roots
> beginning to move like legs,
> my leaves like arms,
> the pistil the head. I walk
> out of the pool
> until I reach my utmost weariness
> in a dance of the fading power
> of my roots—when I lie down
> silently to die and find myself
> afloat again.

A distinct contrast is evident in this imagery of a pacific existence in the pond, sustained by sun and water, with the preying crocodile, nosing through the swamp in "Ritual Three." But Ignatow has more in mind than such discrepancies between the gentle and the predatory, though we should do well to remember them. If the initial stanza can be considered—and I think it must be—as a purposeful abandonment of familiar human life and the preferred acceptance of a symbolic death and rebirth (contained within the progression of the poet's dreaming), then its basic motive, as the next stanza indicates, is a quest for that cast-off humanity in its pristine form which can be discovered only if approached in an evolutionary scheme from a lower species of life, in this instance, a water plant. The effort of the plant to leave its placid condition, its expenditure of strength to engage in the dance, to move as a man does, and finally to die in exhaustion and be returned to its original position in the pool can be understood both as a celebration of life's energies and, equally, as the compulsion to extend the effectiveness of those energies.

Yet this endeavor terminates in failure and results, with stanza three, in an apparent awakening from the dream, for Ignatow now meditates more consciously on the unlikeliness of ambitious evolutionary desires: "I see no fish crawling / to become man. The mountains / have been standing / without a single effort / to transform themselves / into castles or apartment houses." In other words, the nonhuman, whether animate or not, harbors no wish to become human or to be an instrument or production of the human: lesser creatures and things are content to remain themselves. Man alone aspires, and to his ideal of himself Ignatow turns in the following lines. "Amid silence," which signifies the otherness, the difference between man and the rest of creation, the poet erects "a statue / in my image" and directs his supplications to it:

> I love you, man,
> on my knees. To you
> I will address my pleas
> for help. You will save me
> from myself. From your silence
> I will learn to live.

The statue's lack of response puts the burden of aid on the poet himself; he may create and venerate an idealized image, request its help, yet it is merely an image, whose muteness enables Ignatow the better to hear his own questions, realize the humanity he must sustain for himself. The next stanza clarifies his responsibilities and designates the sole route he can travel. This way does not involve a thoroughgoing metamorphosis or transformation into something else; like the fish and the mountains, he will stay what he is, though he does not enjoy their natural integrity or self-unity and needs to search for that completion:

> I was shown my only form.
> I have no hope
> but to approach myself,
> palm touching palm.

The sense of touch, which Ignatow returns to in the stanza following, suggests how rudimentary and exploratory are the regions of experience he traverses here. His hand taps "on a wall," with the result that he gains an awareness of his "humankind" at the primal levels of the sensory order. Yet such awareness denotes a self-awareness which the wall, in its cold solidarity, never knows. The wall stands as an entity at one with itself, while the poet, as a man, has to bear the pain of division, of self-consciousness and individual isolation; others may touch his solitude as he touched the wall, simply confirming their and his separateness: I feel my humankind, / secretly content / to suffer. / I too am a wall." This willingness to suffer, so crucial to Ignatow's final affirmation of existence, implies a resignation to the demands of necessity as the price of being human, of recognizing the array of possibilities available to a person and to nothing less. The poem closes with a night vision of cosmic proportions and the poet assumes, in an intense, exhilarated mood, the terms of his human life, including both its vitality and potentiality ("fire"), and its unavoidable end in death ("dumb"). Emphasis falls not on mortality as a defeat, but on the given span of existence as an essential bond with the universe and nature, in which death is incorporated:

> The stars are burning overhead.
> Excited, I understand
> from a distance:
> I am fire,
> I'll be dumb.

We should recall, in regard to these recent poems, Ignatow's references to a life without perspective and observe how, in spite of the odds, it becomes for him a viable, if always trying, form of being. The conclusion of "Six Movements on a Theme" proclaims the unity of a single existence; the poet remains inseparable from the most important and the least significant details of his existence, so that finally he must be identified with all of them as they shape a unique world of events, acts, dreams, loves, and pains, finishing in a death wholly his own. "Secretly," "The Life Dance," "Three in Transition," "For My Daughter in Reply to a Question," and "Walk There," among other poems, investigate, celebrate, and test in a variety of ways the relationship between self and the occurrences to which it is subject, in the interest of perceiving, comprehending, and preserving their bonds of attachment. Alone, in "Secretly," Ignatow indulges himself in the contemplation of his foot; his eye examines it scrupulously from every angle as if noticing it for the first time and absorbs its appearance in motion, while his mind elaborates its function in the journeying of his life. The surprising analogy he draws between this bodily member and a bird ("In profile shaped like a bird's head, / the toes long and narrow like a beak, / the arch to the foot / with the gentle incline / of a bird's body / and the heel thick and stubby / like a starling's tail") may also remind us how birds are associated in certain of his poems with freedom and independence, the potentiality for movement. Further, this likeness develops a double vision of his existence, the continuation of which seems fatiguing on the surface, Yet, covertly, he is transported by the strength, resilience, and fleetness of his birdlike foot:

> The full weight of my body
> today walking on it
> supporting me in my weariness
> it can perform its flight,
> its shape delicate, light,
> swift-seeming, tense and tireless
> as I lie on a bed, my foot
> secretly a bird.

Looking even more closely at the mysterious ties which confer a true, personal intuition of authentic being-in-the-world (to borrow that familiar term from existential philosophy and psychiatry), "The Life Dance" is a spontaneous exercise in joy derived from participation in the harmonious creative upwelling of nature's rich resources. Elated by the sight of a spring "bubbling out of the ground," Ignatow's "mind / too begins to spring," which then coaxes him into physical activity ("small hops"). Gradually, he abandons self-consciousness and engages in a vigorous dance whose motions and gyrations appear to dramatize a symbolic language he cannot himself translate:

> Is anybody watching?
> I care and don't care,
> as I hop, and soon
> because nobody is looking I'm leaping
> and twisting into awkward shapes,
> letting my hands make signs
> of a meaning I do not understand.

Abruptly Ignatow shifts inward to thought about his intense efforts, acknowledging in them a wish to strike far into the roots of existence, to seize and uncover by whatever means possible that underlying unity of origins which binds him to the reality of the world with the same intimacy as a hand clasped in friendship or the breath keeping him alive:

> I am absorbed in getting at what
> till now
> I had not been aware of.
>
> There is a feeling in the world
> I sometimes think I'm grasping.
> I find myself holding a hand or
> as I take a deep breath
> I think it is there.

This unity with earth is echoed in the ending of "Night at an Airport," written around 1940 but appropriately printed with these later pieces. Here the flux and form of our individual lives both originates in and imitates the patterns of recurrent turbulence and calm to be found in nature:

> We have our beginnings
> in breeze or storm, dancing or swirling;
> and are still when the wind is still.
> We have earth and return to it—
> everlasting as a thought.

Ignatow takes earth for our birthplace and our only home, the ground of our return and last repose. His statement and acceptance of this view certainly grow from the struggle toward affirmation of and union with existence he has maintained since departing the sinister void of the "Ritual" poems. In keeping with his commitment to a position of determined but gentle agnostic humanism—if such a phrase will do to describe what is a living response at every moment to the actualities of his experience—he desires also to adjust himself to the value of suffering and to the impending promise of death. He handles the first of these two requirements deftly and handsomely in his own brief moral coda to *The Divine Comedy*:

> Dante forgot to say,
> Thank you, Lord, for sending me
> to hell. I find myself happier
> than when I was ignorant.
> I am left helpless
> but more cheerful.
> Nothing could be worse
> than to start ignorant again.

> And so I look to you
> to help me love my life
> anew.

Such love proves to be everywhere in evidence in Ignatow's recent poems, but precisely for this reason the unavoidable termination of life requires assimilation into his total vision without simultaneously destroying it. In "Three in Transition," dedicated to the late William Carlos Williams, he muses on the enigmatic "beauty / in leaves falling" and wonders: "To whom / are we beautiful / as we go?" The seasonal passage into death he notes in the second stanza is a part of the very process of life, for as he gazes at the night sky from a field a sense that the rhythm of his respiration, of breath in and out of his lungs, is one of both living and dying overcomes him:

> Silently
> I breathe and die
> by turns.

The last portion of the poem focuses specifically on Williams's death, and, as in "Night at an Airport," Ignatow envisages this event as the entirely natural conclusion to an existence and perhaps as a release into the free, elemental energy of the universe. Nature or the physical cosmos is plainly asserted as the veritable location of human life and death:

> He was ripe
> and fell to the ground
> from a bough
> out where the wind
> is free
> of the branches.

With "For My Daughter in Reply to a Question" and "The Hope," as well as the two "Coffin" poems from the section of new work of the past decade which completes *Poems 1934-1969*, Ignatow persists in exploring various possibilities of this theme of death. The answer he gives to his daughter's query about human mortality rests finally on the indisputable uniqueness of each person; the singularity awarded to an individual, preserved and cherished by him, will secure his special place which the years to come cannot remove. (We can remark here an obvious contrast to the attitude taken in "The Song," discussed earlier, where time erases everything.)

> There'll never be another as you
> and never another as I.
> No one will ever confuse you
> nor confuse me with another.

> We will not be forgotten and passed over
> and buried under the births and deaths to come.

"The Hope," however, concentrates less on identity and more on conditioning, a toughening procedure that takes the poet into a natural setting at
evening where he must do without the comforts and shields provided by
civilization to insulate him from the inclemency of the elements. His intention is to endure the hardships of this situation, which threatens his life,
and so achieve a new alliance with raw nature that indicates vigor and an
ability to maintain himself in proximity to death:

> If I live through the night
> I will be a species
> related to the tree
> and the cold dark.

Some proof of the success of this venture for Ignatow can be discerned in
the "Coffin" poems (the first in order of appearance bears no title in *Poems
1934-1969*, while the following piece is called "First Coffin Poem"). A kind
of surrealist touch, the lightness of fantasy, rules his approach to mortality
here, suffusing the dreamlike quality of both poems with a strange humor-
ousness. The initial, untitled piece steps directly into the realm of the irrational and absurd, its very lack of a designation adding to the reader's shock:

> They put a telephone in his coffin
> with an outside extension
> and were not surprised
> when the receiver was lifted
> and there were sighing sounds:
> Hair growing? Skin shrinking?
> Larvae coming into being?
> When those above asked for an answer
> they received none and went down
> and opened the grave. They found
> the receiver back in its cradle.

Our feelings of improbability are utterly vanquished by Ignatow's mastery of
tone, atmosphere, and detail; we are captives of the same curiosity as his
band of odd, anonymous investigators. The next stanza reveals them inde-
fatigably at work, repeating the activities we have already observed but at
last resorting to stricter measures as one member decides to remain in the
grave "and peck through / a hole bored in the wood" of the coffin. The
others then enact their telephone routine once more and bring up their
companion, whose news is unexpected. His succinct declaration needs to

be understood in view of the fact that he has voluntarily stayed close to
death, so that his descent into the grave, his "observations" there, and his
return amount to a certain type of vicarious or symbolic death and rebirth
motif which results in new knowledge for him, knowledge which takes the
form of self-discovery. What he says to the rest of the group offers nothing
to those avid for particulars yet is abundant in suggestiveness about man,
the limits of whose being clearly cannot be fathomed or circumscribed:

> he stared long at his colleagues
> and said finally, as if to himself,
> I am a mystery.

If the sighs overheard from the coffin carry possible connotations of satisfaction, or of sleep and fulfillment—though they must, in the end, retain
their air of ambiguity and resist strict definition—Ignatow's straightforward
address in "First Coffin Poem" will not seem totally unexpected to the reader.
He opens with a statement, however, as startling as the one with which the
preceding poem began. In this instance death's presence and potentiality
within an individual's existence, concretely realized as the coffin which,
throughout the poem, is shifted about like ordinary furniture while the poet
tries to incorporate it naturally into his daily affairs, is recognized and assimilated. The poem again aims at bizarre, Surrealist evocations but does so
deliberately to manipulate the reader into sharing the author's vision.
Ignatow's speech marvelously mixes congeniality, practicality, and whimsy,
which permits him to maneuver a bright surface of ideas and, at the same
time, prove with genuine seriousness the relations between life and death:

> I love you, my plain pine box,
> because you also are a bench,
> with the lid down. Can you see
> my friends in a row seated
> at ease with themselves?
> I am in a coffin
> and it has been set against the wall
> of a living room. It is just before
> dinner and several friends are standing
> about with glasses in their hands,
> drinking to the possibilities
> that life offers.
>   The coffin also
> could be placed as a table
> in front of a grand sofa, with food
> and drinks served on it, and an ashtray.

Because death is inescapable it should be brought into the center of life's
events, not ostentatiously but simply, pragmatically; the "possibilities" of
an existence can only be valued and sought out by remembering its limited
duration. Ignatow's outlook in this poem puts us in mind of the similar
attitudes held by Wallace Stevens in "The Emperor of Ice Cream" and William Carlos Williams in "Tract," both poems containing funeral directions
which treat death as a commonplace conclusion rather than a special occasion. As the poem continues, Ignatow replies to those who might find his
various uses for the coffin "gruesome" and would prefer to substitute "an
actual coffee table" by demonstrating that it

> . . . would prove
> how rigid we must be about ourselves
> and cause us to languish, caught
> in a limitation. We must make one thing
> do for another.

Whatever else these lines may imply, they point, as did the previous poem,
to the constant aura of mysteriousness remaining, ineradicable, in human
life and to the fluid borders between living and dying. Ignatow enjoins us to
be flexible, to allow death access to the intimacy of our lives so that perhaps, like the sighs escaping the coffin, life can somehow infiltrate death
and humanize it. If the two states remain compartmentalized, "rigid, we will
never enter fully into the realities of what we are now, and what we are
steadily and inexorably becoming:

> I am hope, in urging you
> to use my pine box. Take me to your home
> when I die imperceptibly. Without fuss
> place me against the wall in my coffin,
> a conversation piece, an affirmation of change.
> I am, sincerely yours.

Moods of determined persistence and of celebration dominate several
other poems at the close of *Poems 1934-1969*. Chief among them are "Walk
There," the final piece in *Rescue Me Dead*, and "While I Live," "Morning,"
and "Feeling with My Hands" from the section of newer work. The recurrent metaphor of the walking journey appropriately returns to finish *Rescue
the Dead*, for as we saw earlier in Ignatow's epigraph for the book ("I feel
along the edges of life / for a way / that will lead to open land") his entire
enterprise in the poems of this collection—in the complete body of his
writing as it exists up to the present moment, for that matter—shapes into
a personal quest conducted along the very boundary lines of his existence,

with all the attendant perils which threaten nerves, vision, and seem to negate the prospect of going on, in search of an honest, manageable means of being, a path that leads toward a horizon. The route chosen circles down into darkness, disorder, and bestiality, both as they appear in the prevailing assumptions (frequently unconscious) of contemporary society and as they break in upon and besiege the poet's own consciousness. Ignatow makes this descent and climbs out again into daylight. "Walk There" really needs no discussion; it dramatizes in sharp detail the poet's continuing progress out of the "dark wood" which will eventually result in his arrival at the "open land" of his epigraph, a place where life's possibilities still await him:

> The way through the woods is past trees,
> touching grass, bark, stone, water and mud;
> into the night of the trees, beneath
> their damp cold, stumbling on roots,
> discovering no trail, trudging
> and smelling pine, cypress and musk.
> A rabbit leaps across my path,
> and something big rustles in the bush.
> Stand still, eye the nearest tree
> for climbing. Subside in fear
> in continued silence. Walk.
> See the sky splattered with leaves.
> Ahead, is that too the sky
> or a clearing?
> Walk there.

Just as Ignatow handles various objects in nature while passing, in the lines above, to feel a tacit kinship with them and refresh the awareness of his own solidity, so in "While I Live" he hears the language with which the physical universe—in trees, grass, and flowers, in the life-giving warmth of the sun—speaks to him. But he also recognizes "the darkness in language" and thus prepares to face the end that will come to him as to every living thing, "only that I may endure the necessary / ecstasy of my personal death." That conclusion, however, is not yet, he insists in the poem's strong, positive climax:

> I am labor, I am a disposition to live.
> Who dies? Only the sun
> but you must wait
> while I live.

Ignatow performs an act of human definition in "Morning," a longer, more detailed piece, delineating himself as a person apart from, though not alien to, the natural world he inhabits, represented here by the birds whose song he listens to as he awakens: "I am not their flesh and they sing." He proceeds to distinguish his brain as the agent bestowing "identity" on him, deciding his actions, carrying out the rapid processes of his thought, furnishing the words he employs ("where have I learned to know them / as quickly as you think them?") to name things, parts of his body, or to designate the kinds of emotions or states of being he experiences. Language further extends his potentialities by offering the opportunity for dialogue, for conversation with himself as well as with others:

> I am a talker, hearing myself
> and replying to myself. I have a companion
> and I am on my feet,
> walking where I can be heard.

And, not unexpectedly, we watch him moving again along the by now familiar track that opens out of the present into the unknown before him: "the road between the woods leading somewhere, / sending its emptiness ahead." But this "emptiness" contains ominous overtones, for the birds are suddenly "silent" and the poet realizes how delicately constituted is his selfhood, how easily endangered with annihilation:

> Silent birds, are you listening to my voice
> giving me my self? Are you recording
> your listening to me? Are you birds then?
> And when will you sing again?
> My brain will have birds to record itself
> and it falls silent, my voice halts.
> There is silence
> and I could fade again.

Danger passes, however, and the final stanza starts on a climactic note in support of the poet's existence and that of the birds. Ignatow uses these closing lines to announce a fascination with basic sensory operations, with the fundamentals of experience in which mind and senses collaborate, as if here, at "the beginning," to borrow his words, the reality and worth of living as a man in the physical universe might be tried. Momentarily, he seems to adopt the guise of a second Adam; but rather than an innocent Adam born into paradise, he is a man who has descended through all the levels of a fallen or imperfect world and resolved to come back, to initiate the venture once more:

> They live, I live,
> they sing, I hear them sing.

> No, this is not happiness.
> It is the beginning,
> it is curiosity,
> it is touch, by ear.
> It is sight,
> it is a coincidence of brain and body.
> I can be happy
> in this knowledge.

Characteristically, in his most recent statement in a poem of his poetic convictions, Ignatow emphasizes both human movement and sensory responsiveness, beginning with the title, "Feeling with My Hands." Poetry must for him activate life and reply to it at the very threshold of experience; it has to be an integral part of the living flow and thus devoid of rhetoric or metaphysical pretensions. Ted Hughes, writing of East European poets such as Vasko Popa (Yugoslavia), Miroslav Holub (Czechoslovakia), and Zbigniew Herbert (Poland), speaks of certain human fundamentals from which they have tried to develop their work. Whatever differences of circumstance and history may exist between them, and between their situation and Ignatow's, something of what Hughes says has an unmistakable relationship with our poet's outlook and efforts:

> The attempt these poets are making to put on record that man is also . . .
> an acutely conscious human creature of suffering and hope, has brought
> their poetry down to such precisions, discriminations and humilities that it
> is a new thing. It seems closer to the common reality, in which we have to
> live if we are to survive, than to those other realities in which we can
> holiday, or into which we decay when our bodily survival is comfortably
> taken care of, and which art, particularly contemporary art, is forever try-
> ing to impose on us as some sort of superior dimension.[12]

Ignatow does not regard *Poems 1934-1969* as either a "collected" or definitive edition of his work; indeed, a supposition of this kind would allow some readers and critics to mark an end to his career. So, in spite of the extraordinarily rich, abundant achievement represented by this book, we must leave David Ignatow energetically, forcefully in process, with the words and images from "Feeling with My Hands" in which he depicts at once the poetic object he intends and himself active within it. His voice and gesture, compelling, unassuming, yet vibrant with earned humanity reach toward us as we read:

> Will this poem be able to think and breathe
> and have sex? Will it be able
> to lift a finger to call a waiter

for the menu? Will it have hopes
of a future life? Will it have friends
among other poems? Oh yes, will it
be able to write other poems?

I do not want it to rest on its merits.
I want others to look through it
to see me breathing and taking food
and embracing my wife, telling her
she has lovely teeth. This poem
should have an erection and everywhere
should say hello and be a friend
and not hesitate to tell other poems
what it thinks about them. Be pleasant
but be truthful. Be happy but fear not death.
Here it is and I am still talking
and feeling with my hands.

(1974)

NOTES

[1]Scott Chisholm, "An Interview with David Ignatow," *Tennessee Poetry Journal* III,
2 (Winter 1970), p. 27.
[2]Ibid., p. 27.
[3]See "On Writing," *Tennessee Poetry Journal* III, 2. (Winter 1970), pp. 14-15.
[4]Ibid., p. 14.
[5]Chisholm, "An Interview with David Ignatow," p. 25.
[6]Ibid., p. 22.
[7]Ibid., p. 23.
[8]Ibid., p. 27.
[9]I am indebted in part here to Ignatow's discussion of the poem. Ibid., pp. 31-33.
[10]Ibid., p. 32.
[11]There are similarities in this treatment of and insight into violence between Ignatow
and the extraordinary French poet Henri Michaux. See, for example, the latter's
"Chez les hacs," in *Selected Writings of Henri Michaux*, ed. and trans. Richard
Elmann (New York, 1968).
[12]Introduction to Vasko Popa, *Selected Poems* (Harmondsworth, Middlesex, 1969),
p. 9.

16

A Reading of
Galway Kinnell

*The little light existing in the mystery that surrounds us comes from ourselves: it
is a false light. The mystery has never shown its own.*
——JULES RENARD

. . . le Rien qui est la verité
——MALLARMÉ

All things are one thing to the earth . . .
——KENNETH PATCHEN

GALWAY KINNELL'S FIRST COLLECTION, *WHAT A KINGDOM IT WAS* (1960), CAN
be viewed in retrospect now as one of those volumes signaling decisive
changes in the mood and character of American poetry as it departed from
the witty, pseudo-mythic verse, apparently written to critical prescription,
of the 1950s to arrive at the more authentic, liberated work of the 1960s.[1]
Our recent poetry shows how closely and vulnerably aware of the palpable
life of contemporary society poets have become, for, increasingly during the
past decade or so, they have opened themselves as persons to the complex,
frequently incongruous, violence-ridden ethos of the age in an effort to
ground the poetic imagination in a shared, perceptible reality. This kind of
openness—a sensitive receptivity in which the poet, to borrow a phrase of
Heidegger's about Hölderlin, "is exposed to the divine lightnings" that can
easily exact their toll on nerves and emotional balance—extends, in many
instances, beyond matters of social and political experience to naked
metaphysical confrontation: with the universe, the identity of the self, the

possibilities of an absent or present God, or the prospect of a vast, over-whelming nothingness. In such poets as Theodore Roethke, Kenneth Patchen, John Berryman, Robert Lowell, James Wright, Anne Sexton, James Dickey, W. S. Merwin, and Sylvia Plath, for example, with all differences aside, the pursuit of personal vision often leads toward a precipitous, dizzy-ing boundary where the self stands alone, unaided but for its own resources, before the seemingly tangible earth at hand with its bewildering multiplic-ity of life, the remoteness of space, the endless rhythms of nature, the turns of night and day, and within, the elusive images of memory and dream, the irrationality and uncertainty of human behavior, the griefs and ecstasies that living accumulates. Here the poet—and Galway Kinnell is certainly of this company—is thrown back upon his own perceptions. His art must be the authoritative testimony to a man's own experience, or it is meaningless; its basic validity rests upon that premise.

"Perhaps to a degree more than is true of other poets, Kinnell's develop-ment will depend on the actual events of his life," James Dickey remarked prophetically in a review of *What a Kingdom It Was*.[2] For what we encoun-ter as an essential ingredient in his work as it grows is not only the presence of the poet as man and speaker, but also his identification, through the-matic recurrences, repeated images revelatory of his deepest concerns and most urgent feelings, with the experiences his poems dramatize. In what follows we shall try to see how Kinnell, using the considerable imaginative and linguistic powers at his command from the beginning, explores relent-lessly the actualities of his existence to wrest from them what significance for life he can. Through the compelling force of his art, we find ourselves engaged in this arduous search with him.

With the advantages of hindsight we should not be surprised when we notice that the initial poem of *What a Kingdom It Was*, aptly entitled "First Song," is located out of doors—in Illinois cornfields with frog ponds nearby—and that in the course of its three stanzas there is a movement from "dusk" into night. A large proportion of Kinnell's poetry is involved with the natural world, for he is drawn to it in profound ways, has been since childhood, and it provides him with an inexhaustible store for his imaginative meditation, if that phrase will do to distinguish a kind of thinking through images and particulars that is integral to the poetic act. But Kinnell's images from nature will become increasingly stark and rudi-mentary, their bonds with the ordinary range of human sympathies ever more tenuous, as he matures. Indeed, his poems about killing a bird for Christmas dinner, shooting buffalo with a murderer for companion, moun-tain-climbing, camping out alone in the mountains during winter, exam-ining fossils in the cliff above a frog pond, seeking to define himself by identifying with porcupine and bear, bring him finally to the contemplation

of what it is to be human in an extreme, one might say primitive situation. Under such fundamental circumstances he faces himself and the
conditions of the world simultaneously, without mediation or disguise. It
should be said, however, that Kinnell employs other means than nature
for cutting to the bone of existence, though intimate acquaintance with
other living creatures and with the earth is of primary importance to his
work.

Likewise, the imagery of darkness or blackness, mentioned above, plays a
prominent part in many poems. The night with its infinite interstellar spaces
reminiscent of those in Pascal or Mallarme haunts Kinnell, heightening his
sensitive awareness of immense emptiness and void in the universe. In "First
Song," though, these stringent realities are softened, almost sentimental-
ized, by pleasant details of smoky, twilight cornfields, croaking frogs, and a
small group of boys making "cornstalk violins" and "scraping of their joy" as
night falls. Pleasurable nostalgia fills the poem, yet the final lines perhaps
disclose something more, an indication of life's mixed blessings, a prediction of pain as well as exultation:

> A boy's hunched body loved out of a stalk
> The first song of his happiness, and the song woke
> His heart to the darkness and into the sadness of joy.

However muted this passage, however conventional its emotion, it does
reflect, in the poet's backward look across time, a recognized moment of
anticipation of those paradoxes of living which the years afterward must
inevitably make manifest.

A number of the poems that follow enter more precipitously on the confusions and conflicts only hinted at in "First Song." At the risk of emphasizing the obvious, one should note how these poems dramatize through crucial incidents in the author's youth the passage from a state of ignorance
and innocence into a state of experience which derives from a firsthand
knowledge of guilt, violence, hypocrisy, and death.

Unavoidably, in treating this difficult awakening to experience, Kinnell
comes up against the disturbing incongruities a boy senses between the
spiritual or religious training he has received and the harsh facts of the
world he begins to meet. "First Communion" and "To Christ Our Lord"
explore this area but do not exhaust it for Kinnell; it is a major concern of
his first book. The former poem focuses on the boy's estrangement from
church religion. His remoteness from the formal pieties is evident in the
opening lines, which start by defining the physical distance from home to
church "way over in the next county" and move immediately to a completely secular recollection of having made "the same trip" the preceding
year "carrying a sackful of ears to collect / The nickel-an-ear porcupine

bounty." The contrast between the spiritual realities supposedly represented by the church and the tough-minded, earthy attitude of the porcupine hunters who slice off the ears of their prey to collect a reward hardly needs remarking, though it prepares for the manner in which the interior of the church and the sacrament of communion are conceived in the next lines—a totally material manner:

> Pictured on the wall over dark Jerusalem
> Jesus is shining—in the dark he is a lamp.
> On the tray he is a pastry wafer.

The perception here doesn't seem to get beyond the tangibility of the objects: all is what it appears to be and nothing more. But the picture of Jesus is described with an ambiguity and use of detail linking the lines with many later ones in Kinnell's poems. At first, the portrait has merely a material resplendence, the quality of the painting; then that resplendence plays upon the light/darkness imagery we associate with the prologue to St. John's gospel. Yet in terms of the kind of symbolic weight with which Kinnell continues to endow his images of light and lamps and flames, and his contrary images of darkness and night, the figure of Jesus is fundamentally implicated with human hopes and desires to escape the "dark Jerusalem" of the world. But these implications are cut short with the terse line reducing the communion wafer to a lump of perishable pastry. Kinnell next recounts the journey home from communion: the adults exchange pleasantries about the preaching but soon resort to local gossip of a slightly salacious kind. Once more the boy recalls the porcupine bounty and compares the worth of the two trips. His choice, never made explicit, seems indisputably the more verifiable value of the money: "The last time over / The same trail we brought two dollars homeward. / Now we carry the aftertaste of the Lord."

The last stanza shifts to external nature and renders it, in part at least, in sacramental terms. The season is autumn; life flares forth in a final display of vitality; sunlight appears to lend the prairie grass intimations of "parable" to the observer, but one which refers to nature's unalterable cyclical pattern. Decline and death are sure to follow:

> The sunlight streams through the afternoon
> Another parable over the sloughs
> And yellowing grass of the prairies.
> Cold wind stirs, and the last green
> Climbs to all the tips of the season, like
> The last flame brightening on a wick.
> Embers drop and break in sparks. Across the earth
> Sleep is the overlapping of enough shadows.

The last line above functions obliquely, implying seasonal transition, the sinking toward winter, and at the same time serves to bring us away from external nature to the boy in his bed preparing for sleep and turning his final waking thoughts to the communion day just past. Addressed to Jesus, these thoughts constitute a rejection of the "disappointing shed" where "they"—doubtless the adults, minister included, whose professed beliefs and practices stir no feeling of the sacred in the boy —"hang your picture / And drink juice, and conjure / Your person into inferior bread." Christ is, then, both something less and something more than these parishioners believe. The poem ends with his resolution "not [to] go again into that place. . . ."

If Christ is not to be found in any truly apprehensible form in churches, His spirit and example still persist in the boy's mind, influencing the view he takes of his experiences and actions. The sharp discrepancy between what Jesus represents for the boy and the very different acts which exist-ence seems to force upon him creates the inner tension of the beautiful poem "To Christ Our Lord." In the loveliness and terror of Kinnell's presen-tation of the winter landscape on which the poem opens there are evident at once the hard, puzzling contrarieties that compose life at any moment. Wolves hunt elk at Christmastime, tracking them over the frozen land, thus demonstrating an iron natural law of survival. Kinnell sketches the scene in swift strokes for the first three lines; then, without finishing his sentence, he offers a view of the Christmas dinner preparations. No com-ment is necessary for the reader to see that both man and wolf maintain themselves by adherence to the same law: "Inside snow melted in a basin, and a woman basted / A bird spread over coals by its wings and head."

The allusion to a crucified figure in the shape of the outspread bird is not accidental but is a particular instance of the cosmic image that brings the poem to its moving climax. The boy, listening to the grace said before this Christmas meal, wonders at the contradictions between his Christian and his human positions, for it is he who has been responsible for killing the bird. He remembers vividly how, as he hunted this creature, there alter-nated within him the dictates of conscience and the animal instinct of hunger which drives the wolves after elk. Hunger and the sense of necessity tri-umphed, causing him perplexity. Kinnell captures the feeling of pursuit, the winter dawn, the agonized choice and its result as they are recalled with the swiftness of the events themselves:

> He had killed it himself, climbing out
> Alone on snowshoes in the Christmas dawn.
> The fallen snow swirling and the snowfall gone,
> Heard its throat scream as the rifle shouted,
> Watched it drop, and fished from the snow the dead.

> He had not wanted to shoot. The sound
> Of wings beating into the hushed air
> Had stirred his love, and his fingers
> Froze in his gloves, and he wondered,
> Famishing, could he fire? Then he fired.

Though he repudiates the deed and wishes to love rather than kill, he has learned that, strangely, he harbors both impulses. But he is further disillusioned by the conventional prayer of thanksgiving which "praised his wicked act," an act that, in his mind, is opposed to everything Christ stands for. Finally, recognizing that there is "nothing to do but surrender" to the contradictions of the world and "kill and eat" as others do, he submits, though "with wonder." This "wonder" is an awe and puzzlement at the tragic mixture of love and death inherent in creation and brings on the expansive vision with which the poem concludes. In the closing stanza the boy again wanders "the drifting field" of snow (whose constantly changing shapes suggest the elusive, unstable character of reality) at night still searching for a meaningful reply to his questions. His querying of the black reaches of space, scattered as in Mallarmé's memorable phrase, with "la neige eternelle des astres," at first wins only silence, vacuity; but suddenly he sees the distant constellation of the Swan which, like the bird roasting outspread upon the coals, mimes the figure of the crucified Christ:

> At night on snowshoes on the drifting field
> He wondered again, for whom had love stirred?
> The stars glittered on the snow and nothing answered.
> Then the Swan spread her wings, cross of the cold north,
> The pattern and mirror of the acts of earth.

There can be little consolation or resolution in this image with its indications of death, but there is a certain understanding, possibly the beginnings of acceptance. A darkened universe returns to the watcher an enlarged symbol of the actuality he has so painfully met; the crucified figure, Christ or bird, is the proper image for the world's conditions.

I have discussed these poems in some detail not merely because they merit it for their obvious high qualities of language, imagery, and rhythm but because the experiences central to them are unquestionably of importance to Kinnell in his progressive stripping off of innocence, illusion, and his achievement of a hardened, stoic attitude. We catch an early glimpse of this attitude, or the need for it, in "Westport," a poem which ostensibly deals with a rugged westward journey, undertaken through some unavoidable compulsion. Not so oddly, if we consider what Kinnell has been saying in these other early poems; the speaker admits to the taxing and unpleasant aspects of the trip yet also confesses that these are its peculiar rewards as well:

> "Yes," I said, "it will be a hard journey . . ."
> And the shining grasses were bowed towards the west
> As if one craving had killed them. "But at last,"
> I added, "the hardness is the one thing you thank."

The travelers go their way, and in three brief lines finishing the poem they find darkness descending, listen to the desolate sounds of the landscape and wind. Their fate appears mysteriously implicated with the harsh but durable existence of nature:

> Now out of evening we discovered night
> And heard the cries of the prairie and the moan
> Of wind through the roots of its clinging flowers.

Obliquity is Kinnell's method here, a sign of even freer, more allusive writing to come. Like the travelers, the reader confronts the rich opacity of "night," the startling, potentially frightening "cries of the prairie" and wailing of the wind that readily remind him of pain; set against these dark or negative qualities there is that last phrase describing the tenacious hold on life of the "clinging flowers." These details are meant to remain suggestive but ambiguous, just as they would be in their actual setting, for the very possibilities in them to stir the imagination. Kinnell wishes such elements of experience to approximate the external circumstances of the world they mirror because he knows they cannot provide any meaning but what we read in them for ourselves. Or as Whitman says, "All truths wait in all things."

The chief poems in this first book, and those most relevant to Kinnell's development and more recent inclinations, are "Easter," "The Schoolhouse," "Seven Streams of Nevis," "The Descent," "Where the Track Vanishes," "Freedom, New Hampshire," "The Supper after the Last" (all of these but "Easter" appear in the third section of the volume), and the long poem "The Avenue Bearing the Initial of Christ into the New World." I do not intend to slight the other poems, but those named are clearly the most notable for range and vision, and in several instances for manner and technique. Also apparent in these poems is Kinnell's preoccupation with the larger metaphysical themes previously in evidence and now increasingly at the forefront of his interests. Death, suffering, the will to elude the body's mortality, and the brute facts of the actual World: Kinnell's imagination turns these themes over and over, dwelling on the insoluble enigmas of life's significance or lack of it as these emerge in the process of his own living.

"Easter,"[3] the most conventional in form with its rather neat quatrains, rhymes and off-rhymes, again, as in "First Communion" and "To Christ Our Lord," separates what the poet takes for the shallowness of official Christianity from what he perceives as the true meaning of Christ—that He is symbolic of the ubiquitous pain, victimization, and death of man and all other living things. Just as the hunted bird of "To Christ Our Lord" was transformed into an emblem of the sacrificed Jesus, so in the present poem the "virgin nurse," who has been "Raped, robbed, weighted, drowned" in the river, exemplifies His death yet another time. The poem is crowded with subtle ambiguities, resonances, and ironies, for Kinnell elicits effects from the particulars he uses on both literal and metaphorical levels at once. The second stanza, for example, begins in a matter of fact way: "To get to church you have to cross the river, / First breadwinner for the town. . . ." And for the banal, unspiritual townspeople, satisfied with the comforts of thoughtless, routine belief, the statement has merely literal application. But in terms of the victim whose body rides in its depths, the river is reminiscent of the Jordan and likely the Styx, too; throughout the poem it symbolizes a dimension of death beyond the reach of the living. The myopic sight of the townspeople, who view these waters only with the eyes of commerce and gain, fails to comprehend them, as the poet's vision does, as the means of redemption, though a natural rather than a supernatural one: "its wide/ Mud-colored currents cleansing forever / The swill-making villages at its side."

In contrast to the muddy river which purifies the towns along its banks and the lives within them, there is heard the "disinfected voice of the minister" preaching his Easter sermon. But his remarks are irrelevant; he speaks to his parishioners neither of their deaths nor of the nurse's murder, "he is talking of nothing but Easter, / Dying so on the wood, He rose." The story is too familiar so the congregation, inattentive, put their minds to something more immediate, a "gospel" from the headlines which at least quickens their pulses—"Some of us daydream of the morning news." Others, more distracted or uncomfortable in hard pews, are rendered by Kinnell wittily, though a bit pretentiously, in parody of Easter's original significance:

> Some of us lament we rose at all,
> A child beside me comforts her doll,
> We are dying on the hard wood of the pews.

After a stanza commenting on death's omnipresence, the poem returns to the river where, with the ironic reminder that many of Christ's disciples were fishermen, "with wire hooks the little boats are fishing" to recover, in a spurious attempt at resurrection, the body of the nurse. The last five stanzas are addressed by the poet to the dead woman and convey his own notion of her redemption. If her corpse is not hauled up from the river, she must find her true communion in the sacrament of its muddy currents (". . . drink well of the breadwinner") and be carried by them in what seems a movement toward liberation that is also an identification with water as an element of both death and purification. Surprisingly, Kinnell urges her not to regret "That the dream has ended," to reflect on her life and see it for what it was, what she dimly, when alive, thought it actually might be—a kind of hell. Only in death is there the hope of serenity or repose:

> Turn
> On the dream you lived through the unwavering gaze.
> It is as you thought. The living burn.
> In the floating days may you discover grace.

In "Easter" and the poems following it Kinnell contemplates human experience against the silent, puzzling background of earth, universe, and death, particularly as it can be witnessed in the character and fate of others. In "The Schoolhouse," a learned but isolated country schoolmaster who once taught the poet and who wrestled with problems of knowledge and belief; in "Seven Streams of Nevis," the seedy, outcast lives of seven individuals through whom the poet seeks the seven virtues and the purpose of human affliction; in the death of a friend while mountain-climbing in "The Descent"; in the implications of the path to a deserted Alpine cemetery in "Where the Track Vanishes"; in the death of his brother in "Freedom, New Hampshire"; in the tragic, desperate but resilient lives of the poor Jews and Negroes in the New York ghetto in "The Avenue Bearing the Initial of Christ into the New World." A single exception is "The Supper after the Last," a complex poem of a fierce, apocalyptic sort which assumes the aspect of hallucinated vision.

By comparison with most of these poems "Easter," in spite of its subject, appears cool, detached, objective, for Kinnell's approach to his material grows more personal and intense as he continues to write. In a stanza such as the following from "Seven Streams of Nevis" the formal structure strains outward under the tremendous emotional force generated from within, so that, as in certain poems by Baudelaire, Yeats, Lowell, or Kunitz, for example, the language seems barely able to contain its pressure:

> O Connolly! O Jack! O Peaches!
> When you fall down foaming in fits
> Remember with your scrawny wits
> And knee up laughing like leeches:
> You are just flesh but you will be
> —One rainy day—faith, hope, and charity.

The second section of this poem departs somewhat from the strictness of
the first to develop one long stanza rising to its own powerful climactic lines
but more suited to the meditative nature of Kinnell's vision as he nears a
symbolic source from which the uncontrollable energies of life spill forth.
Leaving behind the horror and suffering of the seven lives he has examined
in the opening part, the poet, alone, climbs Ben Nevis in western Scotland,
the highest peak in England, which takes on in the poem the features of a
sacred mountain, soaring into the heavens, fixing a metaphysical center
point in the universe with access to the divine world and to the infernal
regions.[4] At this locus some knowledge of the ultimate origin and design of
existence should be obtainable; that is the motive behind the poet's climb.
But the knowledge that is forthcoming can only be called somber and chill-
ing awareness; there is no mystical revelation or illumination. The entire
stanza abounds in the imagery of darkness and blackness, only occasionally
contradicted by images of light. The poet starts the ascent of Ben Nevis "in
darkness" reflective of his own ignorance of final answers, as well as indicative of the literal time of day. Climbing, he comes upon the seven streams,
"well foreknown," that in their separate courses and movements suggest the
terrible headlong rush toward disaster of the seven persons already portrayed:

> One sang like strings, one crashed
> Through gated rocks, one vibrated, others
> Went skipping like unbucketed grease across
> Hot stones, or clattered like bones, or like milk
> Spilled and billowed in streamers of bright silk,
> Irises glimmering a visionary course—
> Me grimping the dark, sniffing for the source . . .

The "source," discovered in the next lines, turns out to be a still, "dark"
pool "Whose shined waters on the blackened mountain / Mirrored the black
skies." And stressing again the darkness that seems less a temporary absence
of light than the very negation of it distilled from mountain, water, and sky,
the poet carries his search forward to the middle of the pool, the calm eye of
the world's hurricane, the heart's chaos:

> . . . I rode out on
> Dark water under the darkness of the skies,
> And the waves ringing through the dark were the rings
> Around the eye itself of the world, which,
> Drawing down heaven like its black lid, was there
> Where merely to be still was temperate,
> Where to move was brave, where justice was a glide,
> Knowledge the dissolving of the head-hung eyes;
> And there my faith lay burning, there my hope

> Lay burning on the water, there charity
> Burned like a sun.

The primary revelation as the poem moves toward its climax and conclusion is that the cosmos, and thus men's lives, is dominated by darkness. The
poet arrives at a midpoint, a place of recognitions which is his version of
Eliot's "still point of the turning world," but what he recognizes is the sheer
human strength and virtue that the acts of living demand. He discovers no
divine source as Eliot does. Darkness surrounds men, the pool and the empty
black heavens above; it is Kinnell himself who bestows the light there is in
his "faith," "hope," and "charity" with regard to the human situation. A
person apparently must create his own virtue by traveling to the center of
himself, accepting himself, and realizing his isolation in the world. We are
close, I think, to Yeats's recommendation at the finish of "A Dialogue of
Self and Soul" when he proclaims himself rightful judge of his own acts:

> I am content to follow to its source
> Every event in action or in thought;
> Measure the lot; forgive myself the lot!

Kinnell ends with a request that approaches prayer, asking the "pool of
heaven" to give "the locus of grace"—which I presume to be a condition of
awareness similar to the one the poet has achieved—to

>   seven who have
> Bit on your hearts, and spat the gravels of
> Tooth and heart, and bit again; who have wiped
> The thumb-burst jellies of sight on a sleeve
> (The visions we could have wrung from that cloth)
> And sprouted sight like mushrooms—O seven
> Streams of nothing backgazing after heaven,
> In the heart's hell you have it; call it God's Love.

The seven in their agonized lives, so powerfully and graphically asserted
throughout the poem, are allied here to such great tragic figures as Oedipus
and Lear, whose suffering and blindness result in another kind of penetrating vision of reality. They are brought to knowledge of their nothingness
which still thirsts for meaning, solace, transcendental resolution ("backgazing
after heaven"). The "locus of grace" offers, in the last line, a shocking disclosure that echoes in part the conclusion of "Easter," where life is referred
to as infernal: "In the heart's hell you have it; call it God's Love." These
words can be interpreted variously. One might say Kinnell implies that God
wills the suffering of individuals out of the paradox of a divine love whose
goal is their purification and salvation. If we isolated the line and elicited

from it a Christian meaning, we could indeed say something of that sort. But I cannot locate anything else in the poem, or in the rest of Kinnell's work for that matter, which would sustain this reading. It appears more likely that, severe though it may be, Kinnell extends to us "the heart's hell" as the fundamental human reality we have to live with, and from which we must summon our own virtue. Heaven is an illusion, looked on with nostalgia, which worsens our state by measuring it against an impossible ideal. Poetry, Kinnell tells us later, in the second of his "Last Songs" from *Body Rags* (1968), should incorporate the specifically human faults, the things that make man part of this world, not an eternal or paradisiacal one (there are some resemblances in this, of course, to Rilke and Wallace Stevens):

> Silence. Ashes
> In the grate. Whatever it is
> that keeps us from heaven,
> sloth, wrath, greed, fear, could we only
> reinvent it on earth
> as song.

Obviously, neither in "Seven Streams of Nevis" nor "Last Songs" is Kinnell praising man's fallibility, but he continues to insist on realizing it as integral to what man is. If we return to the phrase "God's Love," the final words of the poem, I think we find it suggests first of all the poet's bitterly ironic criticism of the idea of a benevolent Creator who could will misery and death for His largely helpless creatures; further, it emphasizes his conviction that the love and value to be found in the tumult of earthly existence are in man's ravaged breast: God's love is simply what man makes it.

In "The Descent" and "Where the Track Vanishes" Kinnell gets nearer the looser structures of more recent poems. The two pieces juxtapose or alternate various scenes and incidents as the means for tracing out the theme of death and the pattern of ascent and decline which he perceives in all the particulars of nature and in man. More and more, in line with European poets such as Rilke or Yves Bonnefoy (whose poems he has so beautifully translated),[5] he envisages death as something like a negative presence, awaiting its appointed moment to emerge from beneath the surface of each individual life. This vision extends to the whole creation; it cannot be denied but must be faced with strength and tenderness, as this passage from "Where the Track Vanishes" points out:

> My hand on the sky
> Cannot shut the sky out
> Any more than any March
> Branch can. In the Boston Store

> Once, I tried new shoes:
> The shoeman put my feet
> In a machine, saying Kid
> Wrig yer toes. I
> Wrigged and peered:
> Inside green shoes green
> Twigs were wrigging by themselves
> Green as the grasses
> I drew from her
> Hair in the springtime
> While she laughed, unfoliaged
> by sunlight, a little
> Spray of bones I loved.

It is no more possible for the poet, as a man, to avoid participation in the life of nature than it is for a tree: both are wedded indissolubly to earth. Under the green light of the now old fashioned X-ray machine used to test the fit of shoes Kinnell watches, with a boy's fascination and an adult's understanding, the skeleton beneath the skin, his own mortality; suddenly, movingly, it recalls for him a girl whom he once loved and an affectionate gesture they shared. She takes form not in any ordinary description of her features but as an image of delicate, almost frail being lifted momentarily from the world like the season and surroundings in which he remembers her. The elegiac quality implicit in the last lines strengthens the impression of the evanescence of affection and, more emphatically, of personal identity, which also occupy Kinnell in "Freedom, New Hampshire."

The place "where the track vanishes" in this poem is a ruined mountain graveyard, "a heap of stones / Mortared with weeds and wild flowers— / The fallen church." Though everything here decayed long ago, and there would seem to be little chance of visitors, still a track is worn through the grass, ending among the gravestones. Perhaps, the poet muses, it is the crippled French peasant, leading his twelve goats up the mountainside to pasture, who has cut this path, but it is far from certain. Kinnell proceeds to another section filled with mythologies of the cosmos, the constellations, and finishes with a stanza opening out to the vastnesses of space. If the symbolic implications of herdsman, goats, cemetery, and ruined church were not quite pinned down for the reader till now, this last stanza does not permit him to mistake their purpose, though of course they remain essential as specific, literal details of actuality too, in keeping with Ezra Pound's belief that "the natural object is always the *adequate* symbol." At this point the peasant becomes the "Herdsman," doubtless referring to the northern constellation Bootes but likewise certainly representative of Christ with His twelve disciples (somewhat ironically presented here as goats) ascending the night sky toward the stars, riddlingly described as "A writhing of lights," in search of the ever elusive "fields" of paradise. The stanza introduces both Christian supplication and pagan goddesses of fertility and renewal to delineate the ceaseless human desire for transcendence or rebirth. Looking back on the cemetery, where Kinnell imagines the dead merging with one another in the common soil, and the "fallen church," we note how they reinforce the main interests of the poem by indicating the universality of death and absorption into the earth, and by implying that creeds grow outworn. Nonetheless, the longing to go beyond the confines of mortality endures, the track climbs up. The three closing lines possess a dark ambiguity. They hint at a primal level of being which is associated with the earth, is at once the state of origins and the state of return; the poet conceives this as the source of our lives and mythologies and their conclusion. Existence begins to manifest itself constantly in Kinnell's work as unerringly cyclical in form:

> Fields into which the limping Herdsman wades
> Leading his flock up the trackless night, towards
> A writhing of lights. Are they Notre Dame des Neiges
> Where men ask their God for the daily bread—
> Or the March-climbing Virgin carrying wheat?
> Where the track vanishes the first land begins.
> It goes out everywhere obliterating the horizons.
> We must have been walking through it all our lives.

Similarly, "The Descent" is constructed upon the symbolic pattern of human aspiration or ascent and the inevitable gravity of nature and fate that compels man downward to conclude in death and the earth. Designed in four parts, the poem alternates between a mountain-climbing expedition that results in tragic death and two moments in the Seekonk Woods—one the poet's recollection of childhood, the other a visit to the same location years later. All of these events demonstrate aspects of the cyclical scheme Kinnell intuits. At the outset he says of the string of mountain-climbers, seeing them on the slopes as if from below though he is really in their company: "it must have seemed / A lunatic earthworm headed for paradise"— already emphasizing the basic urge for transcendence the poem unfolds. One climber, Jan, a former member of the Resistance, tries to shortcut by jumping a crevasse and falls, mortally injured. Through some oddity or dimming of the dying man's vision he mistakes the declining moon before him for the rising sun behind, a misconception the symbolic properties of which Kinnell puts to use:

> Then he whispered, "Look—the sunrise!"
> The same color and nearly the same size
> But behind his back, the new sun

> Was rising. When the moon he was
> Staring at set in the mountains
> He died. On the way down the ice
> Had turned so perilous under the sun
> There was no choice: we watched while he went down.

The confusion of Jan's vision becomes for Kinnell a dramatic way of introducing into the poem the theme of human illusion in conflict with the undeviating cyclical pattern of sunrise and moonfall, ascent and de-cline, or birth and death, to which man and nature alike are subject. The conflict arises because the individual longs to retain his identity by re-birth or resurrection elsewhere; for while renewal occurs in the sense that new lives begin, death destroys each unique being, disperses the self into the undifferentiated whole again. As Kinnell writes near the close of "Free-dom, New Hampshire," meditating on the loss of his brother, "But an incarnation is in particular flesh / And the dust that is swirled into a shape / And crumbles and is swirled again had but one shape / That was this man." So within the context Kinnell establishes in "The Descent" both mountain-climbing and what Jan thinks he sees are signs of man's wishes and illusions, while Jan's fall and consequent death, the sinking of the moon, and the fact that the sun's heat melting the ice makes the slopes treacherous, forcing the climbers to let Jan's body sled down the mountain alone, are actualities which complete the cycle. This pattern recurs in the second section, where the poet remembers lying hidden in grass "In Seekonk Woods, on Indian Hill" when someone fired a shotgun at nearby crows. His reaction was instantaneous, boyishly impulsive, and touching:

> Two crows blown out from either hand
> Went clattering away; a third
> Swam through the branches to the ground.
> I scooped it up, splashed the ford,
> And lit out—I must have run half a day
> Before I reached Holy Spring. (Anyway,
>
> I thought it was holy. No one
> Had told me heaven is overhead.
> I only knew people look down
> When they pray.) I held the dying bird
> As though, should its heartbeat falter,
> There wouldn't be much heartbeat anywhere.
>
> After a while I touched the plumes
> To the water. In the desert

By the tracks I dug a headstart
Taller than myself. I told him,
"Have a good journey, crow. It can't be far.
It'll be this side of China, for sure."

Thus the boy's childish but shrewd thought that heaven must be beneath the ground because the dead are laid to rest there and the praying head inclines this way contributes to Kinnell's symbolic scheme, as does the simple baptismal gesture the boy bestows as an unconscious allusion to rebirth. The poet is led to think again of his dead friend Jan, of the possibility that he might have kept a grip on life: had he been turned "to the sun / Might not the sun have held him here?" He replies to his own query with a rhetorical question stressing the contrarieties that work upon a person, pulling him in opposite directions:

Or did he know the day came on
Behind, not glancing back for fear
The moon was already dragging from his bones
The blood as dear to them, and as alien,

As the suit of clothes to a scarecrow
Or the flesh to a cross?

At this moment he can comprehend his friend's "descent," announced in the poem's title and grasped naively by the poet in his boyhood, for what it is, the unavoidable rounding off of the course of existence: "To his valleys / Rivers have washed this climber to the sun / The full moon pestled into earth again." Then the last two stanzas of this section play upon the important thematic suggestiveness of height and depth, light and darkness. The paradisiacal realm, however, is no longer located where boyhood had it, underground; the poet has learned what men believe, or imagine, that it is a luminous celestial dimension ("Heaven is in light, overhead, / I have it by heart"). By way of contrast, the realities of death, burial, nightfall, and the earth to which life is joined are brought forward:

Yet the dead
Silting the darkness do not ask
For burials elsewhere than the dusk.
They lie where nothing but the moon can rise,
And make no claims, though they had promises.

Formal religion makes these "promises," yet from this sleep comes no awakening; only nature, contained in the image of moonrise, continues its eternal circle. The milkweed seen growing at the start of the second stanza

puts us in mind of the hopes and plans of men, who try to launch themselves
beyond the graveyard soil of their beginnings but become merely "drab,"
don't succeed in resolving the enigmas of existence or rising above them,
and fulfill their lives only by extinction. New life springs from the deaths of
others and progresses toward the same goal, that is the clear assertion emerging from the abundant detail of Kinnell's writing:

> Milkweed that grow beside the tombs
> Climb from the dead as if in flight,
> But a foot high they stop and bloom
> In drab shapes, that neither give light
> Nor bring up the true darkness of the dead;
> Strange, homing lamps, that go out seed by seed.

The final portion discovers Kinnell back at the scene of the crow shooting, attempting to recapture something of that moment in the past which is
for him still redolent with grace. He seeks the spontaneous, honest feeling
for the numinous that was his as a boy, but it has vanished beyond recovery.
Instead, he looks upon a changed landscape; Indian Hill has turned into a
subdivision, the crosslike TV aerials on the rooftops exhibit the secular
interests now presiding over this once (for the poet) sacred spot. When he
tries to find his "Holy Spring" he faces the blunt, incontrovertible facts of
nature:

> Fields lying dark and savage and the sun
>
> Reaping its own fire from the trees,
> Whirling the faint panic of birds
> Up turbulent light. Two white-haired
> Crows cried under the wheeling rays;
> And loosed as by a scythe, into the sky
> A flight of jackdaws rose, earth-birds suddenly
>
> Seized by some thaumaturgic thirst,
> Shrill wings flung up the crow-clawed, burned,
> Unappeasable air. And one turned,
> Dodged through the flock again and burst
> Eastward alone, sinking across the wood
> On the world curve of its wings.

With these lines Kinnell draws together the echoes, parallels, and recurrences of his poem. One can say that in a certain sense its construction
reflects the cyclical pattern of existence which is everywhere so plain to him
and dominates his imagination. When he attempts to revive the experience

of his youth, he is answered only by nature with its fertility and its alternating creative and destructive energies. (The scene is reminiscent though hardly imitative of those in Richard Eberhart's "The Groundhog," and there are thematic affinities with Dylan Thomas.) The actions of the crows and jackdaws, moreover, do not really differ from those of humans. We are all "earth-birds," like the "earthworm" mountain-climbers of the poem's opening, vainly scaling the heights or searching for the sacred of which we were once confident. Our desires are no different from the birds' instinctive climbing through the air; we are obsessed with the miraculous, the supernatural that will free us of death and preserve us. The lone bird flying eastward, away from its flock, follows the line of "descent" to earth, recalling Wallace Stevens's "casual flocks of pigeons" at the close of "Sunday Morning" who "make / Ambiguous undulations as they sink, / Downward to darkness, on extended wings." This jackdaw is the counterpart among unself-conscious creatures of Jan, who, dying, believes he sees the sunrise of renewal; the "world curve of its wings" proclaims unmistakably the universality of death, the return to earth. So we are "Strange, homing lamps, that go out seed by seed."

But Kinnell goes beyond these resolutions of imagery, parallelisms of quest and incident, to introduce the figure of Christ at the poem's end, once again clothing Him in an image from the natural world yet symbolically appropriate. He appears, then, as a "fisherbird," who still speaks in the voice of His suffering and despair upon the cross; His cry articulates the agony of every living being, of all who feel the torment of mortality. Concentrating on the idea of the Incarnation, Kinnell sees Christ as the exemplary sufferer in whose speech, passion, and death the pain of others is embodied, manifested as the supreme, heartrending instance of man's "thaumaturgic thirst" for immortality—and its defeat:

> Nor do we know why,
> Mirrored in duskfloods, the fisherbird
> Seems to stand in a desolate sky
> Feeding at its own heart. In the cry
> *Eloi! Eloi!* flesh was made word:
> We hear it in wind catching in the trees,
> In lost blood breaking a night through the bones.

Once more Christ's presence occupies a central position in Kinnell's poetry, and that is in "The Supper after the Last," which is also the piece he selected for inclusion in Paul Engle and Joseph Langland's anthology *Poet's Choice*. His accompanying comment has a special relevance to his imaginative preoccupations at that time, and since:

It is from this poem, "The Supper After the Last," that I want to make a fresh start, and I chose it for this reason. I mean towards a poem without scaffolding or occasion, that progresses through images to a point where it can make a statement on a major subject.[6]

"A poem without scaffolding or occasion, that progresses through images. . . ." Kinnell might have been speaking here about the poetry of Robert Bly, Louis Simpson, W. S. Merwin, Frank O'Hara, Donald Hall, or John Ashbery, among others, and certainly about much of the most important contemporary European and Latin American poetry—in fact, about almost any poetry whose roots lie in the Surrealist or Expressionist traditions of twentieth-century literature. A common concern of such poets is the creation of a poetry which relies less and less upon logical or narrative structure, upon the representation of external events (surely, these are the types of things Kinnell means by "scaffolding or occasion"), but which develops around a highly suggestive grouping of images whose source is inward experience, memory, dream, or vision. The purpose of this technique is to increase the authenticity of poetic statement, to dispense with artificiality, to free poetry from any ties that would prevent it from approximating as closely as possible its sources. Of course, this is not the only kind of poem Kinnell will write in the future, and he does not seem to have converted himself so completely to these artistic strategies as, say, Merwin or Bly; but there can be no doubt that this new direction to his efforts has strengthened, purified, and quickened the poems of his two later collections.

"The Supper after the Last" can best be approached as a culmination of a sort as well as a new start. Themes we have noted in considerable detail in previous poems are not only quite apparent in this one but also reach a fierce, shocking resolution: a ruthless visionary statement that assimilates its predecessors, abolishes the hesitations, hopes, defeated yet renewed desires so evident before. The poem has near-surrealist qualities in its opening lines which bring forward mirage, illusion, and hallucination; but the particulars of water, sky, dragonfly, the bather and his shadow, however puzzling at first, must not be overlooked, for they will reappear charged with meaning. A scene is offered at the start that is deliberately indefinite, that doesn't permit the reader to settle securely on a specific landscape, for land and sea obscurely mingle while the sky overarches them in the mirage; then a brightly colored dragonfly floats down to the desert floor and a bather comes into view, wading in what has already been called both "illusory water" and "The sea [that] scumbles in" and trying without success to destroy that dark reflection of himself which is his shadow. The atmosphere is mysterious, confusing. Kinnell has, in accordance with his prose remarks, confined himself to a mental occasion. The landscape before us has been formed by the inner eye:

> The desert moves out on half the horizon
> Rimming the illusory water which, among islands,
> Bears up the sky. The sea scumbles in
> From its own inviolate border under the sky.
> A dragon-fly floating on six legs on the sand
> Lifts its green-yellow tail, declines its wings
> A little, flutters them a little, and lays
> On dazzled sand the shadow of its wings. Near shore
> A bather wades through his shadow in the water.
> He tramples and kicks it; it recomposes.

Once we begin to read carefully, examining the recurrence and expansion of various details from this scene later in the poem, our bearings grow more distinct. The "illusory water" already seen returns as water reminding us of baptism or the waters of life, both implying faith or renewal. Such significance gains support by the assertion that this water "Bears up the sky," that is to say, metaphorically speaking, it animates or sustains a belief in the transcendent, the otherworldly. This notion of the passage seems less strained when we recall that the poem's title entertains the notion of resurrection: we can assume that it refers to a meal Christ eats after His return from the dead. In part two water is an essential element in another scene that discloses a "whitewashed house" while "Framed in its doorway, a chair, / Vacant, waits in the sunshine." We are not told for whom this chair waits, but undoubtedly it has been prepared for the risen Christ. The next stanza reveals the water in a container, and the invisible world hovers on the verge of visibility:

> A jug of fresh water stands
> Inside the door. In the sunshine
> The chair waits, less and less vacant.
> The host's plan is to offer water, then stand aside.

The anonymous "host," one who awaits the coming of Christ, and so one of the faithful, places the water as a sacramental gesture signifying new life or resurrection and as a token of his belief that it will come through Him. Thus far, the poem establishes an almost hypnotic stillness; the one violent act of the bather kicking in the first stanza is absorbed by the vagueness and fluidity of the mirage. As we observed, the second part opens on a stark, simple arrangement of house, doorway, sunlit chair, and jug of water; but as the host removes himself to make way for his expected guest the poem reaches a turning point that, with the beginning of part three, shatters the calm and jolts the reader's complacency. Suddenly we are shown "the supper after the last" carried on with savage gusto:

> They eat *rosé* and chicken. The chicken head
> Has been tucked under the shelter of the wing.
> Under the table a red-backed, passionate dog
> Cracks chicken bones on the blood and gravel floor.

As this section continues, so does the ferocity of the meal increase. The unidentified figure devouring chicken is, I take it, a particularly brutal portrait of Christ as Death, the universal destroyer whose ravenous jaws and digestive system are transformed into a horrifying image of the Styx down which everything must pass. The message of this Christ, who apparently has been robbed by His suffering and death of the illusion of His teachings, His promises at the Last Supper, is mortality without reprieve. This supper has nothing sacred or life-renewing about it; plainly it is a feast of sheer annihilation:

> No one else but the dog and the blind
> Cat watching it knows who is that bearded
> Wild man guzzling overhead, the wreck of passion
> Emptying his eyes, who has not yet smiled,
>
> Who stares at the company, where he is company,
> Turns them to sacks of appalled, grinning skin,
> Forks the fowl-eye out from under
> The large, makeshift, cooked lid, evaporates the wine,
>
> Jellies the sunlit table and spoons, floats
> The deluxe grub down the intestines of the Styx,
> Devours ill but the cat and dog, to whom he slips scraps,
> The red-backed accomplice busy grinding gristle.

This "emptying" of the eyes can be understood, I think, as one instance in Kinnell's work of the deprivation of spiritual significance from existence, a demythologizing of life and the cosmos we have observed in various poems which here assumes a more stringent character, for it refers to Christ's loss of His transcendental vision. At the outset of part four even the host, the man of faith, falls victim, his "bones . . . / Crack in the hound's jaw" as if to herald the wild man's speech, which begins with ironic reversals of the Gospels. His words inform men of their fundamental nothingness, describe them as creatures of dust who long for immortality, who form from these deep-seated wishes pictures of the eternal, the entirely compassionate and merciful, and insist on the veracity of the pictures because they have imagined them:

> I came not to astonish
> But to destroy you. Your
> Jug of cool water? Your

Hanker after wings? Your
Lech for transcendence?
I came to prove you are
Intricate and simple things
As you are, created
In the image of nothing,
Taught of the creator
By your images in dirt—
As mine, for which you set
A chair in the sunshine,
Mocking me with water!
As pictures of wings,
Not even iridescent,
That clasp the sand
And that cannot perish, you swear,
Having once been evoked!

With the poem's closing part we look again on the desert mirage of the
beginning. The vision of Christ trembles, blurs, "begins to float in water" as
everything now seems illusory, uncertain. Christ is finally named as He is on
the point of disappearing, but His voice continues while His figure blends
into the liquid fluctuations of the atmosphere: "Far out in that mirage the
Saviour sits whispering to the world, / Becoming a mirage." The words of
His parting statement bring back the images of dragonfly, light and darkness. Man strives, He says, to ascend "from flesh into wings," an effort indicative of the will to escape his fate, and He admits that "the change exists." But it is not a permanent change, and obtains only within the boundaries of mortal life, though man wishes it to endure beyond them: "But the
wings that live gripping the contours of the dirt / Are all at once nothing,
flesh and light lifted away." So the Saviour proclaims Himself the idea of
God or the eternal, the objectification of man's desires—"I am the resurrection, because I am the light"—thus recalling, in "The Descent," a similar
expression, of the human will to survive: "Heaven is in light, overhead, / I
have it by heart." But the fading Christ, introducing again the dragonfly we
first saw laying "the shadow of its wings" on the sand, asserts that man's
destiny is analogous to that small creature's downward flight; the earth is his
last home, to vanish is his end. At the poem's finish the Saviour appears in
the dual role of a phantasmal god of unattainable worlds and the architect of
man's death. In spite of his metamorphoses, his struggles toward the "light,"
a man's final transformation brings him to the ground from which he came:

I cut to your measure the creeping piece of darkness
That haunts you in the dirt. Steps into light—
I make you over. I breed the shape of your grave in the dirt.

That moving "piece of darkness" is an individual's shadow, the reflection of his death inseparable from his existence which the bather at the poem's outset tries unsuccessfully to dispel. The poem concludes in the absoluteness of death, an assurance for Kinnell that holds little promise for appeal.

With "The Supper after the Last" Kinnell has not only arrived at decisive technical changes that will influence many of his later poems, but he has also brought a course of thematic exploration to an end. This exploration, concerned with man's spiritual compulsions and aspirations, the forms they take in concrete experience, the illusory convictions they foster, derives its impulse from sources deep within the poet's own psyche, his inner and affective life. By exposing what he believes to be the hopeless falsity of these longings for eternity, and by confronting death as an unconditional fact in a tough, unremitting way, he prepares as the ground for his future writing certain limitations of existence within which his poems must be created. We can surmise, I think, that Kinnell has purged himself in the poems we have discussed of personal anxieties and questionings with regard to death, Christ, the purpose and goal of existence. This is not to say he does not ponder still the elusive, mysterious nature of human life and its stubborn refusal to yield the explanatory meanings for it we seek; but hereafter the realms of transcendence remain a dark void, an inscrutable blackness on which he can cast no illumination, and the person of Christ, as might be expected, no longer occupies him with a few incidental exceptions. He takes a new grasp on the world at hand, on his life here and now in all of its immediacy, or engages himself with the particulars of other lives and surroundings present to him. The poem "Last Spring," from *Flower Herding on Mount Monadnock* (1964), can be read as a statement of his altered interests. The first part describes his dreaming through "a dark winter" and losing his hold on the physical substance of things, accepting their "glitter" as substitute; but this mode of dreaming leads to death, or at least to a loss of contact with actuality. His mind is invaded by "the things / Whose corpses eclipse them, / Shellfishes, ostriches, elephants." But with the movement of seasons into spring and new life the sun's brightness and clarity dissolve the poet's private fancies, his "keepsakes . . . inventions,"

> It left me only a life
>
> And time to walk
> Head bobbing out front like a pigeon's
> Knocking on the instants to let me in.

This attentiveness to being in the world in its full temporal and tangible immediacy is a striking attribute of the long, ambitious poem "The Avenue Bearing the Initial of Christ into the New World." Composed freely, without linear or narrative structure, in a series of fourteen sections focusing on a variety of moments and figures in the life of Avenue C in New York with its teeming ghetto population of Jews, Negroes, and Puerto Ricans, the poem evokes, through myriad impressions of the particulars of daily experience interspersed with the poet's imaginative projection into individual lives and his allusive imagery, provocative ironies, a comprehensive vision of people existing under circumstances of destitution, pain, persecution, and death in a country that supposedly extends promises of refuge, security, equality, and opportunity for those who flee to her shores. Christ does not appear in the poem except in a brief, glancing reference; Kinnell simply uses Him in the title to point up the victimization of persons who had come to America in the hope of achieving a better sort of life. Throughout the poem there is an insistence on the element of betrayal especially of the Jews—though the application is obviously much wider—first by God, who is treated with disgust and rejection because He deceived Abraham (doubtless Kinnell means all the Jews as well) and has nothing but cold indifference to human feelings; He is reduced in a simile from omnipotent deity to repellent insect:

> A child lay in the flames.
> It was not the plan. Abraham
> Stood in terror at the duplicity.
> Isaac whom he loved lay in the flames.
> The Lord turned away washing
> His hands without soap and water
> Like a common housefly.

Then they are betrayed by America, the new world to which they have voyaged in desperate flight from poverty, pogroms, concentration camps, only to find themselves still imprisoned; in spite of this disappointment and constant hardship they exhibit a sturdiness, a will to endure, which is the inherited strength of ages and draws the poet's admiration:

> The promise was broken too freely
> To them and to their fathers, for them to care.
> They survive like cedars on a cliff, roots
> Hooked in any crevice they can find.

Behind Kinnell's poem stand Whitman's *Leaves of Grass*, Hart Crane's *The Bridge*, and Williams's *Paterson*, along with something of *The Waste Land* and *The Cantos*. Like those poets, ours immerses himself in the rich welter of life and does so with sympathy and understanding. As a result, the poem abounds in images rendering with vigorousness and exactitude the very feel of this street, the lives thronging it, from "the eastern ranges / Of

the wiped-out lives—punks, lushes, / Panhandlers, pushers, rumsoaks" to
the old Jew who "rocks along in a black fur shtraimel, / Black robe, black
knickers, black knee-stockings, / Black shoes"; or where

> The old women peer, blessed damozels
> Sitting up there young forever in the cockroached rooms,
> Eating fresh-killed chicken, productos tropicales,
> Appetizing herring, canned goods, nuts;
> They puff out smoke from Natural Bloom cigars
> And one day they puff like Blony Bubblegum.
> Across the square skies with faces in them
> Pigeons skid, crashing into the brick.
> From a rooftop a boy fishes at the sky.
> Around him a flock of pigeons fountains,
> Blown down and swirling up again, seeking the sky.

Such a burst of energy and exaltation, the abrupt takeoff of the pigeons,
wakens thoughts of escape—"To fly from this place"—but these deteriorate
rapidly into nightmare images of failure and death: "To run under the rain
of pigeon plumes, to be / Tarred, and feathered with birdshit, Icarus, / In
Kugler's glass headdown dangling by yellow legs." Indeed, death pervades
this poem, making itself felt just the other side of the hard, marginal lives
Kinnell portrays on this city street, in the seedy rooms and restaurants, in
the market, in the memory of a dead friend, in the figure of the "ancient
Negro" who sings "Over Jordan" outside "the Happy Days Bar & Grill," in
the frightening persons of "Bunko Certified Embalmer, / Cigar in his mouth,
nose to the wind" and the owner of the fishmarket who "lops off the heads, /
Shakes out the guts as if they did not belong in the first place, / And they
are flesh for the first time in their lives," in the occasional reminders of the
concentration camps and the extermination of Jews. But perhaps most resonant with meaning because they touch a more fundamental symbolic level
are the parallel images of the Avenue itself and the East River. Both are
implicated with the flux of life, the current that draws everything toward
annihilation, in the arterial flow of blood through the body which ends
thus: "The lungs put out the light of the world as they / Heave and collapse,
the brain turns and rattles / In its own black axlegrease." The final section
of the poem begins with suggestions of an absent God and the inexorable
passage of life into death, here embodied in the details of the fish:

> Behind the Power Station on 14th, the held breath
> Of light, as God is a held breath, withheld,
> Spreads the East River, into which fishes leak:
> The brown sink or dissolve,
> The white float out in shoals and armadas,

> Even the gulls pass them tip, pale
> Bloated socks of riverwater and rotted seed,
> That swirl on the tide, punched back
> To the Hell Gate narrows, and on the ebb
> Steam seaward, seeding the sea.

In succeeding stanzas the street reappears with its desolation, violence, and irrationality. Then Kinnell resorts to a highly suggestive interweaving of light and dark, familiar because of earlier applications in "The Descent," "Where the Track Vanishes," "The Supper after the Last," and elsewhere. Momentary luminescence is always swallowed in darkness. Even more cruelly paradoxical is the glow of a corpse in the night waters of the river, which has now become one with the Avenue and the sea into whose depths life empties:

> It is night, and raining. You look down
> Towards Houston in the rain, the living streets,
> Where instants of transcendence
> Drift in oceans of loathing and fear, like lanternfishes,
> Or phosphorus flashings in the sea, or the feverish light
> Skin is said to give off when the swimmer drowns at night.

This identification compels the poet to a stanza of summary proportions that makes explicit the poem's crushing ironies, the human frustration and waste, the sacrifice linking the Avenue's population with the murdered Christ, and the cosmic injustice behind these realities:

> From the blind gut Pitt to the East River of Fishes
> The Avenue cobbles a swath through the discolored air,
> A roadway of refuse from the teeming shores and ghettos
> And the Caribbean Paradise, into the new ghetto and new paradise,
> This God-forsaken Avenue bearing the initial of Christ
> Through the haste and carelessness of the ages,
> The sea standing in heaps, which keeps on collapsing,
> Where the drowned suffer a C-change,
> And remain the common poor.

If there is something strained about "C-change," so that it seems rather gimmicky for so serious a passage, the meanings it generates, both with respect to crucifixion and to the irony of Ariel's song in this context, are anything but slight. Yet for all of its grimness, which continues into the closing stanzas with their renewed emphasis on the fugitive and outcast person, on persecution and death, the poem is completed on a note that combines lamentation, hardiness, and a kind of resignation to life's inequities and miseries which even allows, in the face of oblivion, a corrosive laughter:

> In the nighttime
> Of the blood they are laughing and saying,
> Our little lane, what a kingdom it was!
>
> oi weih, oi weih

A considerable number of the poems from Kinnell's next two volumes, *Flower Herding on Mount Monadnock* and *Body Rags*, adhere closely to the lineaments of a specific experience; rather than enlarging on it as some previous pieces do, they attempt to seize it through a literal concreteness or through the more oblique progression of images referred to in *Poet's Choice*. Quite often the two approaches are joined in the same poem, as, for example, in "Middle of the Way." In any event, the desire to articulate what the poet sees, hears, thinks, and dreams with undeviating accuracy, with as little departure from the quality of the original experience as possible, causes him to tighten his language even further; imagery becomes sharp, spare, precise and is set down with an admirable directness that enhances the effect of lyric purity. And the relationship to nature we have observed throughout Kinnell's work increases in importance for him. Like Roethke or Gary Snyder, he is attracted to the nonhuman world, not as a field for intellectual conquest but as the basic context of man's living—the only one he really knows—in which other forms of life manifest their being together with him. This perception comes alive variously in many poems, nowhere with a more moving sense of participation than "In Fields of Summer":

> The sun rises,
> The goldenrod blooms,
> I drift in fields of summer,
> My life is adrift in my body,
> It shines in my heart and hands, in my teeth,
> It shines up at the old crane
> Who holds out his drainpipe of a neck
> And creaks along in the blue,
>
> And the goldenrod shines with its life, too,
> And the grass, look,
> The great field wavers and flakes,
> The rumble of bumblebees keeps deepening,
> A phoebe flutters up,
> A lark bursts up all dew.

In such poems as "Tillamook Journal (2nd version)," "On Hardscrabble Mountain," and "Middle of the Way" he carries his own human solitariness far into forest and up mountainside, there to assimilate whatever he can of nature's existence, separate in its magnitude, its awesome age, its unity that excludes man with his unique self-awareness: "I love the earth, and always / In its darknesses I am a stranger." "Middle of the Way," from which these lines come, demonstrates, as do other poems, Kinnell's persistent use of the imagery of darkness to connote the unfathomable aspects of the universe and his own temporary being within it. This period of isolation in the wilderness, at night by a dying fire "under the trees / That creak a little in the dark, / The giant trees of the world," elicits the beautiful meditative stanzas concluding the poem. The progression of Kinnell's thought is convincingly set forth in images which realize the total experience:

> The coals go out,
> The last smoke weaves up
> Losing itself in the stars.
> This is my first night to lie
> In the uncreating dark.
>
> In the heart of a man
> There sleeps a green worm
> That has spun the heart about itself,
> And that shall dream itself black wings
> One day to break free into the beautiful black sky.
>
> I leave my eyes open,
> I lie here and forget our life,
> All I see is we float out
> Into the emptiness, among the great stars,
> On this little vessel without lights.
>
> I know that I love the day,
> The sun on the mountain, the Pacific
> Shiny and accomplishing itself in breakers,
> But I know I live half alive in the world,
> I know half my life belongs to the wild darkness.

Not only do we get the impression of being there, of the immediacy of Kinnell's reflections under the circumstances, but we also witness the quite personal flow of his thoughts and feelings. While it is sensitive to external setting—the middle section preceding these stanzas is cast in the abbreviated form of a prose journal recording the day's events in the mountains— the poem moves rapidly into the poet's mind in the first lines above, away from the facts of the dead fire, the final wisp of smoke, toward the center of consciousness where specific elements from the outer world (the stars, the worm, the black-winged butterfly, the sun, the mountain, the Pacific) are charged with hidden implications drawn from the non-rational psyche and the emotions to enter into new combinations. Behind them lies the effort to uncover covert impulses, ties, tendencies of the inner self that pass unnoticed while an individual is occupied with daily affairs; in these stanzas they are released to convey the poet's mind on a kind of dream-journey of associated images which culminates in his realization of the double urge in him toward a world of radiance, clarity, and order, and toward a world of impenetrable darkness, chaos, and oblivion. Of course, what I am claiming for this passage in the way of meaning remains implicit in the images themselves, in accordance with Kinnell's wish for a poem lacking logical structure, "scaffolding or occasion," and such images as he offers are not readily exhausted but prove continuously stimulating to the reader's imagination.

"Middle of the Way," however, is only one of many meditative poems from *Flower Herding on Mount Monadnock* and *Body Rags* in which the poet employs linked groups of images, metaphorical statements, and specific details of observation or recollection to speculate on the self's identity, its relationship to nature, time, and, as always, death. Through most of these pieces runs Kinnell's recurrent alternation of night and day, physical actuality and the possibility of nothingness. Occasionally, accompanying these opposing conditions of being and nonbeing, we find the waters of flux and change, the river that glides toward death. In "Poems of Night," a sequence of brief lyrics, the poet quietly, gently traces the features of his beloved as she sleeps, moving his "hand over / Slopes, falls, lumps of sight, / Lashes barely able to be touched, / Lips that give way so easily." Finally, in the last two poems, he perceives a portion of his own existence embodied in the contours of her familiar form; her self has been so deeply bound up with his for a time that in holding her body in his arms he feels he is embracing something fundamental to his own nature: "I hold / What I can only think of / As some deepest of memories in my arms, / Not mine, but as if the life in me / Were slowly remembering what it is." Yet the next poem, which brings morning, fails to provide confidence or hope in these discoveries because the day itself is seen as fragile and doomed, a vessel we float perilously and, at last, in vain upon the darkened flood:

> And now the day, raft that breaks up, comes on.

> I think of a few bones
> Floating on a river at night,
> The starlight blowing in place on the water,
> The river leaning like a wave towards the emptiness.

Kinnell frequently reflects in recent poems on wreckage, either that of the human body, as above, or the ruins of houses, sea wrack scattered along deserted beaches, fossils, burnt out stretches of timber. For him such sights constitute the residue of lives lived, human or otherwise, and so prove worthy of contemplation. Though they are perceptible reminders of perishability, sometimes of suffering, they can reveal as well an innate dignity and strength that confirm the value of what they have been. It should be noted too that the universe as Kinnell now represents it contains destructiveness as a perpetual native element, no less a part of the underlying design of things than the wind, which he often makes a symbol for it:

> The wind starts fluting
> In our teeth, in our ears,
> It whines down the harmonica
> Of the fingerbones, moans at the skull . . .
>
> Blown on by their death
> The things on earth whistle and cry out.
> Nothing can keep still. Only the wind.
> ("Tree from Andalusia")

At the outset of "Spindrift" the poet's attention is fixed on what the sea has washed ashore: "old / Horseshoe crabs, broken skates, / Sand dollars, sea horses, as though / Only primeval creatures get destroyed." Later, in a ritual gesture, Kinnell draws "sacred / Shells from the icy surf, / Fans of gold light, sunbursts"; one of these he is to raise to the sun, source of life and light, and pledge himself to go "to the shrine of the dead." Performing this natural religious ceremony, with its implicit veneration for the principle of life in the cosmos, lie enjoys briefly its sudden manifestation as the sunlight strikes the shell:

> And as it blazes
> See the lost life within
> Alive again in the fate-shine.

But we can only assume the "shrine of the dead" is here, or any place where a man turns his thoughts upon the dead, which Kinnell proceeds to do during the rest of the poem. Section after section, he shifts from one object of reflection to another, apparently at random, yet all the while skillfully accumulating force, particularly through the repetition of key images of wind, light, and shell, as he aims toward a final comprehensive statement. Kinnell studies the iconography (to borrow a term he suggests) of nature's forms, trying to extract the meanings worked by the world into a seashell, a worn root, the motion and sound of the surf; in the latter he reads a message lying beneath every detail of the poem: "It is the most we know of time, / And it is our undermusic of eternity." The waves' recurrence, the sea in its seemingly contradictory aspect of stable sameness and ceaseless change, reminiscent of Valéry's "La mer, la mer, toujours recommencée!", indicates metaphorically for the poet the rhythm which holds together the life of creation. He is then able to remember the death of a friend or relative in the ambiance of that imagery of light and shell given a sacred significance:

> I think of how I
> Sat by a dying woman,
> Her shell of a hand,
> Wet and cold in both of mine,
> Light, nearly out, existing as smoke,
> I sat in the glow of her wan, absorbed smile.

The "lost life," glimpsed earlier as the shell was held to the sun, appears now in this memory of an existence about to be abandoned, a light darkened, revived here as the poet lifts it up to the human warmth of his thought. In the next part we find him "Under the high wind" already mentioned as the sign of flux and destruction "holding this little lamp, / This icy fan of the sun," which is, we recall, his Golden Bough, the token of his permission to visit the dead. The first of the two stanzas shows the fateful wind as it "moans in the grass / And whistles through crabs' claws," and in the second its ominousness grows more immediate to the poet himself: his life is threatened, lies under the same sentence:

> Across gull tracks
> And wind ripples in the sand
> The wind seethes. My footprints
> Slogging for the absolute
> Already begin vanishing.

Existence is, then, constantly being consumed; it vanishes like the smoke, the gull tracks and footprints, into the surrounding, the hurling, eroding wind. The last section introduces an anonymous old man who might be anyone, including a projection of the poet into old age; his "wrinkled eyes" are "Tortured by smoke," which would seem, as in the instance of the dying woman, to specify the minimal amount of life left in him. Physically crippled by his years, what can this man "really love," the poet wonders. Other creatures not endowed with this self-consciousness or the capacity for this type of affection simply exist to the end by instinct and without advance knowledge of death:

> The swan dips her head
> And peers at the mystic
> In-life of the sea,
> The gull drifts up
> And eddies toward heaven,
> The breeze in his arms . . .

Kinnell's answer to his inquiry amounts to a compassionate declaration of acceptance that asks nothing further but binds man to temporal creation. At the close the image of the shell returns, symbolic of all life, refined and polished by its travels through time, sacred because it is what we know, possess for a while, and value supremely:

> Nobody likes to die
> But an old man
> Can know
> A kind of gratefulness
> Towards time that kills him,
> Everything he loved was made of it.
>
> In the end
> What is he but the scallop shell
> Shining with time like any pilgrim?

A more detailed version of this acceptance occurs at the finish of "Flower Herding on Mount Monadnock," where the poet locates in the forest a flower corresponding to his desire early in the poem for one "which cannot be touched," that is, which will be permanent and inviolable. But the flower he discovers is quite mortal. Its life burns up and disappears much as the lives in "Spindrift," though here Kinnell examines its pretensions to durability—in effect, to immortality of the spirit—but these are discounted when death affirms its reality and life's single appeal is to itself. The end of the poem puts us squarely in front of the observable facts, dismisses the unseen aura with which we are tempted to surround them. "No ideas but in things," insisted William Carlos Williams, and Kinnell surely agrees:

> In the forest I discover a flower.
>
> The invisible life of the thing
> Goes up in flames that are invisible
> Like cellophane burning in the sunlight.
>
> It burns up. Its drift is to be nothing.
>
> In its covertness it has a way

Of uttering itself in place of itself,
Its blossoms claim to float in the Empyrean,

A wrathful presence on the blur of the ground.

The appeal to heaven breaks off.
The petals begin to fall, in self-forgiveness.
It is a flower. On this mountainside it is dying.

The poems of *Body Rags* do not alter the direction Kinnell's work has taken thus far, nor do they exhibit any changed attitude toward an existence whose horizon is ringed by death, though the intensity with which he enters into his experience has never been greater. In the haunting meditations of "Another Night in the Ruins" he recalls a night flight over the ocean during which his dead brother's face appeared to him shaped from storm clouds, "looking nostalgically down / on blue, / lightning flashed moments of the Atlantic." These "moments" have their counterparts in the other imagery of light and flame remarked before as significant of the vital energy which is life breaking forth and yet consuming itself, finishing at last in smoke, ashes, darkness. Kinnell's image of his brother catches him brooding on this paradoxical principle and revives the dead man's words:

He used to tell me,
"What good is the day?
On some hill of despair
the bonfire you kindle can light the great sky—
though it's true, of course, to make it burn
you have to throw yourself in . . ."

True to the obliquity of his technique, he proceeds away from the demanding implications of this statement and provides a stanza emphasizing harsh, ruinous change and a nearly hallucinatory intuition of ultimate vacuity with "the cow / of nothingness, mooing / down the bones." But the return to his brother's idea begins with the unexpected appearance of a rooster who "thrashes in the snow / for a grain"; when he uncovers it, he "Rips / it into / flames," an act that matches exactly, in meaning and imagery, the gesture of self-sacrifice (so full of echoes of Christ's death) required by his brother's reasoning to bestow on an existence an importance beyond itself. The symbolic rooster in this metaphysical barnyard, "Flames / bursting out of its brow," urges Kinnell to a point of recognition we have watched him arrive at before: namely, that man is no phoenix ("we aren't, after all, made / from that bird which flies out of its ashes"), there is no rebirth. But he goes further than he has in previous instances by regarding as valid his brother's word and seeing the necessity for the self to assimilate its destiny and death:

```
      . . . for a man
as he goes up in flames, his one work
is
to open himself, to be
the flames . . .
```

"Another Night in the Ruins" is the first poem in *Body Rags*, and with good reason, I think, since many of the pieces which follow reflect the terms of recognition given there. So in "Lost Loves" the poet can "lie dreaming" of women he has cared for, moments in the past, while time heads him "deathward." In spite of these losses and the eventual outcome of his life, he finds it possible to take pleasure in perpetual alteration and to identify himself with the many "lives" and selves passed through in the course of one existence:

```
And yet I can rejoice
that everything changes, that
we go from life
into life,

and enter ourselves
quaking
like the tadpole, his time come, tumbling toward the slime.
```

Poetry, when it is written, is the product of this existence and consequently will bear the marks of the self's struggles, transformations, failures, escapes. Like the scarred hill of the world in which the layers of time past lie fossilized, it contains whatever its author has done or been:

```
The poem too
is a palimpsest, streaked
with erasures, smelling
of departure and burnt stone.
                ("The Poem")
```

The last four poems in the collection, however, to my mind best demonstrate Kinnell's bold and powerful attempt to integrate himself with his experience, and to do it without mediation or protection, exposing himself completely to a direct encounter with his perceivings. The resulting poetry has a stunning force and uncompromising toughness that sometimes leave the reader gasping. Of course, these pieces, which include the long poem "The Last River," "Testament of the Thief," "The Porcupine," and "The Bear," differ from one another in various ways, too, though the latter pair are close in spirit.

"The Last River" shows an evident kinship with "The Avenue Bearing the Initial of Christ into the New World," not merely because of its length but because both poems are concerned with large, specifically American areas of experience. As he did in the earlier poem, Kinnell here employs juxtaposition and collage to accommodate a wide range of material; now, however, the atmosphere is more fluid and indeterminate. The two poems are held together simply by the focus of the poet's consciousness, but in "The Last River" he makes himself felt more definitely as a presence, a person in the poem to whom everything there is happening, than he does in "The Avenue . . .," where he prefers occasionally to be anonymous. So it is his consciousness in "The Last River," shifting and sliding through images and memories, ever changing, dropping below to the levels of dream and nightmare, following the course of the Mississippi southward and, at the same time, floating down the waters of the Styx into the underworld with his Virgil a boy named Henry David, visiting the damned in their torments, and returning to achieve, through the agency of another version of Thoreau, a prophetic vision of national destiny, that is the locus of the poem.

Kinnell starts off by mingling details from his travels in the South and his work with black people in a voter registration program with impressions of a jail cell at night into which he was locked, presumably for this activity among Negroes, or something related to it. An air of sombreness, futility, and malevolence dominates the poem but is alleviated by sudden flashes of grace, instances of dignity and love, usually revealed through images of lightning, fire, or sunlight. The effect of such passages, when they occur, can be startlingly beautiful, implying a kind of revivification, a rebirth into life in its plenitude that comes close to a religious affirmation of living for Kinnell.

> A girl and I are lying
> on the grass of the levee. Two
> birds whirr overhead. We lie close,
> as if having waked
> in bodies of glory.
>
> And putting on again
> its skin of light, the river
> bends into view. We watch it, rising
> between the levees, flooding for the sky,
> and hear it,
> a hundred feet down, pressing its long weight
> deeper into the world.
>
> The birds have gone,
> we wander slowly homeward,
> lost in the history of every step . . .

Then too one must remark the achievement of the descriptive portions of the poem, in which Kinnell, writing in a line of descent from Whitman and the Roethke of *North American Sequence*, catches with a richness and precision of language the strange, poignant lyricism of American rivers:

> the Ten Mile of Hornpout,
> the Drac hissing in its bed of sand,
> the Ruknabad crossed by ghosts of nightingales,
> the Passumpsic bursting down its length in spring,
> the East River of Fishes, the more haunting for not having had a
>   past either,
> and this Mississippi coursing down now through the silt of all
>   its days,
> and the Tangipahoa, snake-cracked, lifting with a little rush from
>   the hills and going out in thick, undernourished greenery.

In the midst of these changing scenes, memories and perceptions sharp with pain, nostalgia, disgust, and intermittent joy, Kinnell centers his imagination on a journey to Hell, hunting some revelation about the life of this country among the condemned dead: "The burning fodder dowses down, / seeking the snagged / bodies of the water buried. . . ." A different sort of Aeneas, he takes "a tassel of moss from a limb" and starts on his way, led by the boy Henry David "over the plain of crushed asphodels" to meet a horrendous scarecrow Charon, who ferries them to the inner precincts of the underworld. Subsequent sections, dramatizing the punishments of such offenders against individual and society as Northern and Southern politicians, the Secretaries of Profit and Sanctimony, and even a well-meaning liberal, whose appearance in this place greatly disturbs the poet, struck me at times as both excessive and too derivative, their immediate ancestor being not Dante but the Ezra Pound of the "Hell" Cantos XIV and XV. For all the likely justice done here to those who deserve it, these tortures do not realize the effect Kinnell wants; the reader turns aside finally with no sense of moral triumph or fulfillment but with feelings of revulsion:

> On the shore four souls
> cry out in pain, one lashed
> by red suspenders to an
> ever-revolving wheel, one with
> red patches on the seat of his pants
> shrieking while paunchy vultures
> stab and gobble at his bourbon-squirting liver,
> one pushing uphill
> his own belly puffed up with the blood-money
> he extorted on earth, that crashes back

and crushes him, one
standing up to his neck
in the vomit he caused the living to puke . . .

Journeying on, the poet and his guide pass "The Mystic River," where
crowds drink Lethean waters that run down "from Calvary's Mountain,"
and an enigmatic "Camp Ground," whose character is not disclosed, for the
mists of the underworld close about Kinnell and his mind lapses into unconsciousness. When he awakens, it is to "a tiny cell far within" his brain, a
jail cell as well, and there he envisages an anonymous man "of noble face,"
identifiable as Thoreau, who in anguish and self-torment, "wiping / a pile of
knife-blades clean / in the rags of his body," tries to expiate the sins of American history:

> "Hard to wash off . . .
> buffalo blood . . . Indian blood . . ." he mutters,
> at each swipe singing, *"mein herz! mein herz!"*

Confessing that he had sought a love above the human, unencumbered by
the flesh, and that he really "only loved [his] purity," Thoreau fades out,
leaving Kinnell with "a letter for the blind" which places upon him his
own guilt, the burden of his obligations as a man. The poem ends with a
vision of "the last river" dividing a black man on one side from a white
man on the other; between them, in the middle, stands a symbolic figure
whose qualities not only erase the obvious differences of pigmentation in
the other two men but also radiate, through the now familiar imagery of
lightning and flame, suggestions of a nearly divine power, harmony, grace.
(One recollects, reading this passage, lines which occur early in the poem:
". . . then lightning flashed / path strung out a moment across the storm, /
bolt of love even made of hellfire / between any strange life and any strange
life. . ."):

> a man of no color,
> body of beryl,
> face of lightning,
> eyes lamps of wildfire,
> arms and feet of polished brass.

The figure speaks, prophesying a national agony, a crisis of relations that
will tax citizens extraordinarily; but as he begins his appeal to men's virtues,
in a horrifying instant, this visionary idol crumbles and is transformed into
the hideous scarecrow Charon, on whose ferry Kinnell previously entered
Hell. Ironically, the "last river" has become that of the underworld:

> . . . he is
> falling to pieces,
> no nose left,
> no hair,
> no teeth,
> limbs dangling from prayer-knots and rags,
>
> waiting by the grief-tree
> of the last river.

The possible implications of this conclusion are numerous, and Kinnell allows the reader to tease them out for himself. One can say, nonetheless, that this collapse of the ideal into the vicissitudes and mortality of the real, like Thoreau's recognition in the poem of the necessary taint of the physical, the humanly imperfect in existence, conforms with the attitude toward experience Kinnell has developed so forcefully in his work. It is noteworthy that both Thoreau and the "man of no color" finish clothed in "body rags," the tattered evidence of their encounters with the rough actualities of the world. Inasmuch as Kinnell identifies himself with his vision and can "choke down these last poison wafers" bequeathed him in Thoreau's parting message (*"For Galway alone / I send you my mortality. / Which leans out from itself, to spit on itself. / Which you would not touch. / All you have known."*), the words and images of this poem, lifted from his own deep-felt moments of experience, are "the prayer-knots and rags" of his life. Though there are a few spots where the poem weakens, especially in parts of the Hell episode, as a whole it leaves, like most of its author's writing, a profound impression, as of something lived through.

"Testament of the Thief," "The Porcupine," and "The Bear" create similar indelible effects but do so with, if anything, more raw violence, undisguised, earthy matter-of-factness—in short, whatever means will permit Kinnell to shortcut poetical niceties and cleave to the bare truth of his perceivings. The truth or vision contained in these poems cannot be readily abstracted; it is extremely personal—indeed, the poems seem to me the most personal Kinnell has written—yet it involves no more than a continuation of his quest for the fundamentals of existence. Each poem of the three appears composed at the very frontiers of experience, the imagination working against any restraints in order to achieve the shocking dimensions of its discoveries. So it is that Kinnell identifies in the poems with fierce, hardened, alienated creatures—thief, porcupine, and bear—shares their mania "for the poison fumes of the real," endures their bodily suffering and death to arrive at a knowledge of himself in them.

"Testament of the Thief" opens with the thief already dead on the gallows. The poem progresses by jumping to two other outcasts—a coolie and a beggar—who sit nearby, undisturbed by the swinging corpse, and then to another pariah, the keeper of an opium den, a specialist in supplying illusions and dreams in which members of society take refuge from reality, and whose attitude involves no moral scruples, only practical business considerations. From section to section stress falls on the elementals of life, on the creative/destructive processes ruling man and beast that have long been a feature of Kinnell's work:

> Under the breeze, in the dusk,
> the poor cluster at tiny
> pushcarts of fire, eating
> boiled beets,
> gut,
> tongue,
> testicle,
> cheeks, forehead, little feet.

Life feeds on life to save itself: it is this hard but basic law of earth on which many of the poem's images concentrate. In the environment of the poor, whose lives are pared to the rudimentary bone, the thief once wandered; the ground where he slept retains the imprint of his body. Kinnell halts the reader here, admonishes him of the basic realities of daily life, and hints, with perhaps an indirect rejection of Yeats's exalted, courtly conception of the poet's role at the end of "Sailing to Byzantium," that the true sources of poetry more properly lie in this place:

> Stop a moment, on his bones' dents,
> stand without moving, listen
> to the ordinary people
> as they pass. They do not sing
> of what is gone or to come, they sing of
> the old testaments of their lives,
> the little meals,
> the airs,
> the streets of our time.

These lines keep to the spirit of Verlaine's " tout le reste est littérature" or Henry Miller's declaration at the outset of *Black Spring*: "What is not in the open street is false, derived, that is to say, literature." Surely, Kinnell's grappling in these three poems with the very blood and bones and guts of creatures, with life and death in their blunt material aspects, demonstrates his imaginative drive to gain utter authenticity in the essentials of his vision. This intention shows up plainly in the actual "testament" the thief leaves, "items" addressed respectively to the keeper of the opium den, the beggar, the coolie, and "the pewk-worm" of torment and mortality who "lives all his life in our flesh." To each of them his legacy must come as an education in harsh reality, the dispersal of hope or illusion; only the "pewk-worm" fits into a different category, and this is indicated by putting the stanza about him in a final, separate section. The "opium master / dying in paradise," a world of inhaled, manufactured dreams, receives the thief's nose, in a key statement we have already seen, "in working disorder, / crazed / for the poison fumes of the real." For the beggar who lies asleep, wallowing in erotic dreams of the "girl friends / of his youth," he offers "their / iron faithfulness to loss." And to the coolie, whose life is hard labor and "whose skeleton / shall howl for its dust like any other" in the common fate of death, he gives, in a burst of extravagant language, "this / ultimate ruckus on the groan-meat," which is to say, the rending chaos of the body. The poem concludes with the thief's legacy to the "pewk-worm," inhabiting man's flesh and slowly boring away at him, consuming him from within, whom "you can drag forth / only by winding him up on a matchstick / a quarter turn a day for the rest of your days," so inseparable has he become from the person of his victim. This worm is, in fact, the determined principle of corruption bred into man's nature; therefore the thief's gift to him, "this map of my innards," signifies a recognition and acceptance of this inevitable condition, infused with wry, grim humor. Giving final, unquestionable support to this testament of the thief is the remembered brutal concreteness of death, his "thief-shadow lunging by the breeze" at the end of a rope and presiding over the entire poem.

Kinnell moves from description through analogy to conclude finally in identification with the porcupine in the poem of that title. First presented as a voracious creature, the porcupine is afterward linked, in the bold, outspoken manner of these recent poems, with humans:

> In character
> he resembles us in seven ways:
> he puts his mark on outhouses,
> he alchemizes by moonlight,
> he shits on the run,
> he uses his tail for climbing,
> he chuckles softly to himself when scared,
> he's overcrowded if there's more than one of him per five acres,
> his eyes have their own inner redness.

This extravagance of tone and statement increases and the porcupine emerges as a fantastic, obsessed animal whose single devotion is to "gouge the world / empty of us, hack and crater / it / until it is nothing if that / could rinse it of all our sweat and pathos." So he is addicted to everything man's flesh has touched and soiled, "objects / steeped in the juice of fingertips / . . . surfaces

wetted down / with fist grease and elbow oil," and in an exuberant fashion
Kinnell claims him as an "ultra- / Rilkean angel," one in whom the tar-
nished things of the world find an honest measure of their value, one

> for whom the true
> portion of the sweetness of earth
> is one of those bottom-heavy, glittering, saccadic bits
> of salt water that splash down
> the haunted ravines of a human face.

In contrast to the imagined creature he has built up thus far, Kinnell turns
suddenly in the fourth part to give a straightforward but quite grisly account
of the shooting of a porcupine by a farmer. But it grows clear that in this
episode, as in the earlier parts of the poem, we are being treated to a display
of persistence, a dogged tenacity toward life which exists to the point of
annihilation. In the end the furious efforts of the dying animal seem no less
astonishing than the poet's previous depiction of his curious inclinations:

> A farmer shot a porcupine three times
> as it dozed on a tree limb. On
> the way down it tore open its belly
> on a broken
> branch, hooked its gut,
> and went on falling. On the ground
> it sprang to its feet, and
> paying out gut heaved
> and spartled through a hundred feet of goldenrod
> before
> the abrupt emptiness.

After a brief stanza in which Kinnell announces that the sacred books of
the ancient Zoroastrians reserve a place in Hell for those who destroy porcu-
pines, the poem shifts its center to the poet's own life. Lying sleepless and
disturbed, he envisages himself as undergoing metamorphosis, "the fatty
sheath of the man / melting off." With the disappearance of his human features, the inward torments of self-consciousness also vanish; whatever pained
his thoughts and feelings before changes into outward aggression. The transformation complete, he has become the porcupine: "a red-eyed, hard-toothed,
arrow-stuck urchin / tossing up mattress feathers, / pricking the / woman
beside me until she cries." Having identified himself thoroughly with this
animal, he can see the aptness of the alteration in terms of his past experience. Pierced with the arrows of his quills, he has suffered, in the woundings
and dyings imposed by existence, like a "Saint / Sebastian of the / scared
heart," indeed, has felt himself disemboweled like the porcupine shot from

> And fallen from high places
> I have fled, have
> jogged
> over fields of goldenrod,
> terrified, seeking home,
> and among flowers
> I have come to myself empty, the rope
> strung out behind me
> in the fall sun
> suddenly glorified with all my blood.

The dramatic horror of such remembrance is matched by the desolate mood with which the last stanza begins. Here Kinnell maintains his altered identity, which should be interpreted not as subhuman but as the human reduced by lacerating acquaintance with life to a level of fierce struggling to keep a hold on it under narrowed, unaccommodating circumstances. In the final sense, his tenacious fight for survival, his determination to forage the world for sustenance in spite of a crippling feeling of personal emptiness, wins respect for this poet-turned-porcupine. And beyond this basic impulse to stay alive, to keep on going, the images of thistled and thorned flowers, so close to the sharp, bristling porcupine quills, imply something more: a rough, wild beauty of bloom and blossom—or translating these into terms of Kinnell's life as the effort to create poems—which the rude contest for existence may yield:

> And tonight I think I prowl broken
> skulled or vacant as a
> sucked egg in the wintry meadow, softly chuckling, blank
> template of myself, dragging
> a starved belly through lichflowered acres,
> where
> burdock looses the arks of its seed
> and thistle holds up its lost blooms
> and rosebushes in the wind scrape their dead limbs
> for the forced-fire
> of roses.

From this dark condition of the spirit, then, there rises an affirming gesture which, rather characteristically for Kinnell, is glimpsed through analogies with nature. What the private implications of the attitude taken at the end of the poem are for him we cannot say, nor is it a matter of importance for the reader. What does matter is that the severe, at times repellent, poetic myth created in "The Porcupine" incarnates a view of ourselves that, left to our own devices, we should probably not be hardy or unflinching

enough to formulate. The same must be said for "Testament of the Thief,"
and certainly for "The Bear." In the latter the quest for identification with
the beast is even more urgent, violent, and terrifyingly absolute; the whole
poem possesses the aura of symbolic nightmare in which the meaning may
prove elusive but the details are dreadfully realistic. The poet goes off at
once on the track of the bear; no hesitations or deliberations are involved,
for every step proceeds with a predetermined and frighteningly rigid logic,
while, nonetheless, nothing appears reasonable or humane. The manufacture of the fatal bait with its vicious sharpened wolf's rib for the bear to
swallow marks the first stage in a hunt of ever more agonizing, distasteful,
yet necessary proportions. As he follows the track of blood from its hemor-
rhage, the poet gradually adopts some of the beast's behavior. The quest is
evidently preparing him through initiatory processes for his last transformation, and these can be both repulsive and hardening:

> On the third day I begin to starve,
> at nightfall I bend down as I knew I would
> at a turd sopped in blood,
> and hesitate, and pick it up,
> and thrust it in my mouth, and gnash it down,
> and rise
> and go on running.

With the exactitude of ritualized dream the hunter-poet, "living by now
on bear blood alone," after seven days sights the dead animal, "a scraggled, /
steamy hulk," and soon, with a ruthlessness and a ravenous hunger that
would do credit to the bear, he is devouring its flesh, assimilating its strength
and nature. At last he opens its hide, merges his identity with the bear's,
and falls asleep in its skin. But the process has not been completed. If this
poem exhibits the qualities of some awful dream from its beginning, then
the sections immediately subsequent to the one in which he enters the
bear's body compose a dream-within-a-dream that brings the hunter-poet
closer to the goal of his quest. For now, wrapped in the flesh and fur of the
animal, sated with its blood and meat, he must dream as he sleeps there that
beast's agonizing death journey, of which he is the cause, as if it were his
own. Once again, in these fifth and sixth sections, Kinnell engages the most
brutal sufferings the self can tolerate:

> 5
> And dream
> of lumbering flatfooted
> over the tundra,
> stabbed twice from within,
> splattering a trail behind me,

splattering it out no matter which way I lurch,
no matter which parabola of bear-transcendence,
which dance of solitude I attempt,
which gravity-clutched leap,
which trudge, which groan.

6
Until one day I totter and fall—
fall on this
stomach that has tried so hard to keep up,
to digest the blood as it leaked in,
to break up
and digest the bone itself: and now the breeze
blows over me, blows off
the hideous belches of ill-digested bear blood
and rotted stomach
and the ordinary, wretched odor of bear,

blows across
my sore, lolled tongue a song
or screech, until I think I must rise up
and dance. And I lie still.

The pain and the persistence resemble what we saw in "The Porcupine." In neither poem can the suffering creature elude its cruel destiny, its torturous death; such are the inexplicable premises of existence which Kinnell's poetry probes relentlessly from the start. But in his recent work he not only takes these realities as they come; he even searches them out with the intention of living them through to the finish, reaching toward the extreme, the rock-bottom of existence, so to speak, in order to find some final principle of being, a hard kernel of self that endures, and turn it to poetic account. So, out of the hideous torments he undergoes in dreaming the bear's death as his own, comes the possibility of poetry—though one almost shies from the word "art" under the circumstances—more than the primitive "song or screech" blown from his exhausted mouth, or the sudden desire to perform a dance of death; it is a deeper, more personal sense of the poem and what animates it that emerges in the closing stanza after the hunter-poet awakens. He sees again the known landscape of winter, yet he further realizes that now he is the bear, and has his own journey to make, strangely nourished by the painful myth he has enacted:

And one
hairy-soled trudge stuck out before me,
the next groaned out,
the next,

the next,
the rest of my days I spend
wandering: wondering
what, anyway,
was that sticky infusion, that rank flavor of blood, that poetry, by
   which I lived?

This powerful dream-poem of the poet's initiation, which seems to me in
spite of its harshness to be ultimately quite strong in its affirmation of existence, completes Galway Kinnell's latest book. It also puts us in mind once
more of the indivisibility for this fine poet of "the man who suffers and the
mind which creates"—a reversal of Eliot's well-known dictum. This indivisibility is a distinguishing mark of the work of many of the most important and forceful younger American poets during the past fifteen years, poets whose "poems take shape from the shapes of their emotions, the shapes
their minds make in thought."[7] Kinnell's growth as a poet has traced such a
pattern in close congruence with the events of his life, his most fundamental perceptions and emotions, the themes and images, obsessing his consciousness. As even a cursory reading of his work would indicate, he is one
of the most substantial, accomplished poets of a very talented generation.
His future poems should not be predicted but awaited with anticipation.[8]
There is something essential of Kinnell himself and of his poetry in these
memorable lines he wrote for Robert Frost:

Who dwelt in access to that which other men
Have burnt all their lives to get near, who heard
The high wind, in gusts, seething
From far off, headed through the trees exactly
To this place where it must happen, who spent
Your life on the point of giving away your heart
To the dark trees, the dissolving woods,
Into which you go at last, heart in hand, deep in . . .

(1970)

NOTES

[1]These changes were, of course, gradual but visible at widely varying points on the
American literary map from the mid-1950s on. Roethke, Patchen, Kunitz, Eberhart,
W. C. Williams, Weldon Kees, and others can be taken as forerunners.
[2]*Babel to Byzantium* (New York, 1968), p. 135.
[3]A good discussion of this poem appears in Glauco Cambon, *Recent American Poetry* (Minneapolis, 1961), pp. 33-36. Necessarily, I echo some of his observations.
[4]For a discussion of sacred mountains, see Mircea Eliade, *Patterns in Contemporary Religion* (New York, 1958).

[5]Yves Bonnefoy, *On the Motion and Immobility of Douve*, trans. Galway Kinnell (Athens, Ohio, 1968). Bonnefoy's epigraph from Hegel is perhaps significant: "But the life of the spirit is not frightened at death and does not keep itself pure of it. It endures death and maintains itself in it." (Translated by Kinnell.)

[6]*Poet's Choice* (New York, 1962), p. 257.

[7]Foreword to *Naked Poetry*, ed. Stephen Berg and Robert Mezey (Indianapolis and New York, 1969), p. xi.

[8]Just as this volume of studies was completed, Kinnell published his extraordinary new *Book of Nightmares* (Boston, 1971), which continues through a group of ten profoundly linked poems many of the preoccupations with existence, death, and nothingness discussed above. Poetically speaking, it is a striking accomplishment and must stand as one of the imaginative landmarks of the 1970s.

17

Donald Hall's Poetry

I wake to sleep, and take my waking slow
—Theodore Roethke

Je ferme les yeux simplement
pour mieux voir
—Philippe Soupault

The recent appearance of *The Alligator Bride*, a volume of new and selected poems, provides a good occasion for looking at the development in Donald Hall's writing, where his work began, and the important alterations it has subsequently undergone. Of the poetic generation of the 1950s Hall is one of the most interesting and influential figures. As an editor, anthologist, and sometime critic, he has helped to shape a sense of current poetic history, its multiple ideas and aims; he has been an open proponent of pluralism in contemporary poetry and opposed to established critical theories and dogmas. Nowhere does he declare his attitudes more clearly and succinctly than in the admirable introduction to his anthology *Contemporary American Poetry* (1962). There he starts by noting the gradual downfall of the New Criticism as the "orthodoxy" dominating American poetry from "1925 to 1955," and then rightly observes that "typically the modern artist has allowed nothing to be beyond his consideration. He has acted as if restlessness were a conviction and has destroyed his own past in order to create a future. He has said to himself, like the policeman to the vagrant, 'Keep moving.' "

For present purposes I should like to shift attention from the general applicability of this statement and regard it instead as perfectly suitable to

Hall's own career as a poet. Indeed, he has, in his own writing, and certainly in the life of imagination and feeling which lies behind it, charted the kind of course he detects in the work of many of his contemporaries, a course that demands at some crucial juncture radically decisive gestures, the destruction of a "past in order to create a future." That past in Hall's case becomes quite evident in his first two collections, *Exiles and Marriages* (1955) and *The Dark Houses* (1958), though the latter reveals tangible growth and the desire for change. The initial book, however, shows how closely he adhered to the then prevailing requirements of—in his own words—"symmetry, intellect, irony, and wit" derived from Eliot's criticism and the thought and practice of various modern critics. In a recent lecture, *The Inward Muse*, Hall remarks that he "grew up in the thick of the new criticism" and as he worked on his early poems "could sometimes hear the voice of Mr. Ransom" (whom he did not know) reminding him to be appropriately ironic; he adds that "it took ten years to get rid of that voice."[1] Doubtless, other poets of Hall's generation have known the same or similar experiences. In the later 1950s, however, the break with the critical establishment began, first with the arrival of Ginsberg and the Beats, but soon rejections came from every quarter. As it appears now, this movement has delivered poetry back into the hands of poets.

Hall's early poems, of which he wisely retains only a few—and these usually revised—in *The Alligator Bride*, are not wholly devoid of interest, especially since the reader can glimpse in them some of the areas of experience most meaningful to the poet and certain themes persisting in his work. But one can dismiss without regret, as Hall does, the slick, witty pieces such as "The Lone Ranger," "A Novelist," "Conduct and Work," "Apology," "Syllables of a Small Fig Tree," "Some Oddities," "Carol," "Cops and Robbers," "Nefas Tangerine," "Six Poets in Search of a Lawyer," "Lycanthropy Revisited," and various others, including the long poem "Exile" (winner of the Newdigate Prize at Oxford), which does reappear in the later collection, only reduced from one hundred to six lines. Formal skills, dexterity, irony, and intelligence are all on view here, along with occasional echoes of mentors, but the best one can say for these poems is that they exhibit a gift for knowledgeable, polished versifying; today they seem dated and very slight.

More support can be mustered for several other poems which must have emerged from deeper sources in the poet and, correspondingly, touch profound, truly sensitive chords of feeling in the reader. Some of these are poems of New Hampshire, where Hall spent summers on his grandparents' farm from the time he was a small boy. The annual visits, the farm labors, his love for his grandparents and complex attachment to the slowly dying way of life they knew provide material for quite a few poems in his first book and after. It is also instructive, as well as pleasurable, to read the fine prose memoirs of these farm experiences, published in 1961 as *String Too Short to Be Saved*; from this book the background and many of the details in a poem such as the moving "Elegy for Wesley Wells" (his grandfather) become clear. That poem and "Old Home Day"—both of them shortened and revised— are the best of the early New Hampshire pieces and the only ones Hall has salvaged. In the first version the "Elegy" lost something of its force through lengthiness; in its present form it is still long, but the dead farmer, his past, and the history of the region he inhabited have become more intimately and vitally related. We realize soon after the poem's beginning that Hall is writing from England; his distance from his home country not only increases the sense of loss but also offers the perspective of exile which sharpens his vision of the contours of Wesley Wells's life and inheritance, finally con- firming his solidarity with it. The opening effectively renders the atmo- sphere of absence and deprivation death creates which has now descended upon the farm:

> Against the clapboards and the window panes
> The loud March whines with rain and heavy wind,
> In dark New Hampshire where his widow wakes.
> She cannot sleep. The familiar length is gone.
> I think across the clamorous Atlantic
> To where the farm lies hard against the foot
> Of Ragged Mountain, underneath Kearsarge.
> I speak his name against the beating sea.
>   His dogs will whimper through the webby barn,
> Where spiders close his tools in a pale gauze
> And wait for flies. The nervous woodchuck now
> Will waddle plumply through the world of weeds
> Eating wild peas as if he owned the land,
> And the fat hedgehog rob the apple trees.
> When next October's frosts harden the ground
> And fasten in the year's catastrophe,
> The farm will lie like driftwood,
> The farmer dead, and deep in his carved earth.

Following this passage, Hall shifts to historical considerations, to the rich- ness of this region before the Civil War, which "took off the hired men" who cultivated the fields, so that in time these lands returned to their origi- nal state "thick with ashy pine." The poem continues by recounting the steadily worsening fortunes of the inhabitants—those who remained—and through the bizarre, disturbing image of an abandoned railroad and loco- motive evokes the departure of progress and prosperity. (A more detailed description of this engine and its setting occur in *String Too Short to Be Saved*.)

Deep in the forest now, half-covered up,
The reddened track of an abandoned railroad
Heaved in the frosts, in the roots of the tall pines;
A locomotive stood
Like a strange rock, red as the fallen needles.

Recalling the daily and seasonal routines of the farm that formed the basis for his grandfather's existence for so many years, the poet achieves an essential, durable picture of the man to be retained in memory, one which incorporates the honesty, stability, and unobtrusive heroism of that life:

I number out the virtues that are dead,
Remembering his soft, consistent voice,
His gentleness, and most,
The bone that showed in each deliberate word.

The poem's closing portions show Hall keeping a solitary vigil "on England's crowded shore" and realizing that his ties are to that "place and people" far off "in dark New Hampshire"; he ends envisaging his grandfather's body carried to the cemetery for burial.

"I cannot see the watch on my wrist / without knowing that I am dying," Hall writes in a poem from his second collection, *The Dark Houses*; and that acute sensitivity to time and mortality, acquired in part at least from his New Hampshire experience, develops into a constant element of his work. The most accomplished of the early poems seem possessed by intimations of death, loss, isolation, and guilt. In the shortened, rearranged version of "Old Home Day" the initial stanza blends images of man and landscape in a condition of general decay:

Under the eyeless, staring lid,
And in the pucker of a mouth,
Gullied hayfields cave together
And crumble in the August drought.

And from the lengthy, rather tedious original text of "Exile," once a poem of four pages, Hall has extracted what were three parenthetical couplets set in the middle of different stanzas to make brief yet highly suggestive summaries of personal dilemmas. Each stanza designates a relationship valued by the poet which has now been violated, either through death, through the poet's own betrayal, or through the changing circumstances that influence an individual's life. None of the violations is elaborated in much detail; instead, a simplicity of language and description stimulates the reader's imagination, permitting him to tease out the possibilities and to discover similarities in his own experience. The final couplet, while it depicts a particular moment of knowledge, the realization that a person grows away from even his deepest roots and that he will return to the place of his origins only to find it alien and strange because he has himself altered, should not be understood merely as a third instance of perplexing loss in the poem. For if we view the three stanzas in sequence, we comprehend a certain kind of movement. In the first couplet death deprives the poet of a good friend, still in his boyhood. In the second, and most complex, he breaks a relationship with a girl while he yet loves her—out of what hidden motives we are not sure—and suffers a period of remorse, then dismisses the incident from consciousness, though it obviously has not vanished since he must include it at the center of the poem (this experience turns up elsewhere in Hall's early poetry). Finally, in the concluding stanza, he visits his birthplace and thinks it has changed completely. What appears of primary importance in the poem, I believe, is that all of these events cause alterations in the poet, and the last couplet with its rhyme of grew/new emphasizes the continuity of change in each life. The exile of the title denotes an unavoidable, recurrent aspect of existence: time and death exile us, and we even exile ourselves from others, yet we grow and mature from such experiences, always impelled forward by the promise of what is yet to come. Loss, then, creates the possibility of gain, and so, in this light, the third couplet slides ambiguously between estrangement and potentiality:

> A boy who played and talked and read with me
> Fell from a maple tree.
>
> I loved her, but I told her I did not,
> And wept, and then forgot.
>
> I walked the streets where I was born and grew,
> And all the streets were new.

"Wedding Party," a poem Hall uses to begin both *Exiles and Marriages* and *The Alligator Bride* (though in a shorter, improved form in the latter volume), takes up this theme of temporal change and erosion and treats it in a slightly fantastic manner, especially as the irrational elements are allowed to dominate in the new, condensed version with its total abandonment of verisimilitude. At the very start imaginative vision dictates the order of details, which are not given as we might expect, for the focus falls at once upon somewhat ominous figures rather than the bridal couple:

> The pock-marked player of the accordion
> Empties and fills his squeeze box in the corner,
> Kin to the tiny man who pours champagne,

> Kin to the caterer. These solemn men,
> Amid the sounds of silk and popping corks,
> Stand like pillars.

This odd group, ruling over the occasion as it turns out, mutes and qualifies the conventional gaiety from the outset. The bride appears after these men, in the last line and a half of the stanza, in a bizarre analogy to the Virgin or some other female saint carried in effigy by a religious procession through a throng of worshipers:

> And the white bride
> Moves through the crowd as a chaired relic moves.

Certainly, the phrase "chaired relic" induces a feeling of strangeness and also—quite importantly—first implies the idea of time, aging, and death so central to the poem's climactic vision. With the end of the initial stanza, then, unpleasant expectations, though as yet indefinite, have been established. In his original version Hall included a middle stanza which identified the poem's speaker as a guest invited at the last moment, a "friend to the bride's rejected suitor," added further unnecessary filler, and finished with "summer twilight" and the threat of an approaching storm. This stanza merely dissipated the curious atmosphere generated by the preceding one and made concessions to ordinariness or normalcy which the reader, intent upon the unreality of the situation, couldn't care about less. Now, with such externals removed, the last stanza immediately picks up and magnifies the disquieting details. The accordionist suddenly assumes the gigantic, terrifying proportions of a god or fate presiding over these ceremonies. Under his spell, as if in a hallucination, the bride's marriage and future life are envisaged as already completed, transformed into a few faded memories, and, by implication, nearing death. (It is perhaps worth noting that in neither version is the groom mentioned.) The storm which breaks, no longer related to the thundershower of the omitted stanza, thus can be understood metaphorically as the tempest of time striking the bride and, I believe, her guests as well, ravaging their lives, while above them looms the accordionist-god, his instrument directing the rhythms of existence, of air in and out of lungs:

> Now all at once the pock-marked player grows
> Immense and terrible beside the bride
> Whose marriage withers to a rind of years
> And curling photographs in a dry box;
> And in the storm that hurls upon the room
> Above the crowd he holds his breathing box
> That only empties, fills, empties, fills.

In *The Dark Houses* Hall's work develops along lines similar to those distinguishing the better pieces in his first book. There are fewer poems that seem all skill and fancy, and more that try to reach those concealed roots of experience on which imagination thrives. Once again, as with most of the superior poems from *Exiles and Marriages*, there is an obvious concern with death, time's passage, and with the missed opportunities for a full existence. In "Christmas Eve in Whitneyville," an elegy for his father, the poet reveals an incisive social awareness which draws ironic pictures of middle-class isolationism on this feast day; each family is locked in its home as if it were a cell:

> Each car is put away in each garage;
> Each husband home from work, to celebrate,
> Has closed his house around him like a cage,
> And wedged the tree until the tree stood straight.

Hall proceeds to summarize his father's business career, how after success he could afford trips to Europe, where, unable to forget work, he "took the time to think how yearly gains, / Profit and volume made the business grow." Now, dying early at fifty-two, he has acquired money but has seen little of life or the world; his comment, recalled by the poet, discloses the regret and ambivalence he feels toward the close of his fatal illness:

> "The things you had to miss," you said last week,
> "Or thought you had to, take your breath away."
> You propped yourself on pillows, where your cheek
> Was hollow, stubbled lightly with new gray.

Reflecting on this devotion to acquisitiveness, Hall comes again to the image of enclosure; the house which resembled a "cage" becomes synonymous with a mode of living that is itself a form of imprisonment. The poet looks elsewhere for liberation and reward:

> This love is jail; another sets us free.

Without anger but in a mood of determination, Hall leaves his father buried among the people who still pursue the same ends he has rejected. For the poet it is a moment of farewell and departure in search of a different, more abundant existence. The imagery of darkness links the town's sleeping inhabitants with the dead who lie in its cemetery. In different ways all of them are denied life:

The lights go out and it is Christmas Day.
The stones are white, the grass is black and deep;
I will go back and leave you here to stay,
While the dark houses harden into sleep.

Certain other poems in this second collection also exhibit social interests and criticism;[2] the best of these are "1934," which treats effects of the Depression in New Hampshire, and "The Foundations of American Industry," a sharp, ironic depiction of wasted life among auto workers whose fathers had labored in government projects during the 1930s. Their jobs are mechanized by assembly line techniques, their leisure is aimless and empty:

In the Ford plant
the generators
move quickly on
belts, a thousand now
an hour. New men
move to the belt when
the shift comes.

For the most part
the men are young, and
go home to their
Fords, and drive around,
or watch TV,
sleep, and then go work,
towards payday;

when they walk home
they walk on sidewalks
marked W
P A 38;
their old men made
them, and they walk on
their fathers.

Notable here is the entirely successful adoption of a deliberately flat, conversational manner, coupled with the type of observation and rhythmical movement associated with William Carlos Williams and, later, David Ignatow. One senses the attempt on Hall's part to "make it new," in Pound's phrase, to look beyond the formal confinements of most of his writing up to this point and reduce the margin between the poet and his material, or to put it in terms of the Imagists, again borrowing from Pound: "Direct treatment of the 'thing' whether subjective or objective." While his later poems—with striking exceptions such as "Woolworth's" and "Crew-cuts" from

The Alligator Bride—rarely venture into areas of social or political commentary, the present piece offers strong hints of the kind of freedom, economy, simplicity, and directness of statement (even when the implications of the imagery arc strange or oblique) Hall will arrive at six years afterward with *A Roof of Tiger Lilies* (1964).

A few more poems in *The Dark Houses* are quite effective in their individual ways and prepare for further achievements. These include "Religious Articles" (shortened, revised, and called "'I Come to the Garden Alone'" in *The Alligator Bride*), "Three Poems from Edvard Munch," "The Three Movements," "Waiting on the Corners" (reduced to the first of seven sections in its later version), "The Presences of Death," and "Revelations, Contradictions" (the last two omitted from *The Alligator Bride*). In each of these poems Hall struggles toward a greater knowledge or seeks a degree of self-knowledge or seeks the circumstances of human existence; gradually he is breaking away from the superficial intelligence that rules his previous writing. The conclusion of "Religious Articles," in which the poet visits an old church he attended in childhood and thinks about the dead members of his family lamenting the deprivation and loss of their lives, urges on him an agnostic, skeptical attitude, but one which will also force him to take up the burden of his own life. The voices of the dead, he realizes, are voices he lends them; as they speak all pretense is stripped away:

> "We who do not exist make noises
> only in you. Your illusion says
> that we who are cheated and broken
> croon our words to the living again.
> You must not believe in anything;
> you who feel cheated are crooning."

And in "Revelations, Contradictions" Hall scrutinizes intently his alternating perceptions of order and disorder, of fragmentation and nothingness with symmetry and fullness of being; between them stands the perceiving self. At the end he is compelled to accept contrariety as a fundamental principle: "Things are their opposites. To understand / Today's solution makes tomorrow's lie."

Pressing further beyond the surfaces and the barriers of false appearance and convention with which experience is frequently masked, the poet confronts emptiness, cruelty and violence, metaphysical terror, and death in the poems inspired by Munch's three pictures, "The Scream," "Marat's Death," and "The Kiss" (the later, shortened versions are most satisfactory), and in "Waiting on the Corners." What Hall says in "The Scream" is true for all of these poems: "Existence is laid bare," and it is an existence turned back upon itself, without spiritual appeal. "The blood not Christ's, / blood of death without resurrection, / winds flatly in the air," Hall observes of the surging background to Munch's agonized figure, and concludes that this picture has "not even the pause, / the repose of art that has distance." Distance. It is exactly such emotional and experiential spacing we have already seen Hall beginning to eliminate from his poetry. The third poem of the original sequence "Waiting on the Corners" brings a new lucidity and intimacy of vision to bear upon the poet himself. In keeping with one of the main themes of the sequence, the poem finishes on a level of psychological and spiritual vacancy, but prior to that conclusion it enters a highly subjective area of the speaker's life, probing and dramatizing vividly in pulsing rhythms a crisis of the self, an excruciating symbolic death and rebirth in the psyche which leaves its victim changed but also emptied out. In its own fashion this poem displays affinities with some of Theodore Roethke's work, "The Return," for example, and with the intense poetry of self-revelation written by Anne Sexton and Sylvia Plath. But it is chiefly significant in terms of Hall's efforts to increase the depth and authenticity of his poetic experience:

> At least once before
> my skin has felt rough fingers
> pull my eyelids down,
> my body laid
> on the floor like clothes.
> I struggled against the pit
> like a bull in the yards.
> I tried
> to lift myself out by willing,
> for I knew what I hated the most.
> After I died, my eyes
> opened to find the colors
> as bright as knives.
> It was necessary to die,
> for a few moments only
> to give up
> whatever I owned, and all
> I might become, and the sight,
> taste, touch, and smell
> of the particular world.
> There, in the pit,
> all willing gone from me,
> no more an animal
> in hatred,
> "You" (I heard a voice)
> "who have lost everything
> want nothing."

The interior concentration of this poem and its reading of a barometer of hidden emotional stresses and dilemmas place it as prophetic of the deliberate turning Hall's work will soon take.

The final poem in *The Dark Houses* is "The Three Movements," and through irregular lines and phrasing, suggestive of the uncertain, searching efforts of the poet's mind, it also leads him toward the brink of anticipated changes in his writing. The poem involves a poetic or imaginative quest to replenish his art, but it cannot be achieved simply by looking to tradition, learning from others:

> It is not in the books
> that he is looking, nor for
> a new book, nor
> documents of any kind . . .

The lack of desire for "a new book" indicates, I think, a wish to reach beyond the restrictions of literary convention. But what he seeks is not available to the poet effortlessly either, occurring like a sudden event in nature:

> . . . nor
> does he expect it to be like the wind,
> that, when you touch it, tears
> without a sound of tearing, nor
> like the rain
> water,
> that becomes
> grass in the sun.

The image that comes to him when he envisages his goal is that of a person, alert, sensitive, resolute, attentive to experience; and it is difficult not to see this figure as a re-creation of the poet's self, in the sense in which, say, Whitman, Yeats, Rilke, or Neruda make themselves over in their art to assimilate more life, more of reality into poetry. In short, Hall recognizes that he must make himself over in order to transform his writing; or, as Robert Bly remarks, "Since the country [America] has no image of a poet as a poet, a poet to develop must learn to imagine himself":

> He
> expects that when he finds it,
> it will be
> like a man, visible, alive
> to what has happened and what
> will happen, with
> firmness in its face, seeing

            exactly what is, without
            measure of change, and not
            like documents,
            or rain in the grass.

In a second stanza he entertains his doubts and hesitations; perhaps what
he requires "is not / for the finding," and the previously dismissed alterna-
tives must be accepted as the only possibilities after all. But in the last stanza
he acknowledges that he has slighted "the movement / that intrigues / all
thinking," a process whereby the covert, the oblique, the unconscious aspects of the mind are drawn into focus; from this "movement" will emerge
the startling, unexpected image of the poetic self whose identity is exact,
unmistakable:

                It is
            the movement which works through,
            which discovers itself
            in alleys, in
            sleep, not
            expected and not
            in the books of words and phrases
            nor the various paints and edges
            of scenery.
            It is, he says,
            familiar when come upon,
            glimpsed as in a mirror
            unpredicted,
            and it appears
            to understand. It is
            like himself, only visible.

    With the awareness of new imaginative resources announced at the close
of "The Three Movements" Hall's poetry departs from past practices and
sets out for unexplored territories of experience. The areas into which he
moves after his own fashion are regions of inwardness, the preconscious,
the peripheries of sleep, the moods of reverie and daydream, which is to say,
wherever the energies of the interior life, the life of images and dreams rich
with association, persist, and what Hall has termed "the vatic voice" can
speak and be heard. In this endeavor he has some remarkably illustrious
modern predecessors such as Whitman, Rilke, Lawrence, Breton, Trakl,
Desnos, Neruda, Vallejo, Eluard, and Roethke, among others, and certain
of his more immediate contemporaries—Robert Bly, James Wright, W. S.
Merwin, for example—who began to create a poetry which, as Bly noted in
an interview printed in *The Sullen Art* (1963), "simply disregards the con-

scious and the intellectual structure of the mind entirely and, by the use of images, tries to bring forward another reality from *inward* experience." Meanwhile, several New York poets, John Ashbery, Kenneth Koch, and the late Frank O'Hara, closely linked with the influential painting *avant garde* (and, oddly enough, originally students at Harvard at the same time as Hall and Bly), were introducing their own modes of irrationalism and surrealist techniques into poetry.

In various essays and lectures Hall discusses the creative process in himself and in the work of other poets (see, for instance, his introduction to *A Choice of Whitman's Verse,* [1968]), and he observes that the critical and technical powers operate instinctively upon the flow of images, intuitions, and details which the mind offers in moments of inspiration. Thus he rejects, in *The Inward Muse,* the "theoretical dualism of *creation* which provides material, and criticism which shapes it." But in a later lecture on *The Vatic Voice: Waiting and Listening* (printed in the *Michigan Quarterly Review,* Fall 1969) he tries to describe the passive attendance on creativity, the coming of words and images in a sudden release, and the nature of this expression from far within ourselves. Hall begins by seeking a fundamental principle:

> A premise: within every human being there is the vatic voice. *Vates* was the Greek word for the inspired bard, speaking the words of a god. To most people, this voice speaks only in dream, and only in unremembered dream. The voice may shout messages into the sleeping ear, but a guard at the horned gate prevents the waking mind from remembering, listening, interpreting. It is the vatic voice (which is not necessarily able to write good poetry, or even passable grammar) which rushes forth the words of excited recognition, which supplies what we call inspiration. And inspiration, a breathing-into, is a perfectly expressive metaphor: "Not I, not I, but the wind that blows through me!" as Lawrence says. Or Shelley's "Ode to the West Wind." We are passive to the vatic voice, as the cloud or the tree is passive to the wind.

For the poet, indeed for any man, it is necessary in Hall's opinion to hear this voice, to listen for it, away from the strictures of logic or reasoning, the demands of practicality, the noise and distraction of our urbanized society, "not only to make poems, or to invent a new theory of linguistics, but because it feels good, because it is healing and therapeutic, because it helps us to understand ourselves and to be able to love other people." Attention to this voice: revives and animates the imaginative life, the apprehension of the world, as Hall says, children know and the poet, among others, needs to rediscover if his work is to achieve depth, resonance, true poetic quality. A few paragraphs devoted to Hall's personal habits, deliberate reliance on dream and reverie as a means of stimulating the imagination and stirring the vatic voice to speech (he notes that the "Two characteristics that distinguish the vatic voice from normal discourse are that it is always original, and that we feel passive to it. We are surprised by it, and we may very well, having uttered its words, not know what we mean.") are of particular interest for the light they cast on experiences in back of much of the poetry included in *A Roof of Tiger Lilies* and *The Alligator Bride*. Then too these disclosures may remind us, as Gaston Bachelard remarks, how in order to comprehend what a poet has formulated from his creative reverie we must join him in dreaming it as we read. One can likewise see resemblances between Hall's intentions and the investigation and experimentation with sleep, dreams, and their imagery conducted by André Breton, Robert Desnos, and other Surrealists.

> Sometimes I have tried to keep in touch with this vatic voice by sleeping a lot. Taking short naps can be a great means of keeping the channel open. There is that wonderful long, delicious slide or drift down heavy air to the bottom of sleep, which you touch for only a moment, and then there is the floating up again more swiftly, through an incredible world of images, sometimes in bright colors. I come out of these fifteen or twenty minute naps, not with phrases of poetry, but wholly refreshed with the experience of losing control and entering a world of apparent total freedom. I wake with great energy. On occasion, I remember phrases or scenes from dreams— either night dreams, or nap dreams, or waking fantasy dreams—take these phrases or images directly into a poem. That happens, but it is not the only virtue of dream. Dream is the spirit dying into the underworld, and being born again.
>
> There is also the deliberate farming of daydream. There is a way in which you can daydream quite loosely, but also observe yourself. You watch the strange associations, the movements. These associations are frequently trying to tell us something. The association is always there for some reason. Listen. When you hum a tune, remember the words that go with the tune and you will usually hear some part of your mind commenting on another part of your mind, or on some recent action.
>
> There is something I want to call peripheral vision, and I don't mean anything optical. If you talk about a dream with an analyst, and there is an old battered table in the dream that you casually mention, he may well say, "What about this table? What did it look like?" Often these little details are so important. When I am listening to something passively speaking out of me, I don't attempt to choose what is most important, I try to listen to all of it. I never know what is going to be the most important message until I have lived with it for a while. Very frequently, the real subject matter is something only glimpsed, as it were out of the corner of the eye. Often the association which at first glance appears crazy and irrelevant ultimately leads to the understanding, and tells what we did not know before.

With these observations of Hall's before us we can better understand the nature of that "movement" of the mind in the act of discovering the materials of a poem. And these materials, whose sources lie in subterranean levels of the self, when gathered and shaped into the final form of the completed poem, will result in a poetry of dream and inward vision, a kind of surrealism already familiar in modern European and Latin American literature, "ultimately a poetry of the deep mind all men share," in Hall's words about Whitman. Emphasis shifts from the techniques of verse making, the outside or external aspects of the poem to "spirit" or vision, the force within the poet animating and relating his images. Obviously, this does not mean that formal considerations are dispensed with altogether—one still finds Hall employing various prosodic devices; but the general tendency is toward greater looseness or openness of form, away from iambics and rhyming. The strength of such poetry depends to a considerable degree on the phrasing, the rhythm and movement of lines as both imaginative *and* musical units within the whole, as well as on diction, imagery, and intensity or authenticity of vision. Its aim is finally, in a paradoxical phrase, to awaken the reader to dreams, which is to say, turn him away from the superficialities that consume his outward existence and indicate the immense hidden reservoirs of life within him. Poetry of this order rehabilitates the powers of imagination, of dreaming on the world, and may even be said to revive a sense of the sacred, as it certainly does in some poems of Hall's, Merwin's, Bly's, Dickey's, and Wright's, though there is no specifically orthodox theological framework involved. The mysterious range of poetic possibilities disclosed to Hall through this transformation of his art is best described, however, by the poet himself briefly but evocatively in "The Poem," placed in the first section of *A Roof of Tiger Lilies*:

> It discovers by night
> what the day hid from it.
> Sometimes it turns itself
> into an animal.
> In summer it takes long walks
> by itself where meadows
> fold back from ditches.
> Once it stood still
> in a quiet row of machines.
> Who knows
> what it is thinking?

What this kind of poetry is thinking is a question readers coming upon it for the first time may well ask, for unlike, say, a Metaphysical poem of witty conceits and learned allusions, it yields little to rigorous logical analysis—a reason perhaps why Surrealism, Expressionism, the contemporary poets of France, Germany, Spain, Italy, and Latin America, with a few exceptions such as Valéry and Rilke, never engaged most of our important critics of the past three decades, while European critics have long been studying them. If that situation in America is being revised now, it is chiefly due to the prose writings of poets themselves and to the extraordinary increase in the enterprise of translation. Hall's "The Poem" stands both as a statement of the sources and procedures of his new work and as an example of it. We understand that this is so, yet at the same time we cannot "translate" the substance of the poem from its images into a more rational and readily assimilable prose paraphrase—that is, to borrow a phrase of James Dickey's, use up the imaginative or creative matter which is the poem by the process of exegesis. Just as this type of poetry originates in the interior life and evokes that life, so the imagery and implications draw inward in the poem, and the reader must follow them toward the center rather than try to pull them away from the poem for inspection and explanation. Of course, I am not saying that the poem means nothing, but that the meaning is implicit, inherent in the particular arrangement of images and movement of lines bearing them. To be sure, this is true of virtually all poems, but we are dealing here with a kind of poem that is purposively irrational, within whose imaginative context meaning emerges only by suggestion, evocation, indirection, or obliquity. Only by living within the body of images, or floating on them, to use Hall's own description, do we approach a point of comprehension; then themes and motifs make themselves felt, patterns of emotion are revealed. As the opening lines of "The Poem" imply, the poetic imagination looks to the "night" world of dream, reverie, the preconscious and the unconscious in preference to the daylight world which demands lucidity, not mystery; rational coherence, not indefiniteness or suggestion. This poem also exhibits what might be called the infinite capacity of the poetic imagination for extending itself, for rejecting any kinds of restriction upon the realms of experience it can partake of—animals, summer meadows' machines: the strange evocativeness of these possibilities for the poem tells the reader something of how such poetry should be apprehended.

In correspondence with these remarks, the dominant mood or atmosphere of the majority of poems in *A Roof of Tiger Lilies* is that of reverie, daydream, or the more enigmatic narrative of the night dream which displays characteristic qualities of ellipsis, condensation, and displacement. Frequently, a poem starts off with an external, objective situation or observation; then gradually, as the poet's mind loosens its narrow or rigid focus, barriers fall, and associations, memories, images begin to assert themselves: the poem thus slips inward, unfolding its interior drama. The themes of these poems remain close to those of Hall's earlier writing, but now they are explored

from within; their roots in the psyche of the poet become essential material
for his work. "The Snow," the first poem in the collection, provides an
introductory illustration. In the beginning stanzas the speaker watches snow
falling outside his window. As it takes over his perceptions, memories are
stirred, then hidden affective resonances until, at the close of the second
stanza, his sight seems blurred, as if he were physically outside in a blinding
snow, though he has really moved inside himself, to the border of his inner
world and its vision:

> Snow is in the oak.
> Behind the thick, whitening
> air which the wind drives,
> the weight of the sun
> presses the snow
> on the pane of my window.
>
> I remember snows and my walking
> through their first fall in cities,
> asleep or drunk
> with the slow, desperate falling.
> The snow blurs in my eyes
> with other snows.

In his lecture *The Inward Muse* (*Michigan Quarterly Review*, Winter 1967),
Hall notes how the poem got started, where it led him, and what he tried to
accomplish during its composition:

> Poems begin any number of ways, but here is a frequent way. It is snowing,
> the first snow of the year. I become sleepy with the snow, I relax, daydream,
> enter that sleepy and almost hallucinating state I recognize as preluding a
> poem; my spirit wanders out of myself into the snow, and phrases come
> into my head. Suddenly, I realize that snow does this to me, every year,
> especially first snow. I must write about it in order to understand it. Snow
> is, in psycho-analytic language, over-determined for me. It is burdened with
> affect, heavy with a nameless emotion. Being over-determined, it must
> have multiple sources. I try to keep my attention diffuse and responsive to
> suggestion, my pen moving, as one thing leads to another down the page. I
> am trying to reach, be true to, exploit—the multiple sources of this over-
> determination.

It must be added that Hall continues by denying that he is merely taking
"dictation of [his] unconscious mind" here, for he insists that such dictation
is too rapid and prolific to be recorded verbatim; instead, the trained critical instincts busily accept and reject words and images as they appear. But
we recognize in Hall's descriptive remarks the first stages of the poem: the

initial direct statement ("Snow is in the oak."), the details ending with the irrational perception that the "weight of the sun" is forcing the snow against the speaker's window, and the drop away from perception into recollection, finally into an indistinct blend of memories unified by snow. The third stanza inaugurates a quest for the implications and associations in the interior or psychic life of the poet; this search leads back to the origins of existence before the poem concludes. At the outset, Hall sees snow as representative of the phase of decline to which all things are destined, and this significance discloses in turn a deep-seated obsession with mortality already evident, as we noted, in the earlier poetry:

> Snow is what must
> come down, even if it struggles
> to stay in the air with the strength
> of the wind. Like an old man,
> whatever I touch I turn
> to the story of death.

Following this passage, snow is viewed as an agent of reversal and transformation, endowing everything it covers with "the substance of whiteness." But the last three stanzas of the poem perform an analysis, after their own fashion, of the poet's response to snow in the attempt to trace the origins of that response at the beginnings of his life. The inevitable fall of snow toward the earth, which previously aroused submerged associations and the fear of death, is now linked to a birth trauma; an individual resists birth as a fall into the world culminating at last in death in the same way as a sick and dying man fights against his end. Hall's method of analysis does not employ rationalistic or logical means, for again be proceeds by reverie, reaching back along connecting strands of emotions and memories to revive within himself the child's sense of reality:

> So the watcher sleeps himself
> back to the baby's eyes.
> The tree, the breast, and the floor
> are limbs of him, and from
> his eyes he extends a skin
> which grows over the world.

> The baby is what must
> have fallen, like snow. He resisted,
> the way the old man
> struggles inside the airy tent
> to keep on breathing.
> Birth is the fear of death.

The final stanza makes at once a flat assertion of perishability—the fate of man as well as of snow—and the poet declares his inability to find what amounts to a pattern that includes survival or revivification. The poem finishes with the removal of the sun and its life-giving rays, and the return of falling snow, accompanied in the last line by a general statement of descent that may recall Rilke's poem "Autumn," with its haunting lines, "We are all falling. This hand's falling too— / all have this falling-sickness none withstands." But the "One whose gentle hands / this universal falling can't fall through" (J. B. Leishman's translation) seems precisely the saving God whom Hall cannot discover behind the locked "door / to the cycles of water":

> Snow is what melts.
> I cannot open the door
> to the cycles of water.
> The sun has withdrawn itself
> and the snow keeps falling,
> and something will always be falling.

"We want to regress in the service of the ego, we want to become as children," Hall affirms in *The Vatic Voice*, and it is exactly such a regression he undertakes in "The Snow" and a variety of other poems. "The Grass," a poem thematically allied with "The Snow," likewise starts with a visual perception which rapidly leads to a hidden chain of thoughts compelling the poet's imagination to merge with the essences of nature. Like Roethke in his greenhouse poems and his childhood sequences of *The Lost Son* and *Praise to the End!* Hall wishes to uncover the identity and significant relation of things with himself in the intimacy of an imaginative or visionary union with them.

> When I look at the grass
> out my window in rain,
> I know that it happens
> again. Under
>
> new grass,
> among stones and the downward
> probe of trees,
> everything builds
> or alters itself.
> I am led
> through a warm descent
> with my eyes covered,

> to hear the words
> of water. I listen, with
> roots of
> the moist grass.

The process of identification with the earth, grass, and roots of trees simultaneously initiates a fall toward sleep, the lapsing into a reverie or daydreaming state ("I am led / through a warm descent / with my eyes covered") which successfully blocks the ordinary rational operations of the conscious mind and permits the poet to listen for a more fundamental voice within himself, a voice that will disclose his relationship with the natural world. The speech he wants to hear is formed from "the words / of water," and when we recall the traditional associations of that liquid element with birth, purification, fertility, and renewal, the character of Hall's search in the poem becomes more obvious. "For things as for souls," Gaston Bachelard writes in *The Poetics of Reverie*, "the mystery is inside. A reverie of intimacy—of an intimacy which is always human—opens up for the man who enters into the mysteries of matter." So the dream which engages the poet here draws him into a profound participation in the life of the elemental cosmos, where he may learn its secrets of rebirth for himself. In the poem's final image he has felt himself to be a living part of nature, his nerves and sensibilities resemble the roots of grass vibrant with expectancy, waiting for the life-renewing voice of water to fill them. Unlike "The Snow," then, "The Grass" pursues a course of descent which concludes without any definite resolution but hints strongly at the imminent arrival of animating energies, potentialities for existence.

Water, that element containing such affective stimulus for Hall, has some of its central attributes enumerated in "The Sea," where, in this expanded form, it appears as the universal feminine, womb of life, image of serenity or repose, identified also with earth, and is a destroyer as well—in short, something possessing the qualities of the paradoxical figure of Durga:

> She is the mother of calms
> and the hot grasses;
> the mother of cliffs
> and of the grinding sand;
> she is the mother of the dead
> submarine, which rolls
> on a beach among gulls.

No wonder that in his poem "The Child" Hall envisages a boy whose inner ear waits for the whispers and stirrings—as the mature poet does in "The Grass"—of the primal waters. His recommendation in *The Vatic Voice* of

the reanimation of childhood's uninhibited imaginative modes of perception and invention—a recommendation which has, of course, been made
and put into practice by a considerable number of modern poets and painters—and the desire to accomplish it finally brings him to the persona of
that boy, whose actual existence was long ago terminated in time and personal history but who has yet remained an inhabitant of the unconscious
life of the adult. In "The Child" that lost figure of the poet's youth revives.
Hall's interest, however, plainly does not consist in awakening particular
memories, scenes, or incidents from his past; such details of recollection as
one finds in the poem are generalized. The awakening here is an arousal of
the latent sensibilities and imaginative powers of the child—Hall was, recognizing them now for what they are and can offer. Suddenly, this boy's way
of seeing and feeling the world, his essential but acutely sensitive solitude
on which the impressions of experience register with purity, his primitive,
unspoiled awareness of a proximity to the roots and origins of his being (in
the image of the cave and the repeated image of the pool)—and I think to
non-being too—are necessary to Hall as a poet. By delving into himself far
enough to carry the child in him back from sleep, he has acquired the gift of
that child's fresh mental and perceptual faculties:

> He lives among a dog,
> a tricycle, and a friend.
> Nobody owns him.
>
> He walks by himself, beside
> the black pool, in the cave
> where icicles of rock
>
> rain hard water,
> and the walls are rough
> with the light of stone.
>
> He hears some low talking
> without words.
> The hand of a wind touches him.
>
> He walks until he is tired
> or somebody calls him.
> Then he leaves right away.
>
> Later when he plays with his friend
> he stops suddenly
> to hear the black water.

From the discussion of these few pieces in A *Roof of Tiger Lilies* ("The Grass" and "The Child" are slightly revised in *The Alligator Bride*) we begin to notice recurrent motifs or thematic patterns that occupy Hall in a large proportion of the poems. Speaking abstractly—for each specific poem is a different, concrete realization the contours of which a statement of theme merely traces—the scheme visible in these poems is the familiar universal one of descent or death and rebirth or recovery. As I suggest, this symbolic scheme appears in a unique form in each poetic instance; the entire pattern is not always in evidence in a single poem. We can credit the manifestation of such themes, I think, to the kind of poetry of psychic exploration which Hall starts to write with this book. While the imagery of reverie or the unconscious as it is used in Hall's poetry helps to create a sense of objectivity, of a general validity, the watchful reader also perceives the poet's personal engagement with the themes and materials of his work—in other words, a subjective necessity which is already clear enough in "The Snow," "The Grass," and "The Child."

Consequently, the figure of the self stands squarely at the center of this recurrent scheme, for the pattern of change or transformation involved in the poems results ultimately in an alteration of the speaker who has experienced the inner dramas they portray. We have observed in "The Child" how the poet has descended into himself to awaken the dormant childhood figure resident there. In such poems as "Cold Water," "At Thirty-Five," "Digging," "Sleeping," "Wells," "Self-Portrait, as a Bear," "The Days," "The Tree and the Cloud," and "The Stump" Hall also presents phases or versions of an inward journey, psychic crisis, or symbolic dying, all in the interest of attaining a regenerated condition, a new mode of apprehending the realities of the world and the possibilities of his existence—in effect, gaining entrance to a new dimension of being. (His two elegies, "O Flodden Field" and "The Old Pilot's Death," project the vision of a new integration or wholeness beyond mortality but are not specifically religious.) While occasionally we are given a few details or incidental aspects of the outward portions of the poet's experience, these poems largely focus on the interior processes and responses to his external life. "Sleeping" serves as a paradigmatic poem for these psychic ventures because it is both an embodiment of them and a comment on their character. In the poem's second section Hall, napping briefly, is startled by a momentary vision of death and dissolution:

> I was lying on the sofa to rest, to sleep
> a few minutes, perhaps.
> I felt my body sag into the hole of sleep.
> All at once I was awake and frightened.
> My own death was drifting near me
> in the middle of life. The strong body

blurred and diminished into the dark waters.
The flesh floated away.

As before, water has the aspect of a primal source and also of death. Here
the threatening dream of personal destruction and annihilation prepares
for Hall's convictions about the descent into the unconscious life of the self
in the closing stanza:

> The shadow is a tight passage
> that no one will be spared
> who goes down
> to the deep well.
> In sleep, something remembers.
> Three times since I woke
> from the first sleep,
> it has drunk that water.
> Awake, it is still sleeping.

These final lines disclose the poet's persistence in his explorations,
and the waters which at first seemed to promise nothing but death have
become waters to be drunk and suggest healing or renewal. The "shadow,"
in Jungian or analytical psychology, is an unconscious opposite of the
ego or conscious self and contains qualities consciousness has repressed,
"aspects," in the words of M.-L. von Franz from *Man and His Symbols*
(edited by Jung), "that mostly belong to the personal sphere and that
could just as well be conscious. In some aspects, the shadow can also
consist of collective factors that stem from a source outside the individual's
personal life." In this poem it is clear that Hall continues his efforts to
probe the recesses of his inner world so that an experience which initially appears both negative and terrifying may be turned to more positive account in the end. Confrontation with the shadow is an ordeal, a
rite of passage within the self which must be undergone before the way of
integration can open; the last line of the poem implies that what the
shadow concealed has been brought to consciousness, recognized, and
assimilated.

Several poems locate changes in nature which inaugurate or promote
changes in the self. In "The Tree and the Cloud" Hall remarks the differences between them: when the tree is cut down it becomes various other
things, while the cloud goes through metamorphosis, "becomes other clouds."
Consequently, the tree teaches us the solidity of matter, but the elusive
quality of the cloud taxes, and thus develops, our sensibilities—or so I understand the poem's conclusion:

> The tree is hard to the hands.
> To touch the cloud
> hardens the touching.

"The Stump" and "Digging," more ambitious poems, exhibit an intimate relationship, a communion really, between the person of the poet and the life of nature. Both pieces achieve visionary experience, though in quite separate ways, for in "The Stump" it is earned as the result of the poet's gradual approach to and contemplation of the object, while "Digging" starts almost immediately on the plane of dream or surrealist vision. Beginning descriptively in "The Stump," Hall offers details of the cutting down of a dead oak tree on his lawn in mid-winter. Nothing unusual occurs in this first section until the last stanza, where an odd mood of exultancy suddenly seizes the poet at the thought of the felled tree. This elation is, of course, indicative of the responses of the unconscious, affective being to a seemingly routine external event; in his inward self what is taking place assumes for the poet the preliminary stages of a symbolic drama:

> Yet I was happy that it was coming down.
> "Let it come down!" I kept saying to myself
> With a joy that was strange to me.
> Though the oak was the shade of old summers,
> I loved the guttural saw.

With the second section the "nude trunk" is reduced by a man with a saw to the stump of the poem's title. But, strangely perhaps, the stump is resistant to his attempts to plane it down to smooth wood, even with the ground, and at last he abandons the task, leaving in section three only the poet to observe, then draw near the stump, with his imagination dilating upon the latter's properties:

> Roots stiffen under the ground
> and the frozen street, coiled around pipes and wires.
> The stump is a platform of blond wood
> in the gray winter. It is nearly level
> with the snow that covers the little garden around it.
> It is a door into the underground of old summers,
> but if I bend down to it, I am lost
> in crags and buttes of a harsh landscape
> that goes on forever. When the snow melts
> the wood darkens into the ground;
> rain and thawed snow move deeply into the stump,
> backwards along the disused tunnels.

Now the stump's altering appearances, whether viewed close-up as an infinitely extending and rugged topography or seen in the larger perspective of the effects of seasonal change, dominate the poet's mind. The imagery of "rain and thawed snow" penetrating the wood "along the disused tunnels" can only recall Hall's frequent employment of water symbolism with its cycle of recurrence and renewal. If the last section of the poem remains descriptive at the outset, certain phrases there prepare us, as does the reference to water, for the imaginative leap into another dimension of experience taken in the two closing stanzas. Weathering blackens the "edges of the trunk," but at the center of the stump's upper surface "there is a pale overlay, / like a wash of chalk on darkness." Next we are told that "the desert of the winter / has moved inside" the stump. In the first passage the trace of chalky whiteness is set against the darkness in a manner highly suggestive of both purification from and resistance to the negative or deathly connotations of the encroaching dark. The second passage, which shows the sterility of winter passing far into the stump, implies its absorption by the tree—a step that precedes any possibility of rebirth.

At this point a radical break occurs in the poem's continuity. Suddenly we are witnesses not of the familiar stump in the yard, but of an exotic visionary world, abundant with new life, rich with the magical promise of voyages like those of Baudelaire or St.-John Perse, filled with an exquisite dream detail reminiscent perhaps of parts of Rimbaud's *Illuminations*. Only in the final lines does the stump emerge again, but transformed forever by the vision of which it has been the focus:

> There is a sailing ship
> beached in the cove of a small island
> where the warm water is turquoise.
> The hulk leans over, full of rain and sand,
> and shore flowers grow from it.
> Then it is under full sail in the Atlantic,
> on a blue day, heading for the island.
>
> She has planted sweet alyssum
> in the holes where the wood was rotten.
> It grows thick, it bulges
> like flowers contending from a tight vase.
> Now the stump sinks downward into its roots
> with a cargo of rain
> and white blossoms that last into October.

In the terms of Hall's imaginative transfiguration the stump takes on the form of the crippled ship which, planted with flowers by the mysterious, anonymous fertility goddess of the concluding stanza whom we can best simply identify as a revitalizing principle of nature or existence, is rendered capable of making its voyage to an "island" of unknown character. What matters here, anyhow, is not an explanation of the voyage or its end but the transforming, life-giving energies that underlie the poet's dreamlike images. The entire pattern of descent and renewal is contained in the last three lines, where the stamp, heavy with water, "sinks downward into its roots," and by doing so sends up durable "white blossoms." By recognizing this cyclical pattern of death and rebirth, the poet has uncovered the meaning of his own strange desire early in the poem to see the tree cut down; thus we comprehend that attention to these processes or events in nature has its correspondences in the "deep mind," where similar patterns are followed.

In "Digging" the poet imagines himself returned home in the middle of the night after a long day of ecstatically pleasurable work in his garden. The atmosphere of the day and the garden exude potentiality and fecundity: "when lilies / lift themselves out of the ground while you watch them." From here on the poem assumes the aspect of a symbolic dreaming which concentrates explicitly on the transformation of the speaker through his assimilation by and participation in the fundamental cycles of nature. Shrunk to the size of a seed, he is carried by a South wind until he falls "in cracked ground." Death, the way back into water, and an awakening that partially reminds us of Adam's after Eve was created follow this imagery of sexuality and fertilization. The luxuriant blossoming consequent upon these separate stages is directly explained as the integration of the self, which might lead the reader to think of the "green shoot" rising from the poet's side in Jungian fashion as the Anima, the female principle within the male, which needs to be in harmonious balance, with the Animus in order to achieve wholeness:

> The dirt will be cool, rough to your clasped skin
> like a man you have never known.
> You will die into the ground
> in a dead sleep, surrendered to water.
>
> You will wake suffering
> a widening pain in your side, a breach
> gapped in your tight ribs
> where a green shoot struggles to lift itself upwards
> through the tomb of your dead flesh
>
> to the sun, to the air of your garden
> where you will blossom
> in the shape of your own self, thoughtless
> with flowers, speaking
> to bees, in the language of green and yellow, white and red.

"The well is an archetype, one of the gravest images of the human soul,"
Bachelard writes in *The Poetics of Reverie;* Hall's "Wells," with its obviously
quite personal significance, certainly bears out the French philosopher's remark. In this poem, as in "At Thirty Five" and "Cold Water," there is considerable evidence of private dilemmas—the implications are at once sexual,
domestic, and spiritual—which cannot be circumvented (indeed, a situation of impasse seems indicated) but must be lived through, endured, and
finally gone beyond in the effort to rescue the self from stultification or
oblivion. "Wells" also shares with "The Stump" and "Digging" the imagery
of nature's efflorescence as a means of expressing a new flowering of the self
and reestablished bonds with earth or the world. The initial stanzas create
the impression of withdrawal, fear, and impotence; the ladder may be interpreted both as a phallus (as can the tree, partially, in "The Stump" and the
head of the musk-ox and the boat in "The Long River," for example) and as
the way of ascent from the self's isolation, of communication with external
reality and the being of others:

> I lived in a dry well
> under the rank grass of a meadow.
>
> A white ladder leaned out of it
> but I was afraid of the sounds
>
> of animals grazing.

Help, when it comes, arrives in the form of sexual love and brings with it a
blossoming of life, a revived fertility which draws the speaker out of his
solitude into new relationships; he has found a well of sustaining waters
that is not his alone:

> I crouched by the wall ten years
>
> until the circle of a woman's darkness
> moved over mine like a mouth.
>
> The ladder broke out in leaves
> and fruit hung from the branches.
>
> I climbed to the meadow grass.
> I drink from the well of cattle.

(It is also possible to view the well in its first appearance as an image of
entrapment in a domestic or sexual relationship which has deteriorated, become sterile, but from which the speaker hesitates to escape until another
affection frees him.)

"At Thirty-Five" and "Cold Water" are the concluding poems in *A Roof of Tiger Lilies*. They make sense of the poet's inner drama, the problems he must come to grips with in his private life, when read in sequence; though on the surface, except for the fact that they are both expressive of affective or psychic states, there is no close resemblance between them. With "At Thirty-Five" we find Hall in the middle of his life confronting his own dark wood of failures and losses, as well as the prospect of death; the imagery is harsh and violent, filled with overtones of sexual frustration, misdirection, and final destruction:

> At the edge of the city the pickerel
> who has lost his way
> vomits and dies. The river
> with its white hair staggers to the sea.
>
> My life lay open like a smashed car.

The movement or progression of this poem depends upon lightning-like flashes of thought and imagery, sudden jumps in association; it is the kind of poem, as Hall says in a recent essay (*Michigan Quarterly Review*, Fall 1969), that gives us "the expression without the song," where song is taken to signify "the old baggage of ostensible content which, as Eliot says, is never the true content" and so can be ignored. As a result, "images set free from realistic narrative or from logic grow out of each other by association, and poems move by an inward track of feeling." We have already noted such qualities in Hall's work, but it is worth recalling them as we look at this poem, which in its loose, associative arrangement, its "anti-narrative" story (Hall's term), anticipates later pieces such as "The Alligator Bride," "Apples," and "Swan."

The next phase of "At Thirty-Five" constitutes a shift backward, so to speak, first into the decline and ruin of a domestic or amatory relationship, then further back into images of past family life, all linked with the death and decay of relationships and households. Finally, as in the instance of the destroyed auto above, a single line serves both to summarize and punctuate the preceding portion of the poem. If we are puzzled by the interposed, separate lines with their image of a Boeing 707 airliner submerged in the sea yet oddly "intact" after its crash, Hall remarks in his BBC broadcast comments that an image similar to this was so obsessive with him at one time in his life he believed it to be the memory of an actual scene. He adds: "My poetry's full of crashed airplanes anyway, usually having to do with women somehow or other." In the present instance the plane clearly refers to the anonymous woman whose countenance undergoes hideous metamorphoses in the nightmare of the opening stanza of this stage of the poem.

The lucidity and calm of the plane's setting suggest, I believe, that she has, after all, survived her agonies and disruptions:

> Windows barred, ivy, square stone.
> Lines gather at her mouth and her eyes
> like cracks in a membrane.
> While I watch, eyeballs and tongue
> spill on the tiled floor
> in a puddle of yolks and whites.

> The intact 707
> under the clear wave, the sun shining.

> The playhouse of my grandfather's mother
> stands north of the shed; spiders
> and the dolls' teacups of dead women.
> In Ohio the K-Mart shrugs;
> it knows it is going to die.

> A stone, the closed eye of the dirt.

We then proceed to discover the poet freed from the confines of his house (so closely identified with the woman above that, as the concentrated imagery implies, the collapse of one is the collapse of the other), walking the streets "before dawn" and receiving unexpectedly a vision of possibilities, perhaps even of the patching of broken bonds, though the images point to an ambivalence, particularly since the resurrected houses are still designated as "wrecks":

> A door clicked; a light opened.
> Houses sailed up
> like wrecks from the bottom of the sea.

Musing on the nature of dreams—of which this vision of restored houses is perhaps one—he reminds himself that lechery, greed, and vulgarity must be counted parts of the world even "if the world is a dream." This chain of thought forces an abrupt, stark view of the existence of the single man, deprived of love and sexual companionship, living in a terrible futility and isolation comparable to the situation evoked at the outset of "Wells." The stanza's importance is magnified once we realize that the poet can imagine this barren condition as his own potential future. Again, Hall follows his stanza with a single line, indicating here that the course of his thinking in this direction has reached termination:

> There are poor bachelors
> who live in shacks made of oilcans
> and broken doors, who stitch their shirts
> until the cloth disappears under stitches,
> who collect nails in tin cans.
>
> The wind is exhausted.

The poem has moved into a dead-end passage where hope and strength appear to be utterly abolished (the collecting of nails in cans is surely an image of complete sexual futility and despair); only some surge of vitality, a marked change in the perspective of life, can salvage the poet. True to the patterns we have discerned in Hall's poetry, this revivification does occur, for the last stanza reverses the negativism, desperation, and deathward leaning of the first. The lost route of the dying pickerel and the river staggering toward the sea become, as the poet awakens from the horrendous dreams of his recent past, a visible path of his destiny on which he can proceed, aided by the surprising surrealist vehicle of the trolley car that carries him rapidly to the forest of "new pine" where another life awaits him (in "The Dump" from *The Alligator Bride* a similar trolley leads to a colony of old men like the bachelors above):

> In the middle of the road of my life
> I wake walking in a field.
> A trolley car comes out of the elms,
> the tracks laid down through an acre of wheat stubble,
> slanting downhill. I board it,
> and cross the field into the new pine.

From its very opening, "Cold Water" may be read as a deliberate continuation of "At Thirty-Five," with its setting the forest of pine into which the poet disappears. It is a poem that in its early details, as well as in the startling turn it takes in the two closing stanzas, is devoted to a search for abandoned beginnings. Unlike its immediate predecessor, "Cold Water" follows a perfectly straightforward narrative line, broken only by the sudden appearance of the Iroquois elders and the realizations and decisions their coming generates in the poet. As we have seen so often in Hall's poems, however, and can observe equally in the work, say, of James Wright, Louis Simpson, W. S. Merwin, William Stafford, or Galway Kinnell, natural details, objects, or gestures accumulate a significance beyond themselves, become expressive or symbolic in terms of their poetic context, that is, but do so unobtrusively. In this instance the "dammed stream," the shoe full of "cold water," the "shade / of a thicket, a black pool, / a small circle of stunned

drowsing air," when looked at within the structure of the entire poem, seem
necessary stages in the kind of initiatory ritual process thematically proposed there. That we find ourselves engaged more with some deep layer of
the poet's thought than with a literal landscape becomes rather obvious in
the second and third stanzas where the imagined act of fishing turns suddenly real:

> I step around a gate of bushes
> in the mess
> and trickle of a dammed stream
> and my shoe fills with cold water. I
> enter the shade
> of a thicket, a black pool,
> a small circle of stunned drowsing air,
>
> vaulted with birch which meets overhead
> as if smoke
> rose up and turned into leaves.
> I stand on the roots of a maple
> and imagine
> dropping a line. My wrist jumps
> with the pain of a live mouth hooked deep,
>
> and I stare, and watch where the lithe stripe
> tears water.
> Then it heaves on my hand: cold,
> squaretailed, flecked, revenant flesh
> of a Brook Trout.
> The pine forests I walked through
> darken and cool a dead farmer's brook.

While it would be a mistake, I think, to insist too strenuously on the
symbolic properties of various particulars in these stanzas, they still remain
enormously suggestive, especially in view of what is yet to come. The dammed
river, the unpleasant experience of the soaked shoe, the black pool (which,
of course, evokes the other pools, wells, and subterranean waters in Hall's
work), and the atmosphere of lassitude and stagnation surrounding the pool
combine to create an impression of withdrawal to the vicinity of origins,
the beginnings of existence, though at first it may appear to be a *cul de sac*,
a place of stultification. But if we remember that at the finish of "At Thirty-
Five" the poet went off into the forest, presumably to begin his life anew,
then the situation described above can be understood as the regression required if an individual is to reach the starting point of self-transformation.
This sort of journey backward which precedes the self's purification and

integration recalls familiar instances in such poems as Frost's "Directive" and Roethke's "The Lost Son." Strangely enough, too, the forest clearing in Hall's rendering has something of the shape and character of a cathedral, but not a man-made one—a cathedral formed by nature ("vaulted with birch which meets overhead") and thus the appropriate location for the consecration of the self to its true destiny.

The imagined gesture of casting a line which quickly and enigmatically turns into the physical act of catching a fish can perhaps best be comprehended as the initiatory movement by the poet that breaks the spell of torpor dominating the forest clearing and, more pointedly, his inner being. Certainly, this effort and its success call forth the Indian elders; having satisfied a preliminary requirement, the poet has readied himself to be led by them, in spite of hardships, to the heart of "the mystery," and so to a confrontation of the possibilities of achievement or defeat in the struggle to win rebirth:

> I look up and see the Iroquois
> coming back
> standing among the birches
> on the other side of the black pool.
> The five elders
> have come for me, I am young,
> my naked body whitens with cold
>
> in the snow, blisters in the bare sun,
> the ice cuts
> me, the thorns of blackberries:
> I am ready for the mystery.
> I follow them
> over the speechless needles
> of pines which are dead or born again.

We may ask why Hall chooses an American Indian initiation ritual, which introduces a boy into men's tribal activities and their religious significance, as the means for presenting aspects of his own psychic procedures. A primary answer would probably be that he did not choose it in the sense of a rationally calculated selection, but that such images originally came unbidden and recommended themselves for their imaginative implications. We can obtain a further answer from Hall's comment on two passages from poems by Robert Bly and Louis Simpson in the introduction to his *Contemporary American Poetry*; he could as easily be talking of his own poem as of theirs when he says, "This new imagination reveals through images a subjective life which is general, and which corresponds to an old objective life of shared experience and knowledge." The mythic and religious attitude toward life, which was once (with Indians and medieval Christians alike) a common property of the outward existence of the community, and thus had all its members as participants, has been abolished from the external world of modern man by science, technology, urbanization, and widespread agnosticism. But since this attitude corresponds with and reflects the fundamental nature of the self, it cannot be completely vanquished; instead, it goes underground to become an active part of a person's unconscious mind and dream life. The conclusion of Hall's poem acquires strength and conviction as a result of these images of trial and rite of passage, for we can feel that he is engaged, in an inner way, with a progression of the self which is not merely his alone but a central feature of the larger life shared by humans in all times and places.

The twenty-five recent poems gathered in *The Alligator Bride* continue in the vein of the work we have examined in *A Roof of Tiger Lilies;* indeed, as we might expect, certain themes and imaginative preoccupations, because they are charged with personal meaning for Hall, declare themselves again. "The Blue Wing," for example, links the relationship with women to the crash of a plane; the final stanza with its wreckage and residue of bones implies a symbolic dying which is survived through the parabolic arc of death and rebirth which the last three lines describe:

> The tiny skeleton inside
> remembers the falter of engines, the
> cry without
> answer, the long dying
> into
> and out of the sea.

Similarly, "The Dump" and "The Train," using the imagery of trolley lines and railways, are poems of movement away from the past. The first of these, mentioned previously, terminates somberly in a "graveyard of trolleys," populated by old men, "in narrow houses full of rugs, / in this last place," where quite obviously they wither into death. In "The Train" memory presents itself as "a long shape / of darkness, tunnel / huddled with voices, hunger / of dead trees, angels" from which a train emerges gliding off into the distance. A woman's head and arm, growing less and less discernible, extend from a window in gestures of farewell:

> The train curves tightening
> the light hair to itself
> and diminishes
> on a Sunday morning down
> the track forever,

> into memory, the tunnel
> of dead trees.

Death, metamorphosis, the abolition of or escape from the past, and renewal or ascent into a fresh, hitherto unknown dimension of being form
the thematic concerns of most of Hall's new poems, so that they constitute
a distinct extension of the preceding work, sometimes overlapping it but
also breaking into further territories. Close in feeling to the poems of departure, division, and the death of relationships which entails the abandonment of a whole segment of life is the negative continuation of these experiences of severance into static situations, terrible in their desolation and
lack of promise for any future, and so for any hope of fulfilling the poet's
sense of self-identity and destiny. "The Dump," with its crowd of wasted
lives, qualifies as a poem of this type as well as a poem of escape from the
past; in effect, it is a record of failed deliverance. The figures of "Make Up,"
originally depicted in details recalling their bodily, even erotic natures, drift
away from living and harden into "Ghost / stone, and the stone / daughter"
at the end. The woman of "Sew" busily stitches from her "church of scraps"
an image of a man suited to her ideals and in her myopic fashion endows it
with life, "until it stands up like a person / made out of whole cloth"; but the
short closing stanza, spoken by the poet, reveals how far she has missed
knowing what he is. Frustrated from rising into the amplitude of existence,
he remains solitary, neglected if unharmed, among the untested possibilities of his dreams:

> Still, I lie folded
> on the bolt in the dark warehouse,
> dreaming my shapes.

Like Roethke's "Dolor" and Karl Shapiro's "Office love . . ." from *The Bourgeois Poet*, poems of the same bleak but oddly humorous spirit, "The Repeated Shapes" focuses on the emotional depression Hall associates with
modern technical efficiency—in this case, the shiny emptiness of public
sanitation. The line-up of urinals, to Hall's slightly hallucinated eye, appears as a uniform row of old men with whom, in his own despairing mood,
he acknowledges family ties. Here, as elsewhere in these poems, the awareness of waste and futility is nearly overwhelming:

> They are my uncles,
> these old men
> who are only plumbing,
> who throb with tears all night
> and doze in the morning.

On a note of historical authenticity the smashed airplane returns in "The
Man in the Dead Machine," this time as a Grumman Hellcat fighter plane
"High on a slope in New Guinea," where its pilot brought it to rest undis-
covered "among bright vines / as thick as arms." While the human remains
in "The Blue Wing" seem plainly those of a woman, these are, of course, as
indicated by both title and details, a man's, and Hall devotes an entire stanza
of close description to "the helmeted / skeleton" still strapped rigidly upright in the pilot's seat decades later. Then, as we have had occasion to note
before, the poet without warning completes the poem in a stanza that changes
direction and casts on the figure of the pilot and his fate quite different
meanings:

> Or say that the shrapnel
> missed him, he flew
> back to the carrier, and every
> morning takes his chair, his pale
> hands on the black arms, and sits
> upright, held
> by the firm webbing.

The first two-thirds of the poem simply provides a grim, matter-of-fact piece
of reportage from which there can be no issue but the unvarnished account
of what is observed. But with the reversal of actual death and the assertion
of a daily reenactment of another sort of death, we are no longer in the
realm of inanimate external objects like fallen airplanes and skeletal figures; instead, a monstrous ritual of inner existence, confined by the structure of its habitual gear, has been disclosed. The reader cannot help but feel
that, in some ways, this fate is far worse than the one of the poem's opening,
for the living pilot of the last stanza does not really live but each day endures a death, while life itself waits . . . elsewhere, beyond. Not surprisingly,
Hall's most frighteningly graphic poem of imprisonment, self-torment, and
utter despair, "The Corner," is printed immediately after "The Man in the
Dead Machine." In this piece the self has succumbed to anonymity and
descended to the condition of a maddened animal, but in the manner in
which only a human can. The horror of the situation is compounded by the
concluding revelation of the impossibility of relief, even through death:

> It does not know
> its name. It sits
> in a damp corner,
> spit hanging
> from its chin, odor of urine
> puddled around.
> Huge, hairless, grunting,

it plays with itself,
sleeps, stares for hours,
and leaps
to smash itself on the wall.
Limping, bloody, falling back
into the corner, it
will not die.

"The Alligator Bride" shares with the poems we have been discussing manifest elements of guilt, separation, destructive energy, and death, but it weaves more completely the fabric of an irrational or surrealist fable, with a group of characters which includes a sinister cat, the bride herself, and the speaker. Hall's BBC notes disclose how the poem began as "fragments" he had written down which finally were drawn together by the introduction of "the strange figure of a dead stuffed alligator in a bride costume," and it developed until it became "a macabre little story," containing, as he realizes, materials from his own life. Knowledge of his biography is not important, however; for, as he says,

> The story, and the characters, are there, and the story is one that, if you leave yourself open to the language of dreams, is available to everyone. That is, it has the same sort of general availability that a story like Beauty and the Beast has. You have to listen to a poem like this, or read it, as if you were dreaming but keeping your eyes wide open. You have to be alert, but you mustn't be inquisitive. You may not *translate* anything in the poem, you have to *float* on it. At the same time you have to receive every detail. Perhaps this is more demanding than any other kind of poem.

With this advice and admonition in mind we can try to approach the poem on its own terms and stay within the range of allusiveness it establishes. The initial lines of the first two stanzas are connected by a preoccupation with the passage of time, thus reminding us of the poet's obsessive linking of temporal perceptions with his constant awareness of mortality:

The clock of my days winds down.

* * * *

Now the beard on my clock turns white.

In the stanzas which these lines respectively begin, Hall creates a domestic scene, a relationship between the speaker and his cat, who "eats sparrows outside" the window, that leads toward intimacy through the latter's seemingly generous impulse; but at the moment of their communion the cat is losing an enigmatic object she cherishes:

> Once, she brought me a small rabbit
> which we devoured together,
> under the Empire Table
> while the men shrieked
> repossessing the gold umbrella.

We cannot gauge much of the significance of this umbrella beyond the most obvious reasons for its value: it is gold and provides shade, hence perhaps a circle of comfort and security. It appears to be valued as well by the anonymous men who in "repossessing" it are presumably claiming what once was theirs. In any event, this action disrupts the commerce between speaker and cat in the second stanza, where the image of the snowy-bearded clock indicates a rapid flow of time and existence. Now the cat, to all appearances estranged from the speaker (though he can refer to her as "My cat"), continues in a despondent state, not only over her lost umbrella but also for love of the Alligator Bride, who enters the poem in the next stanza, a grotesque, mocking figure that would do credit to a child's nightmare:

> Ah, the tiny fine white
> teeth! The Bride, propped on her tail
> in white lace
> stares from the holes
> of her eyes. Her stuck-open mouth
> laughs at minister and people.

Following a catalogue of food and wine—which also includes the cat and Bride—assembled for the wedding festivities, there comes a swift change of direction as the poem turns toward the speaker as its focal point and as the source of subsequent events. The speaker begins a disclosure of his own malice, in which the cat enjoys a voluntary complicity—apparently as her love shifts into hatred—finding release and termination only in the death of the Alligator Bride. This will to harm or destroy shows itself in images of two very different artificial products of a highly technical age:

> The color of bubble gum,
> the consistency of petroleum jelly,
> wickedness oozes
> from the palm of my left hand.
> My cat licks it.
> I watch the Alligator Bride.

And the stanza after, in its own puzzling fashion, starts off with similar details of imagery, though now they are more widely applied. The odd, inert houses scaled together in "gelatin"—and the speaker's house we learn from the closing stanza is one of these—suggest the same confinement and exclusion of the world that we observed in Hall's criticism of middle-class living in the early poem "Christmas Eve in Whitneyville." In the present instance as well the restrictive conditions of "Big houses like shabby boulders" that "hold themselves tight in gelatin" seem to exert unendurable pressures on those inhabitants who, like the speaker, refuse to be imprisoned in this manner and desire a freedom which is associated with the powers of imagination. The speaker's declaration that he is "unable to daydream," then, makes sufficiently obvious how claustrophobic the atmosphere of this life has become. Need we add what should here be plain: that the cause of this decidedly unpleasant condition is the Alligator Bride, or better perhaps, that it results from the relationship between the Bride and the speaker, who is, after all, the Groom. The inability to "daydream" under these circumstances leads to the violent climax of the poem and to the unsettling aftermath which brings no particular relief:

> The sky is a gun aimed at me.
> I pull the trigger.
> The skull of my promises
> leans in a black closet, gapes
> with its good mouth
> for a treat to suck.
>
> A bird flies back and forth
> in my house that is covered by gelatin
> and the cat leaps at it
> missing. Under the Empire Table
> the Alligator Bride
> lies in her bridal shroud.
> My left hand
> leaks on the Chinese carpet.

However confusing and distressing these events may be, and difficult to unravel with any degree of certainty (and it is in this very respect that their riddling irrationality closely reflects the inextricable mass of motives, thoughts, and acts involved in much more ordinary occurrences), we can readily comprehend how the speaker in pulling the trigger has destroyed himself, or some aspect of his existence, at the same time that he has murdered the Bride. The poem's end does not, however, see him liberated; but in a setting which might even be taken as a dream parody of a murder scene in some Agatha Christie or Ellery Queen detective novel we discover the ravenous cat in vain pursuit of a new prey, the corpse of the Bride, and the guilty speaker, whose "wickedness" (with sexual suggestion?) flows like an open wound to stain the exotic carpet. The air of this situation is one of

bewilderment and irresolution; any final impression of the poem's conclusion must also incorporate the fact that the trio of cat, Bride, and speaker
remain imprisoned in the latter's "house that is covered by gelatin." Whatever the underlying problems might be, the speaker's impulsive course of
action has left damages but no satisfactory achievements, except the release
of violent energy. The poem itself, carefully and subtly composed, effective
in its resonances and its use of detail, is satisfying and stages an intricate
drama of relationships which proves endlessly engaging to the reader's imagination.

"Swan," "Apples," and "This Room" share elements of dream, fantasy,
and narrative with "The Alligator Bride," though the incidents are apt to
seem more disjunct, to comprise less of what could be termed a "story" of
any sort than the latter poem contains. In addition, these three poems point
in affirmative ways, especially through their associations with the world of
nature, toward a new level of life, which is gained, at least momentarily, in
certain love poems such as "The Coal Fire," "Lovers in Middle Age," and
"Gold." Two other poems, "The Table" and "Mount Kearsarge," deserve
mention here because both of them return to the New Hampshire farm of
Hall's youthful experience and manage to accomplish, in distinctive and
quite moving ways, a recovery of the past which confirms it as an essential
ingredient of the poet's existence in the present. The last lines of "Mount
Kearsarge" reveal that Hall no longer needs to live on his grandparents'
farm to be aware of the haunting spectral shape of the mountain; its form
has been absorbed in consciousness and cannot be lost:

> I will not rock on this porch
> when I am old. I turn my back on you,
> Kearsarge, I close
> my eyes, and you rise inside me,
> blue ghost.

Similarly, in "The Table" Hall spends almost the entire poem on recollections of days shared with his grandfather on the farm, and each detail is
lovingly recalled; the finish of the poem, however, is in the present, where
the poet revisits the farmhouse. In an instant of strange, Proustian communication the life which he knew and is not past, the life which the previous
part of the poem has recreated, comes suddenly alive to his mind and senses
as he touches a table in the familiar bedroom and receives a startling perception of his grandfather's dead horse and the busy, humming summer landscape, long gone but existing unchanged. Through the agency of this old
piece of furniture, in which it mysteriously resides, a time that was lived and
felt to the fullest extent has been resurrected in the poet:

>   This morning
> I walk to the shaded bedroom and lean
> on the drop-leaf table.
>   The table hums
> a song to itself without sense
> and I hear the voice of the heaving
> ribs of Riley
> and grasshoppers
> haying the fields of the air.

Divided into five separate sections, though apparently concentrated on scenes and events within one geographical area, "Swan" explores relationships between man and the earth or nature's hidden energies; it also renders the absence or dissolution of such relationships. In its theme, then, the poem has close ties with many of Hall's pieces from A *Roof of Tiger Lilies* discussed previously. At the outset it is winter, a darkening afternoon, as the poet, climbing "Mill Hill," observes a fire in the fields burning off the stubble in preparation for another season's planting:

>   Smoke blows
> from the orange edges of fire
> working the wheat
> stubble. "Putting
> the goodness back
> into the soil."

These details complete the first section and set the precedent for the whole poem: each part, of varying length, is devoted to an individual experience, whether it is almost pure, immediate observation, as in sections one, two, and five; an amalgam of perceivings and inward vision, as in part three; or a mingling of desire and memory into quite specific description, as in part four. Whatever differences exist among these distinct moments of experience, in one way or another each touches the thematic currents we have mentioned, and the reader must draw them together by allowing them to move freely together in his mind. In the passage above the setting at once lends itself to a capacious sense of nature in its entirety, of its cycles, and so of its preparations for renewed fertility to which man contributes here. Such regenerative powers of nature, and the feeling of fundamental, enduring realities that proximity to earth can arouse in a person lead Hall through this poem toward his own physical contact and discovery in the natural realm.

The account of a separate incident, strange and dramatic in character, constitutes the second section and contains one of the two specific references to the bird which gives the poem its title:

> Driving; the fog
> matted around the headlights;
> suddenly, a thudding
> white shape in the whiteness,
> running huge and frightened, lost
> from its slow stream . . .

Seemingly, these lines give us the entire experience, and the stanza trails off inconclusively. The passage recalls perhaps two famous swans in exile in French Symbolist poetry: the swan escaped from its cage and bathing its wings in the just of Parisian streets in Baudelaire's "Le Cygne," and the swan trapped in ice but desirous of the infinite azure of the skies in Mallarmé's sonnet "Le vierge, le vivace et le bel aujourd'hui." In both poems the bird is, to one degree or another, emblematic of the poet tormented by exile and unfulfillment. While I do not wish to imply that Hall had these previous poetic instances in mind, he certainly knows the poems in question, and the present passage may be illuminated somewhat by recalling them. Here, too, it is difficult not to view the significance of the incident, the sudden appearance of a swan out of the thick fog—in which the poet must likewise find it troublesome to make his way—and the details selected to describe it ("running huge and frightened, lost / from its slow stream . . ."), as somehow related to the poet's own condition, a condition that can only be called one of uprootedness, for he is portrayed throughout the poem as always in movement, a kind of wanderer. The stanza's indecisive ending leaves open the possibilities still available for the swan to discover the route back to the stream; the poet is left, like the bird, to maneuver as best he can through the fog toward an unspecified—and probably as yet unknown—destination.

The third section not only stands in the middle of the poem but holds the thematic center as well, tying together important particulars of imagery and providing in its use of the windmill image a focus of the poet's quest for an existence in harmony with nature's rhythms and energies. The mill appears as if seen in reverie or dream; like an agency of nature it channels and lifts the hidden forces of the subterranean world, transforming them in the process. The "dark" on which it draws as a source again recollects the black waters and pools of earlier poems also associated with primal forces or the covert origins of life. Beneath the mill, the network of "tunnels" it taps embraces the world, reaching "to the poles / and down to the center of the earth"; and so this queer edifice seems almost a temple of natural religion through the activity of which great chthonic powers achieve release. The next stanza, of merely two lines, returns to the fire of section one, only then to disclose the mill halted in its operations:

> Fire breaks out in the fields.
> The wheel of the mill does not turn.

The sterility of winter is implied here, for the fire in the initial stanza was witnessed by the poet in December burning "the wheat stubble"; the mill, too, must remain idle during this period. Now the fog reappears as well, and unexpectedly the section closes with a startling flourish of surrealist images:

> The windmill
> flies, clattering its huge wings, to the swamp.
> I make out cliffs of the Church,
> houses drifting like glaciers.

Surely, though the poet does not specify it, the swan somehow merges with the mill as it takes flight—enigmatically, not toward the stream but toward a swamp. It is difficult to determine all this journey may suggest, but in any event it prepares the way for the desolate, frozen, infertile images of church and houses, which replace the natural life and energy symbolized by the windmill with the supernaturalism or abstract theology represented by the church and, following the pejorative connotations of the dwellings in "Christmas Eve in Whitneyville" and "The Alligator Bride," the seclusion from full existence of the bourgeois. The movement of this section traces the abdication of natural modes of being and their replacement by artificial and ideological ones.

The dreamlike qualities of the third part vanish entirely in the next section, to be exchanged for the poet's open declaration of desire for an existence lived in proximity to earth, drawing sustenance of both a spiritual and physical kind from a close working relationship with the soil. He envisages in the daily and seasonal routines of another, ideal individual the life he wishes for himself:

> I envy the man hedging and ditching,
> trimming the hawthorn, burning branches
> while wasps circle in the smoke of their nest,
> clearing a mile of lane, patches of soot
> like closed holes to a cave of fire,
> the man in his cottage
> who smokes his pipe in the winter, in summer
> digging his garden in ten o'clock light,
> the man grafted entirely to rain and air,
> stained dark
> by years of hedging and ditching.

These lines terminate the feeling of restless movement that pervades previous sections, and, of course, the type of living presented here contrasts deci-
sively with what was observed at the close of part three with its glacial houses
and cliff-like church, thus marking a return to harmony with creation. The
"cave of fire" may hint at buried forms of natural energy, not unlike those
the mill reaches, to which the anonymous man, who has blended with his
environment, has access. His identification with nature is so complete that,
in addition to fire, he is associated with the other elements of water, air, and
earth as well: "grafted entirely to rain and air, / stained dark / by years of
hedging and ditching."

The final section, like the second, is brief and inconclusive, but where
the latter offered the desolate, helpless image of the swan lost from its stream
in the fog, this stanza evokes the swan by analogy and now in an affirmative
way:

> The close-packed surface of the roots
> of a root-bound plant
> when I break the pot away,
> the edges white
> and sleek as a swan . . .

By some means, in the transition from the fourth part of the poem to this
last one, the poet has progressed from "envy" of the man whose life revolves
about contact with the soil and what grows there to his own direct physical
relationship with nature or natural process, suggested quite plainly by his
handling of the plant. In thematic and symbolic terms the breaking of the
pot surrounding the plant and the discovery of "the edges white / and sleek
as a swan . . ." is comparable to a moment of rebirth for the poet, who is, as
we noticed, linked to the figure of this bird. The fact that Hall refuses to
complete his poem with a period can only be understood to reinforce the
idea of potentiality which the experience has made manifest. In like fashion "This Room," which is simultaneously the actual dwelling of the poet,
his body, and the metaphorical space of the self's living context, concludes
on an ecstatic note of acceptance by the natural cosmos in the form of
flowers; the sexual overtones of the imagery broaden the implications here
and also look toward the love poems mentioned before and to a volume of
love poetry, *The Yellow Room: Love Poems*, unpublished at the time of this
writing:

> Climbing the brown stairs
> of the air, I enter
> my place. I am welcomed
> by pots of geraniums, green stems

> thick as a thumb, uprushing
> leaves! I live
> in your exhalations, sweet
> tongued flowers!

Of the poem "Apples" Hall says in his BBC remarks, "When I started it, I thought it was about old dead poets. A number of friends of mine who were poets had died all in a year or so, and I wanted to make up a place for them to be. By the time I'd finished the poem, I saw that it was really about other things." The poem is certainly about death, entrance into the underworld or kingdom of the dead, and the beginning of a new paradisaical form of being which consists largely of earthly delights;[3] but poets are not specified as participants, the dead might be anybody. Though ritual elements appear in the circular movement of the dancers at the poem's end, no religious intentions except those implied by the subjective fantasy of acceptance by and habitation within the earth itself can be discerned. The recurrent and resonant image of the apple, together with other particulars drawn from nature, such as grapes, grass, a marigold, and a peacock's feather, keep this poem consistent with those pieces which, like "Swan," seek out an order of harmony with creation." That kind of natural correspondence Hall projects in a vision of the conditions of life after death:

> They have gone
> into the green hill, by doors without hinges,
> or lifting city
> manhole covers to tunnels
> lined with grass,
> their skin soft as grapes, their faces like apples.

The disappearing dead who, in fairy-tale fashion, vanish into the verdant passageways of earth already possess the aspect of renewal, as the analogy between their skin and faces and the fruit specifies. By means of the magical transformations of sight which the "round eye" of a peacock feather—introduced in the second stanza—permits, giving the "curved spot" on the apple's surface the appearance of a "fat camel" and synesthetically changing a "fly's shadow" into "the cry of a marigold," the poet approaches, "looking hard," the world the dead have entered, then swiftly moves into it himself:

> I am caught in the web of a gray apple,
> I struggle inside
> an immense apple of blowing sand,
> I blossom
> quietly from a window-box of apples.

Proceeding through conditions of storm and turbulence seems necessary as a preparation for entrance into the underworld, and the journey is followed by the unmistakable imagery of rebirth within the precincts of this natural paradise, the activities and pleasures of which occupy the last two stanzas of the poem. "Seven beautiful ladies" are provided "each man" and serve him "whiskey"; mysteriously, stories are told by the "rungs of a ladder"; and, not surprisingly, the analogy with apples is announced once more, leading the poem toward its climactic dance about the hill, whose shape derives from that fruit but whose qualities are likewise those of the powerful peacock feather. Within the boundaries of reverie, the poet participates in this ideal cosmos of his imagining:

> Their voices like apples brighten in the wind.
>   Now they are dancing
> with fiddles and ladies and trumpets
>   in the round
> hill of the peacock, in the resounding hill.

Another note of intense revitalization is struck by the love poems in *The Alligator Bride*, which include "The Coal Fire," "Lovers in Middle Age," and "Gold." The last two poems, together with "Waters," which carries oblique hints of sexual fulfillment, and "The Dump," discussed previously, Hall places, with minor changes, in the context of his new book, *The Yellow Room*, a sequence of "poems and fragments" that chronicle a love affair, its complexities and complications, the depths of emotion and awareness it reveals, its rhythm of communion, withdrawal, and reunion, and its painful conclusion in a final separation. The poems of this sequence vary considerably in style, tone, and feeling; certainly they demonstrate a further development in Hall's work, a new delicacy and fineness in many instances that brings his art close in quality to Chinese poetry—or at least to what we apprehend of such poetry in the versions, say, of Ezra Pound and Kenneth Rexroth. And, of course, these poems form a unity among themselves, plotting points along the route of an extraordinarily intimate relationship which, even though it must conclude unhappily, impels the poet to a self-renewal that, one imagines, cannot be destroyed entirely even with the final parting of the persons involved. Obviously then, the poems from *The Alligator Bride* which Hall also uses in the sequence will assume different implications in accord with their various positions there; so, for example, "Waters" becomes much more explicitly sexual in terms of its changed context. "Gold" continues the spatial metaphors noted before in "This Room" and apparent in *The Yellow Room*, but its color symbolism, effective enough in isolation in this beautiful poem, is enlarged by the extension of that symbolism throughout the sequence. In "Red, Orange, Yellow," which appears near the close of *The Yellow Room*, we discover some important explanations:

>For five years of my life, or ten,
>I lived no-color.
>In a beige room I talked
>clipped whispers
>with a lady who faded while I looked at her.
>Even our voices were oyster-white.

This opening easily reminds us of earlier poems of domestic disharmony, but a second stanza provides explicit statements of the warm, vibrant colors the poet associates with the woman he does love and now has lost:

>So I looked for the color yellow.
>I drank yellow for breakfast,
>orange at lunch, gold for dinner.
>Red was the color of pain.
>Now I eat red
>all day. The sky is her yellow.
>Sometimes no-color years
>rise in slow motion,
>like Mozart on drums. Their name is Chumble.
>They smile
>like pale grass, looking downward.
>But red sticks
>needles in my eyes.
>Yellow
>dozes on the beach at Big Sur
>or in the center of my new room
>like a cactus
>that lives without water, for a year.

Even the rending agony of loss receives a bright, burning color and takes its share in a momentous revivification of the self that promises to leave behind certain negative phases of the past. Undoubtedly, torment and despair will recur, but the experience which a poem like "Gold" realizes must, as its brief and stunning last stanza proclaims, inaugurate enduring alterations in the inner life of the psyche and the emotions of both lover and beloved:

>Pale gold of the walls, gold
>of the centers of daisies, yellow roses
>pressing from a clear bowl. All day
>we lay on the bed, my hand
>stroking the deep
>gold of your thighs and your back.
>We slept and woke
>entering the golden room together,

lay down in it breathing
quickly, then
slowly again,
caressing and dozing, your hand sleepily
touching my hair now.

We made in those days
tiny identical rooms inside our bodies
which the men who uncover our graves
will find in a thousand years
shining and whole.

Without entering into further detail about an as yet unpublished book,[4] which may undergo considerable revision, we can still affirm that the fundamental patterns of descent and ascent, death and rebirth, positive and negative polarities are perceptible in these love poems. They also, as previous poems do, find completion in images of stoical suffering and harsh conditions of solitude; one may, however, await beyond them another stage of growth, a new opening out to the possibilities of existence. As the reader looks back over Donald Hall's career, the remarkable strides of his development which follow upon his abandonment of the supposedly correct poetic modes of the 1950s and his subsequent freedom to explore his experience honestly, to say what he needed to say in a voice tested and found to be truly his own, rather than one imposed from without and legislated by alien theoretical criteria, become quite evident. From A Roof of Tiger Lilies through The Yellow Room his work displays that high level of imaginative power and technical accomplishment which has secured him an enviable place among the American poets of his generation.

(1971)

NOTES

[1] I am greatly indebted to Mr. Hall for allowing me to use, in addition to published essays, various unpublished lecture and broadcast materials, and for permitting me to read manuscript versions of his new book, *The Yellow Room: Love Poems.*

[2] For a perceptive discussion of the social dimensions of Hall's poetry, see "Crunk" [Robert Bly], "The Poetry of Donald Hall," *The Fifties,* 3 (1959), pp. 32-46.

[3] The apple here carries very old ties to the traditional paradisaical image of Avalon or Land of Apples. On this island, by some accounts, King Arthur lies buried. See Robert Graves's comments in *The White Goddess* (New York, 1959) and in his edition, *English and Scottish Ballads* (London, 1957).

[4] *The Yellow Room: Love Poems* was published (New York, 1971) after the present collection of essays had been completed.

18

"The Body with the Lamp Lit Inside": Robert Bly's New Poems

PROSE POEMS HAVE BEEN APPEARING WITH FREQUENCY IN THE WORK OF AMERICAN poets for the past few years; there have been special issues of magazines devoted to them, and the poet Michael Benedikt has compiled a large international anthology of the prose poem which will soon be published. The reasons for interest and practice in this form are doubtless many, but they must surely include the increasingly cosmopolitan atmosphere of our poetry in the last decade and a half and the open, exploratory mood of most writers. When Karl Shapiro selected his prose poem "The Dirty Word" as his favorite piece for the anthology *Poet's Choice* (1962), he did so, his accompanying remarks indicate, as an act of defiance, an assertion of freedom from the "habit" of metrical writing. Shapiro had written the poem long before; St.-John Perse had praised it. But its inclusion in the anthology came at a moment which must have been for him one of aesthetic decision, for two years later he published his extraordinary collection of prose poems, *The Bourgeois Poet*.

Had Shapiro been a French poet, there would be nothing startling or newsworthy about a decision to write in this form: some French poets have employed it exclusively or almost exclusively, others have alternated between it and the various possibilities of free or formal verse. At least from Aloysius Bertrand's *Gaspard de la Nuit* (1842) to the present, it has been an integral part of the French poetic tradition. It has appeared in modern German poetry and has been widely used in Spanish and Latin American writing. In American poetry, however, so far as I know, its manifestations have been relatively scarce and scattered, visible occasionally in Williams, Eliot ("Hysteria"), Patchen, and Shapiro, for example. That was the situation until recent years. Now one finds considerable preoccupation and practice with the form among such poets as John Ashbery, Russell Edson, Michael Benedikt, David Ignatow, James Wright, W.S. Merwin, Donald Hall, Vern Rutsala, to name a few, and to the point here, Robert Bly.

I don't propose to offer in this article any general comments on the form of the prose poem itself, which would require a large scholarly acquaintance with European literature I don't possess. From what I do gather, the form is elastic and accomodating: it may be lyric or dramatic, descriptive or narrative, fabulistic or anecdotal—or some combination of these, or something else entirely. Clearly, the poet is freed of the usual concerns of poetic construction in favor of the greater latitude permitted by the unit of the paragraph. But it does seem that each poet who takes up the prose poem does so for particular reasons which give the resulting work a singular, distinctive character. So, for instance, Baudelaire says in the dedicatory letter to *Paris Spleen*: "Which one of us, in his moments of ambition, has not dreamed of the miracle of a poetic prose, musical, without rhythm and without rhyme, supple enough and rugged enough to adapt itself to the lyrical impulses of the soul, the undulations of reverie, the jibes of conscience?"[1] And to move up to the present, Russell Edson writes in a recent essay on the prose poem: "To find a prose free of the self-consciousness of poetry, a prose more compact than the storyteller's; a prose removed from the formalities of *literature*. . . ."[2] Such passages indicate for us the highly individual approaches taken to the form, as well as the sense of a certain kind of liberation, of poetic elbow-room, that goes with them.

Robert Bly is not a newcomer to the prose poem. It is not possible to say when he first attempted to write in this fashion without information from the poet himself, but a look at his first book, *Silence in the Snowy Fields*, discovers two prose poems, "Sunset at a Lake" and "Fall," while the small volume he shares with James Wright and William Duffy, *The Lion's Tail and Eyes*, published the same year, 1962, contains another, "Sparks." So we can guess that Bly has a fairly long familiarity with this type of poem. Recent years have seen him turn to it more often, perhaps as a different and compelling avenue for his imagination's impulses, which in his anti-war poems and his poems of—can we say—mythic and social intent (as in large portions of *The Light Around the Body* and *Sleepers Joining Hands*) were otherwise engaged. Many readers will recognize that *The Morning Glory*[3] is a new, enlarged version of the original chapbook of that title first issued by Kayak Books in 1969 with twelve poems, then reissued in a second edition with twenty poems by the same publisher. The present collection also includes *Point Reyes Poems*, a chapbook initially published by Mudra in 1974, as well as other prose poems gathered from periodicals. Bly's continuing attraction to the potentialities of the form, beyond, that is, the contents of

The Morning Glory, is attested to by the Fall 1975 issue of *Field,* where three prose poems from a new sequence are printed.

In the course of his career as a poet and thinker, Bly's writings have demonstrated a growing concentration of energies in the direction of the public life as it can be probed inwardly, from beneath, as it were, through imaginative submersion in the "deep mind" (to borrow a term from Donald Hall's essay on Whitman) and the articulation of what is discovered in a poetry that is more and more oracular, as well as surrealist (in Bly's sense of the "leaping" Spanish or Latin American Surrealism of Lorca or Vallejo or Neruda) in cast. His latest essays, on the "Mothers" in *Sleepers Joining Hands* and on "The Three Brains" in *Leaping Poetry,* reveal frontiers of concern in the areas of psychology, religion, and something like mystical apprehension (or the bases of it) which are quite congruent with the more extreme metaphoric constructions of a poem such as "Hair" or the title sequence of poems from *Sleepers Joining Hands* with its complex motifs, far-reaching imagery, and its somewhat hermetic air.

Still, a reader who opens *Sleepers Joining Hands* for the first time and begins with the initial group of "Six Winter Privacy Poems" will not feel he has ventured into foreign territory or lost his way, for these poems are instantly recognizable as parts of the poetic and imaginative world which Bly started to make his own out of solitude, reflection, and attention both to place and its images and to the mind and its rich, unbidden images that rise up drenched from a sea of allusion in the beautiful pieces of *Silence in the Snowy Fields.* Here are the beginning pair of those half-dozen winter poems to illustrate the resonance I've indicated:

I
About four, a few flakes.
I empty the teapot out in the snow,
        feeling shoots of joy in the new cold.
By nightfall, wind,
the curtains on the south sway softly.

II
My shack has two rooms; I use one.
The lamplight falls on my chair and table
and I fly into one of my own poems—
I can't tell you where—
as if it appeared where I am now,
in a wet field, snow falling.

The affinity with Bly's earlier poetry—which is emphatically *not* to be taken for duplication or repetition—can be seen even more clearly with a single example from his first book, chosen at random, "September Night with an Old Horse":

> I
> Tonight I rode through the cornfield in the moonlight!
> The dying grass is still, waiting for winter,
> And the dark weeds are waiting, as if under water. . . .
>
> II
> In Arabia, the horses live in the tents,
> Near dark gold, and water, and tombs.
>
> III
> How beautiful to walk out at midnight in the moonlight
> Dreaming of animals.

The prose poems of *The Morning Glory;* and the poems gathered in another new collection, *Old Man Rubbing His Eyes*,[4] with handsome drawings by Franz Albert Richter, seem to me to emerge from the same primal ground of Bly's imagination as the "Six Winter Privacy Poems" or *Silence in the Snowy Fields* or *Jumping Out of Bed*, where the inward being and the outer world of landscape, objects, creatures, or whatever, coalesce. The product of this fusion is mutual enrichment in a poetry which combines precision and accuracy of detail with the freedom of dreaming. A passage from Gaston Bachelard's *The Poetics of Reverie* is apt here and, I think, suggestive of the sort of process that occurs in Bly's mind and art:

> When a dreamer of reveries has swept aside all the "preoccupations" which were encumbering his everyday life, when he has detached himself from the worry that comes to him from the worry of others, when he is thus truly the *author of his solitude*, when he can finally contemplate a beautiful aspect of the universe without counting the minutes, that dreamer feels a being opening within him. Suddenly such a dreamer is a world *dreamer*. He opens himself to the world, and the world opens itself to him. One has never seen the world well if he has not dreamed what he was seeing. In a reverie of solitude which increases the solitude of the dreamer, two depths pair off, reverberate in echoes which go from the depths of being of the world to a depth of being of the dreamer. Time is suspended. Time no longer has any yesterday and no longer any tomorrow. Time is engulfed in the double depth of the dreamer and the world.[5]

In a poem, "To Live," from *Old Man Rubbing His Eyes*, Bly assumes an unexpected perspective on the procedures of what he calls "'Living.'" The descriptive details of the poem point to activities and a kind of pursuit which destroys all individual's existence in rapid movements. Nothing of the quality of life is tasted in this deadly hunger for the fallen "crumbs." But in the midst of this brief poem Bly sets for contrast an attitude of "Floating," one which seems remarkably close in spirit to that of the dreamer in Bachelard's statement above (just as the posture of " 'Living'" would appear to be a fatal extension of the "preoccupations" the dreamer must abandon above in order to enter fully into his reverie):

> "Living" means eating up particles of death,
>   as a child picks up crumbs from around the table.
> "Floating" means letting the crumbs fall behind you on the path.
> To live is to rush ahead eating up your own death,
>   like an endgate, open, hurrying into night.

The poems of Old *Man Rubbing His Eyes* are "floating" poems in the manner Bly implies here, and the same may be said of those in *The Morning Glory*: they are poems of attention, reflectiveness, being, or perhaps of becoming as a state of being, but devoid of will or the pursuit of ends. The "floating" element in this poetry is a type of absorbed passivity and contemplation before a scene, an object, or something else. It is a solitary occupation which dispenses, as Bachelard says, with practical cares and, as I've noted, with the will, in the ordinary meaning of intention, determination, and desire. The effect of such a mental position is a liberation of the mind to dream of the things on which it has come to focus, as in "A Walk":

> It is a pale tree,
> all alone in January snow.
> Beneath, a cottonwood shoot
> eaten pale by a rabbit. . . .
>
> Looking up I see the farmyards with their groves,
> the pines somber,
> made for winter, they knew it would come. . . .
>
> And the cows inside the barn, caring nothing for all this,
> their noses in the incense hay,
> half drunk, dusk comes as it was promised
> to them by *their* saviour.

This poem maintains itself fairly near to the outward setting through which Bly passes, concentrating on specific details that evoke a pervasive atmosphere of winter, a calm, cold landscape, sunk in seasonal torpor, only the cows giving the impression of life. It is on them, and also the pine trees, that Bly's imagination exercises freely, generating something of a presence of their instinctive or fundamental natures: the trees' strange foreknowledge of winter and, stranger still, the promise of dusk made to the cows by an enigmatic, unnamed "saviour." Here as elsewhere in Bly's work the reader is brought not to answers, not to analysis or paraphrase, but to wonder. Finally, if the poem succeeds as it should, he will arrive at a state of "floating" himself, a participation in the timeless dreaming of the poet's vision. The poems of *Old Man Rubbing His Eyes* also turn about a unity of place. Like most of *Silence in the Snowy Fields*, this book has its poetic roots in the farm life and the Minnesota countryside Bly knows so well. "A Walk" is, however, rather modest in its range of associations, its imaginative thrusts. There are poems in this volume which positively soar, "Insect Heads," for instance:

> These insects, golden
> and Arabic, sailing in the husks of galleons,
> their octagonal heads also
> hold sand paintings of the next life.

And there are some poems included which proceed into another dimension, as easily and swiftly as a person steps through a door. This one is called "A Dream on the Night of First Snow":

> I woke from a first-day-of-snow dream.
> I met a girl in an attic
>   who talked of operas, intensely.
> Snow has bent the poplar over nearly to the ground,
> new snowfall widens the ploughing.
> Outside, maple leaves float on rainwater,
>   yellow, matted, luminous.
> I saw a salamander. . . and took him up. . .
> he was cold, when I put him down again,
>   he strode over a log
> with such confidence, like a chessmaster,
>   the front leg first, then the hind
>   leg, he rose up like a tractor climbing
>   over a hump in the field
> and disappeared toward winter, a caravan going deeper into
>   mountains,
> dogs pulling travois,
> feathers fluttering on the lances of the arrogant men.

This kind of departure for apparently new realms through a startling, though frequently unobtrusive, shift or jump of association serves at this point as a means for returning to *The Morning Glory* and Bly's practice of the prose poem. The majority of these poems also being in description which is detailed, objective or factual in character, with the poet sometimes locating himself either at the periphery or in the midst of the observed particulars. The openings of a few poems will demonstrate what I mean:

> A ranger is lifting fingerling trout from a pickup with his scoop. They are weighing the fingerlings for stocking. The man in black boots pours them out of his scoop into a tub set on a scale. . . .
>
> ("At a Fish Hatchery in Story, Wyoming")

> The orange stripes on his head shoot forward into the future. The slim head stretches forward, the turtle is pushing with all his might, caught now on the edge of my palm. . . .
>
> ("A Turtle")

> I am in a cliff-hollow, surrounded by fossils and furry shells. The sea breathes and breathes under the new moon. Suddenly it rises, hurrying into the long crevices in the rock shelves. . . .
>
> ("Sitting on Some Rocks in Shaw Cove, California")

Such openings, with their generally reserved tone and their close attention to a precise rendering of externals, corresponds with the first sentence of Bly's short prefatory note to the book: "There is an old occult saying: whoever wants to see the invisible has to penetrate more deeply into the visible." The invisible, then, the covert images and associations tied to the visible, lifts into view through exacting meditation on what engages the poet in the actuality he confronts or comes upon. We are drawn close again to Bachelard's ideas of dreaming on the world, for as I understand it, perhaps intuitively from Bly's poems themselves, a hidden or invisible reality becomes available to the poet through an imagery which derives from a process of interpenetration of self and object(s) leading the mind to discovery. In a number of Bly's prose poems this transition from observed things to the highly-charged metaphorical structures imaginative reflection generates is quite rapid; some pieces move almost directly into it. "A Hollow Tree" reveals such a quick shift:

> I bend over an old hollow cottonwood stump, still standing, waist high, and look inside. Early spring. Its Siamese temple walls are all brown and ancient. The walls have been worked on by the intricate ones. Inside the hollow walls there is privacy and secrecy, dim light. And yet some creature has died here.
>
> On the temple floor feathers, gray feathers, many of them with a fluted white tip. Many feathers. In the silence many feathers.

In this poem the feeling of factual accuracy lasts for only two sentences, just enough to provide a context for what follows and to lead the reader to

the place where vision takes command. Without laboring the obvious or
trying to reduce the poem's haunting allusiveness by tedious explanation,
one can still point to a pattern of association starting with the suggestive
erosion of trunk or bark which reminds Bly of Siamese temples and carries
him on to an imaginative exploration of—a dreaming on—the stump, its
contents, the feathers, reminiscent of death, perhaps sacrifice, and finally
the awareness of silence, cumulative time and more deaths. A rough sense
of these links does not, of course, explain the poem but may help to chart a
discernible movement.

"A Hollow Tree" creates a slow, grave prose music, contemplative in kind,
which proceeds step by step in its associative development from the beginning gestures of curiosity and observation—that is, from the poet's coming
upon the stump in early spring, leaning down to survey its insides. But other
Bly prose poems are more electric and elliptical in their progressions. In "A
Windy Day at the Shack" the poet's excited mood seems to result immediately from the severe wind- and water-blown surroundings; his mind is bom-
barded with lightning flashes of perception and visionary insight. Another
poem, "Frost on the Window Panes," similar in its volatility, finds the poet
keyed-up, ecstatic, and the poem leaps about weightlessly, as it were, among
its revelations:

> It is glittery, excited, like so many things laid down silently in the night,
> with no one watching. Through the two lower panes the watcher can dimly
> see the three trunks of the maple, sober as Europe. The frost wavers, it
> hurries over the world, it is like a body that lies in the coffin, and the next
> moment has disappeared! In its own skin the mind picks up the radio sig-
> nals of death, reminders of the molecules flying all about the universe, the
> icy disembarking, chill fingertips, tulips at head and foot. I look in the
> upper panes and see more complicated roads . . . ribbons thrown on the
> road. . . .

The deep reverence Bly feels for the natural world is everywhere evident
in these prose poems, as well as in Old *Man Rubbing His Eyes*. Water, trees,
hills, grass, shells, tumbleweed, wind, rain, a bird's nest, tidal pools draw his
reflective gaze and stir his imagination toward dream. These are recurrent
elements of the world his poems make; each is accorded its dignity, the
focus of the poet's sensory attentions and his descriptive powers. Bly says, in
"Grass from Two Years," "When I write poems, I need to be near grass that
no one else sees"; and again in the same poem, further on: "the branch and
the grass lie here deserted, a part of the wild things of the world, noticed
only for a moment by a heavy, nervous man who sits near them, and feels he
has at this moment more joy than anyone alive." Other creatures too elicit
his regard. We discover them in poem after poem: fish, an octopus, a turtle,

lobsters in a restaurant window, circus elephants, a blue heron, sea lions, gulls, a salamander, a dying seal, a starfish, a porcupine, steers. Wherever such creatures appear, the lines of relationship are traced; nowhere more beautifully, I think, than in "Looking at a Dead Wren in My Hand," a haunting, memorable achievement:

> Forgive the hours spent listening to radios, and the words of gratitude I did not say to teachers. I love your tiny rice-like legs, that are bars of music played in an empty church and the feminine tail, where no worms of empire have ever slept, and the intense yellow chest that makes tears come. Your tail feathers open like a picket fence, and your bill is brown, with the sorrow of an old Jew whose daughter has married an athelete. The black spot on your head is your own mourning cap.

Yet a poem equally fine, though quite different in location and detail, is "Sunday Morning in Tomales Bay." Bly combines here vividly observed particulars of setting and creature (fog, heron, sea lions) with sudden associative transitions, all of which gives the poem a rewarding, highly-charged energy. Though the poem is a bit long, I quote the whole of it to convey this impression:

> The blue sky suddenly gone—we are in fog—we drift, lost . . . and there's a machine far away, a derrick . . . it is alive! It is a Great Blue Heron! He turns his head and then walks away . . . like some old Hittite empire, all the brutality forgotten, only the rare vases left, and the elegant necks of the women. . . .
> Where he was, heavy bodies are floating—sea lions! We float in among them. The whiskered heads peer over at us attentively, like angels called to look at a baby. They have risen from their sea-mangers to peer at us. Their Magi come to them every day . . . and they gaze at the godless in their wooden boat . . .
> After a while the boat drifts nearer the fogged shore . . . boulders on it piled up . . . sea lions, hundreds of them! Some on their backs playing, then the whole shore starts to roll seaward, barking and flapping . . . And the heron slowly ascends, each wing as long as Holland. . . .
> The lions are gone, they are somewhere in the water underneath us. At last one head pops up five feet from the boat, looking neither arrogant nor surprised, but like a billfold found in the water, or a mountain that has been rained on for three weeks . . . And the Great Blue Heron flies away thin as a grass-blade in the fog. . . .

We can see from such examples how Bly has discovered in the prose poem a complementary form to the free, variable lines of his other poems. In the prose poem he can elaborate more fully if he wishes, use incident, location, or narrative; he can shift readily back and forth between details of the actual scene before him and the imaginative suggestions or associative leaps emanating from them. This strange, marvelous poetic form possesses great flexibility and almost no restrictions: Bly's only boundaries are the margins of his page. One must consider, I believe, *The Morning Glory* a substantial accomplishment both for Bly, in the canon of his writings, and for the prose poem in America, where it can now be seen coming into its own. In the closing poem of this collection Bly enters a barn assumed to be vacant, only to find it occupied by steers. He speaks of these animals at the conclusion in a manner descriptive of all of his own fine prose poems—in fact, it is applicable to the best of Bly's work in any of his books—pointing up their abundance and life, their deep bond with nature, their strength and resilience, their largeness and freedom of body, their intense yet expansive visionary imagination:

> These breathing ones do not demand eternal life; they ask only to eat the crushed corn, and the hay, coarse as rivers, and cross the rivers, and sometimes feel an affection run along the heavy nerves. They have the wonder and bewilderment of the whole, with too much flesh, the body with the lamp lit inside, fluttering on a windy night.

Wonder, yes, it is here; but these poems have no excess of flesh. The light glows within them by which we can sit down to read.

(1966-1967)

NOTES
[1]*Paris Spleen*, translated by Louise Varèse. New Directions, 1947, p. x.
[2]"Portrait of the Writer as a Fat Man," *Field*, 13 (Fall 1975), p 22.
[3]*The Morning Glory: Prose Poems*. Harper and Row, 1975.
[4]*Old Man Rubbing His Eyes*. Unicorn Press, 1975.
[5]*The Poetics of Reverie*, translated by Daniel Russell. Orion Press, 1963, p. 173.

19

"Of Energy Compacted and Whirling": Robert Bly's Recent Prose Poems

I

READERS OF ROBERT BLY ARE WELL AWARE OF THE DEEP, CONNECTIONS EXISTING between his poems and the ideas he explores, the critical opinions he expresses in his essays and reviews—to say nothing of the relationships between the various larger forms of his literary enterprise: writing, translating, editing, lecturing, and reading his work. The elaborate, detailed scrutiny of Bly's intellectual interests, his reading and the development of his thought I leave to those who are engaged in a comprehensive study. I want to examine here some of his new prose poems, to note some of their striking features, and to point to correspondences of imagery and thought between these poems and several of the author's recent essays, such as "I Came Out of the Mother Naked" from *Sleepers Joining Hands*, "The Three Brains" from *Leaping Poetry*, and "Wallace Stevens and Dr. Jekyl" from *American Poets* in 1976 (edited by William Heyen). These preoccupations of Bly's, not surprisingly, appear in the versions and commentary of *The Kabir Book*, and so this latter volume is also closely involved in any remarks as well.

The concerns fundamental to these poems and essays are surely no novelty to Robert Bly. His work is organic, much as a tree or plant in the natural world he contemplates and loves so well: he strives in it for a healing, an integration of the extreme polarities humans experience (as did such modern masters, say, as Yeats or Lawrence) between the masculine and feminine, the "light" and "dark" or "shadow" sides of personality, between the "reptile," "mammal," and "new" brains; or again, between body and spirit, individual and nature. Always, Bly takes considerable pains to avoid anything resembling a false or imposed unity, a generalization which excludes;

we must, he says in one of his prose poems, "give up the idea of one god."
This is less a call to abandon monotheism, I think, than it is an effort to
arrive at a more expansive, inclusive sense of deity. Indissolubly bound up
with this devotion to balance, to an absorption in all of the differing, contradictory aspects of man's makeup and experience (which we might say in
passing parallels his belief that a truly vigorous associational poetry of the
sort he admires has the capacity to "leap" in its energies from one brain to
another, making use of each of them) is Bly's romanticist, visionary commitment to the singularity, the particularity of each thing, creature, incident; and he often firmly and angrily rebukes the contemporary abstracting, classifying mentality or "mind-set" he notices in politicians, city-plan-
ners, literary critics, and doubtless in many other occupations. In *The Kabir
Book*, to which we can assume the poet gives rather strong assent, the deity
is indwelling, a divine being discoverable within man as he lives in the
physical world—and lost by denying that corporeal nature:

> Fire, air, earth, water and space—if you don't want the secret one, you
> can't have these either.
>
> (poem 4)

> If you want the truth, I will tell you the truth:
> Friend, listen: the God whom I love is inside.
>
> (poem 5)

But the polarities of existence are not easily resolved, though they can be
experienced and named. Bly's writings, whether in poetry or prose, participate in a continuing process on his part, an imaginative and intellectual
pursuit of a very elusive harmony for these age-old conflicts and divisions.

An increased attachment to and practice of the prose poem seems appropriate to the endeavors I've mentioned. Bly's *This Body Is Made of Camphor
and Gopherwood* consists of twenty such poems; it was preceded by *The
Morning Glory* (1975), a larger gathering which included pieces from earlier
chapbooks published by Kayak and Mudra. A very few prose poems were
printed in Bly's initial books, but all the external signs indicate a considerable recent concentration on this form. His books coincide as well with a
widespread growth of interest by Americans in the possibilities of the prose
poem genre, and with the appearance of Michael Benedikt's big, authoritative "international" anthology. Both established and new poets have started
to test the form—and themselves in it—while still, of course, there is some
evident resistance to its introduction. In these pages we can only glance at
some of the qualities which Bly conceives of special value and attractive-
ness in the prose poem, and how his own pieces reflect these conceptions,
in addition to themes and predilections already cited.

In a brief but compelling article, "What the Prose Poem Carries With It" (*American Poetry Review*, May/June 1977), Bly sets forth notions about the prose poem important for a reader of his or anyone else's work of this kind. Contrasting the "quiet and low voice" with the "elevated or 'raised' voice," he indicates that, in his view, "the more original thoughts" have been articulated usually in the former. The prose poem he links with that voice, where "we often feel a man or woman talking not before a crowd but in a low voice to someone he is sure is listening." (This quiet speaking bears some resemblance to the "first" of Eliot's "Three Voices of Poetry," a lyric or meditative voice; but for Eliot the poet in this voice talks to himself, wishes to relieve himself of an inner burden or pressure: the reader merely, as it were, overhears him.) Behind the prose poem also there frequently lies calm or meditativeness, familiar enough to those acquainted with Bly's writings; but then "buried impulses toward joy" rise up through this mood in the prose poem's form as if from an "artesian well." So for our poet the quietly speaking voice, which doesn't seek large pronouncements or effects—though it must necessarily gravitate toward them in dramatic moments—moving within the relative freedom of prose, is capable of releasing "some feelings or half-buried thoughts in us [which] would remain beneath the consciousness, unsure of themselves, unable to break through." He warns of the statues of esteemed dead poets who stand behind an author as he writes, requiring of him sympathy and cooperation in the maintenance of poetic forms stiffened with age and almost incapable of animation or resilience. "The man or woman writing a poem in this century has to deal with these white shapes, either outdoing them by tripling the energy in the poem—Yeats does that—or by doing something they don't notice"—that is, composing the poem in prose.

In the second part of this article Bly discusses the prose poem's content, but he approaches it from a new angle, not in terms of voice or the unconscious or past poetic conventions. Instead, he stresses perception, whatever engages the poet's senses, the immediacy of perceiving something and its accurate transfer into the poem. With characteristic sensitivity he remarks: "I have a feeling that the contemporary poem longs for what takes place only once." The prose poem with its loose formal requirements can at least try to accommodate the unique attributes of a momentary perception, which ordinarily we fail to regard, forget, or absorb into abstract summary or information. "I like the way the prose poem so easily allows the original perception to live," Bly writes, "so that in a good prose poem—just as in a good lined poem—it's possible that every noun would be a singular noun! No one plural noun in the whole poem!" An impossible ideal, no doubt, but perhaps worth working toward. Such a poem would truly be, as Wallace Stevens said, "the cry of its occasion," utterly faithful to the particulars of an experience. Likewise, for Bly it should aid in rejecting the "generalization" into which "we have been pushed too early" in school and elsewhere, our "original perception" forced to disappear in some larger categorical scheme.

Of course, the prose poem is not alone in permitting this desirable truth to individual detail or sensory experience; among other things, that is the province of all literature. And after all, isn't exactly this kind of seeing one of the most impressive elements of this first lined stanza of the first poem in Robert Bly's first book?

> Sometimes, riding in a car, in Wisconsin
> Or Illinois, you notice those dark telephone poles
> One by one lift themselves out of the fence line
> And slowly leap on the gray sky—
> And past them, the snowy fields.
>   ("Three Kinds of Pleasures")

All the same, while the prose poem allows for the sort of creative observation of particulars we see registered in these lines, it further encourages the writer to float about freely in his perceptions by affording him space—blocks of prose paragraphs—where his consciousness can exercise a flexibility not constrained by problems of the line. In such paragraphs, as Michael Benedikt says in his significant introductory essay to *The Prose Poem*, any or all of the other devices of poetry may be called into use—and Bly employs them too. Benedikt also points out that this "genre" of poetry aids our "need to attend to the priorities of the unconscious. This attention to the unconscious, and to its particular logic, unfettered by the relatively formalistic interruptions of the line break, remains the most immediately apparent property of the prose poem." It becomes obvious then that the form makes "association" or "leaping" in which the unconscious plays a leading part, and which Bly defines as "a form of content" in itself, not merely a poetic technician's method but an essential directing of imagination currents in the composition of a poem. Bly's musings in *Leaping Poetry* about Wallace Stevens's early poems have, I think, a value as indirect illumination of the procedures in many of his own prose poems. He notes, "Often in *Harmonium* . . . the *content* of the poem lies in the *distance* between what Stevens was given as fact, and what he then imagined. The farther a poem gets from its initial worldly circumstance without breaking the thread, the more content it has." The key phrase here is "without breaking the thread," for the poem begins with its "original perception," a "fact" of observation or circumstance, which the imagination, the forces and dream logic of the unconscious subsequently transform, transfigure, attenuate to the limit, or compress to an opposite extreme—in short, whatever associational "leaping" and imagery will do—remaining all the while tied, however tightly, to the object or complex of elements with which it originated. Within its framework of the paragraph, the prose poem has ample opportunity for such give and take, expansion from and tension with a certain beginning point. "Rapid association," as Bly calls it, exhibits itself at once in the prose poems of his earlier collection, *The Morning Glory*. In "A Bird's Nest Made of White Reed Fiber" there is swift movement from the title object toward things associated with it by imaginative jumps. The poem proceeds in a breathtaking way from simile to metaphor, likeness to identity; the concluding third sentence is climactic and visionary:

> The nest is white as the foam thrown up when the sea hits rocks! It is translucent as those cloudy transoms above Victorian doors, and swirled as the hair of those intense nurses, gray and tangled after long nights in Crimean wards. It is something made and then forgotten, like our own lives that we will entirely forget in the grave, when we are floating, nearing the shore where we will be reborn, ecstatic and black.

How long a poem stays close to its "initial worldly circumstance" varies with each one. Often, a poem returns to that circumstance in some fashion in the course of its movements, and may then depart from it again; or it may return there at the end; but in any case for the reader the first circumstance or object will have been changed by the imaginative operations occurring in between. To Bly's thinking—as the term "leaping" implies—the author's mind during composition should dance among images derived from different areas of the brain, from both the conscious and unconscious levels. When this activity is accomplished with a great flow of imaginative and emotional power—Bly selects Lorca's poetry as a primary example—"we have," he says, "something different from Homer or Machado; a new kind of poem (apparently very rare in the nineteenth century) which we could call the poem of 'passionate association,' or 'poetry of flying.'"

II

The prose poems of *This Body Is Made of Camphor and Gopherwood* comprise a smaller, more closely knit group than those of *The Morning Glory*; there is less variety, greater intensity of purpose—it can, and in some ways should be read as a sequence. Bly's theme, as the title makes plain, is the body. In poem after poem he explores with precision and strength of imagination the body's relationships of earth, death, selfhood, joyousness, dream, consciousness, and mystical apprehension. This last phrase I use to suggest how the poems progress toward—and not seldom either—one or another state of visionary awareness: for instance, when the poet envisages powerfully the life of protozoa within man's physical structure, in the amazing "The Origin of the Praise of God." At this stage in his career it is no more than commonplace to remind ourselves that Bly's literary impulses contain a sizeable mixture of moral and religious, as well as aesthetic, ingredients, and that his religiousness is involved with psychology and is in no sense conventional. But heterodox visionary qualities are familiar components of American writing and are inseparable from its appeal. "Sometimes the spirit even begins to flow upward a little in the language of the prose poem," Bly admits in the article quoted before. "So prose poems perhaps resemble home or private religion, lined poems are like public churches. The ancient world had both, and, strangely, different gods for the public religion than for the private, which were appropriately called 'Mysteries.' "

In keeping with Bly's comments and speculations on the prose poem, "Walking Swiftly," the opening piece in the book, begins descriptively with "separate events" early in the morning on the farm just beyond his house. The poet wakes to a reality which is clearly familiar, immersed heavily in its own physical properties. But contrast and change set in; and uneasiness on Bly's part leads without transition to sentences about an unspecified "Emperor" and his demands for exotic objects, all of which violate the natural order. The poem continues to a passage about the "heat inside the human body," forces generated in and through man, and seeking proper realization. A final sentence tells us, as in a proverb or the fragment of some parable, how "the artist" expends his energy. My quick summary here breaks up what is in Bly's poem a distinct progression, though not a rational one, from sentence to sentence. It is for the reader to recognize, perhaps after several trips through the text, the way along which these sentences take him, building up a cluster of imagery or thought through one or two, let us say, and then stepping off without warning across a considerable gap to a new one, which presents in turn a quite different, but not unrelated perception or grouping of details. Variations on a pattern of this sort appear constantly throughout these prose poems. Here now is tile text of "Walking Swiftly":

> When I wake, I hear sheep eating apple peels just out screen. The trees are heavy, soaked, cold and hushed, the sun just rising. All seems calm, and yet somewhere inside I am not calm. We live in wooden buildings made of two-by-fours, making the landscape nervous for a hundred miles. And the Emperor when he was sixty called for rhinoceros horn, for sky-blue phoenix eggs shaped from veined rock, dipped in rooster blood. Around him the wasps kept guard, the hens continued their patrol, the oysters open and close all questions. The heat inside the human body grows, it does not know where to throw itself—for a while it knots into will, heavy, burning, sweet, then into generosity, that longs to take on the burdens of others, then into mad love that lasts forever. The artist walks swiftly to his studio, and carves oceanic waves into the dragon's mane.

The "calm" of the poem's setting at first and the contrasting disturbance within the poet betray a fundamental absence of harmony or reconciliation which, as we said, troubles Bly elsewhere and gives impetus to his writing. In this poem, mans dwellings, farmhouses, "buildings made of two-by-fours," are inimical to their environment, sending out tremors that bother a world otherwise balanced within itself. A passage from the essay, "I Came Out of the Mother Naked," helps to explain this negative vibrancy. There Bly reminds us that matriarchal consciousness favors curves and circles, while the patriarchal plans "the ground in huge squares" and "creates straight roads." A little further on he refers to Drinks Water, "an old Dakota [Indian] holy man" who admonished his people of defeat by the whites, "and warned that when that happened, they would have to live in square houses." Bly goes on to quote Black Elk on living in square buildings: " 'It is a bad way to live, for there can be no power in a square. You have noticed that everything an Indian does is in a circle, and that is because the Power of the World always works in circles, and everything tries to be round. . . . Everything the Power of the World does is done in a circle. . . .' " We see as we read these prose poems how essential circular imagery is for the poet; here it is sufficient to note how it clarifies by antithesis the disruptive character of the "wooden buildings" with their square or rectangular design, which is not in conformity with the rounded patterns of the "landscape."

Bly's sudden "leap" to the apparently remote figure of the Emperor adds a sharp new perspective to the poem's theme, for he represents power and domination, and yet he too is a man, driven by human compulsions. He wishes for objects manufactured from other creatures. Readers may want to determine for themselves the significance of eggs and horn: the objects leave room for a variety of interpretations. Does the aging Emperor in fact hope to win renewal from these concocted symbols of life and fertility, constructed at his command? We aren't told; instead, the next sentence reaches out to the surrounding realm of nature to garner images: there wasps and hens behave protectively and oysters, strangely, appear to pronounce judgments, render decisions by moving their shells. The last is, I suppose, a surrealist detail: but we know from Bly's essay on the Mother that "four favorite creatures [of hers] were the turtle, the owl, the dove, and the oyster." The natural activities of these creatures in the poem contradict the Emperor's will. The subsequent passage on the body's "heat" and the forms it takes, while comprehensible in itself, gains in meaning when connected with Bly's article, "The Three Brains." A correspondence seems to me to exist between the different outlets this heat finds in the poem and the identifying characteristics of the reptilian, mammalian, and new brains described in the article, but I won't attempt any investigation here. Indecision about the heat or energy's disposal appears central to the poem's implications. Sheep, trees, wasps, oysters, hens, and so on, do not have such questions raised with regard to them; only man does. The poem ends with the emergence of an artist figure who releases his force (or the heat inside himself) in appropriately harmonic, imaginative fashion. The curved "oceanic waves" of his carving relate him to the "feminine consciousness" Bly believes necessary to human balance and wholeness, for one of the Mother's images is also "the sea," and to the rounded forms of nature in general. He says of the dragon that "in inner life [it] is man's fear of women, and in public life, it is the matriarchy's conserva- tive energy." Surely, the second meaning is the one most applicable to the artist's activity in the poem; but any such. interpretation must be tentative. Bly has advised his readers not to attempt to use "I Came Out of the Mother Naked" as an index to his poems. That seems fair enough; the author should know best, we say. On the other hand, I have obviously not obeyed him in this essay, at least not to the extent of bypassing connections which are too evident to ignore. "Walking Swiftly" reveals itself as a poem divided be- tween conflicting modes of consciousness (masculine and feminine, or light and dark, in the poet's terms) and the manner in which human energy or heat is utilized by each of them. The Emperor remains stolidly patriarchal, demanding the phallic, and also weaponlike, rhinoceros horn, the Apollonian "sky-blue" eggs, and he is, of course, a figure of will and domination. The artist stands perhaps in the antithetical position, or nearly so. In his figure we presumably find a balance of conflicting elements; for the artist belongs to the side of "mother consciousness" and puts will and energy to the service of imagination or art, carving forms harmonious with nature's. But we are talking of a poem, and it does not deliver its secrets to dissection. I believe, however, that Bly conveys some of the implications I've discussed in a fluid, elliptical prose, its language, phrasing, and imagery as full and rich as we would expect to discover in his lined poems.

Each poem in the book emerges from one or another kind of meditation on man's body, I have said, but that is simply the beginning. A poem may lead in any number of directions, become enmeshed in the most intricate webs of experience; and it will usually shift abruptly, yet with apparent ease, from one perception to the next. Quite often Bly starts a poem with an invocation both to his reader and to some of the body's metaphorical com- ponents, thus directly or obliquely, as the case may be, echoing his book's title. Here are some examples: "My friend, this body is made of camphor and gopherwood"; "My friend, this body is food for the thousand dragons of the air, each dragon light as a needle"; "This body holds its protective walls around us, it watches us whenever we walk out"; "My friend, this body is made of bone and excited protozoa . . . and it is with my body that I love." In the final poem he begins with a direct address to a loved one which becomes also, in its way, an appeal for human community, reconciliation and kinship with the world: "I love you so much with this curiously alive and lonely body." Other poems may originate, as "Walking Swiftly" does, in an ordinary or familiar situation, with weather, landscape, objects: "It has been snowing all day. Three of us start out across the fields"; or "The cucumbers are thirsty, their big leaves turn away from the wind." Only a few of them open having already taken a stride into dream or vision: "The horses gallop east, over the steppes, each with its rider, hard. Each rider carries a strip of red cloth raised above his head"; or "Smoke rises from the mountain depths, a girl walks by the water. This is the body of water near where we sleep."

From beginnings such as these Bly gets under way rapidly. Prose paragraphs, as we've noted, supply a medium in which he can attend to particular detail if he desires, or alternate quickly from one dimension of reality to another with no hesitation or explanation, slipping in and out of the factual and the visionary while avoiding some of the conventional problems of technique that might interfere with those motions: he need only decide when and if to use more than one paragraph. In "The Sleeper," for instance, a poem which appears to record an extreme of an extreme withdrawal or self-enclosure, Bly can simultaneously adopt the roles of the dreamer and of an anonymous, transparent speaker who watches from outside, describing what takes place while the first figure sleeps:

> He came in and sat by my side, and I did not wake up. I went on dreaming of vast houses with rooms I had not seen, of men suddenly appearing whom I did not know, but who knew me, of thistles whose points shone as if a light were inside.
> A man came to me and began to play music. One arm lay outside the covers. He put the dulcimer in my hand but I did not play it. I went on, hearing.
> Why didn't I wake up? And why didn't I play? Because I am asleep, and the sleeping man is all withdrawn into himself. He thinks the sound of a shutting door is a tooth falling from his head, or his head rolling on the ground.

Flexibilities of this sort make the prose poem a very suitable form for various poetic or imaginative intentions. Bly can introduce, as he does in "Going Out to Check the Ewes," what one might call different or contrasting manners, place them side by side without advance notice and with no transition between them, and then let them work with, around, and upon each other as the developing poem requires:

> My friend, this body is food for the thousand dragons of the air, each dragon light as a needle. This body loves us, and carries us home from our hoeing.
> It is ancient, and full of the bales of sleep. In its vibrations the sun rolls along under the earth, the spouts over the ocean curl into our stomach . . . water revolves, spouts seen by skull eyes at mid-ocean, this body of herbs and gopherwood, this blessing, this lone ridge patrolled by water. . . . I get

up, morning is here. The stars still out; the black winter sky looms over the
unborn lambs. The barn is cold before dawn, the gates slow. . . .
    The body longs for itself far out at sea, it floats in the black heavens, it is
a brilliant being, locked in the prison of human dullness. . . .

In the first paragraph two sentences are juxtaposed which, so to speak,
call up for the reader separate planes of awareness without any jarring incongruity and in such a fashion that they seem to belong with one another,
or indeed participate mysteriously each in the other. The poem takes for its
point of departure a near-mystical kind of declaration, set in that form of
address we've specified previously. But the body is lowered to the ground
from this metaphoric, visionary height by the second sentence; yet the two
statements don't struggle against one another; they operate as a pair, complementary, necessary companions reflecting the antitheses Bly encounters
everywhere. Moreover, the repetition of "this body" fixes ties between the
sentences, so the ecstatic definition of the first combines readily with the
more earthly harmony of the second. Thinking about these two sentences
and their relationship can help us to grasp the type of subtlety and supple-
ness Bly manages in these poems.
    The next of the poem's three paragraphs maintains that subtlety from the
outset. The opening pronoun refers to the body, which is "ancient, " recalling the dragon image; "bales of sleep" beautifully serves as a reminder of
daily labor, keeping us in mind of the "hoeing" of paragraph one. At the
same time this phrase designates the hidden, unconscious self waiting to be
revealed with coming night, for the workday world is left behind at the
initial paragraph's close. Now night overtakes the poem completely: "the
sun rolls along under the earth," and the reader finds himself confronted
with a sudden abundance of imagery associated both with the feminine
consciousness, or Mother, and with the propulsive force of life and creation. "This body is made of energy compacted and whirling," Bly states at
the beginning of "We Love This Body," and it is quite clear from that poem,
as well as from innumerable instances in others, he means not simply the
human body—though certainly it too—but the entire body of creation, the
physical cosmos and the life or vitality of spirit, soul, psyche, call it what
you will, which infuses, sustains, and orders it. In the poem under discussion those images of energy are plentiful and undisguised, rang from the sun
which "rolls," through "spouts" that "curl" into us (drawing together images
of large or universal energies with those implying their functioning in individuals), the "water" that "revolves," back again to the "spouts," which seemingly even the dead know, finally arriving at a calm and an echo of the title
with an evocation of the body in terms of natural things ("herbs and
gopherwood"). Before the paragraph swings upward again on the diurnal
cycle, the body is praised as a "blessing" and, immediately after, viewed as

solitary, a rocky "ridge" surrounded by, protruding from "water." It is then the poet awakens, as if all that has just occurred were part of his dreaming or else the imagery of forces at work beyond dreams, far off in the inner reaches of being in person and cosmos. Bly goes now to perform the early chores of the farm before daybreak; but even here, in the morning routine, the drawing of detail turns teasingly allusive—sky, unborn lambs, stiff gates seem disturbingly mixed with memories of the night.

In this paragraph's nocturnal journeying we have happened once more on that imagery of the circular mentioned earlier in correspondence with Bly's ideas about "Mother consciousness" and with the Indian sense of "the Power of the World" to which he refers. Bly lists additional images allied to the feminine in his essay: "the night, the sea, animals with curving horns and cleft hooves, the moon, bundles of grain." Furthermore, he argues that "matriarchy thinking is intuitive and moves by associative leaps," to which we can see the poet's should be kindred. "Masculine consciousness," he asserts, following a number of scholars, comes chronologically or historically after the feminine, has for "its main image the bright blue sky surrounding the sun—its metal, gold." It plots straight lines, as implied before, thinks with straight logic, distrusts myth and imagination, proliferates regulations, moral dicta, "and tries to reach the spirit through asceticism." To Bly's way of thinking (as to many another poet's) these masculine values have wrongly created our modern technological civilization and prevailed over it; only now, he tells us, there are indications of change, of righting the balance: "Intuitive gifts are being given." Anyone who has looked at Bly's essay also knows that he names, speculatively, four Mother figures, representative of different energies and impulses. The Death Mother and the Stone or Teeth Mother are icons of danger and destructive forces as real as their positive, creative counterparts, the Good Mother and the Ecstatic Mother. For our purposes, however, in talking of this sequence of prose poems and some of its themes and images, I will be occupied largely with the affirmative aspects of feminine or dark consciousness. And as Bly has remarked: "All men's poems are written by men, already flying toward the Ecstatic Mother. It's possible for a poem to talk about the Death Mother, but I think the energy that brings the words alive belongs to the Ecstatic Mother."

The single sentence paragraph which finishes "Going Out to Check the Ewes" guides us again into regions of metaphor and vision, away from the mundane reference of the poem's title and the descriptive particulars of the barnyard. Yet, as before, connections are present between the rest of the text and what is said at its ending. From the start I have indicated the feeling of dividedness Bly finds prevalent in experience, and it is surely visible in these poems. Of course, some sense of harmony and security makes itself felt in the first paragraph of "Going Out. . . ." A self-unity, the body's supportiveness appear to harmonize existence there. But the imagery of night with its wealth of creative potentiality and energetic expenditure also seems partially imprisoned within sleep or the unconscious. So as morning inevitably recurs at the poem's conclusion the force of those night or feminine energies becomes diminished: division takes hold of the poet's sensibilities— the true or wholly unified body, the human-as-he-should-be, is projected distantly, "far out at sea . . . in the black heavens," with the water and darkness which are among its elemental symbols. Still, it is termed "a brilliant being" too, implying possibly a new kind of radiance or light that reconciles the opposing consciousness, "the Secret One" or inward divinity of *The Kabir Book*, an unrealized God longed-for but secreted behind "human dullness."

The condition enacted in "The Sleeper" is basically the same, especially if we use poem 35 from Bly's Kabir versions as a source of illumination for it. The Kabir poem goes:

> Listen friend, this body is his dulcimer.
> He draws the strings tight, and out of it comes the music of the inner universe.
> If the strings break and the bridge falls,
> then this dulcimer of dust goes back to dust.
>
> Kabir says: the Holy One is the only one who can draw music from it.

In Bly's poem we recall how the speaker (or one aspect of him—he plays a dual role), asleep, is visited by an unnamed man who plays music to him, then places a dulcimer in his hand, but the sleeper refuses to play it and only listens. Questioning himself about this rejection, Bly answers that it has occurred because he hasn't wakened, remains "asleep," not certainly in the limited everyday meaning but in a spiritual sense, which the Kabir poem touches on quite clearly. Earlier I said "The Sleeper" treated a withdrawn state. The dulcimer suggests a music of wholeness vibrating with one's entire being, that "inner universe" of the Kabir version which will be compelled outward if the "Holy One" plays upon it. Bly's sleeper stays exiled in himself, hence he misunderstands even ordinary external sounds as events happening within his own body, or to it, events that are, as the poem shows, destructive or fatal in their significance. Reading his situation in the light of Kabir, we may think the sleeper resembles an unused instrument, falling back to dust, having failed to discover or accept the deity waiting inside him. Obviously, a close affinity exists between this unhappy resolution and the frustration of unfulfillment in the body's "brilliant being, locked in the prison of human dullness."

"How do I know what I feel but what the body tells me?" Bly queries in one of the poems; but the restriction his words could seem to denote must not be taken literally. In "Looking from Inside My Body," the title of which shares the viewpoint of this rhetorical question, recurrent images, objects, details we should by now easily recognize are on display. But the substance of this poem, once we have passed its beginning sentences, is unmistakably visionary: after all, Bly never confines bodily knowledge, here or elsewhere, to basic sensory impressions. Doesn't he tell us in *Silence in the Snowy Fields* that "the quiet waters of the night will rise, / And our skin shall see far off, as it does under water"? Description always gives place to intuition, embodied imagination.

"Looking from Inside My Body" can be called a quest poem, in which the author discovers himself pulled toward two contrary bodies, earth and moon, while confusion, irresolution, and inner division rule. His meditations originate with sunset, the encroaching darkness: "night thickens near the ground, pulls the earth down to it." Bly in his own physical body must remain where he is, a figure composed of card; and so part of it—"down here, thickening as night comes on." This is, all the same, the night of objects, of nature, of other creatures than man too; but in him another element—of spirit—cannot be satisfied with earth alone and yearns toward the moon, locating this second aspect of his being in that lunar image with the feminine associations it bears. Around him he witnesses in the natural world a unity he doesn't possess but must envy:

> There are earth things, earthly, joined, they are snuggled down in one manger, one sweep of arms holds them, one clump of pine, the owlets sit together in one hollow tree. . . .

Again he questions what will happen with night's advent. He faces now the fact that consciousness, reason, intention—all the powers by which he has navigated existence throughout the day—must necessarily be lost, forsaken at this hour: they are all concentrated in the single image of the sun pursuing its routine course—but he has this solar correspondence within that will likewise lose strength. (We remember the Sun is for Bly a central symbol of the masculine or patriarchal disposition.) Yet as such thoughts occur to the poet, the loss of solar energy is suddenly combined with a mystical or religious realization on which the paragraph then trails off inconclusively but not negatively:

> What has been sun in me all day will drop underneath the earth, and travel sizzling along the underneath-ocean-darkness path. . . . There a hundred developed saints lie stretched out, throwing bits of darkness onto the road. . . .

In this rather unexpected turning the poem takes we come near some of Bly's Kabir versions again. Plainly, the actions of the saints in the above passage appear in contrast with what the poet has done so far in the poem.

In curious fashion they toss "bits of darkness" on a road which is in one sense the sun's "path" along the underside of the globe at night but is likewise, I think, the path of individual destiny, the Way, or the "bhakti path" of which Bly speaks in his comments on Kabir. Their gesture is one of reconciliation, harmonizing the polar extremities of light and dark, masculine and feminine which the poet has viewed anxiously in separation.

The end has yet to come; two more paragraphs complete the poem. In the first of them Bly sees himself in the literal situation sketched at the beginning. Nightfall: soon he must retire from the darkened external scene before him, the moon still risen overhead, and enter his room to submit to sleep. Losing this external actuality, he fears that he will surrender all it symbolizes for him. Considerable agitation seems to underlie his anticipated descent into sleep, solitude, incarceration, blackness, and the riddling encounter with "another prisoner" there.

> . . . suddenly my moon will vanish. The sleeper will go down toward utter darkness. . . . Who will be with him? He will meet another prisoner in the dungeon, alone with the baker.[1]

Concluding sentences depict the "moon outside the bedroom," moving through the night sky by itself, "slipping through the arms reached up to it. . . . It will go on, looking. . . ." Several implications at least can be found in this ending, though I cannot cover all of them here. It can be said, referring once again to the Kabir poems, that both external and internal suns and moons exist: the physical bodies in space and the polar opposites in humans, as we say Bly's connotations suggest. Kabir version 13 begins like this:

> There's a moon in my body, but I can't see it!
> A moon and a sun.
> A drum never touched by hands, beating, and I can't hear it!
>
> As long as a human being worries about when he will die, and
>   what he has that is his,
> all of his works are zero.
> When affection for the I-creature and what it owns is dead,
> then the work of the Teacher is over.

Ownership of this sun and moon then is not possible in the usual sense of property or an object. In Bly's poem the quest will be fruitless if that impossible possession constitutes its goal: the sun sinks past the earth's rim; the moon eludes those grasping arms extended toward it. Besides, of course, the correspondences and the basic significance of these celestial entities are inward, reaching to those opposing extremes which need to be merged in order to achieve human wholeness or balance. The saints, being wiser, further along the path, keep repose, "lie stretched out"; the "bits of darkness" they toss on the Sun's route imply a spiritual corrective by means of which these sages work for, or attain, a blending of the antitheses—that very harmony the poet desires. In addition to which Kabir says in another poem not to gaze beyond but to "stand firm" in one's body.

III

Much of my attention till now has been devoted to some poems about "What Is Missing"—the lack of self-unity and of the congruent flow of energies—if I may borrow that half of the poem title "A Dream of What Is Missing." My remarks naturally neither exhaust the subject in those pieces, nor in Bly's collection as a whole. I should like, however, to focus at this point on several poems from the middle and later pages of the book, poems which do realize moments of elation, ecstasy, or fulfillment—a level of intense, heightened perception. This sort of mood predominates in the second half of the sequence and brings the work to a moving, joyous climax.

At the heart of the book the tenth poem, "Walking to the Next Farm," acts as a transitional piece, a bridge to affirmative vision, as well as a companion to the poem that follows, "The Origin of the Praise of God," the most unusual, difficult, and strangely mystical of all. The setting should be well-known to Bly's readers: Minnesota farmlands at midwinter, earth and air heavy with snow. The poet and two others are walking over the fields. Gradually, as is so often the case with these poems, Bly's awareness is brought to bear on a specific quality of the phenomena about him. He abandons other description as extraneous, drawn by his senses, then by intuition, insight, imagination—whatever you wish—to the center of the experience, which amounts to nothing less than some kind of revelation for him. Such is the structure and progression of this starting paragraph:

> It has been snowing all day. Three of us start out across the fields. The boots sink in to the ankles, but go on; our feet move through the most powerful snow energy. There is falling snow above us, and below us, and on all sides. My eyes feel wild, as if a new body were rising, with tremendous swirls in its flow; its whirlpools move with their face upward, as those whirls in the Missouri that draw in green cottonwoods from collapsed earth banks, pull them down with all their branches. And our feet carry the male energy that disappears, as my brother's energy did, in its powerful force field his whole life disappeared, and all the trees on his farm went with it. . . .

In the dreamlike qualities the poem assumes, which are perfectly in keeping too with the weather's behavior, Bly becomes cognizant of what amounts

to a full-scale combat between male and female energies in which the stakes
can be mortality. The men with their physical strength, will, endurance
(even the male sexual attributes of their feet and boots) push through lifting "whirlpools" of snow and the rounded swirls of energy we have come to
identify as inherently figurative of feminine power. Yet if the two sides are
locked in struggle, Bly also glimpses—though the verb is perhaps not adequate to the instantaneous perceiving he experiences—a moment of their
union in his reference to "a new body . . . rising." Ostensibly, this alludes to
the invasion of feminine energy in the whirling columns of snow, but in
view of what the remainder of the poem calls for, it appears rich with prophecy as well. The paragraph proceeds by tracing analogies, instances of the
collapse of masculine objects and individuals into the fierce, revolving "force
field," where they are destroyed. Bly's brother, whose death is included in a
poem close to the end of *The Morning Glory*, is swallowed up here too.
Throughout the paragraph, the fatal, ruinous aggression of matriarchal consciousness perseveres: an engagement with its negative dimensions, I should
guess, the Death Mother or the Teeth Mother.

The following section doesn't offer much respite. There are multiple references to a Tibetan, Huns, Vienna, "the doctor," and Lenin, prefaced by a
depiction of "energy that comes off the fierce man's hair . . . not a halo, but
a background of flames." Bly seems to be concerned to represent here the
involvement of these various persons with the release or frustration of male
forces or concepts. The doctor is most likely Freud, who, Bly notes elsewhere, "could only imagine a great father running the primal horde." This
collocation of figures, activities, and images is for me highly reminiscent of
portions of the poems in *Sleepers Joining Hands*.

But the final paragraph steps back from this turbulence and conflict. The
poet opens with a question, and promptly answers it, giving a reply he believes will lead toward the balance he searches for. Like Yeats, he approves
the embrace of contrarities, rather than a fixed selection between alterna-
tives. The passage returns to imagery, to the poet still walking through the
snow, to the vortices of energy in their costly battle. A three line lyric coda
is appended to this paragraph, a tiny poem of balance or reconciliation in
its own right; and, as we'll see, a similar piece is used as an interlude in "The
Origin of the Praise of God":

> Then what is asked of us? To stop sacrificing one energy for another. They
> are not different anyway, not "male" or "female," but whirls of different
> speeds as they revolve. We must learn to worship both, and give up the
> idea of one god. . . . I taste the snow, lying on a branch. It tastes slow. It is
> as slow as the whirl in the boulder lying beneath the riverbed. . . . Its swirls
> take nine thousand years to complete, but they too pull down the buffalo
> skin boats into their abysses, many souls with hair go down.

> The light settles down in front of each snowflake,
> and the dark, rises up behind it,
> and inside its own center it lives!

What startles the reader is Bly's unexpected denial of the masculine and feminine identities of these "whirls" of force; now he has translated their differences into "speeds" of revolution, envisaging them as operating at fast or slow tempos as the means for explaining their conflict. One shouldn't balk at the change. Bly doesn't write as a philosopher who has restricted himself to the limitations of a special terminology but as a poet free to lend himself to imaginative impulses. The reader will notice that the male/female polarity hasn't vanished anyway from the poems at this point; we shall meet up with it again. In fact, the details of the explorers dragged into watery "abysses" obviously retains associations with the two extremes. Of greater importance is Bly's requirement that we "worship both" energies, abandon the habit of refusing one for its opposite. The small lyric renders this notion quite beautifully—revolutions of light and dark, as with earth's day and night, and the snowflake poised between, secure in its own being.

"The Origin of the Praise of God" is a visionary hymn to the body, its architecture and existence, but most astonishingly this poem travels far beyond the outward, ordinarily visible lineaments and forms to evoke the myriad lives of the cells of which it consists. Bly brings together unforgettable images here to provide a marvelous enactment of the motions and responses of protozoa, the simplest single-celled creatures. In such finiteness and simplicity, and yet with internal complexity, it is not difficult to see an analogy with the previous poem's snowflake. The present poem Bly has dedicated to Lewis Thomas and his book *The Lives of a Cell*.

Starting once more with a simultaneous address to his reader and declaration of the body's composition—in this instance "made of bone and excited protozoa"—the poet claims that only through his corporeal being can he "love" external creation or know his own feelings. He completes the first paragraph with allusions to bodily formation, differentiating the inside ("so beautifully carved . . . with the curves of the inner ear") from the outside ("the husk so rough, knuckle-brown"). With the shift to the next paragraph Bly advances boldly into "the magnetic fields of other bodies—thus announcing a theme of attraction and union occupying him from his poem to the last—and then further, into the responsiveness to such stimuli countless cellular lives within us:

> . . . every smell we take in the communities of protozoa see, and a being inside leaps up toward it, as a horse rears at the starting gate. When we come near each other, we are drawn down into the sweetest pools of slowly

circling energies, slowly circling smells. And the protozoa know there are
odors the shape of oranges, of tornadoes, of octopuses. . . .

> The sunlight lays itself down before the protozoa,
> the night opens itself out behind it,
> and inside its own energy it lives!

The lyric triplet, appearing at the middle of this poem rather than at its
finish, restates the harmony, the integration or balance observed in the
snowflake image. Bly constructs too with scientific accuracy, in that the
one-celled creature does indeed live its own life—is born of fission, feeds
and reproduces by dividing, and finally dies. In the poem the poles of light
and dark lie before and behind it, while the protozoa exists within "its own
energy," just as the snowflake sustains itself at its own central point. Both
become emblems of equilibrium, which Bly has purposely set off by themselves to draw our notice.

It is necessary to recall as well the magnetism of bodies coming into proximity to one another in the quoted passage, with the extraordinary, complicated reactions caused inside of us, of which we can be scarcely conscious
except in terms of general effect. The poet looks outward momentarily to
introduce a couple approaching each other—to put us in touch again with a
familiar circumstance—then turns once more to the swarming cellular reality within, seeing the compulsions, the synesthetic impressions, the huge
movements of microscopic bodies in light of a religious "pilgrimage." Details
of Christ's tomb, the stone blocking its entrance, and a reference to the
Resurrection are worked into a scheme of rebirth or renewal for the persons
of whom these cells are a part. As the individuals unite, so the "clouds of
cells" in each of them, mutually attracted or magnetically compelled, journey toward their bodies' boundaries. In the union of persons opposites fuse,
contrarities and antitheses are overcome, they find completion. Inside them
the cells perform a dance of ecstasy, of mystical achievement. Here we must
not forget that the God for whom both Bly and Kabir are looking lives in
them and has to be discovered initially in mortal, physical existence, not
afterwards. This lengthy concluding portion of the poem dramatizes an experience of the inner deity; it is sanctioned at the close by a sage figure
whose final question clarifies for the reader the route Bly's visionary pursuit
in this prose poem sequence has traced:

> So the space between two people diminishes, it grows less and less, no one
> to weep, they merge at last. The sound that pours from the fingertips awak-
> ens clouds of cells far inside the body, and beings unknown to us start out
> in a pilgrimage to their Saviour, to their holy place. Their holy place is a
> small black stone, that they remember from Protozoic times, when it was

rolled away from a door . . . and it was after that they found their friends, who helped them to digest the hard grains of this world. . . . The cloud of cells awakens, intensifies, swarms . . . the cells dance inside beams of sunlight so thin we cannot see them. . . . To them each ray is a vast palace, with thousands of rooms. From the dance of the cells praise sentences rise to the throat of the man praying and singing alone in his room. He lets his arms climb above his head, and says, "Now do you still say you cannot choose the Road?"

Evidently, much more could be contributed to any thorough reading of this poem. I can't pretend to have dealt with its scientific sources, but my remarks have, I hope, touched some of its essential intentions. The theme of union in "The Origin of the Praise of God" prepares for consideration of some of the later poems in the book. For obvious reasons I must skip over pieces which are excellent and worthy of close, appreciative study in order to give attention to a few of the last. I will, however, pause to quote one of them, "The Pail," because in its opening paragraph Bly reflects in a personal way, and even retrospectively, on the quest for and accomplishment of revelatory experience. These ecstasies are hard won, in an austere environment. They have occurred through an inward communion with the physical body and have taken him through a type of death and rebirth. Still, I quote this lovely poem for a second reason: because there are so many examples in it of the perceiving and recording singular events for which Bly believes the prose poem possesses such a capacity. As he sharpens our sensibilities by imagining the lives of protozoa our naked eyes can't see, so he trains us to regard carefully, lovingly, what is visible that we often neglect:

Friend, this body is made of camphor and gopherwood. So for two days I gathered ecstasies from my own body, I rose up and down, surrounded only by bare wood and bare air and some gray cloud, and what was inside me came so close to me, and I lived and died!

Now it is morning. The faint rain of March hits the bark of the half-grown trees. The honeysuckle will drip water, the moon will grow wet sailing, the granary door turns dark on the outside, the oats inside still dry.

And the grandfather comes back inquiringly to the farm, his son stares down at the pickup tire, the family lawyer loses his sense of incompetence for a moment, in the barn the big pail is swung out so as to miss the post.

In poems such as "We Love This Body" and "Wings Folding Up" the results of choosing the right "Road" are disclosed in the acknowledgment of a pervasive, affirming "energy compacted and whirling," which cannot be dissipated, present even in "the forehead bone that does not rot, the woman priest's hair still fresh among Shang ritual things. . . ." Progress on this path brings its initiates or pilgrims to love—of one's body, of another person, of nature in its abundant particulars. Lavishing our affections, we are repaid in kind. Bly offers numerous sections of fine lyrical writing out of this newly wakened spirit:

> We love this body as we love the day we first met the person who led us away from this world, as we love the gift we gave one morning on impulse, in a fraction of a second, that we still see every day, as we love the human face, fresh after love-making, more full of joy than a wagonload of hay.
>
> ("We Love This Body")

> Is this world animal or vegetable? Others love us, the cabbages love the earth, the earth is fond of the heavens—a new age comes close through the dark, an elephant's trunk waves in the darkness, so much is passing away, so many disciplines already gone, but the energy in the double flower does not falter, the wings fold up around the sitting man's face. And these cucumber leaves are my body, and my thighs, and my toes stretched out in the wind. . . . Well, waterer, how will you get through this night without water?
>
> ("Wings Folding Up")

This second passage confirms all abiding unity with and love for self and creation; it is, further, both realistic and prophetic in its assessment of an "age" of difficult transition, when institutions and traditions are losing their once vital hold on human experience, when their explanations for that experience no longer command as much genuine or durable conviction as they did. But Bly has shaped for himself a harmonious bond with nature to serve as a support, and he can now recollect how "the energy in the double flower does not falter."

We learn something of this double flower's significance from the book's penultimate poem, "Snowed In." A Minnesota winter again supplies atmosphere—and more. The poet has retired to his writing shack, a setting for other Bly poems. Coming through the door, thick snow flying about him, the first thing he notices on sitting down "is a plant in blossom." In the arrangement of his perception and thought, observation leads to meditation, which in turn takes flight into imaginative vision:

> The upper petal is orange-red. The lower petal paler, as if the intensity had risen upward. Two smaller petals, like country boys' ears, poke out on either side.
>   The blossom faces the window where snow sweeps past at forty miles all hour. . . . So there are two tendernesses looking at each other, two oceans living at a level of instinct surer than mine . . . yet in them both there is the same receiving, the longing to be blown, to be shaken, to circle slowly upward, or sink down toward roots . . . one cold, one warm, but neither wants to go up geometrically floor after floor, even to hold up a wild-haired roof, with copper dragons, through whose tough nose rain water will pour. . . .

> So the snow and the orangey blossoms are both the same flow, that starts out close to the soil, close to the floor, and needs no commandments, no civilization, no drawing rooms lifted on the labor of the claw hammer, but is at home when one or two are present, it is also inside the block of wood, and in the burnt bone that sketched the elk by smoky light.

Flower and snow, apparent opposites, thrive on and manifest the same convoluted energies we have seen throughout. The flower's color intensifies as it grows upward, the flakes of snow whirl violently down. Bly identifies both with "oceans," an image recalling the poet's catalogue of things linked with the Mother or feminine consciousness—curving, flowing, rounding things which avoid sharp angles, corners, and logical procedures. Both flower and snow wish in their natures to be driven by this whirling force, this circular "Power of the World" (to use this term from Bly's Black Elk quotation) which exists and functions prior to, aside from, even against, the mathematically calculated ordering of "civilization," "commandments," or buildings laid out in squares and rectangles—we remember "Walking Swiftly." The force does favor unity and relationships between individuals, and has always visited the artist—even the prehistoric, anonymous cave painter—with its presence. In the poem's final section the double flower is, as elsewhere, man and woman, poet and loved one. Bly renders them objectively as he begins, but in the second sentence he alters the distance, applies personal pronouns. This conclusion acquires the strength of intimacy against a background of ageless, ubiquitous cosmic energy; and here, as the cell and the snowflake do in the miniature lyrics about them, this couple knows the joy and grace of accepting their bodies, the tie that unites them, and of living from the profound, balanced center of themselves. "So inside the human body there is the seed," Kabir version 4 says, "and inside the seed there is the human body again."

> A man and a woman sit quietly near each other. In the snowstorm millions of years come close behind us, nothing is lost, nothing rejected, our bodies are equal to the snow in energy. The body is ready to sing all night, and be entered by whatever wishes to enter the human body singing. . . .
> ("Snowed In")

After this paragraph no one will be surprised to learn that the last poem in the collection is even more openly and personally a love poem. "The Cry Going Out Over Pastures" is a lover's declaration—one of both longing and satisfaction—resonating through his natural surroundings, a world of trees, river, birds, pastures, from which, at least partially, he takes his sense of selfhood; and it is a statement of love that is "prudent" and also wild "beyond all rules and conventions." The latter half of the poem roves back in memory to the lovers' first meeting, yet returns at once, in the same sentence, to the immediate moment. There Bly recognizes the unavoidable claim death makes but countenances it with the renewing energies of life, the circling path being follows, bringing with this acceptance a transcending "joy [as] when the bee rises into the air above his hive to find the sun, to become the son, and the traveler moves through exile and loss, through murkiness and failure, to touch the earth again of his own kingdom and kiss the ground. . . ."

   Those words apply to more than the poet's elatedness at this instant; they can be said to summarize metaphorically the arduous journey he has undertaken to arrive at this animated condition. Bly's latest prose poems stand as a fine, coherent achievement, a little of the fullness and intricacy of which I hope has been conveyed here. Much can still be discussed about the style of these poems, their employment of assonance, alliteration, internal rhyming—in brief, their music—and other poetic devices; but a watchful reader will discover them. Poem 10 from Bly's Kabir versions seems a very apt concluding comment on the prose poems of *This Body Is Made of Camphor and Gopherwood*:

> Between the conscious and the unconscious, the mind has put up
>   a swing:
> all earth creatures, even the supernovas, sway between these two
>   trees,
> and it never winds down.
>
> Angels, animals, humans, insects by the million, also the
>   wheeling sun and moon;
> ages go by, and it goes on.
> Everything is swinging: heaven, earth, water, fire,
> and the secret one slowly growing a body.
> Kabir saw that for fifteen seconds, and it made him a servant for life.

                                                                    (1981)

NOTES
[1] Bly has recently mentioned in a letter to the author that the other prisoner and "the baker" refer to the story of Joseph's imprisonment and dream interpretation, Genesis 40.

20

Everything That's Luminous

"I WANT IT OPEN / HANGING / OPEN," HILDA MORLEY WRITES IN A POEM ENTITLED "The Poem" (*New Directions* 27), comparing it to a damaged human body whose innards are on view. This specimen is in real danger of becoming a cadaver ("Can it be saved? Only by some / miracle!"): but the analogy, which might have suggested the old cliché about the "cooked" and the "raw" in contemporary verse, takes on an unexpected transformation in the second half of the piece:

> All open
> but each aspect of it crystallized
> in sharpness
>   as the heart   the lungs the liver
> are   separate & together in the body
> isolating and surrounding them

This crystallization, which preserves the sharp, true intricacy of detail and holds the living flow of experience, of thought and perception, in the music of its articulation, is a new radiant body brought into being by Morley's own "miracle," the extraordinary accomplishments of her acute sensibilities, powerful imagination, and a consummate skill in her craft.

The tradition in which Hilda Morley has placed herself squarely, and to which she adds lustre, is that rich original vein of American writing presided over by Pound, Williams, and H. D. and including the Objectivist poets and those of the *Origin* and Black Mountain groups. Such a location for her work is not surprising: she is the widow of the composer Stefan Wolpe and taught herself for a time at Black Mountain College. The sense of open or "organic form" a reader associates with the essays of Olson or

Levertov, for example, poems to be a clear influence on her art; and behind them, of course, the "measure" of Williams's late work, as well as something of the combined fluid delicacy and sinewiness of H. D. About the weight of such figures and forces on another's poetry, however, one can never be sure. It would appear that music has also exerted its influence, and if is certain that painting and sculpture are of considerable importance to Morley, who has built many poems around them.

It is a shameful comment on our present-day literary situation that Hilda Morley's work has been largely neglected, that a great deal of it has gone unpublished, in spite of the author's productivity and her wide circle of acquaintance. The Kiwanis Club atmosphere of writing programs, bulletins, and university press series which gives prominence each year to the newest batch of dull, windy, unimaginative manuscripts ("parlor poetry" is what I believe Marvin Bell rightly calls it) can hardly be receptive to the sort of poems Morley offers. As a result, she has thus far only two books: *A Blessing Outside Us* (Pourboire Press, 1976), almost impossible to obtain except from the author, and *What Are Winds and What Are Waters* (out this fall from Matrix Press).

Several kinds of material seem nearly obsessive for Morley, and she returns to them again and again, not repeating herself but indeed appearing to find them continually valuable as poetic resources: among these are places, art objects, and her relationship with Stefan Wolpe. Stated so baldly, such materials may look limited—but a reading of the poems should quickly dispel that notion.

Poems of place are for Hilda Morley seldom simply that: they are not versions of travelogue. Frequently they involve relationships, with friends, lovers, but aspects of the landscape, certain of its details noted with accuracy, are as much a part of the complex of experience the poem holds within itself as are the human participants. At the end of "Siesta," for instance, the Mediterranean setting, weather and air, appear to exert themselves actively in the passionate bond of the lovers in their room, so inside and outside merge, and a strange confusion reigns for the man:

> Breaking of surf came down
> inside that room,
>   spray of
> a sky smouldered in constellations,
>   the Venus
> flushed & angry delivering
> August
>   What would you like?
> she asked,
>   To know where I am, he said

In "Mt. Ste.-Victoire" Morley observes her mountainscape through Cézanne's view of it: her opening blends these visions:

> Old savage   among the little hills
> we saw you   who nourished Cézanne's eyes
> From childhood
>   blue-grey
> lion   among the rocks
> your mane trembles   grey & darker
> grey
>   moving   stopping short & moving
> closer

After three sections in "Ibiza," each rendering the poet's pleasure in the particulars of sea and land and sky, trees and flowers, she concludes on a note so different as to throw all that has gone before into a different perspective: "Only for us now that which is / beautiful is not enough." The reader is left to go through the piece again in the light of this statement. just as the lavish praise of detail is called into doubt by undisclosed feelings which surface at the finish of "'Ibiza," so Morley can imagine two people creating an appropriate location out of their relationship with one another, a setting in correspondence with their warmth of emotion and conversation. Here is "Landscape," dedicated to the poet Jonathan Williams:

>   Where we sat
> the desert disappeared: a moviehouse
> a restaurant   a cab   a coffeehouse
>
> Where we talked the earth was broken
> A line of green sprang up
> and made a shape. The soil
>
> was watered.   Where we sat
> the sky seethed for a little
> while   then opened
>
> cleared   then let
> a wind that smelled
> of wild herbs growing
>
> on rocks beside the sea
>
> come through

In poems treating artists or works of visual art-and there are quite a few of
these in the body of her writing- Hilda Morley always draws the experience
of an aesthetic object into a larger dimension of awareness or resolve, a
dimension entered, however, only by contemplation of the art work, the
specific qualities of which suggest the way for getting there. Thus a lovely
poem, "The Turner Exhibition," begins:

> That weight inside the body
> must be shifted,
>   Turner
> showed me that

And "The Niké of Samothrace," a deeply-moving piece which incorporates
the author's grief and memories of her husband, finishes in this triumphant
and transfiguring image of the statue's wing, an image carrying both poet
and reader beyond loss and pain to the edge of expectant change:

> That wing that rises
> above her in the fullness
> of her courage
>   knows nothing
> that cannot be transformed,
>   knows of
> no water unstirring

In "Matisse: The Red Studio," to select another example from among
Morley's poems on art, one sees the very process of relating the elements
discerned and valued in the painting to modes of perceiving and thinking
about actualities of experience outside the picture. The poem starts by announcing the delight of "space moving in unbroken / curves," which liber-
ates the eye of the viewer who follows it. But there is more still to this
freedom, Morley insists, and the poem pursues it back into the space of the
painting and out once more, through an analogy, into the larger frame of
the natural world with its figures of blackbird and gull, and the ubiquitous
"light," a recurrent luminescence, whether glancing touch or broad glaze,
that is this poet's sign of grace. I quote the last two-thirds of the poem so the
reader can trace its course for himself:

> What is free here is not
> the eye only
>   not space only, but our-
> selves swerving & shifting,
>   a sense of gravity

that's root & stumbling-block also
                              There's no one in
the studio & yet each object
is known & lived
                    & every possible
displacement taken care of,
                              each hollow
sudden in the curvature
of space accepted
                    as on this April 22nd
the blackbird's voice disturbs
the rounding of the air
and in that drop we learn the broken
shape,
       the gull's
spurt over the water,
                        his slanted
edge of wing
                    inside the light
                              complaining

Hilda Morley has written a great many poems about Stefan Wolpe, her experience of life with him and his genius for existence, finally about his illness and death, and their aftermath: the poet's suffering and her determination to go on. A number of these pieces have been gathered and arranged into appropriate sections in *What Are Winds and What Are Waters*, a book of impressive power, of lyric and meditative achievement which should be read as a whole. *A Blessing Outside Us* also contains some of these poems: I have chosen one of them, "Another Fire," not because it can be representative of the others—each is unique—but because it bears that imagery of light we saw in the Matisse poem, here seen as deriving from another source. "Another Fire" begins in everyday imagery of weather and city streets (Morley is everywhere superb in her handling such particulars), but there is a progression away from them through the altering details or light: from flashing pools of rainwater to the moon's whiteness and on to the origin of lunar brilliance in the sun. At this point the poem returns to the streets, the person of the poet struggling through the darkness of a night that is as much internal as external, and the desire for light and warmth, for the sun's fire, that comes as memory revives the nearly god-like, luminous shape of the lost beloved. Here, as in all of Hilda Morley's poems, one needs to appreciate the auditory and structural mastery that guides her in the disposition of lines, clustered or hovering free, their music and detail brought into a beautiful interweaving.

Damp streets
            What was the sun's
light flashes between rainfalls:
                        an explosion
of whiteness rising
out of puddles
            (the dark street)
            flashing
of an enormous wing
            Where the moon is
a swan on fire perhaps:
                        a white eagle
in reflection,
            & the moon itself surprising
above the city
            whiter
than the sun
            reflecting
in that heat another
fire
      beyond coldness,
beyond freezing
            to me walking
in this darkness
            where I stumble
& recover & in these shadows moving
always toward a possibility
of that burning
            I knew once
in the sweating of your body & the eyes'
brilliance that could never
be quenched I thought
                        & the little suns pouring
out of the fingers
of your hands

These "suns," light that is perceived and the active eye that perceives it—
("Let the eye then, eye / take, take everything / it can. Never give over. /
Pull the world inside," she says elsewhere)—are not for this poet merely or
only aesthetic but rather are constitutive of a moral, redemptive dimension
without which human existence lacks fullness, whether such plenitude or
completeness is found in the creative nobility of Joan of Arc and Goethe,
Turner and Cézanne, Wolpe and Charles Olson, or in some simpler, everyday occasion. In the extraordinary poem "That Bright Grey Eye," Morley
fuses symbolic, heroic, and mundane aspects—Blake's eagle, the piercing

vision of her (dead husband, the "fiery" sunlit New York streets, and the humble persons of an old woman and a grocery store cashier—into a complex whole at the center of which a moment of gentleness and charity between the last-named figures provides living substance for the implications of light: so much so that the final portion of the poem seems touched with an elemental sacredness.

>   The pavement
>   trembles with light pouring
>   upon it.
>   We are held in it.
>   We smile
>   I hold my breath to see if
>   the cashier in the supermarket
>   will be gentle with the old lady who cannot
>   read the price-tag on
>   a loaf of bread.
>   Then I breathe freely,
>   for yes, she is helpful, yes, she is
>   kind.
>   Outside on
>   the pavement, the light pouring itself away
>   is the light in the eagle's
>   eye   or the eye of a child
>   (I saw it in a man's eye once:
>   but he's dead now more than
>   four years)
>   Drawing heat out of
>   surfaces,
>   the light is
>   without calculation,
>   is a munificence now,
>   is justified.

The handful of poems I've quoted and discussed so sketchily here can barely indicate the imaginative and technical fullness of Hilda Morley's writing. Her achievement is yet to be measured, cannot be measured so long as a large part of this poetry remains unpublished or is scattered in the pages of various little magazines. For me, her work has been a most remarkable discovery, and I think she has clearly earned the company of the finest contemporary poets and must be discussed in the tradition of Olson, Oppen, Niedecker, Creeley, and Levertov, to name a few. To keep in mind what she stands for and how she seeks it, how a poem may be the live bodying-forth of quest and goal, I will finish with a long passage from "Still-Life," prompted

by a viewing of late Cézanne water colors: I hope many readers will, in turn,
seek out Morley's art:

<pre>
              Everything that's luminous
        & soaring moves,
                          moves upward
        there & blows us with it
                          All that is physical
        & weighted, or might be
        subject to decay
                      turns into
        a vapor, a cloud,
                      an energy
        of movement, of light in itself,
                                but vapor
        that's solid,
                      cloud that's tangible
        light that's substance
                          & I say—Praise,
        praise is what it is, making
        the apples, the flask, the bottle
        & the wall behind them soaring
        & full & luminous at once,
                              filling
        the spaces in our body with movement
        & light,   no single
        interstice untouched.
</pre>

                                                (1982)

21

"The True and Earthy Prayer": Philip Levine's Poetry

We live
the way we are
　　　—P.L., "The Sadness of Lemons"

THE POETRY OF PHILIP LEVINE, FROM *ON THE EDGE* (1963) TO HIS TWO LAT-EST collections, *Red Dust* (1970) and *They Feed They Lion* (1972), has always displayed technical skill, a dexterous handling of both formal and, more recently, informal modes, and a command of the resources of diction and rhythm. Yet these aspects of technique seem in a way second-ary, absorbed as they are by a central, driving intensity peculiar to this poet's approach. Such intensity leads him to a relentless searching through the events of his life and the lives of others, through the particulars of nature as these signify something about the processes of living, the states of existence, in order to arrive not at Eliot's transcendence, Roethke's "condition of joy," or Whitman's ideal of progress and brotherhood (though the sharing of suffering and the common ties of humanity are basic to Levine's attitude) but to the sort of awareness suggested by Yeats's phrase, "the desolation of reality": an unflinching acquaintance with the harsh facts of most men's situation which still confirms rather than de-nies its validity. If this is a difficult prospect we must acknowledge how familiar it has become of late through the poems of Robert Lowell, David Ignatow, James Wright, Allen Ginsberg, and Galway Kinnell, to men-tion a few obvious names. In the writing of these poets, as in Levine's, the range of human sympathies, the frankness, perseverance, and sensi-tivity create of themselves an affirmative, life-sustaining balance to the bleak recognition of religious deprivation, war, social injustice, moral and spiritual confusion.

Levine's early poetry is taut, sharp, formal but gradually alters to accommodate his desire for greater freedom in line length and overall construction. A prominent theme of his first book is the reversal or defeat of expectations. Put another way, it motivates a struggle on the poet's part to view life stripped of the vestiges of illusory hope or promise, a type of hard spiritual conditioning which helps to engender his fundamental responsiveness to the dilemmas of the poor, embittered, failed lives of the "submerged population" (the late Frank O'Connor's term) in modern society, a responsiveness that accounts for much of both the energy and the deep humaneness of all his work. A firm grip on existence itself takes priority for Levine from the start, though with it necessarily comes an acceptance of pain and the admission that failure, defeat, and imperfection—but not surrender!—are unavoidable in men's affairs. The penetrating look he gives himself in "The Turning" from *On the Edge* points the direction he follows to maturity, which depends on the realization of flaws as well as the capacity to exist, to continue, made sturdier by this self-knowledge:

> . . . no more a child,
> Only a Man,—one who has
> Looked upon his own nakedness
> Without shame, and in defeat
> Has seen nothing to bless.
> Touched once, like a plum, I turned
> Rotten in the meat, or like
> The plum blossom I never
> Saw, hard at the edges, burned
> At the first entrance of life,
> And so endured, unreckoned,
> Untaken, with nothing to give.
> The first Jew was God; the second
> Denied him; I am alive.

Committed to a fallen, unredeemable world, finding no metaphysical consolations, Levine embraces it with an ardor, anguish, and fury that are themselves religious emotions. In a brief comment on his work contributed to *Contemporary Poets of the English Language* (1970) he lists among his "obsessions" "Detroit" (where he was born, did factory labor, and studied), "the dying of America" (a recurrent theme in various guises), and "communion with others," which incorporates its predecessors as well as specifying what is for him a primary poetic impulse. Writing frequently of persons whose lives are distinct yet touch his own, he increases his consciousness and imaginative powers, and a chord of compassion and understanding reverberates within and beyond the boundaries of his poems. This is not to say that Levine puts himself out of the picture or chooses a mask of impersonality, but that his presence in a poem, whether overt or concealed, constitutes an enlargement of personality, a stepping out of the ego-bound "I" into the surrounding life. Paradoxically, he reaches inward, far into the recesses of the psyche, at the same time he reaches outward, thus fulfilling a pattern of movement Robert Bly has long advocated as essential to a modern poetry rich in imaginative potentialities.

Among the poems of Levine's initial volume, this self-extension appears most complete when he adopts the voices of different persons—the Sierra Kid, four French Army deserters in North Africa, the unnamed officer of "The Distant Winter"—to replace his own. Another sort of identification, of a crucial kind for the line of development his work pursues, occurs in the title poem "On the Edge," and also in "My Poets" and "Gangrene." In these instances he does not assume the role of another speaker but takes up the question of a poetic vocation and the destiny of poets in society today. In one shape or another, each of these poems really considers the problem of speechlessness, the lacerating irony of the mute poet imprisoned by circumstances which thwart or oppose his art, making its practice unlikely or impossible. So Levine sorts through the probabilities of his own future. The poet/speaker of "On the Edge" describes himself as the insane, alcoholic Poe of the twentieth century, born, as Levine was, "in 1928 in Michigan." This latter-day Poe plays the part of an observer who doesn't write, only watches the actions and prevarications of nameless people. In the last stanza he repeats a refusal of his art, though we are provided in its statement of alienation, perceptiveness, and silence with a poetry of angry eloquence:

> I did not write, for I am Edgar Poe,
> Edgar the mad one, silly, drunk, unwise,
> But Edgar waiting on the edge of laughter,
> And there is nothing that he does not know
> Whose page is blanker than the raining skies.

This abstention from writing, or persecution for telling the truth by means of it, occupies the other poems mentioned. Levine's effort here is to indicate the need for honest speech, the conditions which militate against it, and the frustrating atmosphere of separateness the poet faces. Thematically, the poem "Silent in America" from *Not This Pig* (1968), Levine's second collection, brings such matters to a critical climax and to a moment of transformation and decision. Though it is not the first poem in the book, dramatically speaking it should be thought of as a pivotal piece, for its procedure and resolution make possible what Levine is doing elsewhere in the same volume: breaking down those barriers which prevent him from entering areas of otherwise lost

or unapprehended experience requisite to the poetry he wants to write. At
the outset the poet announces his silence, which fashions for him a state of
remoteness and solitude that border on anonymity. Watching ordinary
things—a sprinkler wetting a lawn—stirs him toward utterance, but he stays
quiet. A doctor's examination uncovers no defect. Details of nature engage
him with the elusive tracery of their being; still, the animate *something* he
notices in trees, water, and flowers defies his wish to name it, and thus his
muteness persists. Locked in isolation, Levine now falls victim to inner torments, to his "squat demon, / my little Bobby," a splintered apparition of the
self who plagues him with insatiable sexual demands. The poem develops
rapidly toward hysteria and derangement until the poet bursts out with a
negative cry of resistance. A section ensues in which he articulates the aims
of his writing—to give voice to the varied experience of lost, unknown, or
forgotten individuals he has met, speaking with and for them—but he is
likewise forced to assent to the fact that each person remains finally imper-
vious to total comprehension and communion. The following passage handsomely summarizes Levine's intentions and concerns:

> For a black man whose
> name I have forgotten who danced
>   all night at Chevy
>   Gear & Axle,
>   for that great stunned Pole
> who laughed when he called me Jew
>   Boy, for the ugly
>   who had no chance,
>
>   the beautiful in
> body, the used and the unused,
>   those who had courage
>   and those who quit—
>   Rousek and Ficklin
> numbed by their own self-praise
>   who ate their own shit
>   in their own rage;
>
>   for these and myself
> whom I had loved and hated, I
>   had presumed to speak
>   in measure.
>   The great night is half
> over, and the stage is dark;
>   all my energy,
>   all my care for

those I cannot touch
runs on my breath like a sigh;
    surely I have failed.
        My own wife
    and my children reach
in their sleep for some sure sign,
    but each has his life
        private and sealed.

    Levine's anxiety arises from the profoundly felt impulse to put his language, as poetry, in the service of others' lives, in addition to his own. The walls of privacy and individuality he cannot traverse cause him regret and a feeling of loss. Yet, just as surely, he *does* speak for others to the very limit of his abilities, not only here but also in the rest of this book, as well as in his subsequent poetry. If he is unable to appropriate the entirety of another life, like a second skin, it is still possible for him to go with others, moving to the rhythms of their existence and assimilating the details which his imagination requires. This kind of correspondence and kinship receives treatment in the closing section of the poem, where Levine meets a friend, H., in a Los Angeles bar and talks with him. H. is perhaps a writer too; in any event, he is described as doing essentially what an artist does: he creates a world composed of half-real, observed figures and half-fictitious ones who fit in with their actual counterparts, and he lives with them in imagination and sympathy. In the tavern Levine senses the presence of a person of fabulous name, apparently a wholly fictive man, conjured by his mind, who imposes himself no less strongly on the poet's awareness and emotion is because of that:

    Archimbault is here—
I do not have to be drunk
    to feel him come near,

and he touches me with his
    life, and I could cry,
though I don't know who he is
    or why I should care
about the mad ones, imagined
    and real, H. places
in his cherished underground,
    their wounded faces

glowing in the half-light of
    their last days alive,
as his glows here.

Whatever his self-questioning, Levine clearly cares, and his expressed wish in the next lines merges his own existence with that of such persons as fill the bar, until all seems to become part of poetry itself: "Let me have / the courage to live / as fictions live, proud, careless, / unwilling to die." So he would have his life speak itself as poems do, tenacious of their being. At the conclusion Levine and H. leave the bar and "enter the city." The poet urges his readers to join him, to blend into the mass of humanity thronging the streets in their restlessness, at last to go "beyond the false lights / of Pasadena / where the living are silent / in America." This invitation is as much a definition of his own poetic pursuits as it is a gesture by which the poet makes his reader a partner to what he sees. Levine will invade those areas of the unspoken life and lend them words.

Rich and complex though they usually are, the poems of Levine's first two collections are relatively direct, proceeding by certain logical, sequential, narrative, or other means which provide the reader with support and guidance. Levine never altogether abandons poems of this sort, but even in *Not This Pig* he begins to widen his fields of exploration to include experiences which manifest themselves in irrational, dreamlike, fantastic, or visionary forms, doing so variously in such poems as "The Rats," "The Business Man of Alicante," "The Cartridges," "The One-Eyed King," "Animals Are Passing from Our Lives," "Baby Villon," "Waking an Angel," "The Second Angel," and "The Lost Angel." These pieces prepare the way for the Surrealist atmosphere of *Red Dust*, the elliptical, disjunctive composition evident there, and further visible in portions of *They Feed They Lion*. Levine has cited the Spanish and Latin American poets Hernandez, Alberti, Neruda, and Vallejo, in addition to postwar Polish poetry, as having presented new possibilities available to him. The freedom, vigorousness, metaphorical and imagistic daring of these poets plainly has had a tonic effect on Levine's more recent writing, releasing him to new boldness and strength.

So, by any but a narrow or restrictive view, Levine's latest books must be judged extraordinarily successful, exhibiting an access of inventiveness and vision. In *Red Dust* the elements of experience move into different focus; they are less "distanced," talked about, or pointed to than rendered dramatically as the very substance of language and image in the poems. The general character of these poems is also freer, more intuitive, and thus occasionally more difficult, unyielding to logical analysis. From the beginning we find an openness in the structure of poems, in the sense that they are not brought to a tidy conclusion but often end in a startling, seemingly irrational—yet, on consideration, perfectly apt—statement. Here is the final section of "Clouds," a poem which gathers considerable momentum by associative leaping among apparently random details whose disconnectedness actually pulls together a grim portrait of the contemporary world. Over the shifting scenes and figures the aloof clouds travel, absorb, and spill out their rain, giving the poem coherence while at the same time implying a universal indifference to which the poet responds with vehemence in the striking lines at the close:

> You cut an apple in two pieces
> and ate them both. In the rain
> the door knocked and you dreamed it.
> On bad roads the poor walked under cardboard boxes.
>
> The houses are angry because they're watched.
> A soldier wants to talk with God
> but his mouth fills with lost tags.
>
> The clouds have seen it all, in the dark
> they pass over the graves of the forgotten
> and they don't cry or whisper.
> They should be punished every morning,
> they should be bitten and boiled like spoons.

In poems of this sort the components are set down in combinations which resist or contradict ordinary rational expectations for them. The reader, thus perceptually thrown off balance, has the option either to give up or give in, and so to see and feel the particulars of experience fused in vivid, evocative ways. Gradually, the shifting shapes, the elisions and abrupt juxtapositions will disclose their significance, if the reader will only accept them on their own terms. As indicated previously, Levine's social and moral preoccupations retain their urgency, but, as in the work of the Spanish-speaking poets he admires, such interests tend at times to be integral with the immediate, elliptical, or surreal orderings of imagery and statement. Frequently now, the poems seek out specific details of landscape, cityscape, even vegetation and animal life, though these directly or obliquely correspond with aspects of human existence. Sensitivity to place—whether Detroit, California, or Spain (where Levine lived for two years recently)—the imagination exercised on what is perceived there, leads readily into poems of large expressive force. The figures inhabiting these pieces may be quite separate and distinct, with Levine himself only a transparent or invisible speaker (though, of course, an indirect commentator, sometimes a savage one), as in "The End of Your Life" or "Where We Live Now"; or they may involve the poet openly, as he tries to define himself and his life, or when he captures a moment's affective resonance, a mood charged with implications, of the kind we

observe in "A Sleepless Night," "Told," "Holding On," and "Fist." In
"Noon" he draws self and others together beautifully within the frame of
a landscape:

I bend to the ground
to catch
something whispered,
urgent, drifting
across the ditches.
The heaviness of
flies stuttering
in orbit, dirt
ripening, the sweat
of eggs.
      There are
small streams
the width of a thumb
running in the villages
of sheaves, whole
eras of grain
wakening on
the stalks, a roof
that breathes over
my head.
      Behind me
the tracks creaking
like a harness,
an abandoned bicycle
that cries and cries,
a bottle of common
wine that won't
pour.
At such times
I expect the earth
to pronounce. I say,
"I have been waiting
so long."
      Up ahead
a stand of eucalyptus
guards the river,
the river moving
east, the heavy light
sifts down driving
the sparrows for
cover, and the women
bow as they slap

> the life out
> of sheets and pants
> and worn hands.

In this poem, as in many of Levine's newest, man's common attachments with earth, his relationship with objects, the hard, painful climate in which most lives are lived, are evoked through a skilled interweaving of images, the particulars of the world suddenly caught up to view, suffused with the "reek of the human," to borrow a phrase from Donald Davie. "How much earth is a man," Levine asks in another poem; his answer indicates an indissoluble, fateful bond: "a hand is planted / and the grave blooms upward / in sunlight and walks the roads." In the three angel poems from *Not This Pig*, which create a little sequence among themselves, the realm of transcendence, of the spiritual ideal, dissolves or collapses before the spectacle of flawed earthly reality. What aspects of the spiritual can become evident belong not to a hidden or remote sphere but radiate, if possible, from the ingredients of day-to-day mundane affairs. So, in Levine's work, life is circumscribed by the finality of death, but this inevitability is countenanced with toughness, stoicism, staying power. As he says of his fist in the final stanza of the poem bearing that title:

> It opens and is no longer.
> Bud of anger, kinked
> tendril of my life, here
> in the forged morning
> fill with anything—water,
> light, blood—but fill.

Between the poems of *Red Dust* and those of *They Feed They Lion* no alterations occur in Levine's attitude toward such matters; two poems, "The Space We Live" and "How Much Can It Hurt?", are even reprinted from the earlier book. In general, however, Levine employs less of the dense irrational or associative manner so prominent in *Red Dust*, though with no loss of concentrated force. The opening poems, "Renaming the Kings" and "The Cutting Edge," for instance, dramatize personal incidents in a direct, sequential way quite appropriate to the experiences. These pieces, along with several others, examine the poet's encounters in the midst of natural settings, with each occasion revealing some facet of a relation between the things of earth and a man—a relation sometimes assuring and harmonious, sometimes disturbing or painful. In "The Cutting Edge" a stone under water gashes the poet's foot; he casts it out of the stream and hobbles away. Later he returns, discovers it, and pauses to wonder before deciding what to do with it:

> I could take it home
> and plant it in a box;
> I could talk about
> what it did to me
> and what I did to it,
> or how in its element
> it lives like you or me.
> But it stops me, here
> on my open hand,
> by being a stone, and I send
> it flying over the heads
> of the fishing children,
> arching alone above
> the dialogue of reeds,
> falling and falling toward water,
> somewhere in water to strike
> a conversation of stone.

A very different type of "conversation" takes place in "To a Fish Head Found on the Beach Near Málaga," where Levine, walking alone, comes upon the ravaged body and head, hanging by its shred of bone, then confides his "loneliness," "fears," and torments to it. The result of his strange speech makes him sense the contours and characteristics of his own face and head, and, at last, "throw the fish head to the sea. / Let it be fish once more." The poem's concluding lines assert the speaker's comprehension of the unalterable cyclicism of existence, the ironic necessity of destruction for renewal:

> I sniff my fingers
> and catch the burned essential oil
> seeping out of death. Out of the beginning,
> I hear, under the sea roar, the bone words
> of teeth tearing earth and sea,
> anointing the tongues with stone and sand,
> water eating fish, fish water,
> head eating head to let us be.

This volume also includes sequences of varying length, as well as groups of obviously connected poems. "Thistles," the longest of them, dedicated to the poet George Oppen, is composed of discrete pieces each of which focuses on a singular occasion, perception, or ambiance of feeling. The same may be said for the shorter sequence, "Dark Rings." These poems are not bound tightly together, though the thistle appears in the first and last pieces of that sequence, and the "dark rings" refer not only to a specific detail in one poem but also to images in most and the mood of all of them. Yet their swift, free, occasionally abbreviated notation and arrangement give an impression of accuracy, deftness, and assurance in the handling of experience. The poems are full of nuances and overtones which linger on. One must place with these sequences most of the poems in the book's second section, dealing with Levine's Detroit life among the automotive workers and the abandoned, hopeless, silent figures we have seen him desirous to know and to speak for. The angels return in this section in shifting but always earthly forms, evanescent protective spirits hovering about the poet, presences in his closet, or incarnate in someone of his acquaintance, as in the fourth poem of "The Angels of Detroit" group. Here "the angel Bernard," trapped and frustrated by the massive industrial system for which he labors and cannot escape, writing poems no one will read, aching for love, release, even death, awakens as always to find himself surrounded by the debris of manufacture, our values and lives rupturing from the shapes of steel and rubber in which we have conceived them:

> At the end of the mud road
> in the false dawn of the slag heap
> the hut of the angel Bernard.
> His brothers are factories and
> bowling teams, his mother is the
> power to blight, his father
> moves in all men like a threat,
> a closing of hands, an unkept
> promise to return.
>   We talk
> for years; everything we
> say comes to nothing. We drink
> bad beer and never lie. From
> his bed he pulls fists
> of poems and scatters them
> like snow. "Children are guilty,"
> he whispers, and the soft mouth
> puffs like a wound.
>
> He wants it all tonight.
> The long hard arms of a black woman,
> he wants tenderness, he wants
> the power to die in the
> chalice of God's tears.
>
> True dawn through the soaped window.
> The plastic storm-wrap swallows wind.

'37 Chevie hoodless, black burst
lung of inner tube, pot metal
trees buckling under sheets.
He cries to sleep.

Such a poem gives notice of the incredible strength, the economy and
muscle with which Levine endows the majority of his poems. Two of the
most amazing and powerful pieces, "Angel Butcher" and "They Feed They
Lion," bring the book's second section to a climactic level of prophetic vision; the latter poem is dazzling in its syntactic, linguistic, and dramatic
invention, its use of idiomatic effect. But both poems need to be read in
their entirety and are too long for quotation here. It remains now simply to
say for the purposes of this brief commentary that Levine's poetry, praise-
worthy at the start, has developed by momentous strides in the past decade.
His new poems make it impossible for him to be ignored or put aside. He
stands out as one of the most solid and independent poets of his generation—one of the best poets, I think, anywhere at work in the language. It is
time to begin listening:

Can you hear me?
the air says. I hold
my breath and listen
and a finger of dirt thaws,
a river drains
from a snow drop
and rages down
my cheeks, our father
the wind hums
a prayer through my mouth
and answers in the oat,
and now the tight rows of seed
bow to the earth
and hold on and hold on.

(1976)

LANNAN SELECTIONS

The Lannan Foundation, located in Santa Fe, New Mexico, is a family foundation whose funding focuses on special cultural projects and ideas which promote and protect cultural freedom, diversity, and creativity.

The literary aspect of Lannan's cultural program supports the creation and presentation of exceptional English-language literature and develops a wider audience for poetry, fiction, and nonfiction.

Since 1990, the Lannan Foundation has supported Dalkey Archive Press projects in a variety of ways, including monetary support for authors, audience development programs, and direct funding for the publication of the Press's books.

In the year 2000, the Lannan Selections Series was established to promote both organizations' commitment to the highest expressions of literary creativity. The Foundation supports the publication of this series of books each year, and works closely with the Press to ensure that these books will reach as many readers as possible and achieve a permanent place in literature. Authors whose works have been published as Lannan Selections include: Ishmael Reed, Stanley Elkin, Ann Quin, Nicholas Mosley, William Eastlake, and David Antin, among others.

SELECTED DALKEY ARCHIVE PAPERBACKS

FOR A FULL LIST OF PUBLICATIONS, VISIT:
www.dalkeyarchive.com

SELECTED DALKEY ARCHIVE PAPERBACKS

CAROLE MASO, *AVA.*

LADISLAV MATEJKA AND KRYSTYNA POMORSKA, EDS.,
*Readings in Russian Poetics: Formalist and
Structuralist Views.*

HARRY MATHEWS, *Cigarettes.*
The Conversions.
The Case of the Persevering Maltese: Collected Essays.
The Human Country: New and Collected Stories.
The Journalist.
Singular Pleasures.
The Sinking of the Odradek Stadium.
Tlooth.
20 Lines a Day.

ROBERT L. MCLAUGHLIN, ED.,
*Innovations: An Anthology of Modern &
Contemporary Fiction.*

STEVEN MILLHAUSER, *The Barnum Museum.*
In the Penny Arcade.

RALPH J. MILLS, JR., *Essays on Poetry.*

OLIVE MOORE, *Spleen.*

NICHOLAS MOSLEY, *Accident.*
Assassins.
Catastrophe Practice.
Children of Darkness and Light.
The Hesperides Tree.
Hopeful Monsters.
Imago Bird.
Impossible Object.
Inventing God.
Judith.
Natalie Natalia.
Serpent.

WARREN F. MOTTE, JR.,
Oulipo: A Primer of Potential Literature.
Fables of the Novel: French Fiction since 1990.

YVES NAVARRE, *Our Share of Time.*

WILFRIDO D. NOLLEDO, *But for the Lovers.*

FLANN O'BRIEN, *At Swim-Two-Birds.*
The Best of Myles.
The Dalkey Archive.
Further Cuttings.
The Hard Life.
The Poor Mouth.
The Third Policeman.

CLAUDE OLLIER, *The Mise-en-Scène.*

FERNANDO DEL PASO, *Palinuro of Mexico.*

RAYMOND QUENEAU, *The Last Days.*
Odile.
Pierrot Mon Ami.
Saint Glinglin.

ANN QUIN, *Berg.*
Passages.
Three.
Tripticks.

ISHMAEL REED, *The Free-Lance Pallbearers.*
The Last Days of Louisiana Red.
Reckless Eyeballing.
The Terrible Threes.

The Terrible Twos.
Yellow Back Radio Broke-Down.

JULIÁN RÍOS, *Poundemonium.*

AUGUSTO ROA BASTOS, *I the Supreme.*

JACQUES ROUBAUD, *The Great Fire of London.*
Hortense in Exile.
Hortense Is Abducted.
The Plurality of Worlds of Lewis.
The Princess Hoppy.
Some Thing Black.

LEON S. ROUDIEZ, *French Fiction Revisited.*

LUIS RAFAEL SÁNCHEZ, *Macho Camacho's Beat.*

SEVERO SARDUY, *Cobra & Maitreya.*

ARNO SCHMIDT, *Collected Stories.*
Nobodaddy's Children.

CHRISTINE SCHUTT, *Nightwork.*

JUNE AKERS SEESE,
Is This What Other Women Feel, Too?
What Waiting Really Means.

AURELIE SHEEHAN, *Jack Kerouac Is Pregnant.*

VIKTOR SHKLOVSKY, *Theory of Prose.*
Third Factory.
Zoo, or Letters Not about Love.

JOSEF ŠKVORECKÝ,
The Engineer of Human Souls.

CLAUDE SIMON, *The Invitation.*

GILBERT SORRENTINO, *Aberration of Starlight.*
Blue Pastoral.
Crystal Vision.
Imaginative Qualities of Actual Things.
Mulligan Stew.
Pack of Lies.
The Sky Changes.
Something Said.
Splendide-Hôtel.
Steelwork.
Under the Shadow.

W. M. SPACKMAN, *The Complete Fiction.*

GERTRUDE STEIN, *Lucy Church Amiably.*
The Making of Americans.
A Novel of Thank You.

PIOTR SZEWC, *Annihilation.*

ESTHER TUSQUETS, *Stranded.*

LUISA VALENZUELA, *He Who Searches.*

PAUL WEST, *Words for a Deaf Daughter* and *Gala.*

CURTIS WHITE, *Memories of My Father Watching TV.*
Monstrous Possibility.
Requiem.

DIANE WILLIAMS, *Excitability: Selected Stories.*
Romancer Erector.

DOUGLAS WOOLF, *Wall to Wall.*
Ya! & John-Juan.

PHILIP WYLIE, *Generation of Vipers.*

MARGUERITE YOUNG, *Angel in the Forest.*
Miss MacIntosh, My Darling.

REYOUNG, *Unbabbling.*

LOUIS ZUKOFSKY, *Collected Fiction.*

SCOTT ZWIREN, *God Head.*

FOR A FULL LIST OF PUBLICATIONS, VISIT:
www.dalkeyarchive.com